The State and the Mass Media in Japan, 1918–1945

The State and the Mass Media in Japan, 1918–1945

Gregory J. Kasza

UNIVERSITY OF CALIFORNIA PRESS
Berkeley · Los Angeles · London

University of California Press
Berkeley and Los Angeles, California

University of California Press, Ltd.
London, England

Much of chapter 4 has appeared as Gregory J. Kasza, "Democracy and the Founding of
Japanese Public Radio," *Journal of Asian Studies,* vol. 45, no. 4 (Aug. 1986), pp. 745–
767. Reprinted by permission of the Association for Asian Studies, Inc.

Library of Congress Cataloging-in-Publication Data

Kasza, Gregory James.
  The state and the mass media in Japan, 1918–1945.

  Bibliography: p.
  Includes index.
  1. Mass media policy—Japan. 2. Government and the
press—Japan. 3. Japan—Politics and government—1912–
1945. I. Title.
P95.82.J3K37   1987   302.2'34'0952   86-25095
ISBN 0-520-05943-3 (alk. paper)

Printed in the United States of America

1   2   3   4   5   6   7   8   9

Contents

Tables

Preface

The most distinctive political characteristic of the twentieth century is an unprecedented expansion of the power of states over their subjects. All empirical indicators of state size, finances, and authority point to the universality of this phenomenon. The modern state, composed of the institutions that make and enforce legally binding commands over society, is everywhere coming to direct more and more aspects of social existence. The military dominance of states is now such that the overthrow of a regime by unaided civil forces has become a rarity, and in most countries the state is the largest employer, industrialist, financier, and publisher. The process of state development has in recent decades come to appear all but irreversible. Sizable reductions in state control over society are now rare, occurring mainly in countries defeated in war; steady declines almost never transpire except where the state apparatus was initially imposed by a foreign power. Given the significance of this phenomenon, it is hardly surprising that the historical causes and the impact of growing state domination have become major topics of research. Political scientists have resurrected the state as a central concept in their work, and recent scholarship is increasingly concerned with the debate between statist and liberal doctrines of development and social justice. Scholars of many ideological and methodological schools evidence a growing awareness of the need to better comprehend what has become the most striking political feature of the modern world.

This book, a case study of the expansion of state power in imperial Japan, is designed to shed light on many central questions related to modern state development. Why have constitutional and legal codes largely failed to play their traditional role in limiting state authority? How have modern technology and bureaucratic organization contributed to the increase in state power? What has motivated efforts to increase state control over society? What kind of civil resistance has state expansion provoked, and what conditions determine the effectiveness of that resistance? The study seeks insights into these and many other facets of the subject matter from three perspectives. Substantively, it focuses on state control over the mass media: radio, film, and the periodical press (newspapers and current events magazines). Temporally, it focuses on the period between the two world wars. Theoretically, it focuses on the relationship between political regimes and the control policies they pursue.

The substantive focus on a particular field of public policy permits the examination of state control on a concrete level, linking institutions and ideology to the actual exercise of power. Though the complexity of the subject matter does not allow coverage of all important policy fields, a focus on policy toward the mass media partly compensates for this shortcoming, since the autonomy of the media is closely tied to that of many other social institutions. The size of contemporary countries and the anonymity of social relations between their inhabitants make it impossible to organize large-scale activities, for any purpose, without resort to the mass media. Political groups must rely heavily upon the media to win support and mount opposition to those in power. The media supply schools with educational materials and scholars with essential vehicles for research. Religions need the media to propagate their doctrines, and artists to exhibit their work to the public. Economic groups too are dependent on the media if they are to organize and pursue their interests. Furthermore, media organs are businesses themselves, and as such they are often directly affected by economic policies or indirectly compromised by state control over related industries. A focus on the mass media thus provides a partial view of state control in all these spheres of action, unveiling perhaps more of the overall picture than any other single policy field. In the context of imperial Japan, the study of media policy brings to light all the important shifts that occurred in the state-society relationship.

The temporal focus on the interwar period is also vital, since this period constitutes a critical turning point in the development of modern state power. The experience of World War I, the first total war, generated new state control strategies to prepare for defense or aggression; these were reflected in the work of Nagata Tetsuzan and his army colleagues in Japan beginning in the 1920s. Ideologically, new statist doctrines of the left and right for the first time successfully challenged the liberal principles dominant in political thought since the nineteenth century. The Bolshevik Revolution and the impact of European fascism combined to produce statists across the political spectrum, radical leftists demanding all-powerful workers' states, conservatives seeking new powers to crush the left, and right-wing extremists with their own ambitions for the advance of state power. All these political forces were active in Japan, as in so many other countries in this period. Finally, the postwar and 1929 depressions further undermined the legitimacy of liberal economic systems, calling forth new modes of state intervention to combat economic hardship and social disruption. It is significant that states were able to respond to these many catalysts with new technological capabilities. The interwar years witnessed the first wide diffusion of air transportation, motor vehicles, and countless novel forms of weaponry—not to mention radio and film, two centerpieces of this study.

In the short space of some thirty years, then, a remarkable array of stimuli and means for the growth of state power appeared in concentrated form. No country in the world could remain unaffected, and Japan felt the full brunt of all these elements. From the relatively liberal origins of her first modern state in the late nineteenth century, Japan underwent a profound metamorphosis between the wars, culminating in a statist revolution in the late 1930s. The course of this great transformation illustrates the impact of many pivotal historical influences shaping state development in the twentieth century.

The principal theoretical focus is on the relationship between political regimes and their control policies in the late imperial era. This raises perhaps the most important issue concerning modern state-society relations: to what degree is the burgeoning of state power affected by the rule of different forms of government? Interwar Japan witnessed the rule of two distinct regime types: the relatively democratic regime that governed for most of the 1918–1932 period, and the military-bureaucratic regime that dominated from 1937 to 1945. Although certain hypotheses immediately come to mind regarding the likely regime/policy connection in each case, in fact this connection proves to be quite problematic in both instances.

Traditionally, democratic regimes have been associated with the protection of civil autonomy from state encroachment. Indeed, the democratic period in prewar Japan was often characterized as embodying the *Zeitgeist* of *jiyūshugi,* or, literally, "freedomism." Yet the reputation of democracy for safeguarding autonomous social action has become somewhat tarnished in recent years. Theorists as diverse as the classical liberal Friedrich Hayek and the socialist Michael Harrington have argued that many similarities exist between the state control policies of democratic and non-democratic regimes. In a few cases, such as the government of Salvador Allende in Chile, state control has grown dramatically in a democratic context. More typically, there has been a gradual but steady increase in the state's functions in contemporary democracies. This raises a number of important issues. How do elected officials reconcile more and more penetrating state controls with political democracy and the conditions needed to sustain it? Does growing state power tend to be qualitatively different in democratic systems? Are democratic regimes able to implement new control policies through democratic mechanisms, or do new powers tend to strengthen the authority of non-democratic state institutions? These are some of the questions to be examined in the framework of prewar Japanese democracy.

The connections between military-bureaucratic regimes and rising state social controls are also complex. Presumably there will be fewer scruples of principle limiting the growth of state power under such regimes, but their ability to implement elaborate new programs of social control has been widely questioned. They tend to lack the organizational resources of regimes ruled by a single mass party as well as the popular legitimacy of democracies, making the imposition of new controls more difficult. Furthermore, the vested interests of military and bureaucratic elites make it appear unlikely that they would adopt policies seriously undermining the status quo. For these reasons, military-bureaucratic regimes, even those employing high levels of coercion against outright opponents, are not generally reputed to be great innovators in the realm of statist programs. In many countries they have even acquired a conservative image when their policies are compared to the more ambitious control schemes executed by populist leaders or revolutionary parties.

In recent years, however, this image too has begun to fade. In parts of Latin America and the Middle East, the passive conception of military rule has been shaken by the appearance of military-bureaucratic regimes out to effect far-reaching social change. The Japanese regime of 1937–

1945 provides perhaps the most direct historical precedent for the post-war military mass-mobilization programs observed in such countries as Egypt and Peru. No military regime on record has gone farther to discredit the notion that military and bureaucratic career patterns must lead to a conservative social outlook, and few regimes of any type in recent history have exerted a commensurate degree of control over society.

The research is presented as an historical narrative in order to highlight patterns of policy development. The two major parts cover the democratic and military-bureaucratic periods, respectively. Each provides background information on the political regime and a full description of policy toward the mass media, encompassing the policymaking process, the legal and institutional framework of controls and statistical evidence of their enforcement, and, to gauge the impact of state policy on a concrete level, a content analysis of media expression on a few key topics.

While the historical approach allows due emphasis on factors especially salient in the Japanese case, it does pose the danger that the treatment may become anecdotal and the findings difficult to compare to the experience of other countries. Two steps have been taken to avoid these pitfalls. First, the treatments of both the democratic and the military-bureaucratic regime are capped by chapters placing the Japanese record in a comparative perspective. Second, systematic guidelines for gathering relevant data have informed the narrative throughout. To be precise, all pertinent information was collected on state interference with six basic managerial decisions that might be made by any mass media organization:

1. The decision to found, buy, sell, or continue to operate a media enterprise.
2. The decision to set a price on media products.
3. The decision to fix the substantive contents of media products.
4. The decision to expand or contract the level of output.
5. The decision to hire or fire employees.
6. The decision to acquire materials needed to operate.

The autonomy of newspapers, current events magazines, radio stations, and film companies was examined through the levels of state control over the making of these basic decisions. In the Appendix, the findings are briefly summarized for each medium under each of these decisions for both the democratic and the military-bureaucratic period. This overview should facilitate systematic comparisons between the two regimes as well as enable other scholars to make use of this material for broader comparative purposes.

Invaluable help was received from many colleagues in Japan in the course of this project. Professors Ishida Takeshi and Uchikawa Yoshimi of the University of Tokyo served as excellent guides through the labyrinth of Japanese history. They also provided the introductions and bibliographical direction so essential to completing research of this kind. Others who gave generously of their time were Mr. Mimasaka Tarō, a former editor of *Nippon Hyōron,* Professors Okudaira Yasuhiro and Itō Takashi of the University of Tokyo, Mr. Takamasa Ono of Japan's Supreme Court Library, Mr. Ishizaka Takashi of NHK's Integrated Broadcasting Culture Research Institute, and the librarians at Tokyo University's Institute of Journalism and Communications Studies.

Special thanks go to those who were patient enough to labor through rough drafts of the manuscript, rendering advice and critical reactions when they were most needed: Professor Thomas R. H. Havens of Connecticut College, Professor Ishida Takeshi, Professor James McClain of Brown University, Professor James Crowley of Yale University, and Mr. Takejima Yasushi of NHK. I owe a very special debt of gratitude to Professor Hideo Sato of Yale and the University of Tsukuba, who served as a mentor for this project over several years, and to Professor Juan J. Linz of Yale, who spent countless hours reviewing early drafts with the author and greatly enhanced the comparative and theoretical dimensions of the research.

The project would have been impossible without financial support from the Social Science Research Council and a Fulbright-Hays award administered by the Department of Health, Education, and Welfare. Another kind fellowship offer from the Japanese Ministry of Education was declined. Financial assistance was also provided by Whitman College and by Indiana University's Office for Research and Graduate Development. My deepest appreciation goes to all these institutions.

As is customary, Japanese personal names are written with the surnames first throughout the text. In addition, full official titles and the names of important state offices have been capitalized to highlight the roles of key bureaucratic actors.

PART I

Democracy and Liberty under Party Governments, 1918–1932

CHAPTER I

The Meiji Heritage

It was during the reign of Emperor Meiji (1868–1912) that Japan witnessed the creation of its first modern state and its first periodical press. A brief review of Meiji press policy forms a necessary background to the interwar period, since the establishment of party government in 1918 occurred within the Meiji constitutional framework. Not only the constitution and basic press codes but also many administrative practices of great consequence were carried over into the democratic era.

EARLY MEIJI PRESS POLICY, 1868–1889

The overthrow of the shogunate in 1868 brought to power a modernizing elite of ex-samurai from Japan's western provinces that struggled successfully to institutionalize its authority over the next twenty years. This was a period of arduous challenges to the new leadership, and the press frequently sided with its opponents. Yet although governments restricted the press in numerous ways to safeguard their authority, the Meiji elite nonetheless provided a relatively auspicious foundation for press autonomy in modern Japan.

Until the promulgation of the constitution in 1889, press legislation changed rather frequently in ad hoc response to political crises; provisions of the principal codes are outlined in table 1. The occasions for their enactment can be described briefly.[1] The 1869 decree set conditions for the reemergence of periodicals after existing journals had been shut down the previous year. Most of those closed had recently been established by ex-officials of the shogunate opposed to the Meiji Restoration. Prior to the 1860s, despite a thriving book industry, the only precedents for periodicals were one-page flyers printed on wood blocks to report earthquakes, lovers' suicides, and other sensational events; as a rule, these did not involve political expression. The Meiji elite might have organized an official press monopoly, but instead it not only permitted but encouraged the founding of private journals from 1869. The government bought copies of Tokyo newspapers and distributed them nationwide, provided special postage rates for publications, and supported the opening of tabloids in many provinces where there was initially no press at all.[2] If one goal was to foster subservient journalism, the leadership also saw the press as essential for the rapid dissemination of Western technology, needed to modernize the country.

The legislation of 1873 was provoked by a severe split within the elite itself over whether to invade Korea. When those favoring immediate conquest resigned, the new code was issued to handle the expected crescendo of criticism as they joined the civil opposition. Enforcement was far from perfect, however. A reactionary clique of resignees prepared to launch a military revolt, and their press organs urged the assassination of state leaders and the overthrow of the regime.[3] This led to the still tougher regulations of 1875. During the rebellions that followed in 1876 and 1877, the Home Ministry instituted emergency police controls over all war reporting.

The severest newspaper restrictions of the early Meiji years were those imposed in 1883 to defuse the Freedom and Popular Rights Movement. Having pledged itself to write a constitution, the government sought to shield this project from outside party pressure. In the early 1880s, many newspapers were arranging party affiliations. It is estimated that in 1882 the two major opposition parties were backed by a

1. For more detailed treatment, see Midoro Masaichi, *Meiji Taishō Shi I: Genron Hen;* Richard H. Mitchell, *Censorship in Imperial Japan;* James L. Huffman, *Politics of the Meiji Press: The Life of Fukuchi Gen'ichiro;* Jay Rubin, *Injurious to Public Morals: Writers and the Meiji State.*
2. Okudaira Yasuhiro, "Nihon Shuppan Keisatsu Hōsei no Rekishiteki Kenkyū Josetsu," May 1967, pp. 107–8. This was the third of seven articles by Prof. Okudaira appearing in the journal under this title. They are hereafter cited by the author's name, the abbreviated title "Nihon Shuppan Keisatsu," and the date of the issue.
3. Okudaira, "Nihon Shuppan Keisatsu," June 1967, p. 42; Midoro, *Meiji Taishō Shi I,* p. 41.

TABLE I   STATE RESTRICTIONS ON THE PERIODICAL PRESS, 1869–1890

	1869	1873	1875	1883	1887
Required to publish					
License	x	x	x	x	
Notice					x
Security deposit				x	x
Debarred from publishing					
Foreigners			x	x	x
Women				x	x
Minors				x	x
Convicts/probationers				x	x
Owners and employees of a banned or suspended journal				x	
Legal obligations					
Submission of copies	x	x		x	x
Mandatory corrections	x	x	x	x	x
Political censorship restrictions	x	x	x	x	x
Revelation of news sources				x	
Legal responsibility for content					
Owner			x	x	x
Manager			x	x	x
Editor	x[a]	x[a]	x	x	x
Author			x	x	x
Printer				x	x
Administrative sanctions					
Suspend/ban publication				x[b]	x
Seize printing equipment				x	x
Judicial sanctions					
Maximum prison sentence	—[c]	—[c]	3 yrs	3 yrs	3 yrs

Sources: Midoro Masaichi, *Meiji Taishō Shi I,* pp. 31–32, 119–26, 373; W. W. McLaren, ed., "Japanese Government Documents," pp. 534–35, 539–50.

Note: The table covers only those restrictions provided for by statute. The regime's first ordinances were brief and may not have included all those restrictions actually enforced.

[a]Only the editor was specifically noted, but all infringing the regulations were declared responsible for violations.

[b]This power was added by administrative decree in July 1876.

[c]No specific term of imprisonment was codified in the law.

total of 64 newspapers, while the state-supported party was championed by only 21.[4] Enforcement of the 1883 code was harsh. From 1883 to 1887, 174 periodicals were suspended from publication for varying periods, and another 4 banned altogether, while 198 journalists served

4. Midoro, *Meiji Taishō Shi I,* pp. 112–13.

time in prison.[5] Having jailed many opposition leaders and banished others from Tokyo, the government relaxed its newspaper ordinance in December 1887, as the constitutional project neared completion. For the first time, officials abandoned the licensing system and required only advance notice of intent to open a journal.

There has been much scholarly debate over the repressiveness of the early Meiji state. George Akita has argued that government restraints were of modest proportions, while Richard Mitchell has judged them more harshly, characterizing the penal system as an "embryonic Gulag Archipelago."[6] Assessments will vary depending on the standard of judgment. If repressiveness is measured according to the size and resources of the opposition, the state's actions were more than sufficient to hold its adversaries at bay in the 1880s. Seen from a broader perspective, however, it seems more noteworthy that the Meiji founders never wavered in their acceptance of privately operated journals with an independent political role. In a country with no precedents for an autonomous periodical press voicing critical political commentary, there were 647 newspapers and magazines set in operation by 1889, 164 of them treating current events. Even during the Satsuma Rebellion of 1877 and the most repressive period, the mid-1880s, the growth of a critical press suffered only minor and temporary setbacks.

Early Meiji policy thus represents a considerable liberalization of prior practices, and the passage of time has only reconfirmed its comparatively liberal character. To discuss the autonomy of a civil periodical press at all it is first necessary for one to exist. Most new states founded in the mid-twentieth century have prohibited privately operated newspapers altogether, and the Meiji leaders might have followed a similar course. The foreign and domestic threats facing the regime could have been used to justify a state monopoly over political publications. Not only did early press organs serve the opposition, but their combative, partisan character was untempered by any tradition of fairness or responsible reporting. Concocted stories abounded (for example, false reports that government leaders had fallen in battle), and scurrilous tales of officials' private lives were commonplace. Yet the government, with its eye on contemporary Western patterns of development, did not adopt the out-and-out statist program so typical of new states in the twentieth century. Its press policies stand instead among the relatively

5. Ibid., pp. 86–87; Nihon Teikoku Shihōshō, *Keiji Tōkei Nenpō*, nos. 8–14, 1882–1888.
6. Mitchell, *Censorship*, p. 96.

liberal practices of other modern states created in the nineteenth century, when a more liberal outlook prevailed among founding statesmen than is generally the case today.[7]

THE PRIMACY OF
ADMINISTRATIVE POLICYMAKING

The early Meiji state not only set important legal precedents but also developed certain habits of governance destined to have a lasting impact on media policy. Most critical of these was the wide discretion granted to administrators in making and implementing the law. One episode in bureaucratic policymaking is especially useful for illustrating the origins of administrative dominance and its implications for the emerging conception of the state.

As noted above, the 1875 Newspaper Ordinance was issued to counter seditious criticism from the reactionary press. The law failed to attain its object, however, due to a large loophole. Although it authorized the prosecution of editors, it did not permit the state to close a journal. When one editor went to jail, another would replace him and carry on under the same owner; some journals even took to hiring straw men to serve the jail sentences. In this way state control was rendered ineffective. How would officials correct this deficiency?

The government first considered amending the Newspaper Ordinance so that a journal could be banned if its editor was convicted. The Council of Elder Statesmen (Genrō-in) objected, however, since this would inflict punishment before appeals had been heard.[8] Judicial practices were a tender spot because the Japanese wished to convince the Western powers to abandon their extraterritorial rights. To circumvent this objection, in July 1876 the executive simply enacted a decree: "If newspapers, magazines, or other news publications already approved are recognized as disturbing national peace, the Home Ministry shall prohibit or suspend their publication."[9] This strategy bypassed the judi-

---

7. For an alternative interpretation that sees Meiji media policy as highly statist and leading naturally to the more severe media controls of the late imperial era, see Mitchell, *Censorship*. My own reading, to be developed further below, is that Meiji policy was comparatively liberal and that the radical controls of the 1930s involved a sharp and conscious rejection of the Meiji legacy. Akita's analysis of the Meiji elite as relatively liberal is found in his *Foundations of Constitutional Government in Modern Japan, 1868–1900*.

8. Okudaira, "Nihon Shuppan Keisatsu," August 1967, p. 79.

9. Reprinted in Okudaira, "Nihon Shuppan Keisatsu," September 1967, p. 56.

cial system and allowed bureaucrats to close a journal as a purely administrative measure, that is, Home Ministry officials could now abolish press organs on their own authority. The alleged malefactor had no opportunity to defend his journal as he might defend himself in court: the administrator's decision was final, leaving no route of appeal.

When this decree was challenged in court, it was ruled that the right to stop publications was "inherent in the government." Upon appeal, the Supreme Court concurred, stating that the Home Ministry inherently possessed whatever authority was required to fulfill its duties regarding public peace. The decree had merely publicized and transposed into statutory form a preexisting administrative right.[10] When the publishers of banned journals reapplied for permits under other titles, the Home Ministry again pleaded for a new law to stop the practice, but the Legislative Bureau (*Hōseikyoku*) advised the ministry to "dispose of this matter conveniently within the realm of its own competence."[11] In December 1876, the ministry summarily announced that it would deny permits to anyone whose publications had previously been banned, and the matter was settled.

This episode illuminates the early Meiji conception of the state-society relationship. The first fact of political life is that the state possesses certain intrinsic functions, one of which is to keep order. It is assumed that the existing state is the legitimate repository of these functions. All means necessary to perform them fall within the state's legitimate rights, and officials are the sole judges of what means are necessary. The only real limit to the power of the state is self-restraint. No political facts beyond the state's inherent functions and rights (such as the natural rights of individuals or of regional or corporate groups) need enter the equation for legitimate authority. Under this system laws and decrees merely publicize the form that authority will take; they are not methods of legitimizing power itself. This outlook borrowed heavily from Japan's pre-1868 political traditions, but it was also strongly influenced by European (especially German) theories of inherent state administrative rights:

> According to the *Rechtsstaat* concept, the state is a legal personality analogous to, but significantly different from, the legal personality (*juristisch Person*) of private law. Its distinguishing characteristic is its possession of sovereignty, which . . . implies at least the power to govern and the power to define its own competence and that of its organs. As a legal personality, the

10. The legal rulings on the decree are analyzed in ibid., pp. 57–59.
11. Quoted in ibid., p. 60.

state is considered to be the subject—that is, possessor—of rights and duties (*Rechtssubjekt*), which are defined in the constitution and in other organic legislation by a process of autolimitation (*Selbstbeschrankung*).[12]

Since Japan had no constitution, in the sense indicated, before 1889, the boundaries of autolimitation were redefined with every ordinance. Autonomous social activities were but a residual zone that officials had thus far chosen not to invade.

A concomitant of administrative license was the fuzzy language in which legal regulations were framed. The two principal justifications for sanctions against the press were to keep public order and to safeguard manners and morals. Typically, both concepts were first applied to newspapers through bureaucratic decrees and only later were incorporated into the major legislation of 1883.[13] It became common for the frontier of state policy to be staked out by piecemeal administrative innovations; more formal statutes sanctioning these innovations would be enacted later or not at all. The two vague prescriptions of public order and manners and morals would remain at the heart of media censorship until 1945. Unless they were applied consistently over a long period, which was frequently not the case, publishers could not anticipate their meaning in practice. All that "disturbing national peace" signified to the press was that if officials disliked a story they could penalize the journal. This brand of catchall prohibition maximized administrative leeway in enforcing the law.

The expansion of state power by granting administrators wide discretionary authority was a logical development given the prevailing theory of the state, the concrete historical circumstances, and the convenience of administrative measures. Administrative flexibility relieved officials of having to frame or amend general statutes every time increments of real power were added, and, by facilitating quick policy decisions and execution, it minimized resort to laborious trial procedures. These are great advantages for a regime facing serious challenges in the process of consolidation. Yet with the onset of constitutionalism, the unfettered administrative rule of the early Meiji period created a predicament that was to plague Japan throughout the imperial era: how could bureau-

12. Frank O. Miller, *Minobe Tatsukichi: Interpreter of Constitutionalism in Japan*, p. 10.
13. The "manners and morals" clause had first been added by decree on 12 October 1880: see Okudaira Yasuhiro, "Ken'etsu Seido," p. 145. The first version of the concept of public order in press regulations was in the Home Ministry's decree of 5 July 1876, in which the ministry declared its rights to ban journals and suspend them from publication.

cratic prerogatives be reconciled with the basic constitutional principle
of rule by law?

THE CONSTITUTION
AND PRESS CONTROLS

The 1889 constitution contained two potent mechanisms protecting
the autonomy of the press: the legislative powers of an elected lower
house of parliament, and an independent judiciary. Article 29 affirmed
that "Japanese subjects shall, within the limits of law, enjoy the liberty
of speech, writing, publication, public meetings, and associations."[14]
"Law" was by definition a statute approved by both houses of the Diet.
Ministerial regulations did not qualify as laws and therefore, according
to this article, they could not interfere with the press. The judiciary was
made sufficiently independent to resist pressure from the police or the
cabinet. Itō Hirobumi, who supervised the constitutional project, wrote
of the difference between the courts and the administration: "In the
judiciary, law is everything, and the question of convenience is left out
of consideration."[15] Though all judges were employees of the Ministry
of Justice, their tenure was protected by the constitution except in cases
of criminal misconduct, the terms of which were fixed by law. In a
celebrated case in 1891, the Supreme Court demonstrated its independence by rejecting the cabinet's entreaties to condemn to death a would-
be assassin of the visiting Russian Crown Prince and instead ruling for
life imprisonment.[16] In sum, only a law passed by elected officials could
limit the autonomy of the press, and the prosecution of offenders would
be adjudicated by an independent court system.

This protective shield was not as generous as it first appears, however. The insertion of civil liberties in the Meiji constitution was not
based on theories of natural right, social contract, or popular sovereignty. The liberties of subjects had the status of gifts bestowed by the
Emperor, the constitution was proclaimed on his authority, and its
provisions were said to flow from Japan's unique "national polity,"
rooted in an unbroken imperial line descended from the mythical Sun
Goddess. The founders conceived of the public interest not as a sum of
privately defined goods or a common ground between them, but, rather,

14. All translations of the constitution are from Itō Hirobumi, *Commentaries on the
Constitution of the Empire of Japan*.
15. Ibid., p. 111.
16. Midoro, *Meiji Taishō Shi I*, pp. 169–70. This was the so-called Ōtsu Incident.

as an indivisible good pertaining to the whole society, an outlook shared by many of Europe's monarchical and post-monarchical bureaucracies.[17] In their view, individual liberty was truly legitimate only insofar as it was used to serve this overriding public interest, which it was the task of the state to identify and preserve. If the Meiji leaders unleashed autonomous human endeavor in many fields, they did so because their analysis of the West convinced them that such liberalization would serve the public interest by creating a "rich nation and strong army." Justification for individual freedom as a good in itself was lacking.[18] Accordingly, liberty of the press was far from absolute, and the constitution itself restricted journalism in a number of ways.

Some of these restrictions have been common even to the world's most liberal press codes. Article 32, for example, placed military regulations higher than the soldier's constitutional liberties, and the military denied active-duty servicemen the right to engage in political writing or discussions.[19] This plank has been in many legal codes, to shield the

---

17. The Japanese term *chōtōhashugi* (to be above parties and factions) may be a translation of the German *Überparteilichkeit*.

18. The logic of the founding fathers is captured in the following passage on the autonomy of religious beliefs taken from Itō Hirobumi's *Commentaries*, pp. 58–60:

> the doctrine of freedom of religious belief, which dates back four centuries, first received practical recognition at the time of the French Revolution and of the independence of the United States of America. . . . [it] is to be regarded as one of the most beautiful fruits of modern civilization. . . . Freedom of conscience concerns the inner part of man and lies beyond the sphere of interference by the laws of the State. To force upon a nation . . . a state religion is very injurious to the natural intellectual development of the people, and is prejudicial to the progress of science by free competition. No country, therefore, possesses by reason of its political authority, the right or the capacity to an oppressive measure touching abstract questions of religious faith. . . . As to forms of worship, to religious discourses, to the mode of propagating a religion and to the formation of religious associations and meetings, some general legal or police restrictions must be observed for the maintenance of public peace and order. No believer in this or that religion has the right . . . to free himself from his duties to the State, which, as a subject, he is bound to discharge.

This statement epitomizes the rationale behind Meiji liberalism. The autonomy of a particular social activity is posited as general practice in Western Europe and the United States, which are equated with "modern civilization." This autonomy is not legitimized with reference to moral principles; rather, to deny it would be "prejudicial to the progress of science by free competition." This utilitarian legitimacy drawn from the example of the West is compromised only by the legal duties of a subject, i.e., religions are not to deny conscription, the Emperor, the payment of taxes, or other basic obligations. It was this same reasoning that led to a fairly autonomous periodical press, which was also copied initially from the West, useful for technological development, and referred to as a right "within the bounds of the law."

19. Ibid., p. 67. Disciplinary regulations in the armed forces were a direct responsibility of the Emperor (in practice, of the services themselves), and beyond the competence of the Diet (article 12).

military from political discord and to exclude the force of arms from public debate, but it nonetheless created a long blacklist of potential writers. Furthermore, although in principle trials were to be conducted publicly, the constitution empowered the courts to hold them in secret when necessary to safeguard public order or morality (article 59). The Diet's deliberations could also be closed to the public "upon demand of the Government or by resolution of the House" (article 48). Thus both the courts and the Diet could preclude press coverage of important political happenings. These two provisions as well are found in nearly all countries where a civil press is allowed to function.[20]

More serious were the constitutional powers granted to the bureaucracy, which left an ambiguous boundary between legislative and bureaucratic press authority despite the Diet's formal jurisdiction in this area. Any ministry could issue decrees as a proxy for imperial authority. Their legitimate purposes were "for the carrying out of the laws, or for the maintenance of the public peace and order, and for the promotion of the welfare of the subjects" (article 9). This wide formulation reflected a conscious decision not to limit the administration to execution of the law, as provided for in the French, Belgian, and Prussian constitutions of the day. According to Itō Hirobumi, "Were the executive confined to the execution of the law, the state would be powerless to discharge its proper functions in the case of absence of a law. Accordingly, ordinances are not only means for executing the law, but may, in order to meet requirements of given circumstances, be used to give manifestation to some original idea."[21] Itō thus rejected the dichotomy between policy-making and administration so strongly emphasized by a contemporary of his, Woodrow Wilson. The notion that the bureaucracy should be a mere servant of the non-bureaucratic political elite was not adopted even in theory by the Meiji founders and was explicitly denied by their constitution. Bureaucratic measures could not contravene parliamentary law (article 9), but if laws were written in general terms, administrators could add the specifics, and where there were no laws at all they might introduce "some original idea."

Yet, how could bureaucratic measures affect the press, when it was specifically provided that only Diet laws could compromise the liberties of subjects? The answer is that there were no adequate means to prevent bureaucrats from overstepping their allotted authority. The judiciary,

20. Fernand Terrou and Lucien Solal, *Legislation for Press, Film and Radio*, pp. 282, 286.

21. Itō Hirobumi, *Commentaries*, p. 21.

for all its independence, had no jurisdiction over administrative measures.[22] There was a special system of administrative courts, but the press laws did not provide for this route of appeal. Only constant vilgilance by the Diet could check bureaucratic intervention in press policy, and experience would show that the Diet was ill equipped to play the role of watchdog.

If administrative ordinances were normally to yield to acts of the legislature, the reverse was true in times of emergency. Emergency imperial ordinances could be issued when the Diet was in recess if there was "an urgent necessity to maintain public safety or to avert public calamities" (article 8). If such ordinances were not approved at the next Diet meeting, they then lost their validity. Article 14 further authorized the imperial declaration of a state of siege, which according to Itō was to be used "at the time of a foreign war or of a domestic insurrection, for the purpose of placing all ordinary law in abeyance and of entrusting part of the administrative and judicial powers to military measures."[23] These two articles enabled the executive to use stringent measures against the press in crises. Emergency imperial decrees were employed to restrain the press on four occasions before the onset of party government, only one of which involved a state of war.[24]

In sum, legislative and judicial protection for the press was limited by constitutional clauses on military service, the secrecy of court and Diet proceedings, administrative prerogatives, and emergency executive powers. A final point is that the press had no defense from the Diet itself. The proviso that civil liberties could be exercised only "within the limits of law" meant that parliamentary laws might eradicate press autonomy altogether without violating the constitution. Scholars sometimes cite

22. Itō wrote:

Were administrative measures placed under the control of the judicature, and were courts of justice charged with the duty of deciding whether a particular administrative measure was or was not proper, administrative authorities would be in a state of subordination to judicial functionaries. The consequence would be that the administrative would be deprived of freedom of action in securing benefits to society and happiness to the people. . . . As the object of an administrative measure is to maintain public interests, it will become necessary under certain circumstances to sacrifice individuals for the sake of the public benefit. But the question of administrative expedience is just what judicial authorities are ordinarily apt to be not conversant with. It would, therefore, be rather dangerous to confide to them the power of deciding such questions. (Ibid., pp. 120–21)

23. Ibid., p. 31.
24. Emergency imperial decrees were issued after the attempted assassination of the visiting Russian Prince in May 1891, the day war was declared against China in August 1894, in the aftermath of the Portsmouth treaty negotiations in September 1905, and briefly during the rice riots of August 1918.

this priority of law over fundamental liberties as proof of the framers' authoritarian bent, but this stipulation has been a mainstay of the Western liberal tradition. Even the French revolutionaries' Declaration of the Rights of Man and the Citizen proclaimed the freedoms of speech and the press "except as prohibited by the law," and European constitutional practice has generally developed in accord with this principle; in fact, many European constitutions of the late nineteenth century made no mention of civil liberties at all. It might be assumed that the Diet's House of Representatives, elected by subjects, would not acquiesce in overly oppressive legislation despite its sweeping powers. With the passage of time, however, the validity of this assumption was to be severely tested.

THE DIET AND PRESS POLICY: THE NEWSPAPER LAW OF 1909

The constitution, rather than placating the opposition parties, at first served only to institutionalize their struggle against the founding fathers. The Meiji elite retained control over the cabinet, which was formally appointed by the Emperor according to the founders' advice, while elections gave the opposition dominant influence in the Diet's lower house. From this foothold within the system, the parties strove to use the legislature's power over laws and budgetary increases to extract concessions from the cabinet. Conflict over press restrictions was especially heated since the Diet included many journalists, some of whom had served time in prison for censorship violations. In the beginning, then, the battle lines over press policy were drawn as might be expected; most elected officials pressed for more liberal treatment, while the Meiji founders were generally opposed.

The Meiji elite easily won the early rounds of this contest. All legal codes in force in 1889 had been endowed by the constitution itself with the status of laws, and the approval of both houses was required to amend or replace them. Consequently, the 1887 Newspaper Ordinance was still on the books, and lower-house reform proposals were blocked by the conservative House of Peers, an appointed body. In the course of twelve Diet meetings during the period from 1890 to 1898, nineteen proposals to reform the Newspaper Ordinance were presented to the Diet, but none met with success. Twice measures passed by the House of Representatives died in the House of Peers, and twice bills consigned to a joint committee were thwarted by the upper-house participants. All proposed revisions would have curtailed or eliminated the Home Ministry's administrative power to ban or suspend publication.[25]

In 1896, the tide turned in favor of journalistic autonomy. Ōkuma Shigenobu, a black sheep among the Meiji elite who favored the party movement, demanded more tolerant treatment of the press as a condition for his entry into the Matsukata cabinet.[26] The Prime Minister subsequently endorsed a bill abrogating the bureaucratic power to ban or suspend journals from publication, and it passed the Diet in March 1897. The bill did empower the courts to stop publication, but this was still a liberal change: from 1890 to 1896, bureaucrats suspended press organs on 654 occasions; from 1897 to 1908, with this power confined to the judiciary, only 21 journals were suspended. The disparate effects of administrative and judicial implementation could not be clearer. All in all, this was a major victory for the House of Representatives and a vindication of those determined to work for change within the constitutional system. Surprisingly, however, despite a continual rise in the Diet's influence, the 1897 reform was not followed by further liberalization of the press code.

What began as yet another attempt by representatives to loosen state controls in 1909 ended by reversing the liberal trend of the previous two decades. The Newspaper Law passed in that year was a landmark piece of legislation that would endure until 1945. The original bill would have reduced prison sentences, ended the judicial power to dissolve publications, opened pre-trial proceedings to newspaper coverage, and eliminated security money for periodicals appearing fewer than four times monthly.[27] Its sponsor, Matsumura Kōichirō, had been a political reporter for the *Ōsaka Asahi Shinbun*. In lower house committee, Justice and Home Ministry officials criticized the measure, and it was then delegated to a subcommittee of five representatives, all press people.[28]

Working in consultation with bureaucrats, within days the subcommittee produced a comprehensive Newspaper Law that defeated most objectives of the original proposal.[29] The bond money system was toughened by doubling the required amounts, the judicial power to terminate

25. Uchikawa Yoshimi, "Shinbunshi Hō no Settei Katei to Sono Tokushitsu," p. 61.
26. Ibid., p. 63.
27. It is reprinted in ibid., pp. 93–95.
28. Eight members of the original eighteen-man committee were active in the newspaper business, seven of these in management: ibid., p. 78.
29. Ibid., pp. 82–83. The Newspaper Law is reprinted in Shunbara Akihiko, *Nihon Shinbun Tsūshi*, pp. 124–29.

a publication remained intact, and treatments of pre-trial criminal proceedings were still disallowed, despite a slight relaxation in wording.[30]
The only new leniency in punishments was a reduction of the penalty
for publicizing secret pre-trial proceedings and official documents, from
imprisonment to simple fines. Furthermore, the draft authorized administrators to ban particular editions of a journal from circulation and to
seize all copies without resorting to prosecution. This major innovation
soon became the principal source of bureacratic power over the press.
The Newspaper Law was approved overwhelmingly by the full committee and was passed by both houses in March 1909, without significant
amendment.

The scantiness of criticism of the new legislation is remarkable. One
scholar found virtually no discussion of free expression during the Diet's consideration of the bill.[31] Another, who examined newspaper reactions, concluded, "What is astounding is the fact that there was not even
one criticism of the Newspaper Law from the contemporary press either
during the process of Diet deliberations or after its promulgation."[32]
Indeed, the Ōsaka Asahi newspaper editorialized on 15 May 1909 that
the law was neither a step forward nor backward, remarking that the
administrative right to seize particular issues was largely justified by
journalistic abuses.[33] What brought about this atrophy of the liberalism
so prominent in the press and the Diet just ten years earlier, when the
1897 reform had stricken a similar power from the books?

Passage of the Newspaper Law is best explained by three factors: the
new willingness of the Diet opposition to work for change within the
existing constitutional framework; a corresponding shift in the politics
of the mainstream press; and the appearance of socialist intellectuals
and a workers' movement that were anathema to the establishment as a
whole. Since these changes set the stage for a discussion of media policy
under party governments, each deserves further comment.

The Newspaper Law reflects a reconciliation of sorts between the
Meiji founding elite and its principal civil opponents of the late nineteenth century. The Diet opposition, thanks in part to a restricted electorate, was mainly made up of political and economic elites on the outs.

30. Whereas the old ordinance had banned all information "related to the pre-trial
examination," the law now specified the "contents of the pre-trial examination," presumably allowing general information on the crime, so long as it was not specifically prohibited by the prosecutor. One impetus for the original reform proposal had been the prosecution of fourteen Tokyo newspapers for reporting the murder of a restaurant hostess in
December 1908.
31. Shunbara, Nihon Shinbun Tsūshi, p. 130.
32. Uchikawa, "Shinbunshi Hō no Settei," p. 85.
33. Shunbara, Nihon Shinbun Tsūshi, p. 131.

Election to the legislature had afforded these men considerable influence within the state, and by 1909 party politicians in the lower house had held important cabinet posts. While persisting in their drive for full-fledged party government, they discovered certain common interests with the Meiji leadership, above all a shared desire to control labor. They were not averse to police laws apparently aimed at this new opposition group, and consequently they did not uphold the liberal cause in 1909 as had once been anticipated (indeed, feared) by the constitution's framers.

The conversion of opposition leaders into adherents of the constitution was accompanied by similar changes in the orientation of the press. Journalism shed much of its political character and developed into a multifaceted business largely independent of the parties. Journals downplaying politics in favor of more general subject matter had appeared as early as the mid-1870s. They were long called the "little newspapers" in deference to the politically inclined heavyweights dominating the periodical press. But the commercial bent of the little newspapers infiltrated most of the press after the Sino-Japanese War (1895), with contents shifting toward human interest stories and the society page as journals competed for readers.[34] Political commentary was not abandoned, and the press retained its basically critical stance vis-à-vis the state. But purely informative reporting gained ground over partisan editorializing as the press retreated from party affiliations, and censure lost its radical edge as the major journals followed leading politicians in their propensity to criticize from within the constitutional order.

Both legislators and journalists accepted the Newspaper Law mainly because they were convinced by government spokesmen and recent trends in enforcement that its primary targets were political radicals and pornographers. Though the socialist and labor press was still minuscule, conservative state elites emphasized the need for preventive measures. Premier Katsura Tarō wrote in 1908:

> We are now in an age of economic transition. Development of machine industry and intensification of competition create a gap between rich and poor and this becomes greater and greater; and according to Western history this is an inevitable pattern. Socialism is today accepted by only a few but if it is ignored it will someday spread. Obviously therefore it is necessary to propagate public morals. What we call social policy will prevent socialism from taking root.[35]

34. Uchikawa, "Shinbunshi Hō no Settei," p. 65.
35. Quoted in Kenneth B. Pyle, "The Technology of Japanese Nationalism: The Local Improvement Movement 1900–1918," p. 55.

State officials focused the Diet's discussion of the Newspaper Law on the campaign against radicals. For example, the Home Ministry's Criminal Affairs Bureau Chief defended the judicial power to terminate publication as follows:

> Naturally, if one looks at past examples, the cases in which the courts have handed down a verdict of stopping publication have been extremely flagrant, one or just a few each year. . . . In other words, in cases where a periodical embraces from the start the objective of carrying articles harming manners and morals or encouraging radical socialism, and when even one or two punishments [that is, fines or imprisonment] give rise to absolutely no prospect of reform, the courts prohibit further publication. In fact, the application of this clause is extremely rare, as I have just said.[36]

Recent experience could only confirm this statement. According to Professor Uchikawa Yoshimi, every political journal closed on court orders from the legal reform of 1897 to passage of the Newspaper Law in 1909 had been connected with the labor movement or socialism.[37] Even the new administrative right to ban particular editions appeared to be aimed at obscenity and the left. Journalists had no prior experience with this precise administrative power, and their subsequent protests confirm that they did not anticipate the enormous impact it would have on the mainstream press.[38]

Since the new law was to govern newspapers, and those magazines covering current events, for the next thirty-six years (purely artistic, scientific, and statistical magazines were regulated under the Publication Law of 1893), its principal tenets are enumerated here for reference:

Banned from publishing and editing were active-duty military men, minors, convicts and probationers, and those residing outside the empire, but women were no longer disqualified.

To found a journal a person had to notify officials ten days in advance, report the names of the owner, publisher, chief editor, and printer, and post a security deposit if current events were to be covered. Local authorities could suspend a publication until it met these requirements.

---

36. Quoted in Midoro, *Meiji Taishō Shi I*, pp. 238–39.
37. Uchikawa, "Shinbunshi Hō no Settei," p. 79.
38. According to the law of 1883, circulation could be stopped only if there were an administrative decision to close down the publication altogether. Under existing law, police could stop circulation only if the issue in question were prosecuted in court, and this happened only in blatant cases of illegality. The Home Ministry's spokesman defended the need for change, arguing that by the time the ministry decided to prosecute it was often too late to remove the offending issue from circulation: Midoro, *Meiji Taishō Shi I*, p. 238. He did not indicate that the new power might be used against mainstream journals for offenses too minor to be prosecuted.

Inspection copies had to be sent to the central Home Ministry, local government, and the local and regional prosecutors' offices simultaneously with publication.

Forbidden contents included preliminary trial proceedings, closed judicial hearings and Diet deliberations, unreleased state documents or petitions to the state, incitement to crime or vindication of a criminal, desecration of the imperial family, matters undermining the constitution, advocacy of changes in the political regime, anything subversive of public order or manners and morals, and information banned by the Army, Navy, or Foreign Ministers within their areas of competence.

Corrections of false or defaming stories submitted by the affected party had to be published without charge in the same length and size of print as the original report.

The Home Minister could stop circulation of any issue threatening public order or manners and morals, and prohibit further publication of similar contents by the same journal.

A court of law could terminate a journal carrying items banned by the Army, Navy, or Foreign Ministers, disturbing public order or manners and morals, or violating the clauses on the imperial family, political regime, or constitution.

Legal responsibility for the contents of an article was shared by the chief editor, subordinate editors who worked on the article, and the author, and, for some offenses, the publisher and printer as well.

Maximum prison sentences for various offenses were *three months* for inciting crime or vindicating a criminal, or for an editor who lied about his legal qualifications; *six months* to the publisher, editor, and author for disobeying a judicial writ to cease publication, disturbing public order or manners and morals, or violating a Home Ministry prohibition on certain contents; *two years* to the publisher, editors, and author for items banned by the Army, Navy, or Foreign Ministers, and to the publisher, editors, author, and printer for articles violating clauses on the imperial family, political regime, and constitution. Other offenses were punished with fines, including the knowing sale or distribution of a banned edition.

The institutional, ideological, and legal legacy of the Meiji founders has often been blamed for inviting the more statist media policies of later years, and this proposition will be closely examined in the chapters that follow. At this point, however, at least three observations can be made bearing upon such an historical assessment. First, the Newspaper Law was hardly a Draconian measure as press codes go. The clauses on personnel restrictions, notification of intent to publish, inspection copies, and forbidden contents have been fairly standard even in the press laws of democratic regimes.[39] Only two provisions stand out as departures from the liberal norm. One is the demand for a security deposit, instituted by only a few countries in this century (for example, Lebanon, Egypt, Colombia).[40] The other is the administrative right to seize offending editions, which liberal regimes have generally permitted only in times of emergency, if at all.[41] Yet this did not constitute a system of pre-publication censorship, and short of revolutionary rhetoric, the law allowed severe reproofs of government policies and officials.[42] It certainly did not prevent a large segment of the press from furthering the cause of democracy during the next decade.

A second observation is that the Meiji constitution had shown itself compatible with even more liberal directions while the founding fathers still dominated the cabinet. The newspaper code of 1897 turned out to be the most liberal framework for press controls ever legislated in imperial Japan. Finally, the system provided later party governments with ample opportunity to rewrite the press code—as will be shown, it was they who chose not to take advantage of it. Of the various political elites to rule Japan in the imperial era, the Meiji founders must be remembered as the only ones to leave the press freer from state control than they had found it.

DEMOCRACY AND THE MASS MEDIA: INTRODUCTORY REMARKS

In 1918 Japan's first party cabinet of lower-house representatives took control of the Meiji state. Most theories of political democracy posit an intimate relationship between this form of government and the autonomy of the mass media. At a minimum, support for democracy implies a belief that subjects of the state should have some input into the making of its policies. Consequently, the central empirical feature of a modern democracy is that subjects choose many top state officials from among competing candidates in elections permitting a genuine expression of the popular will. Neither the presentation of diverse candidates

39. See Terrou and Solal, *Legislation*, pp. 259–328.
40. Ibid., pp. 71–76.
41. Ibid., pp. 335–36.
42. Police confiscation was so inefficient that in practice it was not even an effective form of pre-circulation control; see chapter 2.

nor a meaningful formulation of electoral choice is possible without some degree of media autonomy. In fact, many conceptions of political democracy point to media autonomy as a constituent element of the regime type. For example, Robert Dahl's criteria for a polyarchy in a large contemporary country include freedom of expression, access to alternative sources of information, free and fair elections, and institutions for making government policies depend on votes and other expressions of preference; these requirements could not be met in the absence of autonomous media organs.[43] The close logical association between democratic procedures and the autonomy of the mass media clearly leads one to expect liberal policies from democratic regimes. As Alexis de Tocqueville wrote, "censorship of the press and universal suffrage are two things which are irreconcilably opposed and which cannot long be retained among the institutions of the same people."[44]

Democratic practice, however, has often confounded these theoretical expectations, and prewar Japan illustrates a much more complex relationship between democracy and the mass media than is indicated above. Japan's elected leaders, though they did not impose an extreme system of mobilization, nonetheless acted to restrict media autonomy rather than to enhance it. Notwithstanding de Tocqueville's assertion, the Japanese Diet approved a Peace Preservation Law stiffening press controls simultaneously with universal manhood suffrage. Controls instituted over the new medium of film were even tougher than press restrictions, requiring state censorship before public exposure. And radio, first established during the democratic period, was the most tightly regulated of all, confined to a public-interest monopoly that denied autonomous political expression. What makes this record significant is that it has not been at all unusual among democratic systems. In fact, democratic practice tends to point away from the dominant theoretical perspective toward a minoritarian viewpoint that posits at best a tenuous connection between democracy and liberty. As Isaiah Berlin expressed it:

> Self-government may, on the whole, provide a better guarantee of the preservation of civil liberties than other regimes, and has been defended as such by libertarians. But there is no necessary connection between individual liberty and democratic rule. The answer to the question "Who governs me?" is logically distinct from the question "How far does government interfere with me?"[45]

43. Robert A. Dahl, *Polyarchy*, p. 3.
44. Alexis de Tocqueville, *Democracy in America*, 1: 190.
45. Isaiah Berlin, *Four Essays on Liberty*, p. 130.

The chapters that follow aim at explaining how it is that a regime led by popularly elected officials comes to impose limits on public expression. Some preliminary considerations of this issue are offered below to direct attention to the principal findings and, in the process, to provide a capsule description of prewar Japanese democracy, which is necessary to appreciate the regime/policy connection.

A logical first reaction to hearing that a democracy has restricted political expression is to ask whether the regime in question is really a democracy at all. This is surely a valid concern in this case, since Japan was experiencing its first democratic system ever, and its traditions were not wholly supportive of the experiment. Furthermore, Japanese democracy evolved within the Meiji constitutional framework, which allowed but did not require party governments. Official ideology remained one of imperial rather than popular sovereignty. The argument for presenting this as a democratic regime can be elaborated in response to the following two questions: (1) How many people had an opportunity to participate in politics? (2) To what extent were elections an effective mechanism for determining government leaders according to the popular will? The brief answers given below indicate that although Japan's prewar democracy did not always meet ideal standards, it appears respectable enough alongside other democratic systems in the real world.

As for the variable of participation, the Diet legislated universal male suffrage in 1925, so that between the elections of 1924 and 1928 the electorate grew from 3.2 to 12.4 million out of a population of 62 million people.[46] The suffrage expanded faster in prewar Japan than in nineteenth-century Britain, and although women were denied the franchise until after 1945, this was also true in France, a country with a much longer democratic past. On the whole, there was little state interference with non-revolutionary political associations and interest groups. Moderate labor and tenant farmers' unions did suffer some police harassment, and several bills to legalize their activities failed to pass the Diet, but controls were not so harsh as to prevent a marked development of these groups. From 1921 to 1931, the labor movement grew from 300 unions with 103,412 members to 818 with 368,975, though this still encompassed only 7.9 percent of all industrial workers.[47] In the same span, tenants' unions grew from 681 to 4,414, with over 306,000 members.[48] Direct party organization of the electorate was shallow compared to that

46. *Nihon Kindaishi Jiten,* pp. 766, 839.
47. Ibid., p. 908.
48. Ronald Dore, *Land Reform in Japan,* p. 72.

of some European mass parties, but perhaps not so unlike that of parties in the United States or most developing countries.[49] The parties relied heavily upon local notables to muster electoral support, especially in rural areas.

Concerning elections, the evidence is that they provided meaningful if somewhat indirect popular control over government. The Meiji founders bequeathed a system in which a group of Elder Statesmen or *Genrō* (nine men held this formal title) advised the throne regarding the appointment of the Prime Minister. What characterized the democratic period is that except for the 1922–1924 break all appointed chief executives were presidents of one of the two largest parties in the (elected) lower house.[50] The *Genrō* were first pressured to accept party government in 1918 by the parties' skillful use of their power in the Diet and by the rice riots of that year, which underlined the need for governments with popular support. The democratic cause was further aided after 1922 by the fact that the last remaining *Genrō*, Saionji Kinmochi, had long supported the parties' advance. Nonetheless, the connection between elections and formation of the cabinet continued to be filtered through this middleman. When a Prime Minister died in office, Saionji would replace him with the next leader of the same party; when a cabinet resigned due to some policy failure, he would select the head of the largest opposition party. In either case, the Emperor (who had no personal say in the matter) formally appointed the new Prime Minister. As is often true in parliamentary cabinet systems, elections had no bearing on the transfer of power.

If the incoming Prime Minister's party did not control the lower house, however, he would have to call elections or see his programs defeated, since the House of Representatives had to approve all laws and additions to the prior year's budget. Several months would elapse between formation of the cabinet and elections, and the new Prime Minister generally used that time to put his own party's bureaucratic dependents in charge of key police offices and prefectural governor-

49. To be specific, there was nothing like the organizational network of Germany's Social Democratic Party, which in a town of 10,000 people could boast of sports societies, a first-aid organization, a party choir, labor unions, a shooting club, a construction company, a consumers' cooperative, youth and children's groups, a newspaper, and a paramilitary corps: William Sheridan Allen, *The Nazi Seizure of Power: The Experience of a Single German Town, 1930–1935*, pp. 15ff.

50. Some scholars now restrict the democratic period to 1924–1932. I favor the more traditional boundary of 1918 pursuant to the analysis of Tetsuo Najita. It seems unnecessary, however, to argue the point here, since virtually all major media policies to be discussed under party governments were formulated in the 1924–1932 interval.

ships. State patronage and a partisan enforcement of electoral laws then favored the appointed government in the subsequent elections, which never failed to provide the new cabinet with control over the lower house.[51] Despite electoral abuses, however, election results suggest that the views of the voters remained paramount. Margins of victory varied considerably, from 56 percent for the winning party to 27 percent for the runner-up in 1920, to a slight defeat for the governing party in 1928, forcing the cabinet to seek the support of independents (see table 2). Furthermore, labor parties won 4.6 percent of the vote in 1928 and 4.9 percent in 1930. The continuing electoral dominance of the two major parties after 1932, when patronage and the police no longer sustained them, also speaks for the primacy of genuine popular choice. There is little record of fraudulent counting after the ballots were cast.

The limitations of prewar democracy having been enumerated, its positive aspects should also be mentioned. The gradual evolution of democratic institutions in Japan was not merely a source of compromises but also a source of strength. The institutionalization of competitive politics among a limited segment of the population followed by the gradual addition of new participants in the political process has been judged the developmental pattern most likely to produce a stable democracy.[52] This was the path to democratic politics taken by the United Kingdom and Sweden. In Japan, gradualism allowed for several decades of accommodation between the parties and other state elites, making for a relatively smooth transition to a democratic regime. This stands in contrast to the sudden and turbulent inception of democracy in Germany and Spain, which, though it allowed those regimes to become more unqualifiedly democratic, proved to be a cause of considerable instability. Another asset from 1925 on was a two-party system in which there were several alternations of power and no deep ideological rifts between the two parties, the type of system prone to the moderate politics of "centripetal competition," to borrow a phrase of Giovanni Sartori's. It is likely that any scholarly observer in the mid to late 1920s would have concluded that the Japanese regime was steadily evolving

51. An exception to the general pattern was the 1924 election called by a transcendental (or non-party) cabinet *before* the appointment of a new Prime Minister; there was relatively little government interference, thanks partly to pressure from Saionji himself. On three occasions, Prime Ministers holding a majority were replaced due to death or incapacity by members of their own parties, and elections were not held at all. Only the first party Prime Minister, Hara Kei, called elections while holding a Diet majority, twenty months after taking office.

52. Dahl, *Polyarchy*, pp. 33–40.

TABLE II PRIME MINISTERS AND HOUSE OF REPRESENTATIVES ELECTION RESULTS, SEPTEMBER 1918–MAY 1932

Premier (Party)	Date of Appointment	Date of Elections	Parties	Votes	Percent of Votes	Seats	Percent of Seats
Hara (Seiyūkai)	Sept. 1918	May 1920	Seiyūkai	1,474,796	56.1%	278	59.9%
			Kenseikai	722,348	27.5	111	23.9
			Others	428,643	16.3	75	16.1
Takahashi (Seiyūkai)	Nov. 1921						
Katō T. (no party)	June 1922						
Kiyoura (no party)	Jan. 1924	May 1924	Kenseikai	869,028	29.4	151	32.5
			Seiyūhontō	732,182	24.8	112	24.1
			Seiyūkai	661,355	22.4	102	21.9
			Others	688,625	23.3	99	21.3
Katō K. (Kenseikai)[a]	June 1924						
Wakatsuki (Kenseikai)	Jan. 1926						
Tanaka (Seiyūkai)	Apr. 1927	Feb. 1928	Minseitō[b]	4,256,010	43.1	216	46.3
			Seiyūkai	4,244,385	43.0	217	46.5
			Others	1,365,801	13.8	33	7.0
Hamaguchi (Minseitō)	July 1929	Feb. 1930	Minseitō	5,468,114	52.3	273	58.5
			Seiyūkai	3,944,493	37.7	174	37.3
			Others	1,033,588	9.8	19	4.0
Wakatsuki (Minseitō)	Apr. 1931						
Inukai (Seiyūkai)	Dec. 1931	Feb. 1932	Seiyūkai	5,706,356	58.6	303	65.0
			Minseitō	3,382,700	34.7	146	31.3
			Others	634,060	6.5	17	3.6

Source: Nihon Kindaishi Jiten, pp. 768–69.
[a]Katō Kōmei formed a cabinet with the joint backing of the Kenseikai, Seiyūhontō, and Seiyūkai.
[b]The Minseitō was founded in June 1927 by a merger of the Kenseikai and Seiyūhontō.

into a more permanent and complete democracy. In sum, elected officials controlled the principal locus of state authority—the cabinet—and were periodically compelled to demonstrate their popular mandate at the polls. The media policies of this period, therefore, must be accepted as the products of a democratic regime. The question remains: how do democratic governments justify controls on political expression?

There is yet another factor that might justify the avoidance of this difficult issue. Even where elected leaders stand atop the state apparatus, they do not monopolize policymaking. Voters never elect more than a small minority of state officials; given the volume and complexity of government business, this means that many policy decisions must be made by appointed administrators. One of the principal findings of this research is that "democratic" media policy in prewar Japan was in fact largely devised by non-democratic state institutions, namely, the bureaucracy.

It would be deceptively easy to attribute bureaucratic influence entirely to the Meiji legacy. The great power of the early Meiji bureaucracy has already been noted, as has the fact that prewar party governments evolved within the Meiji constitutional system. Japanese politics of the 1918–1932 period cannot be addressed in the same terms as the interwar democracies of Spain or Germany, where fresh democratic institutions were created and then demonstrably wrecked to set off politically coherent epochs. The Japanese regime evolved within a preexisting political framework that saddled it with a greater number and variety of non-democratic state institutions than would be found in most democracies. The upper house was staffed by a new peerage that party appointees had only begun to penetrate in the 1920s. An appointed Privy Council advised the throne on imperial decrees, foreign treaties, and legal-constitutional matters. The army and navy enjoyed independent control over their internal affairs and a "right of supreme command" whose proper extent was a subject of much controversy. Yet unlike the influence of these institutions, the sway of the bureaucracy cannot simply be credited to Meiji precedents, for the ministries were left quite vulnerable to political interference.

A turning point in the rise of party power came with the appointment of Seiyūkai Representative Hara Kei as Home Minister in 1906. Hara used his authority over the building of railroads, dams, and other projects to expand his party's constituency, and he made the careers of higher civil servants dependent upon support for his party's objectives.[53]

---

53. See Tetsuo Najita, *Hara Kei in the Politics of Compromise, 1905–1915.*

This practice continued into the period of party governments. The parties did not interfere with the civil service entrance exams, but they used a legal loophole permitting bureaucrats to be sent on compulsory leaves of absence to control promotions to the top administrative posts. Most key bureau and section chiefs, as well as provincial prefects and police heads, were individuals of known affiliation with a major party.[54] Such a high degree of politicization, which is not very common among the industrial democracies, is generally thought to reduce bureaucratic influence over policy, since it provides cabinet ministers with tremendous leverage over their subordinates.[55] Nonetheless, bureaucrats all but monopolized the making of film policy and also took the lead in regulating radio. Their ability to do so may have had less to do with the Meiji patrimony than with more general causes underlying administrative power in modern democracies, and these will receive considerable attention in the pages that follow.

If bureaucratic authority accounts for much of media policy, it does not exhaust the subject. Party governments did indeed assume direct command at several critical junctures, and on each occasion they opted for greater state control over the mass media. The Peace Preservation Law was sponsored by a party cabinet and passed by the House of Representatives, reflecting a widespread determination to suppress the propaganda of radical, anti-system groups. For radio, party Communications Ministers intervened to impose an even more statist policy than that advocated by their bureaucratic staffs. These episodes demonstrate the need to confront the perplexing issue of why elected leaders themselves choose to restrict public expression in apparent violation of democratic principles. If bureaucratic dominance is to be the first theme for analysis, the decisions of elected statesmen to restrain the media constitute the second.

54. Ibid., p. 44. The position of bureau chief (*kyokuchō*) was one step below the vice minister's level, section chief (*kachō*) one rung lower. To give an indication of their numbers, there were six or seven bureaus each in the Home, Finance, and Commerce and Industry Ministries in the late 1920s. Those in the Home Ministry contained on the average five or six sections apiece. For the structure of prewar ministries, see Hata Ikuhiko, *Senzenki Nihon Kanryōsei no Seido-Soshiki-Jinji.*

55. Mattei Dogan, "The Political Power of the Western Mandarins: Introduction," pp. 13–14.

CHAPTER II

The Press

The periodical press grew tremendously in size and quality between 1918 and 1932. The number of journals registered under the Newspaper Law rose during this period from 3,123 to 11,118. Magazines of high intellectual caliber appeared, catering to a growing and better-educated middle-class readership, and a handful of daily newspapers evolved into national opinion leaders. The circulation of the Ōsaka Mainichi Shinbun, for example, grew from 260,000 in 1912 to 670,000 in 1921 and 1,500,000 in 1930.[1] Major press organs acquired greater professionalism and prestige. Ownership patterns had already been drifting away from the one-man operations of the early Meiji years to a corporate format, and the Tokyo earthquake of 1923 spurred this trend, since many publishing houses ruined in the disaster could not be rebuilt by single individuals. In the early 1920s, prominent newspapers introduced entrance examinations for reportorial jobs. In 1921, the Asahi's first exam attracted only 3 or 4 applicants for each slot; in 1928, there were over 500 competing for some ten positions.[2] Columnists now included not only university professors and other leading intellectuals, but even retired bureau chiefs from the state administration.

The new respectability of the press was in part a logical accompaniment to party rule. There were few senior party politicians without journalistic experience; Prime Minister Hara Kei had once been editor

1. Itō Takashi, Shōwa Shoki Seiji Shi Kenkyū: Rondon Kaigun Gunshuku Mondai o Meguru Sho Seiji Shudan no Taikō to Teikei, pp. 435–36 n. 1.
2. Ibid., pp. 436–37 n. 2.

of the *Ōsaka Mainichi Shinbun,* and Katō Kōmei president of the *Tō-kyō Nichi Nichi Shinbun.* Many journals were long-standing supporters of the democratic cause, and newspapers led the drive for universal manhood suffrage.

Press policy is especially illuminating in several respects. First, the Diet and cabinet took a more direct hand in formulating press controls than they did in regard to either film or radio. A major legislative effort to liberalize the press code came within an inch of success, and the press was the medium most affected by the only major media-related legislation that did pass the Diet in this period, the Peace Preservation Law. Press policy thus provides the clearest picture of the thinking of politicians on media controls. A second factor that comes to light is the extent to which the bureaucracy was able to control policy simply through its responsibility for implementing the law. The press was the only medium controlled by a comprehensive Diet law designed specifically for the purpose, and its manner of execution reveals just how far bureaucrats might be constrained by such a formal statute and how much room it left for administrative discretion. Finally, the press was the most autonomous of the mass media, and a study of published political commentary is therefore the best measure of the actual boundaries of permissible public debate. It shows that despite the failure of liberal reform, the existing legal framework permitted wide-ranging expression of critical (but not revolutionary) views on the most important events of the day.

ADMINISTRATIVE AND
JUDICIAL SANCTIONS

The Newspaper Law provided for both judicial and administrative penalties, but the latter saw much more service than the former. The judicial power to close publications fell into virtual disuse—only one journal was closed, this for a violation of public order in 1929. Sentences meted out to individual violators are recorded in table 3. Only sixty-six offenders went to prison in the fifteen years between 1918 and 1932, and no one served more than six months. Fines were the principal punishment; though they did not deter the larger periodicals, they could be highly injurious to weaker publishers. (The more severe court actions pursuant to the Peace Preservation Law are enumerated below.)

Administrative powers were exercised by the Book Section of the Criminal Affairs Bureau of the Home Ministry. This was perhaps the most potent bureau of the weightiest ministry in Japan, controlling

TABLE III   JUDICIAL VERDICTS IN TRIALS OF INDIVIDUALS
PROSECUTED FOR VIOLATING THE NEWSPAPER LAW,
1918–1932

	Sentenced to Prison	Fined	Acquitted
1918	16	629	16
1919	5	193	10
1920	4	143	8
1921	6	210	1
1922	8	128	2
1923	2	226	5
1924	3	280	3
1925	6	189	0
1926	2	255	0
1927	0	197	0
1928	3	179	2
1929	4	404	0
1930	0	262	0
1931	0	197	1
1932	7	169	0

Source: Nihon Teikoku Shihōshō, Keiji Tōkei Nenpō, nos. 44–58, 1918–1932.

Note: The data cover the results of regular trials and summary sentences handed down by the court of first instance (the original tables are titled Zaimei Betsu Tsūjō Dai Isshin Tokubetsu Hō Han Shūkyoku Hikokunin no Ka Kei Sono Ta and Zaimei Betsu Ryakushiki Jiken Tokubetsu Hō Han Shūkyoku Hikokunin no Ka Kei Sono Ta, respectively). Some sentenced to prison were fined as well, but only those suffering fines without prison are listed under "Fined" in the table. Appeals against these sentences were very few and rarely ended in favor of the accused.

police operations nationwide. High scorers on the civil service entrance exams frequently chose to make their careers in this prestigious institution, which attracted the top graduates of Tokyo Imperial University. Local implementation of censorship was handled by the Special Higher Police, responsible also for the oversight of political radicals and social movements.

Bureaucrats exercised two legal weapons against the press. One was to suspend publication of journals for procedural violations, that is, for failure to report the intent to publish or pay the required bond. The other was to ban the circulation of specific editions violating censorship standards, in which case police could seize both the printed copies and the stereotypes. Publishers suffered the material loss on unsold issues and later might be prosecuted in court. Fledgling magazines were especially vulnerable economically, since a weekly or monthly edition involved a greater relative investment than one edition of a daily newspaper. Table 4 documents the use of these sanctions and others described below.

Beyond these two powers, officials devised methods of their own to regulate journalism. Some were to aid the press, while others exacerbated controls, but all were bureaucratic innovations never approved by the Diet. One such device, employed when contents only bordered on an offense, was to issue an informal post-publication warning not to publish a similar article again. Another, used when objectionable passages were few, was to allow a publisher to sell the journal after making deletions; this avoided the full financial injury of a ban on circulation.[3] Deletions were first permitted for books in the early 1920s and were later afforded regularly to magazines. Daily newspapers were denied this option because the need for immediate sale left them no time to make the required changes.

The most important extralegal policy was the pre-publication warning system for newspapers. Officials would notify the journals not to report on certain current events related to public order. The warnings took three forms: *instructions*—publication would probably result in a ban on circulation; *admonitions*—publication might bring a ban on circulation, depending on the social situation and the nature of the article; and *consultations*—publication would not be punished, but a moral appeal was made not to report the incident.[4] One such warning is recorded as early as 1923, and they were probably employed sporadically before then, but it was under party governments that they first saw constant service. Some were dispensed nationwide; others were limited to particular regions. The warnings often counseled against any coverage exceeding official press releases, lending them a mobilizational character beyond censorship. Like deletions, warnings could be of benefit to publishers. The ambiguity of censorship statutes made it difficult to predict the permissible range of reporting on current events, so advance notice could help in avoiding sanctions. Nonetheless, these were bureaucratic attempts to upgrade state control without any legal substructure.

3. Deletions could take two forms. In a *sakujo* sanction, officials decided initially that the offense was not serious enough to justify a ban on circulation and informed the publisher of what should be deleted prior to sale. In *bunkatsu kanpu*, the publication had received a ban on circulation but the publisher requested that he be allowed to cut the objectionable parts and salvage the rest. This latter measure was not begun until September 1927, but the *sakujo* sanction was probably enforced unofficially on a small scale before the 1920s. See Naimushō Keihōkyoku, *Shōwa 8-Nen ni Okeru Shuppan Keisatsu Gaikan*, pp. 115, 118. These reports were printed annually from 1930 through 1935. They will hereafter be cited with the title *Shuppan Keisatsu Gaikan*, followed by the year of issue.

4. "Instructions" is a translation of *shitatsu*, "admonitions" of *keikoku*, and "consultations" of *kondan*.

TABLE IV   ADMINISTRATIVE CONTROLS ENFORCED AGAINST DOMESTIC PERIODICALS SUBJECT TO THE NEWSPAPER LAW, 1918–1932

	Press Organs	Dailies	Bonded Organs	Total Banned Editions	Banned for Public-Order Violations	Post-Publication Warnings	Deletions	Procedural Suspensions	Pre-Publication Warnings Ins–Adm–Con[a]
1918	3,123			513	478	1,080		7	
1919	3,333			200	181	518		3	
1920	3,532			339	327	750		2	
1921	3,980	813	3,056	445	411	529		5	
1922	4,562	865	3,403	98	70	667		4	
1923	4,592	893	3,603	819	771	1,088		3	1– 0–0
1924	5,854	948	4,184	299	267	678	0	6	0– 0–0
1925	6,899	1,012	4,739	175	154	789	0	16	1– 0–0
1926	7,600	1,035	5,089	295	251	884	1	13	0– 0–0
1927	8,350	1,093	5,438	355	331	773	2	17	1– 2–4
1928	8,445	1,150	5,482	389	345	558	4	4	8– 1–5
1929	9,191	1,221	5,917	442	374	998	4	6	2– 1–3[b]
1930	10,130	1,215	5,995	539	504	1,127	6	4	5– 0–4
1931	10,666	1,280	6,290	881	832	1,546	9	11	4–10–1
1932[c]	11,118	1,330	6,301	2,246	2,081	4,348	48	4	44–19–1

Sources: For pre-publication warnings up to 1929: Naimushō Keihōkyoku, Shuppan Keisatsu Hō, no. 8, pp. 135–38. For banned editions, post-publication warnings, and procedural suspensions, 1918–1920: Masu Media Tōsei, vol. 1, document 21, pp. 201–3. All else is from Naimushō Keihōkyoku, Shuppan Keisatsu Gaikan, 1931–1935.

ᵃThe abbreviations refer to "instructions," "admonitions," and "consultations."

ᵇThe data on pre-publication warnings for 1929 are complete only through May.

ᶜThe sharp rise in sanctions in 1932 was not due to the end of party governments in May. Bans on circulation averaged 251 per month January–April, only 150 June–December, and 37 of the 64 pre-publication warnings were given before Inukai's murder.

CENSORSHIP STANDARDS

A further source of discretion lay in the administrator's right to interpret the law's general prescriptions against violations of "public order" and "manners and morals." The full extent of their application will be described in chapter 3. For present purposes it will suffice to note briefly the taboos enforced by press censors under the rubric of public order in 1931: desecration of the imperial family; rejection of the monarchy; propaganda for communism, anarchism, or other revolutionary movements; emphasis on the class character of the state or the law; agitation for terror, direct action, or mass violence; advocacy of independence for the colonies; rejection of the parliamentary system by illegal means; challenges to the foundation of the armed forces; hindrances to diplomacy; revelation of secrets regarding military or foreign affairs; agitation or praise for crime, and impediments to criminal investigations; and matters disturbing the business world or otherwise arousing social unrest.[5] The last entry was a catchall for offenses escaping the other guidelines. These prohibitions are known today mainly through declassified documents. They were not made public at the time, and bureaucrats would not even discuss them in the Diet unless the minutes were stopped. Since the police did not publicize a fixed set of standards or identify the offending passages when an edition was banned, journalists could not know how public order might be construed in regard to any particular story.

More arbitrary yet were the contents of extralegal pre-publication warnings given to newspapers on the reporting of current events. The following were among the instructions or admonitions, which might bring a ban on circulation if disobeyed.[6] At least twenty-three such warnings, with the aim of bolstering public confidence, circumscribed the coverage of bank failures during the depression years of 1929–1932. A second group sought to cover up political crimes. There were nine warnings on offenses of lèse-majesté, starting with one concerning an attempt on the Crown Prince's life in 1923 (the Toranomon Incident), and seven warnings not to report the arrest or pursuit of communist suspects, the first of which was given in June 1928.

A third objective was to conceal events embarrassing to the military.

---

5. Naimushō Keihōkyoku, *Shuppan Keisatsu Gaikan*, 1931, pp. 9–13.
6. Principal sources are idem, *Shuppan Keisatsu Hō*, no. 8, pp. 135–38—these reports were produced from October 1928 to March 1944, usually monthly; idem, *Shuppan Keisatsu Gaikan*, 1931, pp. 44–47; idem, *Shuppan Keisatsu Gaikan*, 1932, pp. 74–78.

Among the dirty linen hidden by at least eleven warnings were the embezzlement of ordnance by military personnel (December 1927), radical statements by young army officers (October 1931), and the suicide of a major in the Shanghai expeditionary force (March 1932). Most critical was the instruction imparted on 16 May 1932 to hush up the complicity of naval officers in the assassination of Prime Minister Inukai (the 5/15 Incident). Items to be omitted from press reports were: the statuses, names, and personal histories of the criminals; anything indicating that the incident was connected with the military; and the motives of the perpetrators and predictions that similar events might recur. The radical cabals of low-ranking officers were omens of danger in this period, but the state endeavored to screen them from the public, even when they cost the life of the last prewar party Prime Minister.

Another very important theme of pre-publication warnings was Japan's military and political thrust into Manchuria starting in September 1931. There were some nineteen warnings in 1931–1932 to gag the reporting of military activities related to Manchuria. Escalation of Japan's involvement was veiled by warnings not to recount troop departures or the calling up of reserves, and fourteen warnings clouded the establishment of Manchukuo as a puppet state. For example, the Home Ministry ordered silence on initial plans for an "independent" Manchukuo (September 1931), the building of railroads (several instances), the participation of Japanese nationals in Manchurian politics and administration (February 1932), transportation and customs duty policy (March 1932), a visit by the Litton Commission to Japanese army officials (April 1932), and the Manchurian Central Bank (May 1932). Often the warnings were lifted after officials announced the event as a fait accompli, impeding criticism until it was without effect. The main purpose sometimes was to mislead foreign countries, but the system also withheld vital information from the Japanese people. Since the founding of Manchukuo was a momentous historical event, state efforts to block information and public debate are highly significant.

A final element of bureaucratic arbitrariness was the use of circumstantial criteria in determining whether or not to apply sanctions in a given case. Reading through banned material, one often finds rather innocuous articles inviting sanctions while more radical pieces were passed over. Moreover, officials admitted that "there are often accounts of absolutely the same content being disregarded in one journal but causing another to be banned from circulation."[7] If simple inconsis-

7. Idem., *Shuppan Keisatsu Gaikan*, 1931, p. 10.

tency was one reason, the consideration of circumstantial factors was another. In 1931, the following circumstantial criteria were in use:

The publication's purpose—academic journals were handled more leniently than those of political groups.

The readership—periodicals aimed at youth or workers were judged especially harshly.

The publication's circulation and influence—substantial journals were the most carefully watched, while those of small radical groups were sometimes overlooked as a harmless outlet for potentially more dangerous elements.

The social climate—enforcement was more severe in times of disorder, such as after the Tokyo earthquake, or around May Day, when the possibility of concrete disturbances was greater than usual.

Geographic distribution—journals sold where there had been violent tenant or labor disputes or a run on the banks received closer scrutiny.

The extent of completed circulation—official action might be waived if the offending issues had already been disseminated.

The proportion of objectionable material—this pertained to how much of the journal violated standards of content.

Given the bureaucratic power to formulate censorship standards, the ambiguity of the standards themselves, and the further discretion afforded by circumstantial considerations, the press control system was in great measure one of rule by men rather than rule by law.

Formidable as this array of controls may appear on paper, the crucial issue is their effectiveness in practice. How far did these measures succeed in constricting public discussion? An examination of the efficacy of administrative controls, the censorship of radical leftist publications, and the permissible range of criticism in the mainstream press will help to answer this question.

THE MODEST IMPACT OF
ADMINISTRATIVE CONTROLS

The chief bureaucratic weapon, the ban on circulation, largely failed to attain its purpose, for two reasons: first, officials were hamstrung by a lenient provision of the law which they could not overturn; second, they were thwarted by the strenuous and often ingenious efforts of publishers to evade enforcement.

As for the legal obstacle, the Newspaper Law required journals to submit inspection copies only simultaneously with publication, and police were not able to seize most offending copies before sale. In 1932, the confiscation rate for 236 select Newspaper Law periodicals banned by bureaucrats was only 25 percent of their total circulation, and figures for later years show this record to be typical.[8] Furthermore, data available for 1933 show that the rate of confiscation for violations of public order was less than half that for offenses relating to manners and morals.[9] Police were helpless to improve on this record because they could not demand earlier submission of inspection copies. They might interpret the Newspaper Law loosely or supplement it with innovative practices, but where the law was specific it could not be contravened. Administrative license thus had its limits.

One implication is that pre-publication warnings could not keep information from the public. Violations were commonplace (see table 5), and the most influential newspapers were among the offenders. Some unlawful editions were circulated before warnings arrived, but many publishers, to stay abreast of their competitors, deliberately ignored the warnings: sensational headlines meant higher sales. Judicial sanctions did not discourage this practice, since they were usually limited to fines inferior to the profits earned from a special edition. However, violations were heavily concentrated around the event in question and fell off sharply afterwards. The official warning on Inukai's assassination was violated 89 times in May 1932, when the crime occurred, but only 5 times more in the same year. A lèse-majesté incident in January 1932 drew 128 violations that month, only 2 thereafter.[10]

8. Idem, *Shuppan Keisatsu Gaikan*, 1933, p. 125. Illegal (i.e., unreported) publications, whose total circulation was unknown, were excluded from the survey. Even for magazines, which circulate more slowly, execution was mediocre. As late as 1935, despite efforts to stiffen enforcement, there were 103 Newspaper Law magazine editions of known circulation banned, yet just 26 percent of the copies were grabbed before sale: idem, *Shuppan Keisatsu Gaikan*, 1935, p. 433. For Publication Law books and magazines, which had to submit censor's copies three days before publication, the rate of confiscation was just 13.7 percent in 1932, and 26.9 percent in 1933: idem, *Shuppan Keisatsu Gaikan*, 1933, p. 124. The police did improve their record in this area—63 percent of all copies of banned books were seized in 1935: idem, *Shuppan Keisatsu Gaikan*, 1935, p. 423.

9. Idem, *Shuppan Keisatsu Gaikan*, 1933, p. 125. Under the Publication Law, only 20.4 percent of books and periodical editions banned for violations of public order were seized in 1933, compared to 44.5 percent of those banned for offenses relating to manners and morals: ibid., p. 124.

10. Figures on both events are from idem, *Shuppan Keisatsu Gaikan*, 1932, p. 73.

TABLE V   NEWSPAPER EDITIONS BANNED FOR VIOLATIONS OF
PRE-PUBLICATION WARNINGS, BY SUBJECT OF WARNINGS, 1931–1932

	Subject Matter	Banned Editions
1931	Military activities in Manchuria	156
	Manchurian-Mongolian independence	41
	Financial conditions of various banks	37
	Radical statements by young army officers	16
	The Manchurian Railroad	11
	Manchurian-Korean air routes	1
	Total	262
1932	Shanghai Incident	437
	Manchurian-Mongolian Incident	259
	Crime of lèse-majesté	130
	Assassination of Prime Minister Inukai	94
	Disturbances of the business world	69
	Arrests under the Peace Preservation Law	52
	Military secrets	39
	Total	1,080

Sources: Naimushō Keihōkyoku, *Shuppan Keisatsu Gaikan,* 1931, pp. 43–44; idem, *Shuppan Keisatsu Gaikan,* 1932, pp. 70–72.
Note: More than one warning may be counted under each subject.

Thus, although the warnings did not curtail initial reporting of big events, they did prevent extended public discussion of them.

Publishers' evasive tactics were another cause of administrative failure. To avoid confiscation, publishers might begin distribution before submitting inspection copies, ship banned issues packaged as other products, deliver censor's copies the day before a holiday or a weekend, when inspection would take longer, or make a second set of stereotypes so that publication could continue if one set were seized.[11] Other tactics were to submit galleys or self-censored copies to officials and then change the contents for final printing; to publish articles by radical writers under pseudonyms; or, if a piece flunked censorship one year, to present it under a new title the next—this did occasionally work.[12]

An accepted method of avoiding sanctions was the use of blank type. Words, sentences, or even whole paragraphs feared to offend the censor were replaced by X's and O's. Sometimes each X or O supplanted one

11. Idem, *Shuppan Keisatsu Gaikan,* 1930, pp. 91–93, and idem, *Shuppan Keisatsu Gaikan,* 1931, pp. 71–73.
12. Taikakai, ed., *Naimushō Shi,* 1: 807.

character of the Japanese language, and readers were challenged to supply the missing words. Prewar readers, including the censors, became quite adept at this. For example, consider the following passage from *Musansha Kyōiku* (Proletarian Education) dated 5 October 1929: "The capitalist landlord class has learned that the Japan *Communist Party* is upholding *abolition* of the *monarchical* system as its immediate policy. Moreover, as the Japan *Communist Party* stresses very justly, the realization of a *communist* society is that our working class overthrow . . . ."[13] In the original, the editor substituted blank type for the italicized words, to escape sanctions for supporting communism or opposing the monarchy. Words such as *communist, revolution, monarchy,* and *Emperor* were frequently X'd out of leftist literature or replaced by euphemisms, for example, *proletarian party* for *Communist Party.* In this case, the blanks were not obscure enough; officials read in their intended meaning and banned the magazine from circulation.

Even the most prestigious magazines were using blank type by the mid-1920s. It was tolerated by officials as a flawed but useful expedient, given their inability to stop illegal issues from circulating. The practice shows that magazines took sanctions seriously enough to exercise self-censorship, but it also demonstrates the laxity of press controls. The missing words symbolized a desire to break the law, and that desire was publicly advertised with every X and O.

SUBJUGATION OF THE RADICAL LEFT

The most common reason for democratic regimes to restrict political expression is to contain revolutionary groups. Many scholars would insist they are justified in the effort. A recent study of the breakdown of democracies held that the "exclusion from political competition of parties not committed to the legal pursuit of power . . . is not incompatible with the guarantee of free competition in our definition of democracy."[14] But though all governments take preventive measures against seditious elements, democracies run a special risk in doing so, for at some point the

---

13. Naimushō Keihōkyoku, *Shuppan Keisatsu Hō,* no. 14, p. 118.

14. Juan J. Linz, *The Breakdown of Democratic Regimes: Crisis, Breakdown, and Reequilibration,* p. 6. An International Press Institute study took a similar stand: "The press is not above the law. There is therefore no suggestion of indicting governments for not granting absolute liberty to the press or for not tolerating attacks which might endanger their existence": "International Press Institute Survey No. IV, Government Pressures on the Press," in *International Press Institute Surveys Nos. I–VI,* pp. 63–69.

severity of repression may betray the regime's most basic principles. A strong argument could be made that Japan's prewar democratic system passed this point of excessive reaction in dealing with a fledgling leftist movement. In practice there were two press control systems in democratic Japan, one of liberal treatment for the majority of mainstream critics, and one of brutal suppression for political extremists.

The regular press laws were applied with special harshness against the left. In 1929, leftist periodicals sustained 241 bans on circulation under the Newspaper and Publication Laws, and the number increased annually through 1932 (see table 6). In 1931, 241 of the 283 newspaper editions banned for violating regular standards of public order were

TABLE VI   DOMESTIC LEFTIST PERIODICAL EDITIONS BANNED UNDER THE NEWSPAPER LAW AND PUBLICATION LAW, BY POLITICAL TENDENCY, 1930–1933

	Communist Party–related	Anarchist	Left[a]	Center[b]	Right[c]	Others	Total
1930	197	45	13	9	3	107	374
1931	305	48		44[d]	11	69	477
1932	543	93		60[e]		2	698
1933	397	50		52		137	636

Source: Naimushō Keihōkyoku, *Shuppan Keisatsu Gaikan,* 1930–1935.

Note: Political tendencies are described as they were in official documents; "center" and "right" are designations within the spectrum of leftist parties and unions. Publication Law violations are included because many leftists used cultural journals for indirect political expression.

[a]These were periodicals supporting the *Rōdō Nōmintō* (Labor-Farmer Party). This was initially a moderate leftist party, eventually infiltrated by revolutionaries. Its inaugural platform called for a minimum wage, an eight-hour work-day, arms reduction, democratic reorganization of the military, and the repeal of laws restricting the rights of labor to organize, strike, and bargain collectively: Beckmann and Ōkubo, *The Japanese Communist Party,* pp. 100–102.

[b]In 1930, these were organs supporting the *Zenkoku Taishūtō* (National Masses Party) and its affiliated unions, a moderate coalition of labor groups striving for legal change.

[c]These were organs supporting the *Shakai Minshūtō* (Social Democratic Party) and its affiliated unions; it was a moderate party backing parliamentarianism and capital-labor cooperation.

[d]This category, combining left and center, comprised organs of the *Zenkoku Rōnō Taishūtō* (National Labor-Farmer Masses Party), formed in July 1931. It advocated parliamentary action as well as "daily struggle," and called for rural relief, an end to unemployment, and more political freedom. It opposed the Manchurian intervention: Naimushō Keihōkyoku, *Shuppan Keisatsu Gaikan,* 1931, p. 90.

[e]Publications of the center in 1932 and 1933 were those related to the Social Masses Party, which was formed in July 1932, combining the forces described in notes c and d above. It claimed to be anti-communist and anti-fascist, and recognized Manchukuo but opposed withdrawal from the League of Nations.

leftist.[15] Some journals were all but driven underground by constant persecution. As of January 1929, the Japan Communist Party's *Musansha Shinbun,* published six times a month from 1925, had suffered 72 bans on circulation.[16]

In this period, sanctions against the left were heavily concentrated against genuinely radical journals. Of all leftist periodical editions banned, those related to communism or anarchism constituted 64 percent in 1930, 73 percent in 1931, and 91 percent in 1932. Typical offenses were the rejection of parliamentary politics for violent direct action, attacks on the monarchy and the military, and the vindication of radicals under arrest. The more moderate groups comprising a large majority of the left were much less frequently molested, though their journals might be banned for supporting strikes, denouncing the tax system, or demanding a moratorium on loan repayments.[17]

The press laws were applied against extremists primarily to control the spread of ideas, not to punish writings connected with violent crimes. Indeed, the campaign against the left was forced to focus on thought control, since there was no pattern of terroristic or violent behavior to combat.[18] An illuminating case was the Morito Incident of 1920. Professor Morito Tatsuo of Tokyo Imperial University published an article on Kropotkin analyzing his condemnation of monarchism and parliamentary government. Morito praised Kropotkin's vision of an anarcho-syndicalist society, though he rejected illegal means to achieve it. The courts sentenced him to three months in prison for disturbing public order under the Newspaper Law, and he simultaneously lost his teaching post. The case was typical in that there was no evidence of riots, strikes, or other crimes being perpetrated under the article's influence. In dispute was the supposition that readers would be so affected as to pose a threat to order.[19] Thus thought control was already part of the

15. The 1929 figures are from Naimushō Keihōkyoku, *Shuppan Keisatsu Gaikan,* 1930, pp. 103, 183, 243; the 1931 figures are from idem, *Shuppan Keisatsu Gaikan,* 1931, pp. 44, 91, 107. There were 262 more non-leftist newspaper editions banned for violations of public order in 1931, but these were for disobeying pre-publication warnings, not regular standards of public order.

16. Idem, *Shuppan Keisatsu Hō,* no. 5, pp. 147–48.

17. Idem, *Shuppan Keisatsu Gaikan,* 1930, p. 104.

18. Communist Party members engaged in a series of bank robberies in October 1932 when starved for funds; the Peace Preservation Law had made contributions illegal. Other than the promotion of strikes, however, there is little evidence of violent crimes before this time. See George M. Beckmann and Ōkubo Genji, *The Japanese Communist Party 1922–1945,* pp. 236–37.

19. In the eyes of the Tokyo District Court, it was enough that the piece might "sow misgivings among the general public regarding the sovereignty of our state or promote a tendency to hold the property rights of the individual in contempt." Quoted in Futagawa Yoshifumi, *Genron no Dan'atsu,* p. 185.

regular censorship system before the Peace Preservation Law elevated it into a crusade.

The Peace Preservation Law of 1925 was the most lethal weapon used against the left. Recent research has disproven the hypothesis that the parties backed this bill only to win conservative approval for universal male suffrage. In fact, party support for such legislation had numerous precedents.[20] The law punished agitation (sendō) for the abolition of private property or changes in the national polity (kokutai) with up to seven years in prison, ten years if violent crimes were advocated or an organization was joined to attain these ends.[21] "Agitation" was another of those vague concepts so common in Japanese law. The Justice and Home Ministries tried to distinguish agitation from simple propaganda by defining agitation as the act of supplying "a special stimulus appealing to the emotions by one's own free will."[22] In practice, it was entirely up to bureaucrats where to draw the line, and publications often fell within their understanding of agitation.

The Peace Preservation Law was first applied against some thirty-seven university students and a labor organizer for planning a Marxist economic revolution (the Gakuren Incident, 1925–1926). Eighteen eventually went to prison, and written materials they had circulated were used as evidence to convict them of agitation.[23] "Thought control" became a major government slogan in the late 1920s, and the Home Ministry's Special Higher Police were often referred to as the "thought police." A comparison of table 7 with table 3 demonstrates that the scope of enforcement of the Peace Preservation Law far surpassed that of the regular press

20. At best, the timing of the Peace Preservation Law and the suffrage act may have been designed to placate members of the Privy Council or the House of Peers who had doubts about expanding the suffrage. See Peter Duus, *Party Rivalry and Political Change in Taishō Japan,* pp. 203–5; Richard H. Mitchell, *Thought Control in Prewar Japan,* pp. 57–62. Mitchell remarks that the Katō cabinet saw the Peace Preservation Law as "one law in a series designed to stem the radical tide": ibid., p. 57. In 1900, the Diet had legislated the Public Peace Police Law, which outlawed the circulation of literature agitating for strikes or walkouts. In February 1922, party Prime Minister Takahashi sponsored a Bill for the Control of Extreme Social Movements originally prepared by his predecessor, Hara Kei. This proposal would have punished communist and anarchist propaganda with up to seven years in prison, but it failed to reach a vote in the Diet. Finally, an emergency imperial decree (referred to as the Peace Preservation Decree) was issued by a non-party Prime Minister after the Tokyo earthquake in September 1923, prescribing ten years in prison for spreading false rumors with the goal of undermining public order. This decree was subsequently approved by the Diet and remained on the books until replaced by the Peace Preservation Law, which borrowed some of its language.

21. The Peace Preservation Law as passed in 1925 is reprinted in *Chian Iji Hō,* document 8, p. 107.

22. Quoted in an analysis by Kiyose Ichirō, a Diet member who argued vigorously against passage of the law: ibid., p. 109.

23. See ibid., document 34, p. 541. The document is a reprint of the appellate court's decision.

TABLE VII   ARRESTS, PROSECUTIONS, AND PRISON SENTENCES
PURSUANT TO THE PEACE PRESERVATION LAW, 1928–1934

	Arrested	Prosecution Suspended	Prosecuted	Imprisoned	Sentences over 5 Years
1928	3,426	16	525	98	14
1929	4,942	27	339	237	40
1930	6,124	292	461	174	29
1931	10,422	454	307	269	18
1932	13,938	774	646	504	87
1933	14,622	1,474	1,285	801	57
1934	3,994	831	496	1,074	88

Sources: Figures for arrested, prosecution suspended, and prosecuted are from *Chian Iji Hō*, pp. 646–47; figures for imprisoned and sentences over 5 years are from Nihon Teikoku Shihōshō, *Keiji Tōkei Nenpō*, nos. 54–60, 1928–1934.

Note: Data on imprisoned and sentences over 5 years are decisions of the court of first instance (*Tsūjō Dai Isshin*). All persons covered in the table were leftists. A lengthy preliminary examination often intervened between arrest and indictment, so those prosecuted in a given year may not have been arrested in that year. Furthermore, trials might last from one year to the next, so court decisions were not necessarily handed down in the year prosecution was initiated. "Prosecution suspended" means that a second arrest for a similar crime could reopen prosecution for the first as well.

code. Mass arrests of communists and other radicals occurred in June and September 1923, December 1925, March and August to October 1928, April 1929, November 1931, and in late 1932. All but the 1923 and 1932 incidents were the work of party governments. The Peace Preservation Law was used exclusively against leftists until 1935, by which time there were few true radicals left to arrest.

In retrospect, the zeal of the anti-leftist campaign may seem difficult to comprehend. Irrational fears akin to McCarthyism undoubtedly affected the response to what was by objective standards a modest threat. The Japan Communist Party had become public enemy number one by the mid-1920s, yet it probably never numbered over five hundred members, and its success at organizing labor was slight.[24] Most of its energy was consumed by internecine quarrels and propaganda efforts, while leftist violence was insignificant from any quarter. Nonetheless, several factors worked to magnify the perception of danger from the left.

In 1918, Japan had intervened militarily against the Bolshevik Revolution, and Soviet communism was viewed as a peril both to Japan and to her interests in Asia. Ever anxious to avert the developmental crises afflicting the West, Japan's leaders could only view as ominous portents

24. See Beckmann and Ōkubo, *The Japanese Communist Party.*

of the future the Soviet-inspired labor rebellions that shook postwar Germany and Italy. One illustration of their impact was Prime Minister Takahashi Korekiyo's proposal of an abortive anti-communist bill to the Diet in 1922, five months before Japan even had a communist party.[25] The Soviet Union substantiated early fears when the Communist International helped to organize and finance the Japanese communist movement, training some of its cadres abroad and supplying them with an inflammatory program. As the ostensible arm of a foreign power, the party naturally appeared more menacing than its modest capabilities would suggest. This would be especially true from the vantage point of the Diet, which had a marked class character; 228 of the 464 representatives elected in 1924 had worked as business executives.[26] Another factor adding salience to the communist threat was the influence of leftist thought in intellectual and university circles. The rhetoric of class struggle permeated many prestigious mainstream journals in the late 1920s, and fellow travelers were numerous among intellectuals alienated by the corruption and conservatism of party governments. They provided the left with more visibility than its numbers warranted.

For all these reasons, elected leaders endorsed a Peace Preservation Law that in objective terms was gross overkill against its projected target, and in so doing they seriously damaged the image of democracy. More conspicuous than revolutionary agitation was the vicious treatment of leftist prisoners. A contributor to *Kaizō* wrote in February 1929:

> Since the Communist incident of last year [the mass arrests of March 1928], we repeatedly hear rumors of "torture" and the cry of "unjust detention." . . . these atrocities, this unjust exercise of police authority, are prone to occur with impertinence when the antagonist belongs to the labor movement or the proletarian class movement. . . . Because I entertain a deep suspicion that the recent unjust exercise of police authority may be influenced directly or indirectly by an imprudent mood among the statesmen who stand above, I would especially like to ask their reconsideration on this occasion.[27]

Even during the greatest showcase trial in Japanese history, the public prosecution of communists in 1931–1932, one of the defendants appeared in court showing wounds from a bad beating. The newspapers

25. See n. 20 above.
26. Ishida Takeshi, "The Development of Interest Groups and the Pattern of Political Modernization in Japan," p. 308.
27. Quoted in Naimushō Keihōkyoku, *Shuppan Keisatsu Hō,* no. 6, p. 68.

picked up the matter and the abuse ceased, but only temporarily.[28] The Diet had unleashed a police campaign that it was ultimately unable to control, and the Peace Preservation Law endured to take its toll of democratic thinkers and statesmen over the next decade.

THE RANGE OF ACCEPTABLE CRITICISM

When a Japanese approached a newsstand looking for criticism of major state policies, what did he find? The purpose here is not to identify a few radical publications eluding the censor, but to gauge the normal boundaries of legally allowed debate. Three mainstream periodicals of high circulation may be used to illustrate these boundaries: the *Asahi Shinbun,* a critical national newspaper with over a million readers, and *Chūō Kōron* (Central Review) and *Kaizō* (Reconstruction), two monthlies printing over 100,000 copies each. Even more than the *Asahi,* the latter two journals provide an excellent test of permissiveness. They were called "integrated magazines" for combining political and social criticism, literary contributions, and neutral reportage, and they prided themselves on a liberal display of partisan argument. In 1933, they would be the only two mainstream magazines outside the cultural field to commemorate Marx's death.[29] Their intellectual appeal and high quality placed them above all competitors—even classified police documents labeled them the "matchless twin stars" of the magazine field.[30] Three content analyses are offered to measure state tolerance for criticism: the *Tōkyō Asahi Shinbun*'s reactions to the Peace Preservation Law, a collection of *Kaizō* articles lambasting censorship, and critical responses to the Manchurian Incident in both *Kaizō* and *Chūō Kōron.*

The *Asahi*'s editorials strongly opposed passage of the Peace Preservation Law.[31] They accused the cabinet of betraying democracy by using the police to thwart popular participation. One editorial, "The Suicide

28. Beckmann and Ōkubo, *The Japanese Communist Party,* p. 219.
29. Naimushō Keihōkyoku, *Shuppan Keisatsu Gaikan,* 1933, p. 226.
30. Idem, *Shuppan Keisatsu Gaikan,* 1932, p. 271. *Chūō Kōron* dated back to 1899, with antecedents under other titles to 1887, and by the early 1920s it had a circulation of some 120,000 copies: see *Chūō Kōronsha 70-Nen Shi,* pp. 3–4. *Kaizō* was founded in 1919, and its attention to labor problems soon boosted its circulation to comparable levels. The journals typically ran several hundred pages in length.
31. The editorials on this issue dated 17 January, 14 February, 5 March, and 12 March 1925 are reprinted in *Chian Iji Hō,* document 7, pp. 100–104.

of the Constitutional Protection Cabinet," suggested that the bill might be a response to the Privy Council's "stupid arguments" against the suffrage bill also before the Diet.

The *Asahi* endorsed the goal of suppressing revolutionary movements but it denounced the Peace Preservation Law for inviting abuses of authority.[32] A call for reform of the House of Peers might be construed as rejection of the parliamentary system, or criticism of military education as repudiation of the draft, bringing moderates into conflict with the law. The result would be "an absolute trampling of human rights and the suppression of speech." The *Asahi* emphasized the precarious position of labor unions under the statute. In a country with neither a trade union law nor recognition of the right to strike, unions per se might be seen as destructive of the property system and the whole labor movement be placed in jeopardy. Many party leaders backing the law had opposed Prime Minister Takahashi's similar bill three years earlier, and the newspaper accused them of a hypocritical about-face now that they controlled the cabinet.[33] One editorial concluded, "In the name of protecting the constitution and for the state [*kokka*] and the people, we hope that the government will not present this evil law, and if it is presented, we demand that the Diet reject it."[34]

In 1928, when Prime Minister Tanaka added the death penalty to the Peace Preservation Law by emergency imperial decree, the *Asahi* again opposed. More biting even than its editorials were two articles by Uesugi Shinkichi, a leading constitutional scholar.[35] Uesugi was a renowned advocate of imperial absolutism who had once written, "It is clear from whatever position one views it, the spirit of our constitution excludes parliamentary government . . . ."[36] Yet he waxed eloquent in attacking the emergency decree. How, he asked, could the government simply decree the death penalty when jurists were debating its abolition? Uesugi denied the gravity of the communist threat, and he disparaged alarmist rhetoric fomenting needless anxiety and soiling Japan's

32. This argument was put forward in the editorial of 17 January 1925.
33. For example, the editorial of 14 February 1925 stated: "The constitutional protection cabinet has put out the Peace Preservation Law, and the Kenseikai, which as a party out of power preached absolute opposition to the Bill for the Control of Extreme Social Movements and buried it, is supporting this evil law. For the party as absolutely the party of government to move to abandon the program [it had embraced] until today is something difficult to excuse in any manner": *Chian Iji Hō,* document 7, p. 101.
34. Ibid., p. 103.
35. Uesugi's articles are reprinted in ibid., document 13, part 5, pp. 193–96.
36. Quoted in Miller, *Minobe Tatsukichi,* p. 301 n. 44.

reputation abroad. A cabinet sponsored bill for harsher punishments had failed to pass the previous Diet, and Uesugi contended that to flout the Diet's prerogatives with an unwarranted emergency decree was unconstitutional. Such a decree would "expose to danger all the rights of liberty recognized in the constitution."[37] College students arrested under the Peace Preservation Law deserved a better education, he wrote, not capital punishment.

Short of revolutionary rhetoric, it is hard to imagine more forceful arguments against the Peace Preservation Law and the emergency imperial decree (which the Diet later approved) than those run by the *Tōkyō Asahi Shinbun*.

The September 1926 *Kaizō* carried an editorial and seven articles criticizing the Newspaper and Publication Laws. The magazine's July issue had been banned from circulation for portraying adultery in one piece and consent to violence in another,[38] and the issue on censorship was linked to a broader movement to liberalize the law. New legislation was pending in the Diet, and the Literary Writers' Association, the Publishing Association, and the Magazine Association had pooled resources to lobby for reform.

Kaizō's editorial emphasized the financial strains caused by bans on circulation—small companies could be ruined by sanctions on consecutive issues.[39] It also denounced the arbitrariness of law enforcement, noting that press controls might someday devolve upon a reactionary cabinet or an unscrupulous Home Minister. The editorial outlined the proposal of the three associations, which demanded more concrete censorship standards, the right to appeal administrative sanctions, and a joint bureaucratic-civil committee to review administrative decisions. The editors averred that "if the present oppression continues, our art and thought will degenerate into an empty corpse completely without spirit . . . ."[40]

The articles attacked the press laws from many vantage points. Minobe Tatsukichi, a democratic-oriented constitutional scholar and Uesugi's rival, argued that literary and academic works should be exempt from censorship, naming a banned novel that he deemed excellent. He joined the other contributors in excoriating the ambiguity of censor-

37. *Chian Iji Hō*, document 13, p. 193.
38. Kobayashi Eisaburō, Matsuura Sōzō, Daigohō Susumu, and Seki Tada, eds., *Zasshi "Kaizō" no 40-Nen*, p. 95.
39. *Kaizō* (September 1925): 1–3.
40. Ibid., p. 3.

ship criteria and calling for a route of appeal.[41] Masamune Hakuchō, a naturalistic novelist, had recently had a line struck from a literary piece in *Kaizō,* his first such experience. He wrote that press controls had never concerned him much, but that if censorship were milder he might have addressed subjects hitherto excluded from his work, perhaps a widespread attitude among non-radical writers.[42] He confessed to a special interest in reading banned books. Another author, Fujimori Seikichi, demanded absolute freedom of expression. He mocked the constitution's treatment of civil liberties:

> "We grant you the freedom of expression. However, you have no right to express what has been prohibited." That is too clear a contradiction in logic. . . . today's system and methods absolutely cannot be imagined as a reality in the cultural epoch of the twentieth century. They resemble barbaric feudal customs. It is a pure and simple right to kill and be excused [*kirisute gomen*]. The attitude is just like that of the old samurai, only since they are state officials it doesn't matter how many they slay.[43]

To kill and be excused referred to the samurai's right over the lower orders in pre-Meiji Japan.

Ōmori Yoshitarō of the Labor-Farmer Party analyzed censorship from a Marxist perspective. "The capitalist class . . . must necessarily force its own scholarship, thought, and art on all of society in order to maintain its supremacy."[44] It was futile to assail press policy with reason and justice when it had such solid economic foundations. "In the end, . . . one cannot perfectly resolve the issue of the ban on circulation, which has such deep roots in capitalist class conflict, if one does not remove its real basis."[45] The Labor-Farmer Party was outlawed in April 1928.

The editorial and three of the articles in *Kaizō* were marred by the use of blank type. Nonetheless, the writers had thoroughly castigated censorship policy and articulated a variety of solutions, from moderate to sweeping reformism to a call for radical change.

The Manchurian Incident was a clash on 18 September 1931 be-

---

41. Minobe also advocated repeal of the prosecutor's right to ban pre-trial information, since it aimed at deceiving the public about current events and forced newspapers to collaborate in the deception. His apparent unawareness of the Home Minister's own illegal pre-publication warning system supports the view that this power had been used very sparingly before 1926. Minobe Tatsukichi, "Shuppanbutsu no Hatsubai Kinshi," pp. 98–101.
42. Masamune Hakuchō, "Hatsubai Kinshi ni Tsuite," pp. 104–6.
43. Fujimori Seikichi, "Hatsubai Kinshi Mondai ni Tsuite," pp. 107–8.
44. Ōmori Yoshitarō, "Kekkyoku wa Keizaiteki Shihai Kankei," p. 102.
45. Ibid., p. 103.

tween Japanese and Chinese troops, arranged furtively by high-ranking officers in Japan's Kwantung Army as a pretext for expanding their control over Manchuria and contiguous areas. In some ways, the response of the press to this issue is a poor measure of state control. The effects of pre-publication warnings and censorship cannot be disaggregated from what by all accounts was spontaneous and nearly unanimous public approval of Japan's aggressive stance.[46] Not knowing that the episode had been stage-managed by Japanese troops, mainstream newspapers and the general public resolutely supported a bellicose foreign policy, just as they had during the Sino-Japanese and Russo-Japanese wars at the turn of the century. Nonetheless, even a self-imposed conformity of opinion on this issue is an important reference point when considering later state controls, and the event's inherent significance justifies a search for criticism.

The experience of *Chūō Kōron* is particularly instructive. Its editorial of October 1931, probably written just after the incident, took a dovish position. It accused elements in Japan of exploiting minor conflicts in Manchuria to impose an aggressive policy. The newspapers were denounced for rousing public antipathy, and the editorial opposed sending troops, stating that Japan's ultimate goals could not be gained by force.[47] The editor received a post-publication warning from the Home Ministry.[48]

The November edition was banned from circulation for Inomata Tsunao's "Monopoly Capitalism and the Crisis in Manchuria and Mongolia."[49] Inomata, a founder of Japan's original Communist Party, had been arrested in the first Communist Party Incident of June 1923, consequently losing his professorship at Waseda University. By 1931, he had abandoned the communists and joined the Labor-Farmer Faction (*Rōnōha*) of Marxist intellectuals then catalogued among the legal left. His essay was so riddled with blank type that it is nearly illegible. A full four pages were ripped out by the editors to avoid sanctions, yet the issue was still banned. It is discernible that Inomata blames capitalism for the contemporary economic crisis and the imperialistic struggle in China,

46. Public support is attested to by the British ambassador: see James B. Crowley, *Japan's Quest for Autonomy*, p. 126. It is also verified by the publications police: Naimushō Keihōkyoku, *Shuppan Keisatsu Gaikan*, 1932, p. 217, and idem, *Shuppan Keisatsu Gaikan*, 1933, p. 203.
47. "Manmō Mondai ni Kansuru Hansei," p. 1.
48. Naimushō Keihōkyoku, *Shuppan Keisatsu Gaikan*, 1931, p. 176.
49. Inomata Tsunao, "Dokusen Shihonshugi to Manmō no Kiki"; Naimushō Keihōkyoku, *Shuppan Keisatsu Gaikan*, 1931, pp. 144, 176.

and he praises the Soviet system for its immunity to the depression and its anti-imperialist policy. Omissions from sentences on the Chinese Communist Party seem to disguise the author's esteem for its battle against Japan and other imperialist powers. Restraints on free expression are castigated, but here again the piece is unquotable due to gaps in the prose.[50]

Chūō Kōron published no further articles as radical as Inomata's on the Manchurian Incident, but it did carry several more moderate critiques. In the January 1932 edition, renowned democratic theorist Yoshino Sakuzō attacked the government's plea of self-defense in Manchuria.[51] The defense of treaty rights did not warrant military action to extract new obligations, expel hostile warlords, and install pro-Japanese figures in their stead. Yoshino argued that the state's position differed from the logic of popular support. While most Japanese saw Manchuria as a "treasure mountain" of needed natural resources, the government was avowing self-defense to avoid the bad name of imperialism. Thus Yoshino discarded the official line and recast the issue in these terms: "Is it bad for us to establish rights in Manchuria for our own existence? This is the urgent problem now confronting us."[52] He lamented that neither the newspapers nor the working-class parties had seriously challenged state policy: "The proletarian parties are silent and the newspapers unanimously glorify military action. In this manner the unity of national opinion has been made complete."[53]

Another moderate protester was Yanaihara Tadao, an economics professor at Tokyo Imperial University, who contributed to both *Kaizō* and *Chūō Kōron*. In *Kaizō,* he portrayed the Manchurian Incident as a clash between Japanese imperialism and Chinese nationalism and cautiously defended the latter. Japan supported the new state of Manchukuo to protect its special rights, but these were unwarranted, and Manchukuo contradicted the national principle behind modern state-building, since Manchurian nationality was related to that of the Chinese. Yanaihara compared Chinese nationalism to the forces of the Meiji revolution, arguing that its anti-foreign component would dissipate once independence was achieved. Japan's interests were better served by promoting Chinese nationalism (and thus, implicitly, by abandoning the puppet state of Manchukuo) than by forging a closed eco-

50. Inomata, "Dokusen Shihonshugi," p. 33.
51. Yoshino Sakuzō, "Minzoku to Kaikyū to Sensō."
52. Ibid., p. 31.
53. Ibid., p. 33.

nomic unit of Japan and Manchuria. After all, Japan's trade with
Manchuria was only 30 percent of its trade with China. Yanaihara
described Japan as an "unreined, unruly horse" in its Asian military
ventures.[54]

In November 1932, six months after the last party Prime Minister
was assassinated, *Chūō Kōron* published a translation of the Litton
Commission's report on the Manchurian situation. Sponsored by the
League of Nations, the report belied Japan's claim of self-defense and
the alleged spontaneity of the founding of Manchukuo. By this time,
however, the journal had reversed its initial editorial position. In December 1932, the editors wrote:

> There is no doubt that our country ought to reject staunchly any demands
> for changes in the present state of affairs, this constituting meddling with our
> freedom of action. We can no longer recognize the interference of Westerners
> in matters pertaining to the Far East or in the great undertakings related to
> the destiny of Oriental peoples. . . .
>
> The establishment of an Eastern Monroe Doctrine is absolutely neces-
> sary. . . . One thing clear in modern history is that peace in the East and the
> felicity of Eastern peoples will begin from the repulsion of unjust oppression
> by Western power . . . .[55]

The state had no power to compel a statement of this kind in 1932.
Despite editorial backing for Manchukuo, however, the publication of
the Litton Commission's report demonstrated a continued willingness
to air other points of view.

There was, then, extensive debate in the press on controversial domestic issues, but much less on the Manchurian question. Judging from
Chūō Kōron's experience, this was partly due to state controls. The
moderately critical essays of Yanaihara and Yoshino were phrased very
carefully to pass inspection, and both writers noted the restraints on free
expression. The censor's impact is also evident in what was not written.
None of the articles, for example, took up the role of the military. Since
the Manchurian Incident was not premeditated in Tokyo, and local
military decisions had turned it into a major crisis, this is truly remarkable. Commentators had to skirt the core of the problem when it most
required attention. As documented in Yoshino's article, however, behind the passivity of the press there was also a dearth of dissension in
civil society. Judging from press treatment of other issues, this may have

    54. Yanaihara Tadao, "Manmō Shinkokka Ron," p. 28; see also Yanaihara,
"Manshū Keizai Ron."
    55. "Tōyō Monroshugi no Kakuritsu," p. 1.

been more decisive than censorship in mobilizing journalistic support for the invasion. Note that the articles reviewed above represent the extremes of criticism in mainstream journals, not the middle range of published opinion.

THE FAILURE OF LIBERAL REFORM

The complacency of the press toward the Newspaper Law lasted only until mainstream journals felt the sting of the administrative ban on circulation. Efforts at liberal reform then picked up where they had left off in the 1890s. The House of Peers shelved a reform bill passed by the lower house in 1912, and subsequent reform proposals were presented at three consecutive Diet meetings between 1919 and 1922, none meeting with success.

The new prestige of the press and its influence with party men set the stage for a major effort at liberalization in the mid-1920s. The prevailing zeal for reform can be grasped from the *Kaizō* articles on press legislation already reviewed. Publishers resented the economic losses from banned editions, and writers railed against "feudal" restraints on their creativity. An organized press lobby drafted guidelines for change, and in December 1924 newspapermen met with sympathetic Diet members to turn these into a new legal proposal.[56] Their bill retained the Home Minister's right to ban particular issues, but only for desecration of the imperial family, items proscribed by the army or navy, agitation for violent direct action that specified the means to be employed, and contents strikingly offensive to manners and morals. The general precept against disturbing public order was dropped. Bureaucrats would have to identify the criminal passages when an issue was banned, and their judgment could be appealed to the administrative court. The judicial power to dissolve publications was to be abrogated, and the editor and printer absolved of all legal responsibility; the publisher alone would be answerable to the law. The bill also relaxed prison sentences. All in all, this was a moderate proposal designed to pass the upper house. It would retain censorship to deal with revolutionary or obscene contents while freeing the mainstream press from police harassment.

In March 1925, the bill passed the House of Representatives almost unanimously. Things looked favorable in the upper house as well, but

56. The press resolution and the proposed bill are reprinted in Midoro, *Meiji Taishō Shi I*, pp. 336–48.

before the peers could consider it, Prime Minister Katō Kōmei announced that his government was elaborating its own bill to replace both the Newspaper Law and the Publication Law, and consequently the lower house draft was never brought to a vote. This was a bitter blow to the press.

The government's own integrated press bill, submitted at the next two regular Diet meetings, reversed the liberality of the earlier reform measure.[57] There was no provision for appeal, censorship standards were increased and again highly abstract, the judicial authority to dissolve publications was retained, and the maximum prison sentence was lengthened from two to three years. Most journalists opposed the bill and it never reached a vote in the Diet.

The great majority of elected officials thus demonstrated their commitment to a more liberal press policy in 1925 but saw their efforts obstructed by the cabinet. This scene has been reenacted in the history of the mass media in many countries. The virtues of liberalism are apparent to all but those who control the levers of power. The same party officials who had voted against an anti-radical bill in 1922 turned into sponsors of the Peace Preservation Law once they had taken charge of the government. The Newspaper Law powers repudiated by the lower house and the press were viewed very differently by a Prime Minister who had those powers at his disposal. Katō, a lifelong admirer of British politics and a champion of the suffrage act, was not ready to sacrifice powers that he relied upon not only to keep order but also to sway election results. The same authority that appears so fearful in the hands of others is perceived as a great asset from atop the roost.

Though the government's own draft failed to pass, its contents are of some interest. Bureaucratic input was evident in its incorporation of several extralegal administrative controls already in use; despite its defeat, however, these controls were not abandoned. The bill would have legalized pre-publication warnings on current events, but these had been employed before 1925 and were used regularly after 1927 despite their illegality. Thousands of newspaper editions were banned from circulation for transgressing these warnings, even though the Diet had refused to approve them. This was a blatant constitutional violation, but if party cabinets acquiesced, there was no institution to termi-

57. The government's original bill, with changes before its second submission noted in parentheses, is reprinted in ibid., pp. 349–60. The bill was first prepared under Prime Minister Katō Kōmei but was presented to the Diet on both occasions by his successor, Wakatsuki Reijirō.

nate the abuse. The practice of demanding deletions before circulation was also inscribed in the bill, but this too had been used earlier and became a regular practice in the late 1920s. The inclusion of these controls in the proposed legislation demonstrates the government's awareness that they required a legal basis, but what can be concluded from their previous use and their amplification after the measure failed to pass? Like the Newspaper Ordinance of 1883, Katō's press law was designed to catch up with administrative practice, not to fix its limits. The bill's failure therefore had no effect on the development of administrative press controls.[58]

In sum, the constitutional guarantee of a free press within the bounds of parliamentary law was partly nullified by bureaucratic power tied to the values and interests of party Prime Ministers. There was a border dispute in the state, arising from the terms of the constitution itself, between administrative and parliamentary jurisdictions. The areas to be monopolized by parliament were mapped out clearly enough, but they had no institutional protection other than the precise dictates of legislation and the watchfulness of the Diet. These proved inadequate to check bureaucratic incursions into most aspects of press policy.

58. Subsequently, Prime Minister Tanaka Giichi organized a Criminal Affairs Council that produced another plan for an integrated press law in August 1928. Minobe Tatsukichi was a member of the council, but an influential newspaper association (21-nichikai) refused to participate due to the increasing rigidity of press controls under the Tanaka cabinet. See ibid., p. 364. The plan contained several liberal features, including elimination of security deposits and the judicial power to dissolve publications, creation of a commission to preside over the levy of administrative sanctions (presumably with civil participation), and allowance for compensation when damage was suffered from illegal sanctions (thus an appeals system was advocated). However, there was no relaxation of censorship standards. The council's plan never produced a legislative proposal. It is reprinted in ibid., pp. 364–66.

CHAPTER III

Film

Film was introduced in Japan in 1896, domestic production starting shortly thereafter. Since there were few theaters, the medium was initially promoted by road companies touring the country. From the outset, film production was in the hands of privately owned, profit-making companies financially independent of the state and generally unconnected to other business sectors. By the mid-1920s, film had become an important mass medium. In 1926, the paying public for films numbered 153.7 million, and there were 15,348 pieces of film presented for mandatory state inspection before public showing.[1]

There was no integrated film control system when the parties took over the cabinet. When the medium began to prosper in the 1920s, therefore, party governments were free to develop a comprehensive policy unencumbered by antecedent legislation. Remarkably, however, the parties never became involved in the regulation of film; the bureaucracy took complete charge. The manner in which this happened speaks to the general problem of bureaucratic power and accountability in democratic regimes. Film policy is also of interest for the elaborate data available on censorship standards and their applications, which offer important insights into the political and social values of state elites. An effort has been made to examine state intrusions into all segments of the industry: production, distribution, import and export, and theater operation.

1. These are official figures from Naimushō Keihōkyoku, *Katsudō Shashin Firumu Ken'etsu Nenpō*, 1927, hereafter cited as *Firumu Ken'etsu Nenpō*. See also Peter B. High, "The Dawn of Cinema in Japan."

BUREAUCRATIC POLICYMAKING:
THE REGULATIONS OF 1925

Before 1925, state control over film was left to the discretion of the Home Ministry's local government and police officials, and it was subsumed under their general authority to regulate entertainment. Films were censored before public showing, and officials in each area determined their own inspection criteria and fees. This was only a small increment to the voluminous responsibilities of the Home Ministry. In addition to its jurisdiction over film and the press, the ministry was in charge of public works, elections, health policy, the licensing of commercial enterprises, fire prevention, Shintō and other religious institutions, public baths, the labor movement and civil political organizations, land development, and the Emperor's public appearances. The Home Minister was sometimes referred to as the unofficial vice prime minister of Japan.

The growth of the film industry led to the centralization and standardization of control in May 1925, when the Home Ministry proclaimed its Motion Picture Film Inspection Regulations.[2] This statute was a unilateral ministerial decree, neither requiring nor receiving cabinet discussion, Diet approval, or the imprimatur of any other ministry. With minor revisions, it guided film administration for the next fourteen years.

The regulations of 1925 required state inspection of all films (and the narrative scripts accompanying silent movies) before public exposure. As a rule, central Home Ministry officials were to conduct the inspection, and their license was good for three years. However, current-events films requiring immediate inspection could be submitted to local government officials, whose approval was valid for three months within their jurisdiction. Bureaucrats could ban or restrict the showing of any film undermining public peace, manners and morals, or health and could revoke the license of a film that had passed inspection. Approved films were marked with an official seal noting any limits placed on public showing of the work. Inspection fees were charged per meter of film, and police could enter and examine any

2. The regulations are reprinted in *Masu Media Tōsei*, vol. 1, document 2, pp. 6–8. A first step toward uniformity was the Rules for the Management of Motion Picture Entertainment prepared by the Tokyo Metropolitan Police in 1917 and circulated to police offices nationwide. Adoption of these norms by other police bureaus was optional. See Taikakai, ed., *Naimushō Shi*, 2: 738.

locale where films were shown. The maximum penalty for violations was a fine of one hundred yen or, in lieu of payment, detention until the amount was worked off.

The purpose of these regulations was not to introduce a more repressive order, but to systematize the Home Ministry's operations. This benefited the film industry, since separate fees were no longer charged in each area, and central ministry approval obviated the need for repeated local inspections.

The decree was issued under the Home Ministry's authority over entertainment, and this had important legal implications. The constitution protected the liberty of speech, writing, and publication against all interference unless authorized by parliamentary legislation. Had films been construed as a form of publication or speech, only a Diet law could have initiated state control. However, by treating films for public showing as "entertainment" rather than "speech" or "publication," the Home Ministry denied the applicability of the constitution and empowered itself to handle the medium as it saw fit. The illogic of denying film the status of speech or publication was not lost on officials. In fact, films sold over the counter for home use were regulated by the same Home Ministry under the Publication Law. But this law required the submission of materials for inspection just three days before public release, and that was not sufficient time to inspect all films destined for public showing. So the ministry expounded the awkward legal interpretation of publicly shown film as "entertainment," thereby stripping film as a mass medium of all constitutional protection and leaving it at the mercy of bureaucratic decrees.

Illogical as this construction may seem, constitutional clauses on the liberties of speech and the press were rarely applied to the cinema or radio anywhere in the interwar period. Even in the United States, the American Commission on Freedom of the Press recommended in 1947 "that the constitutional guarantees of the freedom of the press be recognized as including the radio and motion pictures," reflecting the uncertain legal status of those media at the time.[3]

The initial perception of film as a medium of entertainment rather than information also helps to explain its neglect by parliamentarians. Japan's party governments never challenged ministerial power in this sphere. Film was still a novelty in the 1920s, and few people realized its

3. Terrou and Solal, *Legislation*, p. 30.

full importance. It was only in 1934 that a Diet member rose to protest the bureaucratic lock on film policy:

> the influence of motion pictures is a tremendous thing . . . . it is greater than the influence of lectures or speech and writing. If one reflects upon the influence of motion pictures today, I think it is truly as though the right of legislation were being transgressed for the government merely to handle this at its pleasure by means of arbitrarily manufactured ministerial decrees. It must be said that it is an infringement of the constitution that the basis of the ministerial decree upon which these Film Inspection Regulations depend does not conform to any old laws such as the Publication Law, the Newspaper Law, or the Public Peace Police Law, but is just a temporarily produced article. In short, I must say that you have disregarded the Diet.[4]

Nonetheless, major legislation dealing with film was not passed until the late 1930s, when several European states were also enacting their first film laws. This illustrates another great source of bureaucratic autonomy in policymaking: administrators often have a free hand in policy areas not deemed significant enough to include on the overloaded agenda of modern legislatures.

ADMINISTRATIVE CONTROL IN PRACTICE

The Home Ministry's censors had great leeway in handling films. They could order a total ban on public showing, but this sanction was infrequently applied. More often they labored as editors and cut the offensive segments of a film, approving an abridged version for public viewing. If scissors were inadequate to sanitize a film, officials might return it to its producers with instructions to reshoot certain scenes as a requisite for approval. Even when a film was beyond all repair and destined for prohibition, the censors usually forewarned its sponsors and had the film withdrawn from inspection before they were forced to administer the ultimate sanction. Finally, they might pass a film but restrict its showing to certain regions or viewing facilities (for example, indoor theaters or medical schools). In sum, film inspectors could exercise five options: to ban, to cut, to return for revision, to recommend withdrawal, and to impose locational limits.

Institutionally, film censorship was highly centralized. As was mentioned above, all but current-events films were inspected exclusively at

4. The statement of lower house Representative Hoshijima Jirō in committee hearings, 25 March 1934, reprinted in *Masu Media Tōsei*, vol. 1, document 55, p. 350.

central Home Ministry offices. In practice, very few films were reviewed by local authorities (the number peaked at 10 percent in 1927).[5] In extraordinary circumstances, such as the Emperor's coronation in Kyoto in 1928, film inspectors were dispatched from Tokyo to handle the many petitions for local film endorsement.[6]

If inspection was highly centralized, however, enforcement was entirely a local matter. Local officials were authorized to license and regulate theater operations, censor film advertising, and inspect both films and theater facilities.[7] Police were urged to inspect theater, film, and script before the showing of any film cut by the censors or bound to arouse exceptional public interest.[8] They could also request that a centrally approved film be banned in their district due to special conditions—for example, if the film might inflame local tenancy disputes.[9]

Though the Home Ministry dominated film administration, other institutions were also involved. The Army and Navy Ministries could request special priorities from Home Ministry censors. When additional troops were deployed in Manchuria in May 1928, the army urged extra caution with films touching upon military secrets or discipline, anti-military sentiments, Japanese-Chinese relations, and war atrocities.[10] These instructions were quickly incorporated into film inspection standards.[11] The

5. The number of locally inspected films declined markedly in the mid-1930s: by 1938 only 151 films (0.03 percent) were examined by local officials. This trend accelerated as Japan became further mired in war. The figures are recorded in Naimushō Keihōkyoku, *Firumu Ken'etsu Nenpō*, 1928–1939.

6. See *Masu Media Tōsei*, vol. 1, document 24, pp. 205–8.

7. They were also entitled to limit the length of films shown and the duration of film entertainment programs until February 1932, when policy on these matters was standardized. In 1932, individual films were limited to 6,000 meters and programs to a maximum of four hours: Naimushō Keihōkyoku, *Firumu Ken'etsu Nenpō*, 1933, p. 55.

8. *Masu Media Tōsei*, vol. 1, document 5, pp. 11–12.

9. These solicitations were usually conveyed over the telephone and might be granted or rejected by Home Ministry authorities in Tokyo. If favorably received, they were enforced as areal limitations on the showing of the film: Tajima Tarō, *Ken'etsu Shitsu no Yami ni Tsubuyaku*, pp. 278, 296. These are the memoirs of the Home Ministry's chief film inspector.

10. See *Masu Media Tōsei*, vol. 1, document 25, p. 209.

11. The Military Police also occasionally played a role in film censorship. The MPs were charged by a number of statutes with the protection of military secrets, and they were consulted by Home Ministry censors on the propriety of military-related films. They sometimes took more direct action. In January 1926, a squad entered a theater in Osaka and proceeded to cut some twenty meters of a Home Ministry–approved film, claiming it violated the Military Base Zone Law—apparently an area inside base facilities had been photographed. This action elicited no protest from Home Ministry officials, who advised their local police bureaus to refer such matters to Tokyo to be worked out in consultation with Military Police Headquarters: Naimushō Keihōkyoku, *Firumu Ken'etsu Nenpō*, 1928, pp. 68–69. The role of the Military Police in mass-media censorship is not well documented, but it appears that direct involvement of this sort was rare.

TABLE VIII   ADMINISTRATIVE SANCTIONS IMPOSED UNDER THE
MOTION PICTURE FILM INSPECTION REGULATIONS, JULY 1925–1932

	Total Films Inspected[a]	Bans[b]	Required to Reshoot[c]	Films Cut	Limited by Location	Withdrawn[d]
1925[e]	6,887	11	10	1,239	7	6
1926	15,348	28	44	1,807	87	52
1927	16,101	7	28	1,237	7	23
1928	18,893	8	30	1,445	7	39
1929	16,574	8	39	1,039	2	42
1930	17,430	2	16	1,015	86	35
1931	15,691	6	10	775	27	79
1932	18,436			780	18	96

Source: Naimushō Keihōkyoku, Firumu Ken'etsu Nenpō, 1927–1933.

[a]The figures include Japanese and imported films, films submitted for the first time, resubmissions, and prints of previously submitted films.

[b]The figures include films withdrawn from inspection because sponsors were informed they would be banned. These films are not counted in the "withdrawn" column, except in 1932, when the number withdrawn for this reason is unknown.

[c]The figures include films withdrawn from inspection because sponsors were informed that reshooting was required for approval. All films requiring reshooting were listed as withdrawals from 1928. These films are not counted in the "withdrawn" column, except in 1932.

[d]Some films withdrawn from inspection were removed at the convenience of their sponsors, and not due to official action.

[e]Figures for 1925 cover only the period from July, when the regulations came into force, through December.

Ministry of Education was consulted informally on films for children,[12] and education officials also controlled the choice of films shown in schools. Finally, customs officials inspected imported films as well as publications, and they possessed their own censorship criteria. Films and publications passed through customs were still obliged to undergo Home Ministry inspection before public release. To coordinate the inspection system and to inform other state organs of its activities, the Home Ministry circulated a film censorship bulletin three times a month.[13]

Tables 8 and 9 summarize the administrative sanctions imposed from 1925 to 1932. The overview in table 8 confirms the censors' propensity to avoid outright bans and concentrate their efforts on the cutting room.

12. Masu Media Tōsei, vol. 1, document 8, p. 16.

13. This report contained special censorship instructions from the ministry to its local offices, statistics on the imposition of sanctions, and brief accounts of how particularly pernicious films and those posing unusual administrative problems had been handled. Each issue was printed in 1,600 copies, and the mailing list included the Army, Navy, and Education Ministries, Military Police Headquarters, and Japanese government or military offices in Korea, Taiwan, Manchuria, the South Seas, and Sakhalin. See Naimushō Keihōkyoku, Firumu Ken'etsu Nenpō, 1928, pp. 67–68.

TABLE IX   PAID INSPECTIONS OF FILMS SUBMITTED FOR THE FIRST
TIME AND THOSE CUT UNDER THE MOTION PICTURE FILM INSPECTION
REGULATIONS, BY AREA OF PRODUCTION, JULY 1925–1932

	Japanese Films			Foreign Films			Total
	Inspected	Cut	% Cut	Inspected	Cut	% Cut	% Cut
1925[a]	1,037	205	19%	972	241	24%	22%
1926	2,005	315	15	1,456	374	25	19
1927	2,682	246	9	1,132	216	19	12
1928	2,383	335	14	1,032	266	25	17
1929	2,863	255	8	1,522	306	20	12
1930	3,160	315	10	1,507	201	13	11
1931	3,095	328	10	1,171	202	17	12
1932	2,942	302	10	1,279	207	16	12

Source: Naimushō Keihōkyoku, Firumu Ken'etsu Nenpō, 1927–1933.
[a]July–December.

More precise data show that newsreels almost never suffered administrative sanctions. Only 154 of 19,805 current-events films inspected between 1926 and 1932 were cut, indicating that news film never became a major outlet for political dissidence.[14] It was state policy to exempt news films from inspection fees, along with a few educational films and nonfiction films produced with official cooperation. Table 9 estimates the proportion of other films clipped by the censors. This table excludes films inspected without charge, extra prints of previously submitted films, and those reinspected after their permits expired. In short, all films counted in the table were first-time inspections, and dramatic movies constituted a good portion of them. The annual percentage of these films cut ranged from 11 percent to 22 percent.

These figures paint only a partial picture of policy effectiveness. There are no records of how many films were altered in production based on the director's prior experience with censorship. Nor is it known how many informal phone calls were received at the Home Ministry begging an advisory opinion on a scene scheduled for shooting the next day.[15] Foreign films fared considerably worse than the Japanese, due to differing standards of propriety and to the efforts of Japanese film-makers to abide by national censorship restrictions.

Official records reveal few violations of the film decree. The courts

14. Idem, Firumu Ken'etsu Nenpō, 1927–1933.
15. See Tajima, Ken'etsu Shitsu, p. 292, for evidence of this practice.

dispensed only fifty-seven fines to violators during the entire 1925–1932 period, and data on direct police fines available for 1926, 1927, and 1930 show fewer than five each year.[16] Prior censorship eliminated most infractions. Unlike the case of publications, most illicit films were stopped by bureaucrats before they were shown to the public, and it was not a crime to submit for inspection a film later banned or cut by officials. The only crimes were to show a proscribed film, or to alter a film or script after inspection.

CENSORSHIP STANDARDS

Censorship standards are an illuminating source for the study of state ideology and the state-society relationship. The censor passes judgment on virtually every idea and practice current in society, defining the bounds of heresy and revealing by omission where the state will not intervene. In Japan, the study of censorship is an especially interesting reflection of bureaucratic values. Though the bureaucracy's policymaking role is recognized in many countries, treatments of official ideology are usually limited to the statements of top political leaders—there is simply too little information about the beliefs of administrators. Since Japanese bureaucrats were solely responsible for fixing concrete censorship criteria, however, these provide valuable insights into their thinking.

As noted, the principal censorship guidelines were to protect public order and manners and morals. The ubiquity of these nebulous formulae in prewar statutes is a measure of bureaucratic discretion in applying the law. One or another rendition of the concept of public order or public peace (*annei chitsujo, kōan, chian*) was inscribed in the constitution (articles 8, 9, 59, 70), the Public Peace Police Law, the Criminal Litigation Law, the Administrative Enforcement Law, the Postal Law, the Customs Law, various clauses of the civil and criminal codes, and many other statutes.[17] Administrators themselves confessed to the ambiguity of such phrases, and they had complete control over their meaning in practice.[18]

The frequency of resort to the various standards against films is given in table 10. Note that this table classifies each piece of film cut by the censors, and since one motion picture might be cut in several places, the

---

16. Figures from Nihon Teikoku Shihōshō, *Keiji Tōkei Nenpō*, nos. 51–58, 1925–1932.

17. Naimushō Keihōkyoku, *Shuppan Keisatsu Hō*, no. 6, p. 98.

18. Ibid., p. 97; idem, *Shuppan Keisatsu Gaikan*, 1930, p. 326.

TABLE X   PIECES OF FILM CUT UNDER THE MOTION PICTURE FILM INSPECTION REGULATIONS, BY CENSORSHIP STANDARDS AND AREA OF PRODUCTION, 1927–1932

(J=Japanese, F = Foreign)

	1927		1928		1929		1930		1931		1932	
	J	F	J	F	J	F	J	F	J	F	J	F
Public Safety												
Imperial family	7	3	6	0	0	4	2	3	1	5	2	0
Nation	0	0	0	1	0	0	2	0	10	0	0	0
Constitution	0	0	0	0	0	0	0	0	0	0	0	0
Social organs	10	8	23	35	28	50	150	9	162	52	22	39
Class conflict	9	0	8	11	7	16	79	4	19	3	12	0
National ethos	0	0	3	27	0	5	0	38	1	3	0	1
Foreign affairs	0	8	25	11	0	4	1	3	30	1	8	4
Group conflict	14	0	0	1	10	22	57	2	14	2	13	1
Crime	91	50	208	72	55	30	139	14	46	54	55	67
Public business	24	42	65	96	36	59	30	27	13	35	13	38
Other	59	161	156	80	76	65	265	107	147	52	215	60
Area Total	214	272	494	334	212	255	725	207	443	207	340	210
Annual Total	486		828		467		932		650		550	

Manners and Morals

Religion	9	2	3	0	0	0	21	1	1	4	0	0
Cruelty/ugliness	583	80	473	102	119	42	153	27	103	43	86	41
Sex-related	682	1,119	764	972	663	700	551	356	508	425	541	523
Work ethic	2	0	8	0	0	0	0	0	2	0	1	0
Education	38	18	71	14	43	26	39	3	46	57	40	11
Family	10	9	26	51	26	29	21	4	29	15	21	13
Other	178	47	234	104	187	73	225	55	204	52	199	62
Area Total	1,502	1,275	1,579	1,243	1,038	870	1,010	446	893	596	888	650
Annual Total	2,777		2,822		1,908		1,456		1,489		1,538	
Grand Area Total	1,716	1,547	2,073	1,577	1,250	1,125	1,735	653	1,336	803	1,228	860
Grand Annual Total	3,263		3,650		2,375		2,388		2,139		2,088	

Source: Naimushō Keihōkyoku, Firumu Ken'etsu Nenpō, 1928–1933.

cuts listed here exceed in number those recorded in table 8. The precise contents banned under the concept of public order are discussed below. A few illustrations of the use of these standards have been borrowed from press censorship, in which most of the same criteria were applied.

Imperial family. "Items feared to desecrate the sanctity of the imperial family." This was ever the foremost dictate of state censorship. It shielded from abuse the imperial regalia (sword, jewels, and mirror), Shintō shrines and the Imperial Mausoleum, and all members of the imperial household past and present. This last provision encompassed every Emperor in history, including not a few mythical personages. Thus in 1925 censors cut the samurai drama *Nichirin* (Sun) because they feared that a "princess" in the story might be mistaken for an imperial ancestor.[19] A magazine was stopped from circulation in 1930 for challenging the mythical accounts of the imperial family in history textbooks.[20] Some scholarly writings contradicting imperial mythology were permitted in this period, but they had to be carefully phrased in highly academic language.

A tricky problem was to censor pictures of the imperial chrysanthemum crest, which could not be used as a prop. Flower crests were commonplace on samurai costumes, and the difficulty was to eliminate those that might be confused with the imperial crest. Upon expert advice, it was decided that no flower crest of twelve to twenty-five petals would be permitted unless it was easily distinguishable from the Emperor's chrysanthemum. The prohibited range of petals would otherwise prevent any confusion.[21]

News film on the imperial household was even more delicate. Emperor Hirohito's visit to Kansai in 1929 was preceded by a list of injunctions to local film inspectors: no errors in script or film headings, especially in the specialized language used to describe the imperial family; no mistakes in the order of events on the Emperor's schedule; no films making it appear that the Emperor's attendants are moving forward parallel to him; no shots showing the exhaust from the bodyguards' side car; nothing out of focus, and so forth.[22]

19. *Masu Media Tōsei*, vol. 1, document 18, p. 32.
20. Naimushō Keihōkyoku, *Shuppan Keisatsu Hō*, no. 16, p. 99.
21. Tajima, *Ken'etsu Shitsu*, pp. 255–56.
22. Naimushō Keihōkyoku, *Firumu Ken'etsu Nenpō*, 1930, pp. 84–85. Interestingly, this meticulous censorship of material related to the imperial family was begun only after the Meiji revolution; Richard Mitchell reports that the Tokugawa shogunate issued no rules on treatment of the imperial family in drama or literature: Mitchell, *Censorship*, p. 8.

Nation or state. "Items feared to harm the dignity of the nation (*kokka*)." This category ruled out disparaging treatments of Japan, its culture, or its people; according to Tajima Tarō, the Home Ministry's chief film inspector, these were censored "whether true or not."[23] Since the Japanese were understandably disinclined to produce or import such films, this standard saw little service. It was used against the American film *Thunder in the East,* in which a Japanese naval victory was credited to a British advisor whose virtues were set off against the foil of a bungling Japanese admiral. The French film *Yoshiwara,* named after Tokyo's old red-light district, was also found objectionable. Censors felt the portrayal of prostitution made Japan look uncivilized, and they judged the plot, in which a passionate Japanese heroine committed treason for love of a dashing Westerner, to be an insult to the Japanese people.[24]

Constitution. "Items suggesting or advocating thought which undermines the constitution (*choken*)." This article prohibited denunciation of constitutional state organs, thus protecting the armed forces as well as the Diet from revolutionary rhetoric or extreme abuse. It was also used against films advocating independence for Korea or the other colonies. Under this principle, criticism of conscription and pacifistic Western religious films were cut for implicit rejection of the military. In one case, a narrator of the film *Yonin no Musuko* (Four Sons) was fined for changing the approved script to embellish his account of a mother's agony upon her son's departure for war.[25] This crime of "antimilitarism" was recorded in January 1929.

Oddly enough, even in this period the Diet was less sheltered from abuse than the throne or the military. Censorship did not prevent scathing vilification of government policies, nor did it silence calls for dissolution of the Diet in session. In general, only arguments for complete elimination of the legislature by illegal means were outlawed, though more moderate critiques might be censored if penned by radical political groups. For example, the program of the *Rōnō Seinen Kyogikai* (Labor-Farmer Youth Conference) demanded dispersion of the Diet in 1929, accusing it of bourgeois exploitation, preparations for an imperialistic war, and the introduction of executions for labor leaders under a revised

23. Tajima, *Ken'etsu Shitsu*, p. 263.
24. Ibid., p. 266.
25. Naimushō Keihōkyoku, *Firumu Ken'etsu Nenpō*, 1930, p. 88.

Peace Preservation Law.[26] There was no denunciation of the institution of parliament per se, but censors felt the statement implied as much and so banned it from circulation. As a rule, however, the cabinet, the Diet, and the parties were left open to spiteful remonstrances from anyone unassociated with leftist causes.

Social organs and class conflict. "Items suggesting or advocating the thought of overthrowing the basic principles of contemporary social life" and "Items related to social disputes." Most political and economic radicalism was scrutinized under these clauses. The criterion of social organs opposed the promotion of systemic social change and protected major institutions not enshrined in the constitution. Forbidden items included arguments for the eradication of political parties, capitalism, or the system of private property, and those condemning the principles of free competition and profit. The second standard prohibited films emphasizing class struggle. In practice, the application of the two categories depended on whether the film portrayed criminal thought or criminal action. If a film espoused peasant rebellion in principle, as through the voice of a lecturer, it was clipped under the criterion of social organs; if it depicted actual fighting between peasants and landlords, it fell prey to that of class conflict. Japanese-made films cut under these headings rose significantly in 1929, peaked in 1930 and 1931, and dropped precipitously in 1932. There is no reason to challenge the official interpretation of this pattern, which was that the Manchurian Incident of September 1931 had diverted the attention of filmmakers from the economy to the adventure of foreign conquest.[27]

Though censors began to complain of leftist films in 1929,[28] most were not the work of political activists. Spurred on by the success of *Ikeru Ningyō* (Living Doll), these so-called "tendency films" were produced mainly by the big studios; they drew audiences during the depression and garnered profits for a film industry itself in financial straits.[29] They portrayed the contrasts between rich and poor, but generally steered clear of revolutionary propaganda. Many were set against a backdrop of swords and samurai some decades, if not centuries, in the past.

26. This piece was handled under the Publication Law, which imposed the same standards of public order as the Newspaper Law: idem, *Shuppan Keisatsu Hō*, no. 6, p. 105.
27. Idem, *Firumu Ken'etsu Nenpō*, 1934, p. 2.
28. Idem, *Firumu Ken'etsu Nenpō*, 1930, pp. 4–5.
29. For a concise treatment of tendency films (*keikō eiga*), see Tanaka Jun'ichirō, *Nihon Eiga Hattatsu Shi*, 2: 12–15.

If the encouragement of class struggle was taboo, press censorship was nonetheless fairly tolerant of class analysis. For example, in the August 1929 *Kaizō,* one writer commented: "As far as we the proletariat are concerned, the Hamaguchi Minseitō cabinet differs not a bit in essentials from Tanaka's Seiyūkai cabinet in that it is a government of the large capitalist landlords." Another contribution was titled "The Minseitō Cabinet of Bourgeois Clerks."[30] The magazine suffered no sanctions, and references to the class character of state institutions were not rare in journals passed by the censor.

National ethos. "Items opposed to a firm belief in the nation (*minzoku*)." This principle sheltered the mythical foundations of nationalism. According to Tajima Tarō, Japan's consuming principle was a belief that her people were descendants of the gods, as written in the mythical accounts of the *Kojiki* and *Nihon Shoki.* A purely scholarly film on the racial origins of the Japanese might be permitted, but not if it threatened popular belief in the national ethos. There is no record of such a film ever being produced.

Foreign affairs. "Items feared to damage good will in foreign affairs." This principle eliminated "undeserved" insults to foreign countries or people, and impediments to the realization of foreign policy goals. Such films became a noticeable problem only after the Manchurian Incident in 1931, no doubt due to domestic invective against the Chinese and other international critics of Japanese imperialism.

Group conflict. "Items related to forceful struggles between groups." By this precept the censor cut scenes of fighting between non-class groups such as criminal gangs.

Crime. "Items showing how to commit a crime or how to conceal a crime or criminal which it is feared may lead to imitation." This canon saw more use than any other in the area of public safety. Criminal behavior per se was not forbidden, only such deeds as might be emulated by a spectator. Today many allege that violence in films influences behavior; the Japanese police documented this connection. In 1929, for instance, they found 232 crimes caused by the example of films (89 directly, 143 indirectly). Most were various forms of theft, but there

---

30. Quotations from Naimushō Keihōkyoku, *Shuppan Keisatsu Hō,* no. 12, p. 77.

were also two attempted rapes, two cases of arson, and one homicide. All but thirteen of the perpetrators were under twenty-one years of age.[31] The police thus had definite ideas as to which crimes ought to be cut from motion pictures.

Public business. "Items feared to hinder the execution of public business." This category guarded the censor and other state administrators from criticism. Needless to say, it was interpreted rather loosely. Mack Sennett and the Keystone Cops were said to damage respect for the police and thus were banned under this standard.[32]

The following censorship criteria were employed to protect manners and morals.

Religion. "Items feared to damage the virtuous spirit of religious faith or disturb the praiseworthy customs of religious reverence and ancestor worship." The constitution guaranteed religious freedom as long as it did not disturb public order or the duties of citizenship. Accordingly, not only state Shintō but also other officially recognized religions were screened from abuse by the censor. A notable beneficiary of this provision was the Salvation Army, an occasional target of nasty humor. Unrecognized religions could be handled at the film-maker's discretion,[33] though film inspectors also cut criticisms of religion in which no particular faith was named.

Cruelty/ugliness. "Items related to brutality" and "Items giving rise to offensive feelings." Two censorship criteria are merged here for analysis. The first excluded scenes of blood and gore such as might be found in a war movie. The second prohibited films from depicting, for example, people deformed by disease.

31. Idem, *Firumu Ken'etsu Nenpō,* 1930, pp. 113–15.
32. Tajima, *Ken'etsu Shitsu,* p. 330.
33. Ibid., p. 319. For administrative purposes, the state divided religions into two groups. The first, "recognized religions" (*kōnin shūkyō*), comprised all those formally sanctioned by the state early in the Meiji period: thirteen sects of Shintō, eleven Buddhist religions with fifty-six sects, and a number of Christian groups. For some religions founded thereafter, a second category of groups "analogous to religions" (*ruiji shūkyō*) was used. After 1914, the Ministry of Education regulated the recognized churches, the Home Ministry the second category, though the Home Ministry also maintained special duties in relation to state Shintō. It is unclear from Tajima's work whether both these categories were protected by censorship, excluding only religions belonging to neither, or whether only the recognized religions were protected. On the state's classification of religions and instances of persecution, see Watanabe Osamu, "Fashizumu-ki no Shūkyō Tōsei."

Sex-related. "Items related to illicit sexual relations" and "Items related to lewdness or indecency." Here again two standards are combined. The first was aimed at extramarital sex, while the second was broken down into kissing, dancing, embracing, nudity, flirting, sexual innuendo, pleasure-seeking, and "others." Kissing was rarely permitted in foreign movies, and never in Japanese films except for a mother kissing her child or the like, "because [kissing] in movies is not recognized as a virtuous Japanese custom according to healthy social convention."[34] Just as American audiences once grew accustomed to the one-foot-on-the-floor rule when a couple was filmed sitting on a bed, the Japanese public was treated to kissing scenes shot from the ankles down: two pairs of feet gingerly approached one another, and then the fellow's cigarette hit the floor to remove all doubts as to what was happening from the neck up.

Work ethic. "Items related to the ruin of work." This standard was seldom used, but its content is of some interest. It censored the encouragement of laziness, the notion that work does not pay, and scenes of despair in which a person's economic plight seemed hopeless. Admiration for the carefree "Ginza-man" lifestyle of the Western-oriented wealthy was also cut.[35]

Education. "Items feared to become a hindrance to the development of knowledge and virtue or an obstacle to education" and "Items feared to provoke children's mischievous spirit or to impair the authority of teachers." The first principle prohibited contradictions of what was taught in public schools—for example, an account of faith healing was cut from a religious movie. This criterion was applied mainly to elementary education, but higher learning did not escape unscathed. Einstein's theory of relativity was checked out with professors at Tokyo Imperial University before bureaucrats would license a film about it.[36] The second dictate forbade portrayal of misbehavior that might be imitated by children and of disrespect to the teaching profession.

Family. "Items that strikingly run counter to the customs of a virtuous home." Censorship to defend the family was tied to the myth of Japan as a family nation. Tajima explained:

34. Tajima, *Ken'etsu Shitsu,* p. 330.
35. Ibid., pp. 363–67.
36. Ibid., p. 371.

Individualism does not recognize the supremacy of the national society. Because it denies that the national society rules the individual and, when necessary, may limit the individual's freedom, and stresses that the national society must exist only for the purpose and happiness of the individual, naturally it is contrary to the virtue of the home in our country.[37]

In other words, the individual's submission to his family was the basis of his patriotism and self-sacrifice for the state; the censor guarded the one as he would guard the other. Individualism and other corrupt family practices such as polygamy were regarded as foreign customs destructive of Japanese traditions.

Despite this long list, numerous film cuts were filed in the "other" categories, representing ad hoc decisions or less important standards. This demonstrates the remarkable latitude for bureaucratic application of a statute that spoke only of public peace and manners and morals.

The range of censored topics indicates that officials felt responsible for the whole human being under their charge. They were concerned not only with revolutionary politics or pornography narrowly understood, but also with the family, religion, education, and economic life. Bureaucrats did not recognize a clear boundary between legitimate state interests and an inviolable sphere of civil activity. This reflects a highly paternalistic attitude, an underlying belief that officials were not merely a political elite but a moral elite qualified to oversee every aspect of social life. Administrators did not distinguish sharply between political and moral subject matter. In their view, politics and manners and morals were inextricably related and were to be considered in tandem. Censors discussed eroticism in the same terms (and often in the same sentence) they used to complain of socialist films.[38] The hazy boundary between politics and manners and morals paralleled the absence of clear demarcation between the public and private spheres.

Despite the breadth of censorship standards, however, film regula-

37. Ibid., p. 379.
38. E.g., "In today's situation, erotic love movies are not inferior to [socialist films] in the evil social influence they project; rather, if one looks at things from the point of view of the rise and fall of public spirit, one must recognize that they are even more fearful": Naimushō Keihōkyoku, *Firumu Ken'etsu Nenpō*, 1930, p. 5. See also the volume for 1934, p. 2. This dovetailing of moral and political concerns has been a staple of the Chinese Confucian tradition, and it has had a long history in Japan. In the Tokugawa period, for example, laws prohibiting the samurai from meeting to discuss politics in tea houses were catalogued as controls over morals: see Mitchell, *Censorship*, p. 9. The Japanese term *fūzoku*, translated here as "manners and morals," bears comparison to the French *moeurs* for its comprehensive meaning.

tion was limited to negative control. Bureaucrats blocked objectionable contents from public exposure, but they did not exert positive control (or mobilization) by limiting films to specified themes. The potential film-maker was surrounded by forbidden fruit, but he was not steered into a single path. This paralleled periodical press censorship, but film control was more severe, in that inspection was conducted before and not after public circulation had begun. This factor, combined with the expense and expertise required to make films and the greater difficulty of concealing violations, prevented the medium from ever becoming a prominent vehicle for political debate and criticism.

CHAPTER IV

Radio

Asia's first public radio broadcast originated from Tokyo in March 1925, just four years after the world's first transmission, from Pittsburgh, Pennsylvania. Though the timing of radio's appearance enabled party governments to determine its relationship to the state, the bureaucracy formulated most aspects of policy. Furthermore, when party politicians did get involved, their contribution was to increase state intervention. From the outset, the state imposed tougher controls upon radio than it had on film or the press. The latter media were developed primarily by civil organizations which officials then endeavored to restrain, not always very successfully. In broadcasting, however, more or less autonomous civil associations were never allowed to emerge. Instead, the medium was subjected to a tightly controlled system of mixed civil and bureaucratic management.

An extraordinary rigidity has characterized broadcasting controls in many democracies, and the Japanese case is of considerable comparative interest as one of many statist broadcasting systems forged under elected governments in the interwar period. To some degree even the most liberal regime is compelled to supervise radio more closely than the other media. Technical complexities necessitate legal regulation of the use of wave lengths (which in turn demands a licensing system), and radio also has more immediate military functions bearing on private exploitation than either the press or film. Many democracies have far outrun technical and military imperatives, however, in their zeal to control radio. In fact, it is in the realm of broadcasting that democratic and authoritarian regimes have most tended to converge in their regulatory policies toward the mass media. Since radio became the first source of news to the public in Japan and many other interwar democracies, the prevalence of state and public-interest monopolies in this area has been of great historical moment. "We may still discover," wrote Friedrich Hayek, "that a government broadcasting monopoly may prove as great a threat to political freedom as an abolition of the freedom of the press."[1] This statement may be applicable to interwar Japan, where the radio control system of the 1920s helped smooth the way for military rule a decade later. Though military-bureaucratic elites in the late 1930s had to overcome resistance from publishers and film-makers, they had no need to mold a New Order for radio as they did for these other media; they merely refined the arrangements made by their democratic predecessors.

Fortunately, the making of radio policy is richly documented, affording a rare glimpse into the state's inner workings and the values upheld by policymakers. Connoisseurs of contemporary politics have learned to savor a good tale of bureaucratic intrigue just as an old epic historian must have relished an encounter between Napoleon and the Pope. The players are of lesser stature. Their office titles are certainly more worthy of remembrance than their names. But they are the stuff of which modern state power is made, and as such their activities merit the most careful study.

BUREAUCRATIC PLANNING FOR RADIO

Private petitions for broadcasting permits were first filed at the Communications Ministry in 1921. As executor of the Wireless Telegraphic Communications Law, the ministry required that all radio equipment be licensed. In response to the petitions, two preliminary plans for radio administration were prepared. The first was a Draft Proposal approved by a large body of Communications Ministry officials in August 1923, the second a Research Summary drawn up in the ministry's Transmission Bureau.[2] To the extent that later policy conformed to these two

1. Friedrich Hayek, *Law, Legislation, and Liberty*, 3: 148.
2. In June 1922 the Communications Ministry organized a study group headed by its Transmission Bureau Telephone Section Chief (*Tsūshinkyoku Denwa Kachō*), who had just returned from a research trip to the United States. In August this group produced the

designs, that policy was a bureaucratic artifact. Their common points are discussed below.

MANAGEMENT/OWNERSHIP

The issue of civil versus state management and ownership was much debated, but both plans favored a civil operation. The Research Summary declared that state management was not mandatory because radio, despite its "public character," was not absolutely necessary to society. Moreover, the state had limited capacity to handle such a complex business, and civil operations prevailed in foreign countries except Germany, where there was mixed civil and bureaucratic control. These arguments are of some interest. Absolute necessity is a very liberal standard for state management, though it later pointed to another conclusion when radio's full significance was realized. The state's limited capacity is also a noteworthy point. The mushrooming of bureaucracy and budget to absorb new tasks would be observed on every policy front in the late 1930s, but in 1923 bureaucrats shunned a program demanding a major new commitment of resources. The liberal example of foreign countries was to be short-lived. In Europe, state control would be the rule by 1930. Here, as in so many Japanese policymaking forums, foreign precedents were carefully weighed.

Another plank in both proposals was to license only one station per region. A national monopoly was rejected because the involvement of notables in each area was thought necessary to radio's success. Competing companies in the same region, however, would raise technical difficulties and endanger the stations' economic viability.[3] Officials there-

---

first version of the Draft Proposal related to Privately Established Wireless Telephone (*Hōsōyō Shisetsu Musen Denwa ni Kansuru Gian*). It was then submitted to a more diverse and elite committee of ministry bureaucrats who discussed, amended, and formally sanctioned it on 30 August 1923. The committee comprised mainly officials of the rank of section chief. This method of slowly building a consensus among various offices is a well-known feature of Japanese state decision-making (in some forms referred to as the *ringisei* system). In March 1923, a new Telephone Section Chief took over and reopened the question of the establishment of radio within the confines of the Transmission Bureau. The upshot was the Research Summary (*Chōsa Gaiyō*), apparently finished in the spring or early summer of 1923; it was very influential even though it lacked wider sponsorship. The main points of the Draft Proposal and a complete reprint of the Research Summary may be found in Nihon Hōsō Kyōkai (NHK), ed., *Hōsō 50-Nen Shi Shiryō Hen*, pp. 41–46.

3. A low-power station might operate within the range of a high-power station as long as the two had different functions, e.g., one might be a school network, the other devoted to general programming. Thus they would not be competing for the same audi-

fore advocated that several petitioners combine into a single managerial unit in each area. Ideally, investors would include newspapers, wireless electronics companies, and other businesses, making the stations technically and financially self-sufficient. The enterprises would be under the joint private ownership of the investors. This strategy may have been influenced by events in Britain, where the Postmaster General similarly insisted on a combination of petitioners, though the BBC was from the start a national monopoly.[4]

FINANCES

The financial projections confirm that radio was not seen as just another private business. Both plans banned commercial broadcasting. Its legality under the existing law was doubtful, but the Research Summary's main argument was that "commercials aim at the benefit of the advertiser and are rarely related to the general benefit of the listener" (article 3, no. 7). It advised that operators be licensed only if ready to work for the public interest and not merely for gain. The plans foresaw monopolistic firms, so a profit ceiling was needed to prevent unjust exploitation of the listeners: both plans agreed that profits should not exceed ten percent of capital investment; if there was additional income, listening fees would be reduced.

A ban on advertising has immense consequences for radio's relationship to the state, because it eliminates the readiest and often the only means of economic self-sufficiency. Even non-commercial public networks in the United States appeal for donations on the air, but if commercials were tabooed altogether, a station could not advertise itself any more than it could soap or coffee. The end of advertising is the beginning of radio's dependence on officialdom. This anti-commercial policy prejudiced other aspects of the Communications Ministry's plans. For example, the prognosis for the economic health of several stations in one region would be enormously improved if advertising were allowed. Advertising was also banned from early broadcasting in European democracies such as Britain, Belgium, Denmark, and Switzerland, all of which saw the official imposition of national or local monopolies. In

---

ence. Technical problems included interference between radio signals and the procurement of enough local expertise to run several businesses competently. Moreover, the availability of sufficient capital for several stations in one area was doubtful.

4. James Curran and Jane Seaton, *Power without Responsibility: The Press and Broadcasting in Britain*, p. 136.

countries where two or more civil broadcasters were allowed to transmit in the same area, as in the United States, Australia, and most of Latin America, commercials were invariably their principal source of revenue.

The two plans provided that payments from the producers and owners of radio receivers would help finance the broadcasting stations. The logic was simple. Those who made and sold radios or listened to them were the medium's beneficiaries, so they should pay for it. Manufacturers would pay according to their sales or capital, while receiver owners would pay a monthly fee. Taxes on receiving sets were from the beginning the principal means of financing radio in many countries, democratic and otherwise, including Britain, Belgium, Denmark, France, Switzerland, Rumania, and Turkey. This method opens a Pandora's box of state controls needed to safeguard the flow of income. For example, the Japanese plans required the state to license the production and purchase of receivers so that buyers could be registered for the purpose of collecting fees; those caught with unlicensed equipment would forfeit their right to own a radio. The supervision of producers was necessary to prevent them from selling radios on the sly without proper registration. Without such restraints, the system could not function.

PROGRAMMING/CENSORSHIP

Beyond excluding commercials, both plans restricted entertainment. The Research Summary stipulated that music and entertainment would receive less emphasis than news, weather, and practical knowledge. Since this differed from Western practice, officials appended an explanation. The Japanese character and lifestyle were different from those in the West. Japan was not yet wealthy enough to accommodate a pleasure-seeking way of life, and many Japanese (unlike Westerners) worked all day and well into the night, so radio entertainment should not lure them from their jobs. Radio would have to attract its audience with programming of practical value.

Both plans called for prior censorship of all programs. Each broadcast's contents would be reported one day before transmission. The ministry's local offices would monitor all programs, immediately stopping any illegal presentation. The Research Summary prohibited contents contrary to public order or good morals, including those banned under the press laws.

State mobilization of radio was also justified in the bureaucratic proposals. Broadcasters would have to air any program ordered by the state in the public interest. The Draft Proposal empowered the state to purchase or commandeer broadcasting enterprises if necessary for public peace.

LEGAL BASIS

The statutory framework for radio controls was a paragon of legal sophistry. Both proposals hoped to administer broadcasting under the Wireless Telegraphic Communications Law of 1915, which was not intended to accommodate radio. Logic seemed to dictate a new bill. Civil radio management was difficult to justify before the law's article 1, which read: "The government will manage wireless communications and wireless telephone." Nonetheless, ministerial interests won out over logic. A new law would first require the cabinet's approval, forcing the Communications Ministry to run a gauntlet of bureaucratic rivals anxious to claim radio authority for themselves. From the cabinet, the bill would pass to the Diet, where there might be a scramble to profit from the new medium or where changes might be made in the terms of radio administration.[5] In short, if the Communications Ministry were to monopolize radio policy, a new law would have to be avoided at all costs.

The principal cost was a farfetched interpretation of the existing law. The 1915 statute allowed for civil operation of such facilities as ship-to-shore wireless and experimental equipment "when the appropriate minister recognizes a special need." Since the state technically remained in managerial control of even these facilities, however, how could this clause sanction civil ownership and management of radio? The Research Summary answered:

> as a matter based on the recognition of a special need for the facilities, they are not of course to escape the category of state-managed wireless telephone. However, considering further the relationship to the grand principle of exclusive [state] management of mass communications, broadcasting is not the

5. NHK, ed., *Nihon Hōsō Shi*, 1: 31. Presumably, Diet men might pressure the ministry to license stations in which they had a financial interest or might urge the construction of stations in certain areas to please constituents. State railroad building and other public services had been manipulated politically for years.

sort of report generally sent and received among the masses. Consequently, it does not belong to the category of mass communications. Rather, since one must recognize it as a communication for private use, the approval of civil management [in this case] does not violate the [general] principle of exclusive state management. (article 2, no. 2)

This interpretation would administer radio under the Wireless Tele-graphic Communications Law, while exempting it from the law's provi-sions because it was not a means of mass communication! This last contention was not only absurd but irrelevant, since article 1 of the law made no mention of "mass" communications, but declared state man-agement of "wireless communications and wireless telephone," pure and simple.[6]

These legal acrobatics were partly to defend the Communications Ministry's jurisdiction, but they also aimed at a more liberal policy than a strict reading of the law would permit. This latter fact deserves empha-sis. Bureaucrats in the late 1930s would not be found searching for legal loopholes to enhance civil autonomy. But if this was a liberal interpreta-tion of the law, it also left radio legally defenseless against future incur-sions of state power. Henceforth radio would be the exception in a field where state management was the rule. It would owe its exceptional status entirely to the judgment of the Communications Minister, who at any time might decide that radio was a mass medium after all or that there was no longer any "special need" for civil broadcasting facilities. Broadcasting companies would be formally private but also necessarily subservient to ministerial wishes.

From December 1923 to May 1924, the Communications Ministry unilaterally transformed into state policy nearly all the positions re-counted above, relying entirely upon the Wireless Telegraphic Commu-nications Law. The Tokyo earthquake of 1923 forced the ministry to accelerate its plans, since the torrent of rumors and panic after the disaster highlighted radio's potential utility to the state.

In December 1923, a ministerial decree fixed the broadcasting radius of stations, the wavelength for transmissions, and the cost of a permit to

6. Article 2, sections 1–5, of the Wireless Telegraphic Communications Law lists specific cases in which privately operated wireless facilities may be approved, while sec-tion 6 enables the minister to approve "other" facilities when he recognizes a "special need." Sections 1–5 condition approval upon the facilities not being used for "mass communications," thus the "grand principle." However, the blanket clause covering any "special need" makes no mention of use for mass communications.

operate.[7] A ministry notification (*tsūtatsu*) to its regional offices in February 1924 then provided as follows: Newspaper Law censorship standards would be enforced and no music would be played except at night or on holidays; prior reports of program contents could be made orally, and for certain programs (including news) general content and the announcer's name would suffice; bureaucrats could order official broadcasts; ministerial personnel would monitor all transmissions; and advance ministerial approval was required for the production of receivers. One history of Japanese telecommunications has noted the "police-like" tone of this notification.[8] In May 1924, the Communications Ministry met with petitioners from Tokyo, Osaka, and Nagoya. It announced that there would be no commercials, that only one station would be permitted in each city, that management would be composed jointly of news and electronics firms, and that profits would be limited to ten percent.[9]

This record is a striking illustration of the bureaucratic ordinance powers inscribed in the Meiji constitution. In just a few months, the ministry had instituted a detailed new policy without any external interference, ignoring the Diet's constitutional authority over speech by virtually rewriting an old law to suit its purposes. Before any broadcasting licenses were granted, however, the Kiyoura non-party cabinet fell and the party government of Prime Minister Katō Kōmei took office.

DEMOCRATIC GOVERNMENT AND RADIO POLICY

The new cabinet could have revised the bureaucracy's plans for radio, and there were several good reasons for doing so. The managerial combination of news and production-related investors had run into snags. In Osaka, the attempt by one group of petitioners to secure the single available license was bitterly denounced by the others. Furthermore, the jour-

---

7. By this time forty-one notices of intent to apply for broadcasting licenses had been received by the ministry. The decree was titled Regulations for Privately Established Wireless Telephone for Use in Broadcasting (*Hōsōyō Shisetsu Musen Denwa Kisoku*), and it is reprinted in NHK, ed., *Hōsō 50-Nen Shi*, pp. 47–48. Although the word *rajio* was already part of the Japanese language, the ministry could not depart from the wording of the Wireless Telegraphic Communications Law, which spoke only of "wireless telephone": hence the elongated titles.

8. *Nihon Musen Shi*, 7: 25.

9. NHK, ed., *Nihon Hōsō Shi*, 1: 41.

nal *Musen to Jikken* (Wireless and Experimentation) was founded in May 1924, representing interested parties in civil society. Its contributors argued that radio should develop autonomously before legal controls were imposed, they favored free competition among several stations in each region, and they asked for greater flexibility in programming.[10] Japan's new party government, however, ignored these entreaties.

The Communications Minister, Inukai Tsuyoshi, was a leading party politician, a Diet member since 1890 who would later serve as Prime Minister. Inukai changed only one aspect of the ministerial design. Confronted by vexing squabbles among petitioners, he determined to license only nonprofit, public-interest broadcasting companies.[11] It was the minister personally who instituted this policy, against bureaucratic opposition. The ministry had developed a painstaking consensus against the public-interest option, partly because public-interest firms were judged less dynamic than profit-making companies. When Inukai first submitted his proposal to a body of ranking administrators (the ministry's *Sanjikan Kaigi*), they stuck by the original profit-making design. When Inukai requested that they study the matter again, they refused, asking why an issue apparently settled by their superior was being tendered for discussion at all.[12] The bureaucratic position was clearly more liberal than that of the presiding party minister.

Why did Inukai impose the more statist public-interest format? Basically, he felt the petitioners' bickering was caused by the profit guarantees of the listening fee system—remove the object of greed, and the discord would cease. Inukai had an internal document prepared defending the public-interest option, and it is an interesting measure of the statism/liberalism in his thinking.[13] The paper listed numerous defects of broadcasting for profit: the power of capital would dominate the stations; listeners' fees would remain high to sustain profits; it would be

10. Ibid., pp. 36–38.
11. Japanese companies were legally divided into two groups: Public Interest Juridical Persons (*Kōeki Hōjin*), and Profit Juridical Persons (*Eiri Hōjin*). The public-interest category was further subdivided into Corporate Juridical Persons (*Shadan Hōjin*) and Foundation Juridical Persons (*Zaidan Hōjin*). The foundations were similar to those in the United States: associations making use of a fund perhaps left by some wealthy philanthropist. The Corporate Juridical Persons were a diverse group of organizations recognized for tax purposes as performing a public service. Virtually all the public-interest companies referred to in this study were of the corporate variety. Their financing was varied. Stock flotations, state subsidies, contributions, and the sale of goods and services might all supply income. The state demanded business reports and notice of managerial changes from these companies, but otherwise the mere label Public Interest Juridical Person tells very little about the degree of state control, which varied considerably from case to case.
12. *Nihon Musen Shi*, 7: 32–33.
13. It is reprinted in NHK, ed., *Nihon Hōsō Shi*, 1: 44.

difficult to expand facilities or regulate program content in accord with the public interest; it would endanger public peace and morals; it would complicate official supervision and inflate the state budget; and, should the state decide to purchase the companies, a huge compensation would have to be paid. In contrast, the document noted four virtues of public-interest firms. Since exclusive state management was the general rule for telecommunications, public-interest companies were more appropriate as being more amenable to control. They would maximize the listener's benefit and the public good. They would be less open to the evils accompanying monopolistic businesses. And finally, they would manage programming and other operations in an impartial and just manner, especially important given radio's great social impact.

This position paper shows that the early Meiji public-interest doctrine was still a powerful influence among at least some democratic statesmen of the 1920s. Though the parties were often disparaged as pawns of big business, radio policy was strongly swayed by the taint of illegitimacy associated with civil interests when seen against an overriding public good. Such reasoning was not unique to Japan. In these same years democrats in Britain, Germany, Austria, and other European states similarly restricted broadcasting to public-interest firms (as many do to this day), and with much the same logic. In Britain, for example, the Sykes Committee of 1923 disapproved commercial stations for favoring large companies. Two years later, the Crawford Committee denounced private broadcasting because "no company or body constituted on trade lines for the profit . . . of those composing it can be regarded as adequate," and it successfully urged instead a public commission "operating in the National Interest."[14]

The standard arguments for public-interest radio contain both democratic and anti-democratic sentiments. The notion that a few companies should not dominate a medium with such wide access to the public seems to accord with democratic principles, at least if it is assumed that those public employees who will oversee the medium represent the mass public and not a partial interest themselves; this is an assumption most statesmen seem ready to make. Yet these same statesmen also typically contend that commercial broadcasting will "vulgarize, bowdlerize, and coarsen," as one British group phrased it, precisely because it will produce programs aimed at the mass taste—hardly a democratic point of

14. Quotations from Terrou and Solal, *Legislation*, p. 158, and Curran and Seaton, *Power without Responsibility*, pp. 137–38.

view.[15] The elitist desire to exploit the medium to educate and to raise cultural standards appealed to officials as well as to many intellectuals, and it was evident in Japan in the early decision to restrict programs of popular entertainment.

Petitioners were told of the switch to public-interest companies in August 1924. If bureaucrats disagreed with the policy, investors in Osaka were furious about it. Businesses had pledged to invest large sums in a profit-making enterprise. They argued that profits would not affect the imposition of state control.[16] They also pointed out that public-interest-company law allowed a 10 percent return to investors, but the Communications Ministry denied such compensation. They finally tried to circumvent the policy by setting up a profit-making company to service Osaka's public-interest station by procuring its equipment, collecting listeners' fees, and so forth.[17] The ministry rejected this plan outright. Thus investments in radio were to be donations yielding no gain whatsoever. It is not known how many investors withdrew, or exactly why so many stayed with the enterprises. Some may have counted on future business considerations from the stations, but others were apparently persuaded to support an important cultural innovation without reward.

TERMS OF THE FIRST
BROADCASTING LICENSES

When officials announced the public-interest switch, they also instructed *all* applicants in each city to unite in single enterprises. This accomplished, each group had to obtain two permits from the Communications Ministry, one for recognition as a juridical person, the other for construction of transmission facilities. The permits were issued between November 1924 and February 1925, and they were accompanied by ministerial orders that remained basic to state control during the next twenty years.

The order attached to juridical recognition required ministerial approval for the use of surplus funds, the hiring and firing of top executives, and all major borrowing. A thorough system of reporting required

---

15. Curran and Seaton, *Power without Responsibility*, p. 208. The first director of the BBC declared that to approve commercial radio would be akin to introducing dog racing, smallpox, or the bubonic plague: ibid., p. 205.

16. *Ōsaka Hōsōkyoku Enkaku Shi*, p. 20.

17. NHK, ed., *Nihon Hōsō Shi*, 1: 47–48.

budgetary and operational plans before each business period and an account of business and financial activities afterwards. Bureaucrats could order special reports and participate in company meetings, and the firms had to obey the state's dictates on the construction of new facilities. The state could annul any company decision violating these regulations or the articles of incorporation, or damaging the public interest. Executives responsible for such decisions could be dismissed. In case of noncompliance, the state could rescind a company's permit to exist. The order's last clause allowed the Communications Ministry to amend its contents "whenever necessary for the public interest."[18]

The second order, accompanying the approval of facilities, was more sweeping. It fixed the name, call sign, transmission frequency, electric power, operating hours, and cost of listeners' fees for each station. The ministry could adjust the fees or withdraw the right to collect them. Prior-day reporting of program content was instituted, and the regional Communications Bureau Chiefs could order broadcasts in the public interest. Commercials were banned. Technical personnel had to be licensed and could be dismissed by officials. The state could command changes in broadcasting facilities, restrict or ban their use, assume direct management, or purchase all or part of them. This authority was unconditional. Station operators had to perform all obligations with their own money, including construction of new facilities at the state's behest. The approval of facilities was good for ten years, but it could be revoked in case of noncompliance. This order too could be changed by the ministry at any time.[19]

These two ministerial orders testify to the vast authority claimed by the state over radio. At the time that they were promulgated, none of the other mass media was exposed to anywhere near this rigid a control structure.[20]

THE FOUNDING OF NHK

The Communications Ministry merged the three independent broadcasting companies into a national monopoly, Nihon Hōsō Kyōkai

18. The order accompanying approval of the Tokyo Broadcasting Company is reprinted in NHK, ed., *Hōsō 50-Nen Shi*, p. 164.
19. The order accompanying approval of the Tokyo Broadcasting Company's transmission facilities is reprinted in ibid., pp. 164–66.
20. These orders partly overlap and partly supplement the decree and notification by which the Communications Ministry first made its radio policy official (see pp. 78–79 above), but the earlier administrative ordinances remained in force.

(NHK), in August 1926. The impetus was an opinion paper prepared by ministry officials in late 1925 subscribing to unified national management. The imminent licensing of new regional broadcasters gave the issue a certain urgency at the time. An immediate merger would involve only three companies; to attempt one later would mean negotiating with six or seven. The bureaucrats' primary concern was the rapid spread of radio throughout the country. The original plan of licensing one independent station in each area now seemed a hazard to this ambition. The Nagoya company was financially weak and handicapped by the paucity of local programming. How would stations in smaller cities fare? Short on programming and technical expertise, they would be forced to charge exorbitant listening fees to stay in business. Given their lower power output, reception from any distance would require expensive vacuum-tube receivers, whereas a national system of potent wire relays would reach the cheaper crystal sets. A relay system could best be achieved under unified national management with bureaucratic and civil participation (*kanmin rengō*).[21]

Plans for integration advanced quickly. The opinion paper was followed by a ministerial research report in January 1926, directing bureaucrats to prepare bylaws for a new national company. In another month, the ministry had contrived a hundred-page plan for the merger, including the new firm's articles of incorporation. This plan was presented to Communications Minister Adachi Kenzō in February 1926. Adachi was a Minseitō party leader, a Diet member of twenty-four years' standing. His subordinates asked him to choose between two contingency plans, one for a private company and one for a public-interest firm. Evidently bureaucrats still preferred a profit-making enterprise. Adachi became the second party minister to choose the public-interest alternative.[22]

The Communications Ministry then undertook some behind-the-scenes lobbying. The Vice-Minister of Communications (the ministry's highest-ranking career bureaucrat) traveled to Osaka, where the stiffest resistance was expected, to discuss the merger privately with the chairman of the board. He presented the ministry's amalgamation design as irrevocable and threatened to build another Osaka station if the company refused to cooperate.[23] A new station would obviously mean extinction for the old. Similar discussions were held at the other stations. The Com-

21. On the opinion paper see NHK, ed., *Nihon Hōsō Shi*, 1: 143–44.

22. *Nihon Musen Shi*, 7: 112. Adachi later served as Home Minister in two party cabinets; earlier in his career, he had founded two journals in Korea.

23. NHK, ed., *Nihon Hōsō Shi*, 1: 149.

munications Ministry then formally submitted its unification scheme to the boards of the three companies on 30 April 1926. The existing firms' capital was to be transferred to the new monopoly, allowing investors in the independent stations to retain their stock and their status as owners. Tokyo was compliant. Nagoya agreed in principle while pressing for greater transmission power. Osaka produced a counterproposal.

Given the terms of their license, the Osaka directors could not reject a merger out of hand, but a majority voted to make the consolidated organ a profit-making company, and they were unanimous that the new system should have two poles of equal importance, Tokyo and Osaka. They opposed a p.eponderant central office and insisted that it merely coordinate among the branches.[24] When an Osaka delegation presented these proposals to Adachi, there followed the first of many heated arguments over the merger. The Osaka group retreated on the profit issue since it did not have the other stations' support, but it did elicit a pledge that the central office would have only modest authority. The vice-minister followed with a letter affirming a paternal relationship between the Osaka branch and all new installations to the west. On 8 May, on the basis of his assurances, the Osaka board of directors approved the new system, pending further discussions of particulars.[25]

On 25 May 1926, Communications Ministry officials met with representatives of the three stations to discuss the new firm's articles of incorporation. True to their promise to the Osaka company, the monopoly's branches were granted more authority than in earlier drafts. However, the articles contained the extraordinary proviso that the first executive officers would all be appointed by the Communications Minister. Ordinarily, top executives were to be selected by investors from among themselves, but the articles allowed the minister to fill seventy-four key posts in central and branch offices; his appointees would serve for two years. The ministry announced its choices on 6 August, just two weeks before the scheduled dissolution of the three original broadcasting companies. All eight managing directors (riji), two each for the central office and the Tokyo, Nagoya, and Osaka branches, were retiring Communications Ministry officials.

Objections arose immediately. When directors of the Tokyo company protested to the Parliamentary Vice-Minister of Communications (a Diet representative), he responded as follows: the appointees were to

24. Ōsaka Hōsōkyoku Enkaku Shi, p. 149.
25. Ibid., pp. 158–61.

insure cooperation between NHK and the Communications Ministry; when their terms were up or new branches were founded, ministry officials would again be appointed to executive posts; and if there were efforts to block the founding of NHK over the issue, the ministry was prepared to place radio under state management.[26] The threatening nature of this reply only aggravated tempers further.

On 18 August 1926, two days before the scheduled merger, Osaka delegates presented a petition against the appointments, signed by all of the company's senior executives. The same day, the Tokyo company's board of directors passed a declaration to the same effect. Furthermore, the Tokyo document was actually broadcast that evening on the radio. This was the first and last time a blatantly partisan political broadcast was made by anyone in imperial Japan other than a state official. Leading newspapers strongly backed the petitions. Communications Minister Adachi responded more tactfully than his parliamentary vice-minister. He explained that the ministry's appointments were one-time only, though the need for state-civil cooperation should be considered when future executives were elected. He affirmed the ministry's legal right of direct control but stated it would never be asserted recklessly (tacitly withdrawing the threat of direct state management). He did not, however, renege on his appointments. Thus did a leading party politician collaborate in transforming Japan's only broadcasting company into a quasi-bureaucratic organ. The three independent stations dissolved themselves on 20 August 1926.

Ministerial approval of NHK as a juridical person was accompanied by an official order even more overbearing than those received earlier by the independent stations. Business and budgetary plans now required advance ministerial approval, not merely reporting after the fact. The salaries and duties of executives also needed approval, making it impossible to neutralize NHK's ex-bureaucrats by shifting their tasks to other offices. NHK was given five years to make radio accessible by crystal receiving sets throughout Japan, and the entire cost was to be borne by the company. In addition, all the ministry's earlier powers remained intact.

How did the state and involved civilians evaluate the emergence of NHK? Adachi stated at the first general investors' meeting:

It goes without saying that the broadcasting business exerts an enormous influence on the nation's general culture. Further, when necessary for the

26. Ibid., p. 208.

state (*kokka*), namely, when the state confronts an emergency, broadcasting is a great, unrivaled communications medium that can be used for state duties. . . . I think, then, that it is proper to say that this undertaking for the most part is to be treated as an affair of state.[27]

These remarks show a new respect for the political value of radio. Among other things, the British government's use of broadcasting during the general strike of May 1926 had impressed Japanese officials.[28] Radio policy had evolved accordingly, from the advocacy of regional profit-making companies under fairly independent civil management to support for a quasi-bureaucratic national monopoly using private money. A single national radio network partly run by ministerial veterans promised speedy and integrated expansion and simplified state control.

There was little jubilation among managers of the formerly independent stations. Even the directors of the Tokyo company, who had once favored a merger, were repelled by the ministry's appointments. The former Osaka operators were especially dismayed. Their difficulties in forming a company, due to the ministry's late demand that all petitioners combine; their sense of betrayal at the shift away from profit-making enterprises; the threats used to compel them to forfeit their independence; and an obdurate regional pride, disdaining subservience to the state and to Tokyo, all made them unwilling participants in the merger. Until the day of reckoning it was unknown whether they would vote to dissolve, but the Tokyo and Nagoya companies had already agreed to disband, and this probably decided the issue. An Osaka company director was quoted in the *Tōkyō Asahi Shinbun* on 19 August 1926 as saying:

> The Osaka Broadcasting Company had already had enough of the Communications Ministry's insincere attitude up to now, but lately discussions advanced so rapidly toward a three-station merger that we had resigned ourselves to the irresistible trend of events. But as the Communications Ministry's attitude has actually become arrogant and insulting to us, the argument that it was not necessary to dissolve so readily became widely shared yesterday at the Osaka board of directors' meeting. On the one hand, even we are not about to be silent in the face of Vice-Minister Tanomogi's unspeakably rude bombast [threatening direct state management], and after having ascertained the Communications Ministry's attitude and policy directly in an interview with Minister Adachi today, we have resolved to open

27. Quoted in ibid., p. 196.
28. This was mentioned by the Parliamentary Vice-Minister of Communications in remarks cited in the *Tōkyō Asahi Shinbun*: NHK, ed., *Nihon Hōsō Shi*, 1: 160.

a board of directors' meeting straightaway upon our return to Osaka tomorrow morning to reach a final decision.[29]

Two days later, the Osaka directorate voted for dissolution.

PROGRAM CONTROL IN PRACTICE

Radio expanded rapidly between 1926 and 1932. NHK's branch stations increased from 3 to 19, the number of its employees grew from 395 to 2,249, and the number of radio receivers rose from 361,066 to over 1.4 million.[30] Relay capability for national broadcasts, allowing all stations to air a program from one source simultaneously, was acquired in November 1928. A second broadcast channel devoted to educational programming opened in Tokyo in April 1931 and in Nagoya and Osaka soon thereafter. Despite rapid growth, however, radio was still primarily an urban medium in 1932. In that year 25.7 percent of metropolitan households owned a radio, but only 4.5 percent in rural counties (gun).[31] The rural rate would not pass the 25 percent level until 1940.

State control over NHK's day-to-day operations was extensive. Only in regard to radio did media policy definitely cross the line from censorship to mobilization. Yet in this period mobilization remained rudimentary, and NHK's branches enjoyed significant autonomy from the central office. There was some continuity in state regulation from the three-company period through the founding of NHK, so control measures over the entire span will be examined.

As was noted, the Communications Ministry instituted pre-broadcast censorship in 1924. Local ministry officials initially censored scripts directly on station premises, but this sytem was soon changed to a requirement that program material be delivered to state offices.[32] Oral reporting, often by telephone, was customary for news, lectures, and music, and a

29. Quoted in ibid., pp. 143–44.
30. NHK, ed., Hōsō 50-Nen Shi, pp. 603, 618, 608.
31. NHK, ed., Nihon Hōsō Shi, vol. 1, chart titled Rajio no Nendo Betsu Toshi Gunbu Fukyūritsu, no page number.
32. The responsible local offices were the regional Communications Bureaus (Teishinkyoku) in Tokyo, Osaka, and Nagoya. From May 1925 these branch offices were subordinate to the ministry's central Telephone and Telegraph Bureau (Denmukyoku), which took over administration, and its Engineering Bureau (Kōmukyoku), which handled the technical side of radio. They had been created from the splitting up of the earlier Transmission Bureau. In the text, mentions of notifications from the central ministry to its branches refer to cables sent from the central Telephone and Telegraph Bureau to the regional Communications Bureaus.

general summary of contents was usually sufficient. Programs could be banned, cut, or revised by officials.

In practice, censorship was a cooperative endeavor of state and radio personnel. Instructions on forbidden content were regularly sent to the stations, and they then worked with the sponsors to cut illicit material before filing the program report.[33] Ordinarily, if censors did find something amiss, rather than take official action they merely informed the station and the appropriate changes were made.[34] Coordination was not always perfect,[35] but the informality of telephone reporting and the stations' direct execution of censorship reflect a mutual trust between officials and broadcasting employees. No known statistical records were kept of censorship activities.

State-civil cooperation was also evident in the use of the circuit breaker. There was always a danger that live shows would stray from the authorized script onto illegal ground, so in December 1926, the Communications Ministry ordered NHK to equip its transmitting stations with circuit breakers that could stop a program in progress.[36] These were mandatory even for broadcasts on location outside the studio.[37] NHK's program inspectors operated these devices during all broadcasts.[38] There were two sound monitors in the inspector's room, one carrying the transmission and one a studio monitor. If a speaker wandered from his script, the inspector turned a key, halting transmission. He continued to follow the program on the studio monitor, and when the illegal material ceased he restored transmission power. Direct

33. NHK, ed., *Nihon Hōsō Shi*, 1: 80.

34. *Nihon Musen Shi*, 7: 164, document dated February 1930.

35. For example, a message of 8 December 1925 urged greater punctuality in reporting on news broadcasts; reports were to be made at least one hour before air time: *Masu Media Tōsei*, vol. 1, document 10, pp. 18–19. A notice on 9 March 1933 demanded vigilance in acquiring and reporting scripts for all programs that might touch political subjects: NHK Sōgō Hōsō Bunka Kenkyūjo, ed., *Reiki—Hōsō Hen (1) Taishō 14-Nen–Shōwa 20-Nen*, p. 20. Elaborate, direct state supervision was imposed on broadcasts of ceremonies involving the imperial family: see ibid., pp. 15–17, documents dated 2 November 1923 and 10 December 1928.

36. *Masu Media Tōsei*, vol. 1, document 12, pp. 19–20. The circuit breaker had been required in a document dated 22 May 1925, but it is not clear whether it was actually installed at that time: see ibid., document 1, p. 2.

37. This was required as of February 1920: NHK, ed., *Hōsō 50-Nen Shi*, p. 56. However, special outdoor circuit-breaker facilities had been demanded at least as early as the imperial coronation ceremony of November 1928: see NHK, ed., *Reiki—Hōsō Hen (1)*, pp. 15–16, document dated 2 November 1928, and pp. 16–17, document dated 10 December 1928.

38. In July 1928, the Communications Ministry demanded that one of the members of the board of directors or the station's broadcasting division manager serve as program inspector and that either he or a responsible proxy operate the circuit breaker at all times: NHK, ed., *Reiki—Hōsō Hen (1)*, p. 15, document dated 17 July 1928.

telephones from state offices were installed in the inspectors' rooms to streamline official orders. Communications Ministry bureaucrats also monitored all programs from their own listening facilities, so they were constantly alert for illegal contents.[39]

Use of the circuit breaker at NHK's Tokyo branch is documented for a two-year period starting in April 1931. During that time, there were forty interruptions in twenty-six programs, for an aggregate duration of 16'30".[40] Most were for commercial advertising on nonpolitical shows (for example, lectures on sunburn, rabbit meat, and fig cultivation). Only six programs clearly addressed state policy, all on foreign affairs, and they were cut a total of 4'27". This record reflects nationwide practice, since most programming came through the national relay, and most relay transmissions originated in Tokyo. Prior censorship was obviously very effective, though there may have been more interruptions before 1931, when the censorship system was less polished.[41]

Beyond regular press law standards, virtually any state institution could muzzle radio by conveying forbidden items to the Communications Ministry. In an emergency, any responsible state office could issue a direct order to broadcasters, even to stop a program in progress.[42] The ministries took full advantage of this privilege. For example, in October 1925 the Agriculture and Forestry Ministry banned information on the rice harvest, to avoid price fluctuations. In June 1932 it ordered that broadcasts from the racetrack not include the pedigree or breeding district of thoroughbreds or the amounts bet and paid out.[43] In May 1925 the Imperial Household Ministry sent instructions on reporting the Emperor's medical condition, and in January 1932 it banned speculation on imperial edicts before their proclamation.[44] To expedite administration, direct telephones linked the Home Ministry's Criminal Affairs Bureau to the Tokyo Communications Bureau, and all regional Commu-

---

39. Ibid.; *Masu Media Tōsei,* vol. 1, document 1, p. 3.

40. "Shumoku Tōkei Hyō," made available to the author at the NHK Sōgō Hōsō Bunka Kenkyūjo.

41. On 18 January 1932, there were seven interruptions during two shows, which drew the attention of the *Tōkyō Asahi Shinbun* the next day. Six were interruptions of a stand-up comedy routine, and one was of a lecture on winter sports. Though this incident has been cited in various scholarly sources, it must have been something of a record for the circuit breaker and was certainly not representative of its general use.

42. See the revision of the February 1924 ministerial notification in NHK, ed., *Hōsō 50-Nen Shi,* p. 56.

43. *Masu Media Tōsei,* vol. 1, document 9, p. 18; NHK, ed., *Reiki—Hōsō Hen (1),* pp. 19–20.

44. NHK, ed., *Nihon Hōsō Shi,* 1: 60; *Masu Media Tōsei,* vol. 1, document 36, pp. 220–21.

nications Bureaus to the stations under their jurisdiction. There was also a specially coded telegraph connection between the central Communications Ministry and its branch offices, though here too telephones were used as early as 1930.[45] Such technology was essential to the efficient implementation of controls.

Unique to radio censorship was the categorical prohibition of political argument.[46] Governments could advertise policy, but critics could not attack it, and state institutions were harbored from all censure. The Communications Ministry even banned the reporting of temporary suspensions in its telephone service due to thunderstorms.[47] The writ against criticism of the state gained specificity in response to particular cases. For example, in September 1926, a clergyman on NHK's Osaka station referred to "the army which has destructive objectives" and "armies and warships whose duty is to kill human beings." The regional Communications Bureau Chief was subsequently reprimanded for permitting "careless remarks concerning military duties."[48] More controversial was the lecture by Seiyūkai party figure Mori Kaku upon his return from Manchuria in November 1931. Since the Minseitō was in power, Mori's draft was scrupulously checked; he was told that any deviation from the text would mean the circuit breaker. However, he added the word "recently" to the original sentence "Japanese diplomacy is not respected by China and the League of Nations." The statement thus became a slur against the ruling cabinet. Broadcast inspectors failed to notice, but the Minseitō's indignation soon brought the matter to their attention.[49] Talk of punishing those responsible was quieted only by a change of government in December.

In January 1932, the Communications Ministry tightened censorship of two types of broadcasts, evidently in response to the commotion over Mori's lecture:

1. Expression or content feared to be interpreted as criticism or denunciation of the following: legal regulations; measures based on

45. *Masu Media Tōsei,* vol. 1, document 4, p. 11, and document 23, pp. 204–5; NHK, ed., *Hōsō 50-Nen Shi,* p. 56, document dated 13 February 1930.

46. This was formally inserted in a ministerial communiqué in December 1925, but it had been enforced from the first broadcast: *Masu Media Tōsei,* vol. 1, document 10, p. 19. More detailed reasoning behind the ban is given in NHK, ed., *Rajio Nenkan Shōwa 6-Nen,* pp. 139–42.

47. NHK, ed., *Nihon Hōsō Shi,* 1: 228.

48. Sendai Teishinkyoku, *Hōsō Kantoku Jimu Teiyō,* p. 94 (this document was probably prepared about 1936); *Masu Media Tōsei,* vol. 1, document 11, p. 19.

49. This incident is related in the magazine *Hōsō* (Broadcasting), no. 5 (1939), in an article reprinted in NHK, ed., *Nihon Hōsō Shi,* 1: 137–38.

legal regulations; administrative policies or facilities established pursuant to legal regulations; or the decisions of any lawfully organized meeting or Diet session.

2. Exposition of an opinion or claim tainted with a politically disputatious character that is biased in favor of one party or faction, or expression or content that constitutes an attack on or a rebuttal of such an exposition.[50]

Thus slip-ups were answered by greater diligence.

Needless to say, radical ideas had little chance on radio, but there were a few roundabout cases. In May 1929, a regional lecture on Soviet art and education earned the Communications Ministry's condemnation as "indirect propaganda for the Soviet Russian Revolution."[51] In November 1933, a dramatic performance by the Japan Proletarian Cultural League (its members using aliases) also prompted a ministry warning against this "thought group" which "stirs up class thinking."[52] Such cases were extremely rare. Thought control terminology and concerns increasingly penetrated regular censorship after the Manchurian Incident, but given the standing order against political argument, radio policy did not change much as a result. The uproar over Mori's rather trifling offense shows how tightly the system was run. It is said that Communications Ministry bureaucrats cut such words as *extremely* and *absolutely* in principle lest a statement on any topic invite outside criticism.[53] Even the broadcaster's tone of voice was ordered to be coldly neutral.[54]

50. *Masu Media Tōsei,* vol. 1, document 37, p. 221.
51. Sendai Teishinkyoku, *Hōsō Kantoku Jimu Teiyō,* p. 95; NHK, ed., *Reiki—Hōsō Hen (1),* p. 17.
52. *Masu Media Tōsei,* vol. 1, document 47, pp. 257–58. On November 29, a general notice addressed the "thought problem":

On broadcast content, regardless of whether the show is a lecture, news, fine art, or whatever, you are of course to eliminate anything which introduces an extreme "ism," theory, movement, or actual deed related to the national polity, political system, the economy, or morals, as well as anything which aids or abets related groups and their members. Furthermore, even when it comes to indirect terminology and clever phrasing which at first glance does not seem related to such matters, you must strictly avoid anything feared to foment an atmosphere that would lead one to infer such things, judging from the timing of the broadcast, the context of the speeches, etc. (Ibid., document 48, p. 258)

The pacifistic remarks on the army, the lecture on Soviet society, and the proletarian drama were found on a list of "Important Examples of Problem Broadcasts" covering the years 1925–1936; there were only eighteen cases on the entire list. It is taken from Sendai Teishinkyoku, *Hōsō Kantoku Jimu Teiyō,* pp. 94–96.
53. NHK, ed., *Nihon Hōsō Shi,* 1: 228; in Japanese, the words were *hijō ni* and *mattaku.*
54. Ibid., p. 190, according to a Communications Ministry notice of October 1933.

Though broadcasts for or against political parties were proscribed, including all election campaigning, Diet debates could have become an exception.[55] In August 1925 the original Tokyo Broadcasting Company requested ministerial approval for Diet broadcasts. The Communications Ministry disowned the matter, however, pointing out that "even in England, when the Prime Minister was asked about this during the winter meeting of Parliament in 1925, he replied that the issue required further investigation, and in the United States, though the President's speeches at the opening of Congress and at his inauguration have been broadcast, this has not been extended to legislative proceedings." The ministry gave the Diet the same consideration shown to other state institutions: it could decide on radio exposure for itself.[56]

In December 1925, both houses spurned the proposal. The lower house reasoned that the broadcasts might violate the Diet members' constitutional right of free speech;[57] no other country permitted legislative broadcasts; and if broadcasts from the Diet were to encompass both opposition-party questions and responses from ministers, why not just sanction speeches by the ministers?[58] Finally, inasmuch as the Communications Ministry had repudiated political speeches in general, it would be unjust to grant the Diet a privilege denied to others.[59] The House of Peers reported that opinion was so negative as to preclude the need for thorough study.[60]

55. Elections were preceded by special warnings from the Communications Ministry against any partisan political messages—see, e.g., *Masu Media Tōsei*, vol. 1, document 22, p. 204, a warning of 19 January 1928 just prior to a general election. Professor Nomura of Tokyo Imperial University was set to broadcast a speech about the upcoming general elections on 13 February 1930, but at the last minute ministry officials demanded changes in his address. The professor, who had prepared an evaluation of both ruling and opposition party platforms, refused to budge and his spot was cancelled: NHK, ed., *Nihon Hōsō Shi*, 1: 195. In February 1932, a program in which various party leaders were to announce their platforms was also dropped: ibid., p. 228.

56. NHK, ed., *Hōsō 50-Nen Shi*, p. 278, document dated 7 August 1925. The matter was referred to the chief secretaries of the House of Peers, the House of Representatives, and the cabinet: ibid., document dated 16 September 1925. Meanwhile, the ministry allowed the Tokyo station to make all technical preparations needed to transmit from the floor of the Diet.

57. Article 52 of the Meiji constitution read:

No Member of either House shall be held responsible outside the respective Houses, for any opinion uttered or for any vote given in the House. When, however, a Member himself has given publicity to his opinions by public speech, by documents in print or in writing, or by any other similar means, he shall, in the matter, be amenable to the general law.

58. It is not known how this issue was discussed among Diet members, but it seems likely that the party in power did not look forward to the prospect of opposition attacks on its policies being broadcast around the country.

59. NHK, ed., *Hōsō 50-Nen Shi*, pp. 278–79.

60. Ibid., p. 279.

The ideal of broadcasting without politics was widespread in the
interwar democracies. It was the announced principle in Belgium, Switzerland, Britain, and Weimar Germany as well as Japan. Politicians
feared that partisan control over radio would constitute an unfair advantage. Others would depoliticize the medium for the same reason primary school textbooks are depoliticized: to limit the sphere of divisive
political confrontation. This view was espoused by many radio executives who feared the medium might become a political football.

There are, however, two major shortcomings of nonpolitical broadcasting in democratic systems. The first is that a vital tool of political
socialization is lost. Especially in countries where democracy is just
taking root, radio can serve as a powerful means of promoting democratic values, educating the electorate, and strengthening political parties. In Japan and Germany, these potential advantages were largely
foregone; indeed, one writer has judged radio's neutrality to have been a
major weakness of the Weimar Republic.[61] In Japan, the Diet was probably the freest forum for public debate, especially in the 1930s; had its
deliberations been broadcast, the public's political awareness would
have been immeasurably greater.

The second problem is that where radio is limited to a state or public-
interest monopoly, the ideal of nonpolitical broadcasting is usually a
farce. The state invariably claims the right to broadcast official announcements at will, as it did in Belgium, Britain, Switzerland, Japan,
and other countries overtly embracing the nonpolitical principle. The
result is that allegedly nonpolitical neutrality is in fact biased in favor of
the government's point of view. Even in interwar Britain, to shield the
cabinet from criticism the BBC ignored such controversial issues as the
appeasement policy toward Hitler. Such partisanship became very visible in Japanese broadcasting in the last years of party rule.

Before the Manchurian Incident of 1931, governments made relatively little use of radio. Though general news programs were censored, they were supplied not by the state but by local newspapers
and, after 1930, by the country's two wire services. Due to opposition
from newspapers fearing for their special editions, NHK never developed its own news-gathering capability. Many routine state announcements were broadcast in special time slots or were mixed into the

---

61. John Sandford, *The Mass Media of the German-Speaking Countries*, p. 67. Sandford distinguishes between Weimar "neutrality," understood as the exclusion of politics,
and German broadcasting's postwar "neutrality," which tries to balance the expression of
competing points of view, thus serving the democratic process in a positive way.

regular news. Broadcast requests from local government executives and the Communications Ministry were mandatory, those from other public bodies optional. The first policy announcement by a cabinet member, however, did not occur until Prime Minister Hamaguchi's speech on economic recovery in August 1929, over four years after radio's founding.[62]

The Manchurian crisis was a turning point in the mobilization of radio. The Chinese government undertook a vigorous crusade to convince the world that Japan was the unlawful aggressor, and representatives of NHK and the Army, Foreign, and Communications Ministries joined to formulate a counter-strategy.[63] They concluded that Japan's ability to persuade other countries required united public opinion at home, and radio was mobilized to consolidate public support.

Impressive results were achieved during the twelve months after the incident began in September 1931. There were 228 special lectures and educational programs on the conflict (76 by military men), and 30 programs on its diplomatic ramifications. An additional 56 broadcasts concerned incident-related events, including military maneuvers, troop departures, memorial services for the war dead, and meetings of patriotic societies such as the reservist associations. There were also 30 regular programs on the Children's Hour series devoted to the matter, 42 entertainment shows, and 24 programs on series aimed at women, bearing such titles as "The Power of Women to Guard the Home Front."[64] In one year, a total of 410 programs were presented to mobilize public support, not counting the barrage of special news bulletins that upped news coverage in Tokyo from 40 minutes a day in 1930 to 64 minutes a day in 1931.[65]

The invasion of normally nonpolitical programs is especially noteworthy. A crude example was NHK's petition to the Communications Ministry to start a children's news show, which appeared from June 1932 as "The Children's Newspaper." The entire paragraph describing plans for the program read:

62. NHK, ed., Nihon Hōsō Shi, 1: 195.
63. Ibid., p. 196; Kakegawa Tomiko, "The Press and Public Opinion in Japan, 1931–1941," pp. 541–42. The participants were Lieutenant General Hata Hikosaburō, chief of the Army Research Group (Chōsa Han), Shiratori Toshio, head of the Foreign Ministry's Information Division, Hatakeyama Toshiyuki, the Communications Ministry's Telephone and Telegraph Bureau Chief, and Nakayama Ryūji, managing director of NHK's Tokyo branch, an ex–Communications Ministry bureaucrat.
64. All data from NHK, ed., Rajio Nenkan Shōwa 8-Nen, pp. 6–25.
65. NHK, ed., Hōsō 50-Nen Shi, p. 284.

There is news which holds a special interest for children. For example, the exploits of military dogs; a true story about a [Japanese] child in China whose father is to return home but who persuades his father to let him stay behind for his country's sake and joins a volunteer corps; a youth has a dream of Yamada Nagamasa [an early Japanese pioneer in Asia] and sets out to join the Chinese army, but en route he sees his mistake and seeks help from Japanese soldiers; a young girl escapes from Shanghai and returns to Japan unaided, etc. There is no time to list all of these sorts of military episodes. Even in peacetime, things like a courageous young man rescuing a drowning girl, or those which deeply move children to be filial sons and daughters. We believe that not a few sports and other special news items of interest will be used.[66]

This was but a small dose of what lay ahead.

Beyond blatant political tampering, the state influenced programming in other ways. In accord with official wishes, the broadcast schedule was rather evenly divided among the three categories of information, education, and entertainment. Entertainment topped the 30 percent mark in only six years between 1925 and 1942, in contrast to its 60 percent share in Germany and Britain.[67] NHK's central office fixed norms for the time allotted to various shows (so much to Japanese music, Western music, theater, and so on), and though the branches retained some discretion, national relay programs increased from 17 percent of the schedule in 1928 to 79 percent in 1933, severely constricting the time available for local transmissions.[68]

Radio's servility to the state soon made intellectuals cynical about broadcasting. Feminist novelist Nogami Yaeko wrote in 1932:

Because I sense acutely radio's general power to propagate ideas, or, to go a step further, its enormous power of agitation, I think I would like to hear even information on each day's social events told in the voice of their true social reality, as if they had been filmed as they happened, and not arranged in a montage with mistaken ideology. When I see that radio has been serving as a state organ since the start of the war, this desire becomes all the stronger.[69]

66. Petition dated 19 March 1932, reprinted in ibid., pp. 285–86.
67. Ibid., p. 610; NHK, ed., *Nihon Hōsō Shi,* 1: 183.
68. NHK, ed., *Nihon Hōsō Shi,* 1: 135.
69. Quoted from the journal *Chōsa Jihō* (January 1932), in NHK, ed., *Hōsō 50-Nen Shi,* pp. 293–94. In the same issue, Saitō Ryūtarō wrote: "These days radio is uninteresting. I'm getting tired of it. One restraint after another is imposed by state officials who are like obstinate swine and have no comprehension of things. The best thing would be to liberate it from these restrictions and make it free, but even within the limits of present restraints, one can think of numerous methods preferable to those being used now." (Ibid., pp. 294–95.)

At about the same time, the author Ryūtanji Yū commented: "The lack of interest and enthusiasm for contemporary radio among the intellectual class is just like a burnt-out cinder."[70] There is no evidence, however, of similar skepticism among the general public. The Manchurian Incident produced an unprecedented spurt of new listening contracts as people turned to radio for the latest news from the Asian mainland.[71]

PERSONNEL AND FINANCIAL CONTROLS

The initial influx of bureaucrats set a strong precedent for state control over radio personnel, and official management of radio's finances also strengthened over time. In December 1929, the Communications Ministry demanded prior approval for the hiring of all key employees in the program and technical fields. Program personnel were required to be individuals of "moderate thoughts."[72] By this time, however, NHK had voluntarily hired more ex-bureaucrats than had ever been forced upon it. Each of the seven branch stations had general affairs, technical, and broadcasting divisions. All general affairs managers were ex–Communications Ministry officials, as were five of the seven technical division managers, the other two being ex-navy men. Only the broadcasting division heads had civil backgrounds, and four of them were prominent businessmen chosen to thank investors. All central office division managers were ex–Communications Ministry bureaucrats.[73]

Thus despite some smoldering resentment among investors, the ministry's ties with those actually running NHK were essentially fraternal. The two sides retained distinct institutional identities, and there were

---

70. Quoted in ibid., p. 295, originally from the *Chōsa Jihō* of February 1932. In this same issue, Okuya Kumao, head of the literary section of NHK's Osaka outlet, wrote:

> Those on the left often say that Japanese broadcasting is trying to fulfill its foremost function as an organ for the diffusion of reactionary thought. If one looks at the relationship with supervisory state officials, the scope of the limits on broadcast contents, etc., one cannot disagree with this observation, but it is only the organization and the system which foist [upon radio] varied functions favorable to a reactionary course—it is certainly not inevitable that we must advance along this road. (Ibid.)

71. Year-end statistics for listening contracts show a net increase of 128,469 from 1929 to 1930, 276,830 from 1930 to 1931, and 363,944 from 1931 to 1932. The Manchurian Incident occurred in September 1931. Figures from NHK, ed., *Hōsō 50-Nen Shi*, p. 608.

72. On the policy change of December 1929, see *Nihon Musen Shi*, 7: 165–66. For the state's criteria of competence, see NHK, ed., *Reiki—Hōsō Hen (1)*, p. 22, document dated 28 March 1930.

73. Figures from *Nihon Musen Shi*, 7: 178–79.

contentious issues between them, but most often the ministry was quarreling with its own alumni. This was partly an arranged marriage in which the ministry's initial appointees served as middlemen; they were in position to hire their former bureaucratic colleagues into NHK. But the availability of technically qualified personnel had to be a major factor. Telecommunications had hitherto been a state monopoly, and for many posts there were probably few qualified civil applicants. In any case, there are no signs of an ongoing, deep-seated hostility between NHK employees of civil and bureaucratic backgrounds, and they eventually formed a fairly amicable partnership.

The ministry could veto outside speakers on radio through the censorship system, and the speaker's personal background became an increasingly important factor in program approval. In May 1929, echoing the contemporary anxiety over thought groups, officials demanded that the speaker's occupation, court rank (if any), and educational background be included in program reports.[74] In January 1932, just after the Manchurian Incident, a new command to NHK read: "Hereafter, you will be all the more strict in your selection of performers. Of course, you will avoid anyone who might easily give rise to the least bit of public criticism, and in the broadcasting field also take care to avoid re-using anyone who has caused even minor problems in the past."[75] There were legal penalties for lying and for offending morals or public order over wireless facilities, but there is no record of a violator being punished, which speaks for the thoroughness of censorship and the advance screening of speakers.

Financially, the establishment of radio was probably the best deal the state ever made. Investors saw their money used to finance official plans for radio without receiving a single yen of profit in return. Judging solely by the results, radio's licensing might easily be seen as a clever swindle to finance a government project with private money.

The Communications Ministry made full use of its budgetary powers. The annual budget approval came with written conditions and often with an appended notification containing further orders. For example, the 1929 budget approval declared that NHK's testing and authorization of radio receivers was a "subsidiary business" requiring a ministry permit; the appended notification stipulated that NHK would undergo a detailed audit twice a year. The 1930 notification demanded

74. NHK, ed., *Reiki—Hōsō Hen (1)*, p. 17, document dated 22 May 1929.
75. Ibid., p. 19, document dated 29 January 1932.

the standardization of office structure, salaries, and labor in all of NHK's branches.[76] Thus budgetary powers were used to dictate not only financial but also other matters.

The state's principal financial gain from NHK was control over use of its assets, but there were other benefits as well. The Communications Ministry required NHK to pay 20 sen (or 0.2 yen) annually for each listening contract. In 1928, listeners paid 12 yen per year to NHK, so the ministry's share came to 1.6 percent of NHK's annual income from listening fees. In later years listening fees were lowered, so the ministry's percentage grew relative to NHK's total revenue.[77]

Other offices also took a share of radio money. Economic hard times tempted local governments (under Home Ministry jurisdiction) to impose their own tariffs on radio listeners. In November 1931, the cities of Kyoto, Osaka, and Kobe took a common stand on the issue. Negotiations between the Communications and Home Ministries then compelled NHK to pay local governments the amount of one month's listening fee for every local receiver owner; in exchange, the Home Ministry agreed to nix any further local attempts to tax listeners. When the agreement took effect in 1932, the financial picture looked like this:

Number of paid listener's contracts	1,034,491
NHK's revenue	¥9,310,410 (¥9 annually per contract)
Local government's share	¥775,868 (75 sen annually per contract)
Communications Ministry's share	¥206,898 (20 sen annually per contract)

The local governments' share amounted to 8.3 percent of NHK's revenues, the Communications Ministry's share to 2.2 percent. So NHK turned a profit after all, but not for its investors. Officials of the Communications Ministry and NHK were reluctant signatories to this arrangement with the Home Ministry. The local government money was avowedly earmarked for health projects, but the treatment of disease was not

76. Examples from *Nihon Musen Shi,* 7: 160–62.
77. Listening fees were reduced to 75 sen per month in April 1932 and 50 sen per month in April 1935. The relative expense of owning a radio receiver can be judged in relation to the following Tokyo prices in 1932: one month's newspaper subscription—95 sen; one admission to a movie theater—80 sen; a bottle of beer—34 sen; 500 grams of sugar—22 sen; a pack of domestic cigarettes—15 sen: figures cited in NHK, ed., *Nihon Hōsō Shi,* 1: 176. Radio was still considered something of a luxury item in depression years when some farmers sold their daughters into prostitution to avoid starvation.

part of their responsibility for "the public interest." This was only one example of bureaucratic jousting over radio policy.

INTRASTATE CONFLICTS OVER RADIO

Both the Home and the Education Ministry sought to control various aspects of radio. The Communications Ministry held its ground in 1925 in an accord with the Home Ministry that limited the latter's involvement to clearing censorship requests from certain other agencies. In 1928, however, the Home Minister tried to take over radio censorship by asserting that this task fell under his duty to safeguard public order, and he suggested a new law to shift jurisdiction. The Communications Ministry successfully answered this challenge by sponsoring a revision of the Wireless Telegraphic Communications Law that granted it exclusive censorship authority; this passed the Diet in 1929.[78]

The Education Ministry made its bid in late 1930 when NHK's educational second channel was approved. Education Ministry officials demanded dual jurisdiction, since all juridical persons in educational work belonged to their bailiwick; they also claimed the right to censor educational programs. These arguments were put forth at the bureau-chief level. The Communications Ministry responded that radio was more than just an educational organ and reasserted its own authority over all wireless facilities. Education Ministry control over broadcasting was declared to be "meaningless."[79] The issue was then kicked upstairs to the vice-ministers' level, where it again failed of resolution. Finally, in January 1931, the parliamentary vice-ministers settled the matter in the Communications Ministry's favor; its only concession was to appoint an official consultant with the Education Ministry. This dispute delayed the start of regular broadcasts to schools until 1935, and Education Ministry bureaucrats withheld formal recognition of radio as a tool of instruction until 1941. On both sides, organizational imperatives took precedence over "the public interest."

These bureaucratic border wars are significant for several reasons. First, they exacerbated radio censorship, since the Communications Ministry feared that the slightest negligence might be exploited by its competitors in pressing their claims. Furthermore, the boundaries of

78. In 1933, the same debate was reenacted in an interministerial Thought Policy Committee, but acrimonious exchanges between bureau chiefs ended in a reaffirmation of the status quo: ibid., p. 166.

79. Ibid., pp. 166–67.

such quarrels indicate that they had nothing to do with more liberal treatment for the medium. Regardless of who won, the outcome would have no effect on radio's autonomy from the state. Finally, it is worthwhile stressing that although *state* is often used as a collective noun, it was not a solitary actor with a unified will. For analytical purposes, it is legitimate to isolate a group of institutions according to shared functional traits and label them with one word, but despite the boasts of certain philosophers and statesmen, modern state agencies comprise neither a spiritual personality nor a well-oiled machine of complementary parts. The error of ascribing greater unity to states than the facts warrant is common enough to justify an occasional warning to the contrary.

CHAPTER V

Comparative Analysis

Two salient aspects of media policymaking in Japan's prewar party governments were the prominent role of the bureaucracy and the fact that many elected statesmen themselves actively supported restrictions on public expression. Far from being unique to Japan, these features have characterized the making of media policy in many modern democratic regimes.

POLICYMAKING IN A
DEMOCRATIC-BUREAUCRATIC REGIME

According to Mattei Dogan, policymaking in contemporary democracies is distinguished by increasing executive dominance over the legislature and the growing strength of career administrators, compared to that of politicians, within the executive.[1] Both attributes stood out in prewar Japan. Executive dominance is beyond discussion—91 percent of all laws enacted by the Diet under the Meiji constitution (1890–1947) originated in the executive branch. A similar pattern has prevailed in Western Europe, where government executives have prepared 82 percent of all bills passed by the postwar British Parliament and 87 percent of those approved under the French Fifth Republic.[2] Prewar

1. Dogan, "Political Power," p. 19.
2. Robert M. Spaulding, Jr., "The Bureaucracy as a Political Force: 1920–1945," p. 37; Henry W. Ehrmann, *Politics in France,* p. 306.

Japan's media policies in the era of party governments, when the Diet's influence was presumably at its apex, illustrate the point. The only major media bill initiated by the Diet between 1918 and 1932 was the press legislation of 1924, and this was defeated partly due to the cabinet's opposition. The Diet took no part in formulating or approving policy toward radio and film. The ascendancy of bureaucrats over politicians within the executive was also in evidence. Executive politicians played no apparent role in film policy, made only one substantial modification of bureaucratic plans for radio, and gave in to the bureaucracy in their decision to obstruct the Diet's press bill, which would have curbed administrative prerogatives.

This pattern seems incongruent with the highly politicized character of the bureaucracy. As was noted earlier, the careers of top administrators depended on the favor of party officials. Such politicization should reduce bureaucratic influence, since it enables party cabinet ministers to assert their will on any issue.[3] Party politicians were indeed the prime movers behind some key legislative measures such as the general manhood suffrage act, and Communications Minister Inukai demonstrated the politician's power within the executive branch when he overturned the bureaucracy's plans for profit-making broadcasting firms. Politicians, then, could control policy, but the media record shows that their power usually lay dormant—on the whole, the politician's input was secondary to that of the bureaucrat. The principal reasons are summarized below. To give the case study a broader relevance, the analysis indicates which sources of bureaucratic influence have been typical of democratic regimes and which were peculiar to Japan. Although Japanese bureaucrats enjoyed a few extraordinary prerogatives, on the whole their advantages have been shared by administrators in most democracies.

One prominent reason for the bureaucracy's sway was its superiority in expertise, organization, and personnel. B. Guy Peters lists information and expertise as the greatest advantages bureaucrats possess over politicians in policymaking, and their dominance of these resources is a virtually universal feature of modern democracies. It is frequently cited to explain the widespread decline in the policymaking role of elected officials, especially in Western Europe.[4] Japan's prewar bureaucracy

3. Dogan, "Political Power," pp. 13–14.
4. B. Guy Peters, *The Politics of Bureaucracy: A Comparative Perspective*, pp. 169–70. On the declining power of elected officials, see Anthony King, "Political Parties in Western Democracies: Some Skeptical Reflections," pp. 135–37; Alfred Grosser, "The Evolution of European Parliaments," pp. 449–53; Dogan, "Political Power," pp. 7–9.

was an educational elite, entry and promotion hinging on success in rigorous qualifying exams.[5] Its organizational resources could not be matched by the political parties or by the party executives in charge of government. The offices of party ministers were notably understaffed, and members of the cabinet were forced to rely heavily on administrative line positions below for policy formulation.[6]

The bureaucracy's edge in personnel is well illustrated by the founding of radio. The initial three-station radio structure was launched between November 1924 and March 1925, coinciding with a Diet session, but the cabinet and Diet faced more pressing problems. Premier Katō was struggling to sustain a shaky three-party coalition, and the legislature's attention was focused on the suffrage act and the Peace Preservation Law. Similarly, when bureaucrats proposed the creation of NHK in February 1926, the parties were preoccupied with other matters. Katō had just died and a new cabinet had to be formed. From April 1926, when the ministry's plans for NHK were made public, to the actual merger in August of that year, the Diet never met. Except for a brief exchange in 1923, radio was not even discussed in the Diet.[7] Of course, radio's significance was not obvious to everyone in 1924–1926, but if bureaucrats saw it more quickly than politicians, this was due to the man-hours they could devote to the subject.

A second element favoring administrative influence was a legal system allowing bureaucrats to act with minimal clearance through political channels. Ministerial notifications and decrees were used to fix censorship standards, to set most conditions for broadcasting, and to regulate every aspect of film policy. A single minister could approve a decree, and career officials could issue other types of regulations on their own authority. In principle, parliamentary laws could limit the scope of bureaucratic ordinances, but they rarely did so in practice, due to their lack of concreteness and to the bureaucracy's interpretive skills. Few democratic constitutions have granted the bureaucracy ordinance powers as generous as those inscribed by the Meiji founders, but

5. See Robert M. Spaulding, Jr., *Imperial Japan's Higher Civil Service Examinations,* especially the tables on pp. 260–61, 275–77, 346–48.

6. Tsuji Kiyoaki, "Decision-Making in the Japanese Government: A Study of Ringisei," pp. 462–65, 472.

7. The Communications Minister was questioned in the upper house Finance Committee on 13 March 1923. He was asked if radio would be civilly managed and how many stations would be licensed. The reply confirmed civil management and plans to license two or three stations, one in each of the largest cities; this was consistent with the provisions of the Draft Proposal then under discussion in the ministry: *Nihon Musen Shi,* 7: 21–22.

the growing scale of public business has necessitated the delegation of similar authority to ministries and regulatory agencies in most democratic regimes. Dogan writes:

> Everywhere in Europe, parliaments have been declining in power. Legislative functions have been partly transferred to the executive branch, as seen by the importance of delegated powers which allow the public administration to set regulations. These regulations make possible the implementation of laws in matters that rightfully belong to parliamentary bodies. Laws promulgated as guidelines or decrees issued by the executive also point to this delegation of law making authority.[8]

A third source of bureaucratic leadership was that bureaucrats and politicians were largely agreed on policy objectives. Both party control over senior bureaucratic appointments and the movement of retired bureaucrats into party ranks buttressed this agreement. Ex-bureaucrats comprised 10 percent of the lower house over the five elections from 1920 to 1932. They were even more numerous among party elites: of the eight party Prime Ministers, seven had been civilian bureaucrats, and one a military bureaucrat in the Army Ministry.[9] Administrators and politicians never battled as distinct groups over media policy. The bureaucracy did oppose the liberal press bill that passed the lower house in the Diet meeting of 1924–1925, but it was a party Prime Minister who ultimately blocked the measure. Bureaucratic film controls differed little in principle from the Diet's press regulations of 1909. Party Communications Ministers supported the basic bureaucratic design for radio—they changed the only part they disliked by banning profit-making companies—and no Diet members were so opposed as to obstruct the ministry's plans. If politicians rarely overturned administrative decisions, one reason is that they rarely felt the need. Bureaucratic policymaking was often undemocratic in that the involvement of elected officials was slight, but not generally antidemocratic in the sense of contravening the preferences of party government leaders.

Such agreement between bureaucrats and politicians is not unusual in democratic regimes. A recent survey of Western democracies showed that the main difference between the two concerning state intervention in

8. Dogan, "Political Power," p. 7; see also Grosser, "Evolution of European Parliaments," p. 449; James B. Christoph, "High Civil Servants and the Politics of Consensualism in Great Britain," pp. 45–46.
9. It should be noted that Inukai Tsuyoshi had been a bureaucrat only briefly and never really undertook an administrative career. On the extra-parliamentary careers of prewar Diet members, see Ishida, "The Development of Interest Groups," pp. 306–9.

society was that slightly more bureaucrats favored the status quo, while more politicians advocated change; only 16 percent of the combined respondents favored any major shift.[10] Given this convergence of opinions, it seems improbable that bureaucratic decrees would clash sharply with the preferences of politicians, though the likelihood of this happening differs by country; for example, at present it is less likely in Britain or Japan than in Italy or the United States.

A fourth cause of bureaucratic strength was that the parties lacked a deep organizational base in civil society. This constricted their role in filtering social demands, while increasing that of the bureaucracy. The more diverse and organized party constituencies are, the more interest groups will approach the state through party mediation. When this happens, politicians are inevitably active in formulating policy responses, as they were when periodical press interests channeled their claims through the Diet in 1924. Where organized party penetration of society is shallow, interest groups are more likely to take their demands directly to the bureaucracy, as did the petitioners for broadcasting licenses. When this happened, the parties largely disappeared from the policy picture.

The parties' neglect of radio illustrates their indifference toward developing a wider and better organized constituency. Instead of turning radio into an amplifier for party propaganda, they surrendered the medium to a politically sterile public-interest company under bureaucratic control. There was not one political association among the over one hundred applicants for a broadcasting license. It was not that party governments ignored radio altogether, but the magnitude of their lost opportunity can be appreciated from the fact that the first broadcast from the Diet in session was a speech by Prime Minister Tōjō Hideki in November 1941. So thoroughly conditioned were they within the elitist confines of the Meiji constitutional system that the parties did not seek

10. Joel D. Aberbach, Robert D. Putnam, and Bert A. Rockman, *Bureaucrats and Politicians in Western Democracies*, pp. 119–28. Since the sample included politicians from opposition parties that had never formed a government, some undoubtedly espousing strongly ideological positions, even this finding may exaggerate differences between bureaucrats and the politicians actually running the governments of these countries. The specific result referred to was from the following question: "In general, what is the respondent's preferred degree of state involvement in the economy and society?" The data were gathered on roughly equal samples of bureaucrats and parliamentary politicians in Britain, France, Germany, Italy, the Netherlands, and the United States, and in Sweden from a bureaucratic sample only (N = 1,108). Responses were: much more state involvement and/or social provision—11 percent; some more state involvement and/or social provision—27 percent; present balance—42 percent; some more individual initiative—16 percent; much more individual initiative—5 percent.

to reinforce their preeminence with a stronger mass base. Their failure to do so reflects a startling naïveté regarding the realities of modern power politics, and it greatly facilitated interest aggregation through the bureaucracy, augmenting the latter's policymaking role.

Direct contacts between bureaucrats and interest groups are extensive in most democracies.[11] Joel Aberbach, Robert Putnam, and Bert Rockman found that 59 percent of top Western administrators reported regular interaction with interest groups, compared to 72 percent of politicians.[12] Nonetheless, social interests were much better represented in most interwar Western European party systems than they were in Japan, where industrial labor had yet to find its political voice, and local notables interceded between the mass of tenant farmers and the major parties. Bureaucratic influence thus profited from the relatively immature state of the party system in a way untypical of more highly institutionalized democratic polities.

A fifth reason politicians could be excluded from policymaking is that bureaucrats often planned it that way. The Home Ministry kept film policy out of parliament by treating the medium as "entertainment" rather than public expression. The Communications Ministry denied that radio was a mass medium, in order to regulate it under an existing law and avoid new legislation. It also conducted most of its year-long preliminary study of radio in secrecy. These agencies saw new policy fields as opportunities to expand their personnel, budgets, and authority, and they were naturally reluctant to submit their plans to the cabinet or Diet, where politicians and other ministries might alter them and stake their own claims to the organizational assets being created. Bureaucratic efforts to avoid the interference of politicians are a well-known feature of democratic and authoritarian regimes alike. Peters writes: "In general, we can expect agencies to attempt to get as large a share of the budgetary pie as possible and at the same time seek to maximize their own independence from political control."[13] Administrators use secrecy for this purpose virtually everywhere.[14]

11. On bureaucracy-interest group connections, see Peters, *Politics of Bureaucracy,* chap. 6.
12. Aberbach, Putnam, and Rockman, *Bureaucrats and Politicians,* pp. 213–15.
13. Peters, *Politics of Bureaucracy,* p. 174.
14. "It is not merely in the so-called dictatorial or bureaucratic states that secrecy is used as a weapon. In democratic Western countries the periodic outbreak of enormous scandals involving administrative behavior is probably just a mild indication of what other unsavory patterns the mask of secrecy guards": Joseph LaPalombara, *Politics within Nations,* p. 303.

A sixth cause of the bureaucracy's dominance was its autonomy from the regular courts. Had civil litigants been able to challenge the legality of administrative policies in court, the ministries would have been less free to circumvent the legal prerogatives of the Diet (and the Diet less free to abdicate its responsibilities). Judicial oversight might have compelled the Diet to consider new laws to regulate film and radio. Supervision of the bureaucracy through administrative rather than regular courts has prevailed in many democratic regimes; the practice continues today in Italy, France, Sweden, and West Germany.[15] Such courts can see to it that bureaucrats act in accord with administrative regulations, but they are not ordinarily competent to determine the constitutionality of the regulations themselves in cases where bureaucratic ordinances might violate constitutional law. In Japan, the lack of administrative court jurisdiction over media controls probably allowed an unusually high degree of bureaucratic discretion in interpreting concepts such as "public order," but the administrative court could not have forced new Diet laws to govern film or radio. Bureaucratic abuses of constitutional law can only be stopped by the jurisdiction of regular courts empowered to judge such matters, and these have been lacking in many democracies besides that of prewar Japan.

A final reason for bureaucratic influence over policy was the legitimacy attached to bureaucratic action. The *willingness* of bureaucrats to make full use of the aforementioned advantages was partly due to this legitimacy, which had both historical and legal foundations. In the Tokugawa period, administrative, political, and military authority had been jointly exercised by the samurai without a clear distinction between political and administrative responsibilities.[16] The aura of legitimacy surrounded all functions of the ruling class equally. The Meiji bureaucracy

15. David H. Bayley, "The Police and Political Development in Europe," pp. 330–41, 370. De Tocqueville wrote as follows of the origins of administrative justice in pre-revolutionary France:

> Since the King had little or no hold on the judges . . . he very soon came to find their independence irksome. Hence arose the custom of withdrawing from the ordinary courts the right of trying cases in which the King's authority or interest was in any way involved. Such cases were heard by special courts presided over by judges more dependent on the King, which, while offering his subjects a semblance of justice, could be trusted to carry out his wishes. (*The Old Regime and the French Revolution*, p. 52)

Even in countries where the regular courts exercise some jurisdiction over administrative acts (these include the United States, Britain, Denmark, and Norway), there are usually complementary administrative tribunals that handle most public complaints: Peters, *Politics of Bureaucracy*, pp. 226–27.

16. Edwin Dowdy, *Japanese Bureaucracy: Its Development and Modernization*, pp. xii–xiv.

was initially staffed by ex-samurai, including many protégés of the found-ing fathers, so the sense of legitimacy attached to administrative acts persisted.[17] As was demonstrated by its early press ordinances, the Meiji state explicitly sanctioned unilateral bureaucratic policymaking; indeed, prior to the constitution, the state was little more than a collection of bureaucratic agencies. The constitution legitimized administrative au-thority not only through its grant of ordinance powers but also by mak-ing each minister directly responsible to the throne. This latter feature was complemented by the imperial appointment of all senior career offi-cials, whose status was thus bestowed by the Emperor himself. The no-tion of the bureaucracy as a keeper of the public interest properly above sectarian wrangling could only enhance the formal legitimacy of its poli-cymaking role.

The historical legacy of bureaucratic legitimacy is one Japan shares with most Western European countries, where administration was first conducted by the monarch's personal entourage and then consigned to separate offices entrusted with the royal seal.[18] On this point Japanese and European experience differs sharply from that of the United States. Nonetheless, bureaucratic legitimacy was clearly more formalized under Japan's imperial constitution than in most post-monarchical democratic regimes, more closely resembling Europe's nineteenth-century constitu-tional monarchies in this important respect.

To summarize, though politicians could dominate policymaking when marshaling all of their influence, they were unable or unwilling to exert this influence continuously over most aspects of media policy. The bu-reaucracy was well equipped to govern in this area by (1) its superiority in organization and expertise; (2) its independent authority to issue ordi-nances and other regulations; (3) its basic agreement with politicians on the substance of policy; (4) its extensive interaction with interest groups, owing in part to the thin party base in society; (5) its successful tactics to exclude politicians from decision-making; (6) its autonomy from the regular courts; and (7) the historical and legal legitimacy of its policymak-ing functions.

The question may arise whether the bureaucracy's potency in policy-

17. Reinhard Bendix, *Nation-Building and Citizenship,* pp. 191–93.
18. LaPalombara, *Politics within Nations,* p. 246. In France, once the structure of offices had become complex and the scope of recruitment to them less restrictive, common-ers entering high office automatically received noble status; in Prussia, ennoblement was granted as a special privilege to only the most effective of top administrators: see Hans Rosenberg, *Bureaucracy, Aristocracy, and Autocracy: The Prussian Experience, 1660–1815,* pp. 141–43.

making does not undercut the description of this period as one of democratic rule. Yet despite several extraordinary advantages enjoyed by the Japanese bureaucracy, on the whole the causes of bureaucratic influence were typical of those observed in many democratic regimes. Furthermore, elements especially favoring the prewar Japanese bureaucracy, such as its ordinance powers and formal legitimacy, were counterbalanced by party control over senior administrative promotions, which exceeded that of most democratic ruling parties. If the bureaucracy's weight in policymaking should compromise our customary use of the concept "democratic regime," this assertion would apply to most modern democracies, not only to the prewar Japanese system. Scholars often refer to military regimes as "military-bureaucratic," since uniformed governors are usually highly dependent on their civilian administrators. In the same vein, to speak of "democratic-bureaucratic" regimes would better describe the way that elected governments function in practice.

The reality of democratic-bureaucratic rule has important implications for the assessment of state control over society. Even where the highest offices are elective, control policies may lack the democratic legitimacy associated with government by popular representatives. Controls initiated by elected officials invariably acquire much of their substance from the bureaucrats who administer them. Furthermore, this bureaucratic input is bound to increase as state controls proliferate, because while the bureaucracy expands to manage new functions, the number of elected officials charged with oversight remains fairly constant. The more powerful the state becomes under a democratic-bureaucratic regime, the more bureaucratic and the less democratic it is likely to be. Control measures may even be instituted without the involvement of elected officials at all, making the policymaking process the same as that in an authoritarian regime. There was certainly little difference between the way Japanese press policy was made in the 1870s and film policy in the 1920s. In short, the control policies of democratic regimes do not necessarily possess any quality differentiating them from the acts of non-democratic regimes. In scholarship, this conclusion calls for more comparative studies of policymaking across regime types to better comprehend just how distinctive or indistinctive democratic regimes are in practice. For democratic citizens, it means that the presence of an elected political elite no longer allows complacency about the danger of illegitimate state power.

THE DISPARITY BETWEEN
DEMOCRATIC AND LIBERAL VALUES

Japan's party governments imposed harsher media controls than had the Meiji founding fathers. The autonomy of radio was so severely curbed that it never carried open political discussion. Though film and press controls stayed fundamentally within the framework of the *état-gendarme,* neither was as liberal as Meiji policy. Films were censored before public showing and abandoned to bureaucratic ordinances without constitutional protection. Press policy was exacerbated by the Peace Preservation Law and the beginning of regular pre-publication warnings. Furthermore, it is clear that not all these restrictions are traceable to bureaucratic policymaking. Elected officials were directly involved in limiting radio to a public-interest monopoly, initiating anti-radical legislation, and blocking the liberal press bill of 1924–1925.

In many ways the actions of Japan's party leaders in controlling media expression have been as typical of democratic regimes as the powerful role of the bureaucracy, discussed above. Karl Loewenstein's research shows that legal and institutional curbs on state power in interwar European democracies were generally no more liberal than those in Japan:

Some of the European democracies such as France and England do not possess formal guarantees of fundamental rights as integral parts of their constitutional set-up. Even where a Bill of Rights or similar statements embody the classical concepts of liberal democracy, such as in the Scandinavian countries, in Switzerland or in Czechoslovakia, as a rule the absence of judicial review deprives them of actual enforcement. The combination of fundamental rights guaranteed by a constitutional document with judicial protection against state interference is an almost unique feature of American constitutional law. In addition, in most European countries the customary juristic technique for reconciling constitutional ideals with actual state necessities is that of allowing restrictions of liberal fundamentalism by ordinary legislation of the parliament, or, as was frequently the case in Germany under the Weimar constitution, by way of constitutional amendment. Hence, deviations from the standard principles of abstractly conceived political liberty are more easily accomplished in Europe and seem less repugnant to public opinion than in this country [the United States]. Everywhere in Europe, with the possible exception of England, the residuary spirit of the police state which is inclined to subordinate liberty to the paramount requirements of public order and peace has mollified and vitiated the rigorism of the classic liberal theory, and public opinion thus was and is more tolerant toward legislative limitations of abstract notions of liberty.[19]

Comparative data confirm this analysis in the specific areas of press and radio policy where Japan's elected statesmen played an active role. Regarding press laws, Loewenstein uncovered many parallels to the Japanese experience. Extreme criticism of constitutionally established political bodies was outlawed in Britain, the Netherlands, Belgium, Sweden, Czechoslovakia, and Finland.[20] The circulation of false news or unfounded allegations concerning the state was a crime in France, Finland, Sweden, Czechoslovakia, and Lithuania.[21] The publication of corrections ordered by the state was compulsory in Czechoslovakia, Norway, and Weimar Germany, and the nineteenth-century French regulations still binding in the 1930s were probably the model for Japan's own statutes on the subject.[22] Press controls in the Weimar Republic were much tougher than those in Japan. For endangering public order or slandering the state, newspapers could be suspended for eight weeks, magazines for six months. A 1931 ordinance enabled central and provincial (*Länder*) German states to force periodicals to publish official declarations without amendment or comment.[23] There were also numerous European laws punishing political acts that threatened public order.

The many points of resemblance between Japanese and European democratic radio policies have already been described. The Japanese pattern of public ownership and a minimum of partisan political content has not been at all extraordinary. It is noteworthy that even quite recent data, from 1985, showed radio restricted to state and/or public-interest companies in Austria, Belgium, Denmark, West Germany, Norway, Sweden, Switzerland, and the United Kingdom.[24] Such companies enjoy varying degrees of freedom for political expression, but few permit the same latitude for partisan argument and criticism of the state allowed in democracies with civilly owned broadcasting networks.

Granted that relatively liberal treatment of the press and slight mobilization of the media as active state weapons distinguish democratic polities from most others, the question remains: why do elected officials impose any controls affecting media content?

19. Karl Loewenstein, "Legislative Control of Political Extremism in European Democracies II," pp. 767–68.
20. Ibid., pp. 738–39.
21. Ibid., p. 749.
22. Ibid., p. 750, including n. 112.
23. Ibid., p. 750; Oron J. Hale, *The Captive Press in the Third Reich*, pp. 11–12.
24. *Political Handbook of the World, 1986.*

A first, obvious answer is that not all elected officials are good democrats. No political camp is ever short of half-hearted, self-serving, or ignorant followers. Many advocating elections to the state elite lack an idealistic belief in democratic principles or a good understanding of what their implementation requires. Supporters may favor a democratic regime because its policies advance their material interests, because elections bring certain groups to power and exclude others, or because voting rights are thought to defuse popular unrest. All these motives were operative in the prewar Japanese Diet. The dominant parties primarily advanced the fortunes of landlords and businessmen, many of whom had no qualms about limiting the democratic input of tenant farmers or trade unions or passing a Peace Preservation Law that severely punished propaganda against private property. Their motives thus furthered policies that might not be expected from people cherishing democratic procedures as ends in themselves. Nonetheless, the experience of Japan and other countries demonstrates that media controls in democracies are not always due to a dearth of sincerity or understanding. There are many other reasons why elected officials have consented to controls over public expression, and not all are inconsistent with a basic commitment to democratic values.

Many upholding media autonomy as part of the democratic ideal would compromise it to safeguard a more or less democratic regime in adverse social-historical conditions. Some examples:

1. Access to the mass media for revolutionary groups may be seen as threatening democratic institutions. In a period when democracy was under fire both from leftists aroused by the Bolshevik Revolution and from rightists stimulated by fascism, this was a perception shared by many in Western Europe and Japan. Japanese press censorship was harsh toward revolutionary attacks on the political system, but quite mild toward non-revolutionary union propaganda, showing that media controls were meant to defend not simply business interests but also political institutions.

2. Public criticism of non-democratic state institutions may be viewed as imperiling a democratic regime. The emergence of party governments in imperial Japan was highly contingent upon their acceptance of the Meiji constitution and the institutions it established. It may seem blatantly anti-democratic to jail someone for condemning a monarchy or the military, but if their repudiation might generate a national crisis

jeopardizing democracy altogether, where does the true democrat stand on such an issue?

3. Media autonomy may be thought to undermine a stable democracy in the absence of favorable social conditions such as a high general level of education or standard of living. The uneducated and those with little material stake in society may be seen as easy prey for a demogoguery leading to incompetent governments and ultimately discrediting democratic institutions. Many Diet representatives therefore advocated "gradualism" in the incorporation of new social groups into political life,[25] and this thinking influenced media controls, swaying perceptions of censorship, the bond money requirement for journals, and the limits on partisan debate over radio.

Beyond the compromises imposed by historical conditions, many who cherish democracy may prize other social goods, for example, propagation of a religion or certain marital and sexual practices, which they would have the mass media respect despite the breach of democratic principles. Rousseau, a pioneer of democratic theory, strongly advocated censorship to protect those religious and social mores engendering compassion among fellow citizens.[26] Joseph Schumpeter wrote: "Communities which most of us would readily recognize as democracies have burned heretics at the stake—the republic of Geneva did in Calvin's time—or otherwise persecuted them in a manner repulsive to our moral standards—colonial Massachusetts may serve as an example."[27] Prewar Japanese democrats were not so intolerant or brutal, but they did employ censors to prevent the dissemination of certain opinions on religion, the family, hard work, and sex. As in most democratic countries, the law also punished libel, which brings media autonomy into conflict with the values of privacy and freedom from defamation.

Another reason democrats have endorsed controls over the media is to prevent a small social minority from dominating mass communications, as would sometimes happen under free market conditions. This motive has been especially noticeable in countries where foreigners have managed media industries, but it was reflected in Japan in the concern that radio might fall into the hands of big business. The argument is that a medium with nearly indiscriminate access to the public ought to serve

25. Najita, *Hara Kei*, pp. 22–23.
26. Jean-Jacques Rousseau, *Letter to D'Alembert* and *The Social Contract*, book IV, chaps. VII–VIII.
27. Joseph A. Schumpeter, *Capitalism, Socialism, and Democracy*, pp. 240–41.

the broad interests of that public and that in certain circumstances this is better accomplished by state regulation than by the dominance of a few large private firms.

Beyond the foregoing objectives, elected governments may construe "the public interest" in many other ways to justify media controls. In prewar Japan, the public interests associated with the mass media encompassed crime deterrence, rapid expansion of access to the media (a very democratic goal), practical education, cultural enlightenment, depoliticization, and emergency communications. Should it be protested that the state is itself a partial interest prone to abuse its media powers, the statesman might reply that as the people's elected representative it is his right and duty to act for the public good as he sees it.

In sum, even a committed and knowledgeable democrat may advocate media controls to deal with adverse historical circumstances, to protect other social goods, to prevent a private despotism over the media, or to promote "the public interest" in other ways. Neither the attitudes nor the policies of Japan's elected officials have been unusual in democratic systems; they cannot be passed off merely as products of an immature democratic regime. A recent survey of European democracies showed that 40 percent of bureaucrats and 27 percent of parliamentarians agreed that "The freedom of political propaganda is not an absolute freedom, and the state should carefully regulate its use."[28] Furthermore, such attitudes may well be prevalent among the electorate and media personnel themselves. In Japan, even the liberal press bill drafted by journalists in 1924 did not demand an end to censorship, but only clearer standards and softer punishments. If the public supports media controls, it could easily be argued that its representatives have a democratic duty to follow the popular will.

The Japanese experience demonstrates why for theoretical and empirical precision it is necessary to distinguish between democracy and the concept of liberalism understood in its classical sense. Democracy requires popular election of the top state elite. Liberalism requires that state power be kept within certain bounds. Too often it is assumed that a rather pristine liberalism necessarily accompanies democratic politics,

28. Aberbach, Putnam, and Rockman, *Bureaucrats and Politicians*, p. 177. Polled were 254 senior bureaucrats and 277 parliamentarians from Britain, West Germany, and Italy. The high percentage of bureaucrats concurring with the proposition resulted primarily from the Italian sample—57 percent of Italian bureaucrats agreed or agreed with reservations, while only 33 percent of the German bureaucrats and 22 percent of the British did so. See Robert D. Putnam, "The Political Attitudes of Senior Civil Servants in Britain, Germany, and Italy," p. 107.

and consequently the two values are merged in terms such as *pluralism* or *liberal democracy* (for which there is ordinarily no opposite of *illiberal democracy*). This assumption renders the media policies of many democratic regimes (and, for that matter, their economic and education policies) incomprehensible. It makes it impossible to explain in general conceptual terms the simultaneous support for universal male suffrage and the Peace Preservation Law in Japan, or why there are more privately owned and managed broadcasting networks in Latin America, despite its spotty democratic record, than in Western Europe today.[29] Elected governments have not always embraced a consistently liberal outlook toward the mass media, and many have reconciled controls over political expression with democratic values without any hypocrisy. Conversely, many political actors supportive of liberal policies have not been democrats; this was true of some constitutional monarchists in nineteenth-century Europe and Japan, and, more recently, it applies to some backers of military regimes in Latin America.

As was noted in chapter 1, there is a minoritarian view among democratic theorists that distinguishes clearly between democracy and liberalism. Though this school's origins can be traced to the work of de Tocqueville and Rousseau,[30] some of its most forthright adherents came to the fore during the interwar period, when state control over society under democratic regimes reached unprecedented levels. For example, José Ortega y Gasset argued:

> Liberalism and democracy are confused in our heads, and frequently when we want the one, we shout for the other. . . .

29. In Latin America, virtually every country except Cuba, Nicaragua, and Peru (which has had 25 percent state ownership since the early 1970s) has radio stations under completely civil ownership.

30. Rousseau posited that the expanding power of the permanent body of officials meant the inevitable demise of every republic and even refused to grant legislative powers to the state in consequence. De Tocqueville wrote:

> The Americans hold that in every state the supreme power ought to emanate from the people; but when once that power is constituted, they can conceive, as it were, no limits to it, and they are ready to admit that it has the right to do whatever it pleases. They have not the slightest notion of peculiar privileges granted to cities, families, or persons. . . . These ideas take root and spread in proportion as social conditions become more equal and men more alike. They are produced by equality, and in turn they hasten the progress of equality. . . . The unity, the ubiquity, the omnipotence of the supreme power, and the uniformity of its rules constitute the principal characteristics of all the political systems that have been put forward in our age. . . . Our contemporaries are therefore much less divided than is commonly supposed: they are constantly disputing as to the hands in which supremacy is to be vested, but they readily agree upon the duties and the rights of that supremacy. (*Democracy in America*, 2: 307–8)

>Liberalism and democracy happen to be two things which begin by hav-
ing nothing to do with each other, and end by having, so far as tendencies are
concerned, meanings that are mutually antagonistic. Democracy and liberalism are two answers to two completely different questions.

>Democracy answers this question—"who ought to exercise the public
power?" The answer it gives is—the exercise of public power belongs to the
citizens as a body. . . .

>Liberalism, on the other hand, answers this other question—"regardless
of who exercises the public power, what should its limits be?" The answer it
gives is—"whether the public power is exercised by an autocrat or by the
people, it cannot be absolute; the individual has rights which are over and
above any interference by the state."[31]

Viewing European democracies from the grim perspective of 1938, Karl
Loewenstein wrote:

>Liberal democracy, style 1900, slowly gives way to "disciplined" or even
"authoritarian" democracy of the postwar depression pattern. Critics of
such trends may contend that the cure for which it is intended to serve, may
easily become a disease which ultimately will destroy what is essential in
democratic values. Such objectors are evidently under the delusion that democracy is a stationary and unchangeable form of government. . . . legislation against political extremism, with its attendant inroads into liberal constitutionalism, is only one aspect among many others of the fundamental transformation to which constitutional government has to submit in our time.
State sovereignty—that is, the full display of the coercive powers of the
state—is resurrected while political pluralism is in retreat. Even in democracies, the Commonwealth may again become the Leviathan.[32]

Extreme statements of the problem perhaps, but they are rooted in
evidence similar to that uncovered in interwar Japan.

Democracy, if defined as a set of procedures for choosing the state
elite, demands meaningful electoral choice, and this makes some autonomy for at least one mass medium imperative in any large democratic
polity; without it, no genuine formulation of political preference would
be possible, and the thesis of political democracy would be ruled out by
definition. However, democrats have differed sharply over just what
minimum degree of autonomy for the mass media remains compatible
with democratic politics. Although support for democracy cannot be
reconciled with the most radically statist media policies, democrats have
nonetheless stood at many locations along the liberal-statist spectrum.
The mere presence of democratic institutions does not disclose very

---

31. José Ortega y Gasset, *Invertebrate Spain*, p. 125.
32. Loewenstein, "Legislative Control II," p. 774.

much about the level of state control. Japanese media policy in the 1918–1932 period underscores the need to treat the relationship between democracy and liberalism as an open question, if for no other objective than accurate empirical description. There may be other instances where men of lukewarm democratic affinities like the Meiji founders have proven to be more liberal than their fellow countrymen who came to power by the democratic method.

PART II

Administrative Revolution under Military-Bureaucratic Rule, 1937–1945

Transition to Military Rule, 1932–1937

The 1932–1937 period was one of political stalemate between the parties and the military, with the *Genrō* Saionji maneuvering between them in an effort to sustain civilian governments and a peaceful foreign policy. The political deadlock generally frustrated major innovations in media policy. Nonetheless, some significant changes in media regulations did occur: the Diet initiated several new control measures, the political center and right became prominent targets of censorship, and a monopolistic state news agency was established. Most important, the military and bureaucracy organized a number of interagency cabinet bodies whose mobilization plans came to guide state policy once the first Konoe cabinet had broken through the political impasse in mid-1937. The evolution of these committees from informal discussion groups to dominant policymaking organs provides a key to Japan's subsequent political development.

PARTY DECLINE AND MILITARY ASCENDANCY

The two most familiar methods of changing regimes are forceful overthrow and negotiated agreement. The onset of party rule in 1918 had definite characteristics of the latter in the form of understandings between *Genrō* Yamagata Aritomo and party leader Hara Kei. In the 1930s, however, neither method was employed. There was instead an incremental shift from party dominance toward military-bureaucratic rule. The result was just as surely a new regime configuration, but there was no one moment akin to Hara's appointment constituting *the* point of transition. To differentiate this process from a clear-cut take-over or concession of power, it might be called, borrowing a phrase from Graham Sumner, a "crescive" regime change, that is, one accomplished by piecemeal alterations, none of which signaled a definitive break.

In other respects this regime change paralleled the transition from oligarchic to party rule in the period 1906–1918. At that time the parties had steadily increased their share of ministerial portfolios; now it was they who lost cabinet seats to bureaucrats and generals. Earlier the parties had cracked the bureaucracy's "transcendental" cocoon by linking promotions to cooperation; now party influence was uprooted and the bureaucracy became even more a power unto itself. Mass political activity was not critical to either regime change. The parties' demise was not precipitated by rejection at the polls; the two major parties won 70 to 80 percent of the popular vote and lower house seats in the 1936 and 1937 elections, despite losing control over electoral law enforcement.[1] Both rising elites, however, did call their supporters into the streets on occasion: for example, when the parties incited popular unrest in 1913, and when the military mobilized reservists during the Minobe crisis in 1935. Though there was no systematic resort to violence in either case, both elites also made political capital of violent events perpetrated by others, such as the 1918 rice riots and the 1936 mutiny of junior officers. Violent outbreaks were exploited to accelerate changes that had been some time in the making. The *Genrō* struggled against both regime transformations, but without ultimate success.

As a background to media policy, it is useful to divide the 1932–1937 standoff into two phases: whereas conflict between the parties and military simmered just beneath the surface during the first, it erupted into open confrontation in the second. Phase one covers the cabinets of non-party Prime Ministers Saitō Makoto (1932–1934) and Okada Keisuke (1934–1936). After the assassination of the last party Prime Minister in

---

1. In the election of 20 February 1936, the Minseitō won 39.9 percent of the vote, and 43.9 percent of the seats in the lower house, and the Seiyūkai won 37.6 percent of the vote, and 36.6 percent of the seats. In the election of 30 April 1937, the Minseitō won 36.0 percent of the vote and 38.4 percent of the seats in the lower house, and the Seiyūkai won 35.1 percent of the vote and 37.5 percent of the seats. For the precise results, see *Nihon Kindaishi Jiten*, p. 769. On popular movements in the late 1930s, see Ishida Takeshi, " 'Fashizumu-ki' Nihon ni Okeru 'Kokumin Undō' no Soshiki to Ideorogī."

May 1932, Elder Statesman Saionji nominated these "national unity cabinets," hoping to stabilize domestic politics long enough to cool military ambitions. The label "national unity cabinet" had been used during the wars of 1895 and 1905, and its recurrence reflected the atmosphere of crisis after the Manchurian Incident and assassinations of the early 1930s. As retired military men without party affiliation, neither Saitō nor Okada had a strong political base, so they could not fulfill the *Genrō*'s mandate through positive measures. Their appointment was, rather, a conservative holding action until a new party option became available, perhaps after a well-timed election. In addition to military opposition, Saionji's desire for peace dissuaded him from a quick return to party government; the Seiyūkai, which held a sizable lower-house majority from 1932 to 1936, was strongly pro-imperialist.

The appointment of these weak premiers did stalemate the policy-making process, and few formal initiatives in media policy were even proposed in phase one, but Saionji's strategy failed to stymie either party decline or military aspirations. There were five party ministers in both the Saitō and Okada cabinets, but in the latter the parties lost the key Home and Finance Ministries, and Seiyūkai ministers were expelled from their party for participating.[2] The Saitō cabinet further eliminated the power of party ministers over the civil service by taking measures to insure bureaucrats and police officials against removal for political reasons.[3] The bountiful patronage dispensed by prefectural governors and other officials thus no longer served to cement ties between Diet men and their constituencies.[4] The end of party dependency also engendered unaffiliated cliques of "new bureaucrats" (*shin kanryō*), who developed their own policy orientations. Three became ministers in the Okada cabinet,[5] and some supplanted party connections with close links to military policy planners. Thus Saitō's reform had departified the bureaucracy but not depoliticized it.

The parties' decline was abetted by their inability to agree on a common strategy. Whereas some Seiyūkai leaders insisted on restoring

2. Itō Takashi, " 'Kyokoku Itchi' Naikaku Ki no Seikai Saihensei Mondai 1," p. 59. Itō documents the fact that the loss of influential ministries was a heavy blow to the parties.

3. See Gordon Mark Berger, *Parties Out of Power in Japan: 1931–1941*, pp. 64–65, for details.

4. Ibid., pp. 69–71.

5. Spaulding, "Bureaucracy," pp. 65–66. The three were Home Minister Gotō Fumio, Finance Minister Fujii Masanobu, and Foreign Minister Hirota Kōki, who succeeded Okada as Prime Minister; Spaulding notes that Hirota's placement in this category has been debated.

majority party government, many Minseitō leaders favored a national unity cabinet for affording their party a rebuilding period. Other members of both parties worked for a coalition to restore democracy, as had been arranged in 1924.[6] There was never a resolution of these contrasting approaches.

As party influence waned, military assertiveness grew. In unprecedented fashion, the Army Ministry spoke out on politics unilaterally and publicly in 1934 in a famous pamphlet, *The True Meaning of National Defense and a Proposal for Its Strengthening*. Among other things, the pamphlet declared the creation of a state ministry of propaganda (*sendenshō*) or information bureau (*jōhōkyoku*) to be a pressing matter.[7] In late 1934 the army won formal administrative control over Manchurian affairs, allowing it to experiment with control designs that it would later seek to implement in Japan. The prominent roles of the army and navy in the persecution of democratic scholar Minobe Tatsukichi in 1935 will be described below. In sum, though phase-one cabinets blocked sharp political turnabouts, trends toward party enervation and military activism were equally evident.

An abortive coup d'état by young army officers on 26 February 1936 (the 2/26 Incident) inaugurated phase two of national unity cabinets, comprising the governments of ex-bureaucrat Hirota Kōki (March 1936–January 1937) and retired General Hayashi Senjūrō (February–May 1937). Whereas Saitō and Okada had been genuine conservatives, the Hirota and Hayashi cabinets plainly skewed "national unity" toward greater military power within the state. Only four party ministers served under Hirota—none, thanks to military pressure, in the weightiest ministries—while Hayashi offered portfolios to just three party men, conditional upon their resignation from party rolls. Only one minor-party representative accepted.

Though the chief coup conspirators were executed and theirs was to be the last in a series of violent rightist rebellions plotted in the 1930s, senior military officers nonetheless increased their political activity soon afterwards. In May 1936, the rule that only active-duty officers could become military ministers was reinstated, allegedly to avert the rehabilitation of Imperial Way generals purged for supposed sympathy with the mutineers. Thus if the army or navy refused to offer a minister, no cabinet could be formed; if either withdrew its minister, the existing

6. Berger, *Parties*, pp. 45–58.
7. Rikugunshō [Army Ministry], *Kokubō no Hongi to Sono Kyōka no Teishō*, pp. 251–69.

cabinet fell. The services had not enjoyed this power since 1913, and the army soon used it with impunity.

Army Minister Terauchi resigned to topple the Hirota cabinet in January 1937, the first time a military minister had so undermined a government since 1912. When Saionji then sought to replace Hirota with retired General Ugaki Kazushige, a moderate in the circumstances, the army's ruling triumvirate (the Army Minister, Chief of the General Staff, and Inspector General of Military Education) sabotaged the appointment by refusing a minister.[8] The army's patience with moderate governments was clearly running out. This typifies the way the military services, despite bitter factionalism within, were often able to act as cohesive institutions when dealing with other political elites. In Ugaki's place came ex-General Hayashi, a man more to the military's liking. As Army Minister, Hayashi had been responsible for the 1934 ministerial pamphlet, which repudiated freedom, individualism, and internationalism; it began, "Battle is the father of creativity and the mother of culture."[9] By February 1937, then, one could publicly damn freedom and become Prime Minister of Japan.

Hayashi's elevation signified greater influence for officers loosely identified as the Control Faction.[10] For several years adherents of this tendency had been pressing to strengthen military capabilities through greater state control over society. Their most audacious act had been to offer the Hirota cabinet a radical plan for state reorganization in November 1936. Endorsed by both the army and the navy, its gist was to centralize decision-making in new cabinet organs staffed by military and bureaucratic officials. It proposed that the Cabinet Information Committee, a rather feeble interagency body assembled in July 1936, be fortified and added to the new policymaking complex.[11] This is exactly what would happen four years later, but such designs were premature in 1936.

8. Itō Takashi, *Jū-go-Nen Sensō*, pp. 171–73.
9. Whereas Ugaki had been associated with troop reductions in 1925, Hayashi had illegally dispatched units from Korea to assist the Kwantung Army during the Manchurian Incident: Crowley, *Japan's Quest for Autonomy*, pp. 125–26.
10. The Imperial Way Faction was a rather well-defined group of officers of a particular regional background whose rhetoric tended to emphasize ideological ardor. There was a contrary clique (the *Seigun Ha*) centered on officers from the old Chōshū province, who had dominated the army since the Meiji Restoration. However, the so-called Control Faction was not an organized group; the name refers generally to those officers opposed to regional factionalism and deeply involved in mobilization planning for total war. See ibid., pp. 246–49, 276–79, and also Crowley, "Japanese Army Factionalism in the Early 1930's."
11. For a thorough treatment of this proposal and the reactions to it, consult Ide Yoshinori, *Nihon Kanryōsei to Gyōsei Bunka*, pp. 100–112.

Diet members, spurred by the negative popular reaction to the attempted coup, exhibited a new boldness after the 2/26 Incident. When Army Minister Terauchi appeared for lower-house interpellation, he was severely criticized for the military's forays into politics,[12] and this criticism prompted his resignation shortly thereafter. The succeeding Hayashi government was no more successful at pushing the military's program through the Diet. On 28 May 1937, one month after elections had confirmed their supremacy in the lower house, the Seiyūkai and Minseitō jointly resolved that the government should resign, and Hayashi stepped down three days later.

Thus there prevailed a political standoff throughout the period from May 1932 to May 1937. Conservative cabinets frustrated military ambitions in phase one, whereas an intransigent Diet performed the same function in phase two. Nonetheless, the gradual shift toward a new balance of power among political elites had important implications for media policy. Incremental changes in media politics paralleled the piecemeal steps toward party defensiveness and greater military influence and, more important, the evolving realignment of political elites set the stage for the radical innovations in media policy that were to follow.

THE GROWING STATISM
OF PARTY POLITICIANS

Though the most radical control designs emanated from the military and were opposed in the Diet, the alignment of forces over whether the military or the parties should govern was not identical to an alignment for and against statist policies (or imperialism). As was indicated in part 1, regime and policy preferences are often logically and factually distinct. Many party politicians and journalists joined the military in endorsing stiffer media controls despite their opposition to military government. In later years, some military elements (especially in the navy) would also be found on the liberal side of control questions. In this period, the contribution of the Diet and other civilian groups to the tightening of controls over expression was critical to the development of media policy. The erosion of liberal principles was evident in party

12. One highlight was an exchange between Terauchi and Representative Hamada Kumitarō. Terauchi took Hamada's condemnation of military intervention in politics as an insult to the armed forces and demanded an apology. The congressman replied that he would commit ritual suicide if the Diet judged his remarks to be insulting, but that the minister should disembowel himself if it did not. Terauchi did not insist upon a vote.

platforms and Diet legislation, as well as in positions taken during the Minobe crisis of 1935, which shifted the universe of political discourse sharply to the right.

Despite their rejection of comprehensive military control programs, the increasingly statist attitudes of elected officials were very apparent. In March 1933, the Seiyūkai and Minseitō jointly sponsored a resolution urging the government to suppress radical ideas; it passed by a margin of 218 to 34.[13] The cabinet responded by organizing an elite interministerial Discussion Committee for Countermeasures on Thought one month later. In May 1933, Education Minister Hatoyama Ichirō, a Seiyūkai party leader, set a dangerous precedent by dismissing Professor Takigawa Yukitoki of Kyoto Imperial University. Takigawa, a political centrist, had been fingered as a "red" by two Diet members, one a Seiyūkai representative.[14] At issue were a lecture on Tolstoy and a text on criminal law so respectable that passages had been broadcast on NHK the year before; no matter, in 1933 the book was banned from circulation. The entire law faculty resigned to protest Takigawa's dismissal, but Hatoyama, an ardent advocate of party government, stood firm, and most of the professors eventually returned to work.[15]

In August 1933 the Minseitō announced its "Outline of Countermeasures for Thought," and the Seiyūkai released its own program under the same title in December, calling for "total mobilization" of women to restore domestic morals and tougher university controls to curb radicalism. In March 1934 the Diet passed two proposals of the Discussion Committee for Countermeasures on Thought, one to subject phonograph records to the Publication Law, and the other to stiffen that law's punishments for violations of public order.[16] In May 1936 the Diet

13. *Masu Media Tōsei*, 1: li.

14. These were Miyazawa Hiroshi of the House of Representatives and Baron Kikuchi Takeo of the House of Peers (also to be involved in the Minobe crisis). See Kuroda Hidetoshi, *Shōwa Genron Shi e no Shōgen*, p. 242.

15. See ibid., pp. 241–54, for a concise account of the incident. For more details on official views of the matter and critical press reactions, see *Shisō Tōsei*, documents 26–34. In the end, six resignations were accepted, and two other professors declined to return; the rest capitulated and resumed their duties. Hatoyama, however, was hardly a radical statist. During the Pacific War he was watched by the military as a suspected "freedomist" for his efforts to restore civilian leadership. In 1954, he became Prime Minister of Japan. That this man could be a principal in the Takigawa affair shows how far the political pendulum had swung toward statist values.

16. In lower-house committee, a moderate labor-party representative, Matsutani Yojirō, moved that the public-order penalties be dropped:

We have arrived at a situation in which we must respect the freedom of expression. . . . However, no matter, judging from the various documents and legal bills presented recently by the government, its policy is gradually running contrary to this tendency.

passed another of the Discussion Committee's proposals, to allow police surveillance of released thought criminals, and it approved a new law aimed at illegal rightist propaganda. The latter imposed three years in prison for undermining military discipline, agitating the business world, or confusing the public mind by means of written materials in cases where censor's copies had not been submitted or the materials lacked the publisher's name.[17] Extreme rightists normally eluded the Peace Preservation Law because they accepted the Emperor system, and the Army Minister defended the new bill as necessary to restore military discipline after the abortive coup.[18]

This chronology, though quite incomplete, is indicative of the general trend. The most transparent motive was to silence radical rightist criticism of the parties themselves in a period of violent political crisis. Many party men found themselves in an insoluble dilemma. They realized that media controls victimized some of their own supporters, but they also judged tougher controls necessary to contain the menacing propaganda of the civil right. This dilemma was very visible in the stormy Diet session that followed the 2/26 Incident. Lower house representatives accused the Justice Ministry of harboring "fascist" bureaucrats,[19] they scored the military as a source of seditious literature,[20] and, to much applause, they vilified restraints on free expression (neglecting to note that some restraints they now censured, such as pre-publication warnings, had been introduced under party governments).[21] But when the votes were counted, the law to control illegally circulated radical materials had passed with few modifications.[22] Legislators, despite their

---

The control of expression is becoming extremely severe. . . . Above all, these words "disturbing public order" are exceedingly vague and depending upon the government's discretion they can be interpreted however one wishes. . . . I must say that considering all of our people there is no law more dangerous than this one.

No one seconded Matsutani's amendment: *Masu Media Tōsei,* vol. 1, document 55, p. 354.

17. The bill's formal title was Law for Emergency Control of Illegal Subversive Written Materials (*Fuon Bunshō Rinji Torishimari Hō*). If any person involved in producing a document had his correct name and address on it, it would not be treated under this law: see Naimushō Keihōkyoku, *Shuppan Keisatsu Hō,* no. 91, p. 4.

18. *Masu Media Tōsei,* vol. 1, document 75, p. 415.

19. Ibid., p. 419.

20. Ibid., document 77, p. 625.

21. See ibid., document 75, p. 416.

22. The original government draft had called for up to three years' imprisonment for anyone spreading rumors bound to disturb public order by means other than publications, if the person did so with the intentions listed in the law. This provision was scrapped by the Diet; it was not forgotten, however. The Law for Emergency Control of Speech,

eulogies to free expression, could not bring themselves to roll back press controls and open up public debate. Instead, they bolstered bureaucratic powers once again to deal with the more fearful prospect of a rightist revolution. Thus the radical junior officers, while incapable of effecting a revolution, nonetheless succeeded in paralyzing the liberal opposition. There were other Diet members, however, especially numerous in the Seiyūkai, who were anxious to restore party fortunes not by defeating the right but by adopting its causes. Both the atmosphere of intimidation and this positive shift to the right were clearly visible during the Minobe crisis.

The campaign against legal scholar Minobe Tatsukuchi in 1935 was the most important event in media politics in this period. The immediate issue was Minobe's Emperor-as-organ theory, which held that the state was sovereign and the Emperor exercised his authority as the state's highest constitutional organ. The alternate view was that sovereignty resided in the Emperor himself.[23] Minobe's theory favored parliamentary government because it also declared the Diet to be a direct organ of sovereign state power, whereas the military and other state institutions were labeled indirect organs, their functions delegated from the Emperor as direct organ. In practice, the Emperor's role was largely a formal one hemmed in by constitutional restraints, and Minobe's theory was accepted by most legal scholars and by the Emperor himself.[24]

There was, however, far more at stake in 1935 than an esoteric theory that most of Minobe's attackers had never read. Minobe became a symbol of the *Zeitgeist* of *jiyūshugi* (literally, "freedomism"), a concept referring to all values associated with the prior democratic regime. As a professor emeritus of Tokyo Imperial University, advisor to several

---

Publications, Assemblies, and Associations (*Genron, Shuppan, Shūkai, Kessha Nado Rinji Torishimari Hō*), which passed the Diet in December 1941, provided up to two years in prison for spreading lies or rumors about the "situation." It is reprinted in ibid., vol. 2, document 76, pp. 403–7.

23. Miller, *Minobe Tatsukichi*, pp. 60–67.

24. According to the Ministry of Education, eighteen of the top thirty scholars in public law accepted the organ theory in early 1935: ibid., p. 200. The diary of General Honjō Shigeru, the Emperor's Chief Aide-de-Camp, is filled with the monarch's admonitions on Minobe's behalf. For example, this is Honjō's recollection of the Emperor's conversation on 9 March 1935: "As for me, the military's concern is exceedingly troublesome . . . . It goes without saying that the words of article four of the constitution that the Emperor is the ruler of the state are the organ theory. The opinion that the organ theory stains the sanctity of the imperial house sounds plausible at first, but in reality it is the very debate about this sort of thing that desecrates the sanctity of the imperial house": quoted in Kuroda, *Shōwa Genron Shi*, p. 266. See also David Anson Titus, *Palace and Politics in Prewar Japan*, p. 163.

governments, and member of the House of Peers, Minobe was a prominent and thoroughly respectable spokesman for a way of thinking dominant in Japanese politics for over a decade. He was also one of the
military's most defiant critics. In the November 1934 *Chūō Kōron,* he
castigated the Army Ministry's controversial pamphlet:

> my first impression is that a tendency toward pro-war, militaristic thought
> comes out strikingly throughout the whole thing.
>   It starts at the very beginning with a phrase eulogizing war: "Battle is the
> father of creativity and the mother of culture." We think that "creativity"
> and "culture" can only arise from great individual genius and free research,
> which are mainly the products of peace, and that war to the contrary de-
> stroys these things. . . . The rapid progress of our country that has been a
> wonder of the world since the Meiji Restoration is mainly a result of this
> individualism and freedom. How could one possibly bring about this kind of
> rapid cultural development by binding the people into a slave-like, servile
> existence? Individual freedom above all is the real father of creativity and
> mother of culture.[25]

This was as far as public rebukes of the military were permitted to go in
1934.[26] Every major political force was compelled to take a stand on
Minobe's case and, given his role as a political commentator and the
influence of his books, this meant taking a stand on press controls.

Minobe was first denounced in February 1935, not by the military
but in the Diet. In both houses, government ministers were asked why
his books were not banned.[27] These remonstrances in the legislature
were supported by the right-wing press and by petitions from reservist
branches and other rightist groups. Minobe was labeled a traitor and,
by some, even a communist.

Minobe defended his work in the Diet, and the government was initially unresponsive to the charges. Prime Minister Okada stated before
the House of Peers: "Reading through the whole of Dr. Minobe's work, I
do not believe there are mistakes regarding the ideal of the national
polity. . . . I am not a supporter of the Emperor-as-organ theory, but

    25. Minobe Tatsukichi, "Rikugunshō Happyō no Kokubō Ron o Yomu," pp. 126,
129.
    26. For a rundown of other critical responses to the army pamphlet, see Ishizeki
Keizō, "Kokubō Kokka Ron to Kokutai Meichō," pp. 52–59.
    27. The two Diet interpellators were reservist generals belonging to a patriotic group
called the Meirinkai (The Illustrious Virtue Society). The upper house member, Baron
Kikuchi Takeo, was also an associate of Hiranuma Kiichirō in the latter's National
Foundation Society. According to Kikuchi, the brief against Minobe had been partly
prepared by Minoda Muneki of the Genri Nihonsha (the Principles of Japan Company),
to which Minobe's lower house attacker, Etō Genkurō, also belonged. See Kuroda, *Shōwa
Genron Shi,* p. 257.

when it comes to an academic theory, rather than our speaking out, I do not think there is any course but to entrust the matter to scholars."[28] This statement echoed the general principle of censorship not to intervene in purely academic matters (a principle that was hardly sacrosanct, of course). In the lower house, the Home, Education, and Justice Ministers voiced similar sentiments, and the Prime Minister added that his government did not plan to ban Minobe's books.[29] When Army Minister Hayashi appeared before the Diet in March, however, he took a different line. He denied that the organ theory had had pernicious effects on the army, but he agreed that it had transcended academic debate and become a matter of general concern.[30] This is what Minobe's parliamentary accusers had been insisting,[31] and Hayashi thus undermined the cabinet's plan to ignore the issue as an academic affair. Meanwhile, Representative Etō Genkurō stoked the flames by charging Minobe with lèse-majesté in court, and the clamor in civil society intensified.

It was a combination of party and military elements that eventually secured Minobe's demise. None of these elites seriously entertained the idea of personal rule by the Emperor; they merely used the ideological question as a convenient vehicle for realizing political ambitions. The Seiyūkai sought to exploit the affair to topple the Okada cabinet, accusing it of harboring a treasonous doctrine. If Okada fell, the practice of appointing majority party Prime Ministers might be reinstated, resulting in a Seiyūkai cabinet.[32] In other words, the Seiyūkai would have Minobe's head in order to revitalize democracy! This ploy did not cause the party any ideological disquiet. Its president, Suzuki Kisaburō, belonged to two prominent right-wing societies.[33] It was hardly farsighted, however, to further the party's fortunes at the expense of a leading democratic theorist and thereby to endanger the position of many state officials opposed to militarism. On 23 March, both the Minseitō and the Seiyūkai sustained a motion for clarification of the national polity.

28. Quoted in [Nihon Teikoku Shihōshō], *Iwayuru "Tennō Kikan Setsu" o Keiki to Suru Kokutai Meichō Undō*, pp. 101–2. This was a secret document prepared by the Justice Ministry for its officials in the late 1930s.
29. Ibid., p. 250; Miller, *Minobe Tatsukichi*, pp. 220, 336 n. 43.
30. Miller, *Minobe Tatsukichi*, p. 223.
31. E.g., in the House of Peers' Foreign Affairs Committee (*Gaikō Iinkai*) on 4 March, several days before Hayashi's interpellation, Viscount Mimurodo Yukimitsu argued that the theory had outgrown the status of an academic matter: see Kuroda, *Shōwa Genron Shi*, p. 261.
32. Ishizeki, "Kokubō Kokka Ron," p. 70.
33. The two right-wing organizations were the Emperor Jinmu Society and the National Foundation Society: Miller, *Minobe Tatsukichi*, p. 224.

This had become the slogan of rightists out to expunge the organ theory.

Army Minister Hayashi was trying to outmaneuver the army's Imperial Way Faction, which had been campaigning hard for ideological purity. By supporting the "clarification" campaign, Hayashi protected himself from charges of moral laxity while removing Imperial Way officers from key posts.[34] The Navy Minister joined Hayashi in pressing the cabinet for stern measures. Both were anxious to end the Minobe affair, since it served as a rallying point for more radical military cliques, but they did not mind sacrificing Minobe along the way. No military faction was interested in sparing a man who had minimized the right of supreme command, championed the London naval agreement, lambasted the army's ideological exhortations, and symbolized values impeding the development of a national defense state run by military and bureaucratic elites.

Minobe did have official allies determined to keep him out of prison. Oddly enough, most were civilian officials in the executive branch rather than Diet men. Among them were the Prime Minister, the Justice Minister, and the Emperor himself, all anxious to protect the many high officials with a personal stake in the outcome; Minobe's downfall would leave them vulnerable as subscribers to the same political tendency. These included the Privy Council President, the Cabinet Legislative Bureau Chief, and the Lord Privy Seal. Together with Saionji Kinmochi, they were known as the "senior statesmen bloc" (jūshin burokku).

On 30 March 1935, the Army and Navy Ministers communicated their determination to eradicate the organ theory to the cabinet, which then mandated the Army, Navy, Home, and Education Ministers to suppress the theory.[35] On 9 April, the Home Ministry banned three of Minobe's books. The Diet had just adjourned, and rightist invective had cooled to honor a visit from the Emperor of Manchukuo. Cabinet members sympathetic to Minobe hoped to end the crisis during this lull by appeasing their opponents with halfway concessions. The action against Minobe's books was part of their response. Minobe was cleared of lèse-

---

34. Thus in April 1935 he sanctioned General Mazaki's desire to purge the army of the organ theory, and then in July eliminated Mazaki (an Imperial Way officer) as Inspector General of Military Education. Mazaki's memo condemning the organ theory is reprinted in [Nihon Teikoku Shihōshō], *Iwayuru "Tennō Kikan Setsu,"* pp. 150–51.

35. Ibid., p. 150; Miller, *Minobe Tatsukichi,* p. 228.

majesté, but when he denounced the banning of his books, this opportunity to terminate the controversy was lost.[36] His words to newsmen:

> I bow to the penalty arising from an application of the law. But *Kempō Seigi* is in its twelfth edition and *Kempō Satsuyō* is in its fifth. How is it that though both have been in publication many years it has now become necessary to take administrative action against them? If these works conflict with the law, then all the successive home ministers up to now are properly responsible for overlooking this fact. And, of course, if there are punishable aspects of my theory, then the successive university presidents and ministers of education who took no action all the long while that I lectured on the constitution as a university professor are likewise responsible. How has this come about?[37]

The answer was no secret, least of all to Minobe, who had criticized the abstractness of censorship guidelines as far back as 1926. Ambiguous statutes permitting arbitrary bureaucratic implementation and offering no means of appeal made everyone a potential violator. The same laws originally framed to deal with pornographers and revolutionaries now took their toll of conservatives.

In September 1935, to escape prosecution under the Publication Law, Minobe was forced to resign all public offices,[38] and he was thereby spared imprisonment—in a manner of speaking. By year's end he was barricaded in his house behind a police guard, long since abandoned by most friends, who refrained from contact out of fear for their lives.[39] Minobe was shot and wounded by an assassin entering under false pretenses in February 1936; thus the "bloodless 5/15 Incident," as his downfall was labeled, was not so bloodless after all. His withdrawal from public life was accompanied by formal cabinet declarations condemning the organ theory, a ban on thirty-seven other books of constitutional law, and the resignation of many top state officials associated with his cause.[40] This was an important event in the crescive regime

36. Minobe had also been accused under the Publication Law, and Justice Ministry officials met with him in early April hoping to elicit a recantation allowing them to suspend prosecution. Oddly enough, the one aspect of Minobe's work deemed a potential violation of the Publication Law was not the organ theory per se but his defense of the right to criticize imperial rescripts: Miller, *Minobe Tatsukichi*, p. 230.

37. Quoted in ibid., p. 231.

38. Ibid., p. 242.

39. See the remarks of his son quoted in Kuroda, *Shōwa Genron Shi*, p. 266.

40. Prime Minister Okada was compelled, mainly by the Army Minister, to make two official declarations to "clarify the national polity" in August and October 1935, denouncing the organ theory on both occasions. His diary is quoted to that effect in ibid., pp. 264–65. The thirty-seven legal texts are listed in [Nihon Teikoku Shihōshō], *Iwayuru "Tennō*

change, since it eliminated major obstacles to greater military influence within the state.

The Minobe affair was unique in its profound impact on subsequent expression in the mass media. All interpretations of the crisis, including those of the Home and Justice Ministries and the right wing, agreed that the issue was not so much Minobe's scholarship as the survival of the *jiyūshugi* perspective and its adherents.[41] For some three decades, mainstream journalists and scholars had been fairly tolerant of press controls because debate was allowed within the prevailing constitutional system. Until pre-publication warnings proliferated during 1928–1932, critical commentary short of revolutionary rhetoric had almost always been permitted. The ban on Minobe's books signaled that this era had ended where military sensitivities were concerned, and those sensitivities now extended all the way to constitutional law. If a man of Minobe's stature could be ruined before the eyes of the entire nation, no one was secure.[42]

How did the press respond to the Minobe crisis, which had such fateful implications for all critics of the state? Most big newspapers initially avoided the issue, partly to evade rightist vituperation and partly hoping that the uproar would die down. Diet members had also criticized Minobe in early 1934, but nothing had come of it, and there had never been such a controversy over scholarship before, so in early to mid February 1935 it was reasonable to assume that the issue might go away if it was ignored. According to the Home Ministry, when Minobe's books were maligned in the lower house on 7 February, only the *Yorozu Chōhō* even bothered to explain the organ theory, taking a noncommittal editorial stance.[43] The *Tōkyō Asahi* and *Tōkyō Nichi Nichi* overlooked the incident and were consequently rebuked in a rightist tabloid.[44] What the right needed most was publicity. When the campaign shifted to the House of Peers on 18 February, only the *Teito Nichi Nichi Shinbun* strongly backed Minobe. The Home Ministry again

---

Kikan Setsu," pp. 255–57. Among Minobe's official supporters, the Lord Privy Seal resigned pleading ill health in December 1935, the Cabinet Legislative Bureau Chief resigned in January 1936, the Privy Council President retired in March 1936, and Justice Minister Ohara departed when General Terauchi refused to serve as Army Minister with him in the Hirota cabinet: Miller, *Minobe Tatsukichi,* p. 252.

41. Naimushō Keihōkyoku, *Shuppan Keisatsu Gaikan,* 1935, p. 105; [Nihon Teikoku Shihōshō], *Iwayuru "Tennō Kikan Setsu,"* pp. 88–90; Ishizeki, "Kokubō Kokka Ron," p. 71.

42. On the unprecedented nature of the Minobe crisis, see Ishizeki, "Kokubō Kokka Ron," p. 82.

43. Naimushō Keihōkyoku, *Shuppan Keisatsu Gaikan,* 1935, p. 142.

44. Miller, *Minobe Tatsukichi,* p. 336 n. 41.

found mainstream newspapers taking an "extremely evasive attitude" after Minobe's Diet speech on 26 February and the accusation of lèse-majesté two days later.[45] Regular newspapers tilting to the right, however, were less bashful in condemning his ideas and demanding state sanctions.[46]

No major newspaper solidly supported Minobe as the smear campaign escalated during March. Even sympathetic comments did not extend to a defense of the organ theory. At this point, no one could have imagined the issue would deflate of its own accord. When Minobe's books were banned on 9 April, the *Jiji Shinpō*, *Tōkyō Asahi*, and *Teito Nichi Nichi* registered negative comments, but again most mainstream newspapers stood aloof, and in any case the time for resolute action had passed. Thereafter it was against the law to defend the organ theory in print.

As usual, leading magazines were more daring, but there were no forthright protests like those published when an edition of *Kaizō* was banned in 1925, a matter of far less significance. The *Chūō Kōron* of April 1935 carried an article by Morito Tatsuo, the victim of censorship in 1920, who mocked the accusations of treason against "a moderate constitutional theory that had become a matter of common sense" and noted the irony of "bourgeois" press controls designed to smash Marxism being turned against bourgeois writers.[47] Suzuki Anzō, a student defendant in the first Peace Preservation Law trial in 1926, penned a descriptive history of the organ theory debate in the April *Kaizō* and then, for the same month's *Shakai Hyōron* (Social Commentary), wrote the toughest protest on record. In the latter article Suzuki indirectly upheld the organ theory with references to a 1912 text asserting that the Diet had been intended to obstruct monarchical dictatorship, and he wrote that Minobe's work was doomed for impeding the control policies being advanced on many fronts, that is, for being a liberal doctrine.[48] That Minobe's theory of state sovereignty, which borrowed heavily from nineteenth-century German thought, could be suppressed for its liberalism makes it an excellent yardstick for measuring the statist values of his foes. *Shakai Hyōron* had just been founded by leftist intellectuals; it folded in 1936 when most of them were arrested under

45. Naimushō Keihōkyoku, *Shuppan Keisatsu Gaikan*, 1935, p. 142.
46. E.g., the *Ōsaka Jiji Shinpō* on 7 March, the *Kokumin Shinbun* on 16 March: see ibid., p. 143.
47. Quoted in Ishizeki, "Kokubō Kokka Ron," p. 72.
48. Ibid., pp. 73–74.

the Peace Preservation Law (the Komu Academy Incident). A comparison of Suzuki's sharp remarks in this offbeat journal with the neutral, descriptive character of his *Kaizō* article reveals how cautiously the Minobe affair was handled by a prestigious magazine usually critical of the state. The Home Ministry's survey of press coverage stressed that no legal scholar or critic ever wrote a straightforward defense of the organ theory, even before April when this was still legally permissible. By contrast, not a single rightist journal failed to treat the issue during March, April, and May.[49]

The instinct for self-preservation partly explains the puny response of Minobe's would-be defenders. Rightist groups held numerous rallies and roamed menacingly through the streets of Tokyo during the crisis. Police protection was provided to some of Minobe's threatened associates. According to Frank Miller, the Metropolitan Police warned of terrorism if Minobe were not prosecuted, and there were "riotous disturbances" before the offices of the *Tōkyō Asahi* and *Yomiuri* newspapers.[50] Scholar Kawai Eijirō, one of the few to speak out, described the atmosphere in the *Teikoku Daigaku Shinbun* (Imperial University Newspaper) on 15 April: "By means of threats of [*blank type*] not permitted by national law, the Doctor's mouth has been shut, and things have been brought to a situation where people are not allowed to breathe one word related to this unless they gamble their positions and their lives."[51] The intimidation was enhanced by the claims of many rightist thugs to have masters in high places, for given the presence of respectable as well as vulgar elements on the right, and the close ties between reservists and the military,[52] such claims were plausible.

The psychological impact of the Minobe crisis should not be underestimated. Minobe was a symbol of both liberal and democratic ideals, but only a few individuals had spoken up for either in his defense. Not one key political institution had resolutely defended the organ theory; most had been either mute or antagonistic. Though the timidity and betrayal of liberal and democratic forces are partly explained by physical intimidation, the fear of legal reprisals, factional rifts, and a shift to the right in some quarters, the absence of a single major group ready to offer public resistance remains perplexing. After 1935, Japan's *jiyūshugi* advo-

49. Naimushō Keihōkyoku, *Shuppan Keisatsu Gaikan*, 1935, pp. 158, 163–64, 105.
50. Miller, *Minobe Tatsukichi*, pp. 240, 229.
51. Quoted in Ishizeki, "Kokubō Kokka Ron," p. 75.
52. On the latter point, see Kuroda, *Shōwa Genron Shi*, p. 263, and Miller, *Minobe Tatsukichi*, p. 341 n. 100.

TABLE XI   ADMINISTRATIVE SANCTIONS IMPOSED UNDER THE MOTION
PICTURE FILM INSPECTION REGULATIONS, 1932–1937

	Total Films Inspected[a]	Bans[b]	Required to Reshoot[c]	Films Cut	Limited by Location	Withdrawn
1932	18,436			780	18	96
1933	14,984	13	23	633	25	36
1934	17,468	4	45	651	25	53
1935	21,075	10	41	456	27	51
1936	25,008	6	40	510	27	78
1937	41,560	5	21	395	63	40

Source: Naimushō Keihōkyoku, Firumu Ken'etsu Nenpō, 1933–1938.
[a]The figures include Japanese and imported films, films submitted for the first time, resubmissions, and prints of previously submitted films.
[b]The figures include films withdrawn from inspection because sponsors were informed they would be banned. These films are not counted in the "withdrawn" column, except in 1932, when the number withdrawn for this reason is unknown.
[c]These films were formally listed as having been withdrawn from inspection; they are not counted in the "withdrawn" column in the table except in 1932, when the number withdrawn for reshooting is unknown.

cates, most notably those in the press, were like a guard dog who had retreated backward at the first sign of an intruder; it would be all the more difficult for them to regroup and put up a fight further to the rear.

CENSORSHIP OF THE RIGHT

Administrative sanctions against Japanese films and periodicals generally decreased from 1932 to 1937, despite tougher censorship standards (see tables 11 and 12). Several factors explain the downturn in violations of public order. Aside from the 2/26 Incident, there were few shocking political events after 1933, and this meant fewer pre-publication warnings to newspapers and less provocation for illegal commentary.[53] The

53. The most politically sensitive warnings were related to communist arrests, military radicalism, and Manchurian affairs. Regarding the communists, two warnings in February 1933 and one in January 1934 banned all information on Peace Preservation Law arrests. The 1934 warning specifically forbade the reporting of casualties due to police brutality. Warnings related to the military again covered the radical plotting of junior officers, e.g., November 1934 instructions against reporting a coup planned by Military Academy (Shikan Gakkō) cadets. Warnings also shielded factional conflicts within the army, including General Nagata Tetsuzan's murder by a fellow officer in 1935. Warnings on Manchuria continued to cover up Japan's dominant role in Manchukuo. In December 1933, instructions forbade reporting Japanese involvement in Manchukuo's adoption of an emperor system. In March 1934, there were orders against covering anti-Japanese activities in the area. Most warnings on Manchuria dealt with Japan's penetration of the local economy: Naimushō Keihōkyoku, Shuppan Keisatsu Gaikan, 1933–1935.

TABLE XII   ADMINISTRATIVE CONTROLS ENFORCED AGAINST DOMESTIC PERIODICALS
SUBJECT TO THE NEWSPAPER LAW, 1932–1937

	Press Organs	Dailies	Bonded Organs	Total Banned Editions	Banned for Public-Order Violations	Post-Publication Warnings	Deletions	Procedural Suspensions	Pre-Publication Warnings Ins–Adm–Con[a]
1932	11,118	1,330	6,301	2,246	2,081	4,348	48	4	44–19–1
1933	11,860	1,389	6,676	1,732	1,531	3,379	219	19	44– 9–0
1934	11,915	1,432	7,003	1,185	589	2,242	249	5	45– 1–0
1935	12,101	1,441	7,180	925	653	3,775	171	1	33– 1–0
1936				981	796	3,470	117		
1937				595	498	5,498	94		

Sources: Naimushō Keihōkyoku, Shuppan Keisatsu Gaikan, 1932–1935; idem, Shuppan Keisatsu Hō, nos. 88–110.
Note: Japan was ruled by party Prime Ministers until 15 May 1932. The China Incident occurred on 7 July 1937.
[a]The abbreviations refer to "instructions," "admonitions," and "consultations."

patriotic reaction to the Manchurian Incident undoubtedly dampened political criticism as well; left-wing "tendency" films decreased in number and the press supported an aggressive China policy.[54] Most important was the collapse of the extreme left due to Peace Preservation Law arrests. Journals backing the Communist Party or the related Japan Proletarian Cultural League had all but disappeared by the end of 1934.[55]

Despite the decline in sanctions, however, censors zeroed in on new targets to replace the left. Film censorship stiffened across the board, especially for foreign movies. International tensions increased official antipathy for foreign morals, and there were efforts to uproot from the Japanese language imported words such as *mama* and *papa*.[56] Though sanctions against Japanese films dropped during the early 1930s, foreign film cuts increased and remained high through 1936.[57] In April 1937, inspection fees for foreign films were raised by half, partly because they were "contrary to sympathetic manners and customs."[58] Hitherto unmolested religious groups, both Oriental (for example, Daihonkyō, Tenritsu) and Western (such as Jehovah's Witnesses—Tōdaisha), also became major objects of repression in 1935–1936. Arrests and official denunciations were typically accompanied by wholesale bans on their publications.[59] The fresh assault on conservatives in the political center has already been described with reference to the Minobe crisis.

Of greatest political interest, perhaps, was the extensive censorship of the civil right wing, a topic much neglected in scholarship. Victims of the central political currents of the 1930s have dominated postwar historiography, and most have portrayed the civil right as an ally of rising military-bureaucratic elites, since both opposed leftist and *jiyūshugi* elements. When the right is examined as an object of state policy, however, a greater distance appears to separate state elites from the civil right wing.

---

54. *Masu Media Tōsei*, vol. 1, document 34, p. 218.
55. Naimushō Keihōkyoku, *Shuppan Keisatsu Gaikan*, 1934, pp. 197–98. The disavowal of communism by former leaders Sano Manabu and Nabeyama Sadachika from prison in June 1933 led to a cascade of renunciations from leftist prisoners, disheartening communist sympathizers still active and generating disputes among them that ended up ruining many of their cultural periodicals still in publication.
56. Iwasaki Akira, *Nihon Gendai Shi Taikei: Eiga Shi*, p. 162. Derivations from the German language, however, were soon on the upswing.
57. Cuts of Japanese films numbered 1,228 in 1932, 806 in 1933, 755 in 1934, 472 in 1935, and 629 in 1936; foreign film cuts numbered 860 in 1932, 1,121 in 1933, 1,469 in 1934, 789 in 1935, and 923 in 1936: Naimushō Keihōkyoku, *Firumu Ken'etsu Nenpō*, 1933–1937.
58. Quoted in Tanaka, *Nihon Eiga Hattatsu Shi*, 2: 228.
59. For several official descriptions of the new religious censorship, see Naimushō Keihōkyoku, *Shuppan Keisatsu Hō*, nos. 91–93.

TABLE XIII   THE NUMBER OF ACTIVE RIGHTIST PERIODICALS, BY
POLITICAL/THOUGHT TENDENCY, 1932–1935

	Type of Journal	Total Active Journals	Political/Thought Tendency		
			Pure Japanist[a]	National Socialist	Other
1932	Newspapers	27	11	2	14
	Magazines	32	11	5	16
	Total	59	22	7	30
1933	Newspapers	31	9	4	18
	Magazines	42	16	4	22
	Total	73	25	8	40
					Agrarianist[b]
1934	Newspapers	35	30	3	2
	Magazines	59	52	5	2
	Total	94	82	8	4
1935	Newspapers	43	37	3	3
	Magazines	47	42	2	3
	Total	90	79	5	6

Source: Naimushō Keihōkyoku, Shuppan Keisatsu Gaikan, 1932–1935.

[a]This category is usually rendered as "pure Japanist" (junsui Nihonshugi), occasionally as "Japanist," and once in the magazine classification of 1932 as "pure Japanist/ultranationalist" (the latter term is kokusuishugi).

[b]This category is rendered as "agrarianist" (nōhonshugi) or "agrarian self-governmentist" (nōhon jijishugi).

If some officials manipulated the right as a useful tool, many also perceived it as a threat to public order requiring careful containment.

Before the 1930s, the rightist press was not a major factor in law enforcement or public discourse. In January 1930, police counted only twenty-seven rightist periodicals, twenty-one of them appearing monthly, and officials judged their influence to be "feeble."[60] State documents consistently cite the Manchurian Incident of September 1931 as the principal catalyst for expansion,[61] causing the number of rightist periodicals to double between 1930 and 1932 (see table 13). The end of

60. Idem, Shuppan Keisatsu Hō, no. 17, pp. 21–23. Police described rightist journals generally as those sharing the following guiding spirit: "We recognize an absolute sovereign power based on our national polity and we will defend it to the last, hoping for greater and greater exaltation of imperial honor": ibid., p. 21.

61. E.g., see idem, Shuppan Keisatsu Gaikan, 1932, pp. 152–53. Of the twenty-two leading right-wing journals in mid-1932, ten had debuted after the Manchurian Incident: idem, Shuppan Keisatsu Hō, no. 47, pp. 127–36. Even in the book market, which reacts more slowly to current events, the Manchurian Incident made itself felt before the end of 1931. Nationalist and anti-Marxist books were 12 of the annual total of 614 books related to social thought in 1930, but rose to 69 of 686 in 1931, due to a boom after

TABLE XIV   DOMESTIC RIGHTIST AND LEFTIST PUBLICATIONS BANNED
FOR VIOLATING REGULAR PUBLIC-ORDER CENSORSHIP STANDARDS,
1931–1935

	Political Tendency	Newspapers	Magazines	Books	Propaganda Sheets	Total
1931	Right	15	7	6	15	43
	Left	241	188	181	1,963	2,573
1932	Right	64	42	16	64	186
	Left	349	349	174	2,310	3,182
1933	Right	95	60	23	173	351
	Left	329	306	141	1,866	2,642
1934	Right	216	55	18	203	492
	Left	132	85	28	309	554
1935	Right	105	42	18	117	282
	Left	41	34	16	177	268

Source: Naimushō Keihōkyoku, *Shuppan Keisatsu Gaikan,* 1931–1935.
Note: Newspapers were banned under the Newspaper Law, books and propaganda sheets under the Publication Law, and magazines under both. Violations of pre-publication warnings are not included in the table.

party government was another stimulus for the right, but imperialism was the prime mover. It stirred nationalistic groups to greater efforts and created the readership for new journals of patriotic appeal. Imperialistic issues favored the right until mid-1933; most important were the clash between Japanese and Chinese troops in Shanghai in early 1932, the founding of Manchukuo in July 1932, and Japan's withdrawal from the League of Nations in March 1933. There were no comparable international stimuli in 1934, and the number of rightist journals consequently leveled off in 1935.

The rightist press had suffered few sanctions in the 1920s, but the radical bent of some of the new activists soon became a major concern of the publications police, whose sanctions against rightist journals more than quadrupled from 1931 to 1932 (see table 14). The principal offense was advocacy of violence or revolution, accounting for fifty-one of sixty-four rightist newspaper editions banned in 1932. Other common infractions were subverting military discipline by urging a coup, publicizing military factional struggles, and slandering the imperial house, often by claiming that the Emperor was misled by his advisors.[62]

September: idem, *Shuppan Keisatsu Gaikan,* 1930, p. 88, and idem., *Shuppan Keisatsu Gaikan,* 1931, pp. 69–70.
62. Idem, *Shuppan Keisatsu Gaikan,* 1932, pp. 206, 213–16, 261–62.

Film censors also focused attention on rightist radicalism.[63] The numbers of sanctions imposed on the right and on the left cannot substantiate a judgment on relative degrees of repression; the imprisonment of so many leftists under the Peace Preservation Law places their persecution on a different plane. But the data do show that although some extreme rightist groups had fellow travelers and even a few members in officialdom, their propaganda for violence and revolution was met with systematic countermeasures. The censor's position is illuminated further by a review of the official distinctions drawn between rightist groups and their publications.

During 1932–1935, police divided the right into two main categories: pure Japanism and national socialism. Both were critical of party politics and capitalism, but the national socialist journals were singled out for the extremism of their positive program. Influenced by the thought of Takabatake Motoyuki, Japan's leading national socialist intellectual and one-time translator of Marx's *Capital*, they proposed to eradicate capitalism and replace it with a planned state socialist economy, they were highly critical of private property, and they advocated nationalization of the means of production. Like the early northern wing of the Nazi Party under Gregor and Otto Strasser, Japan's national socialists took their socialism very seriously, and the groups harbored a number of ex-leftists. Their opposition to parliamentarianism was uncompromising.[64]

Though some national socialist ideas found their way into the Japanist camp, as a rule the Japanists embraced more moderate positions. Most rejected party politics but not the Diet (only the Diet was inscribed in the constitution); they were for keeping the good points of capitalism, while compensating for its deficiencies; most supported only a "lukewarm controlled economy"; and many favored the decentralization of

63. Home Ministry film inspector Tajima Tarō wrote in 1938:

Until seven-eight years ago, this kind of so-called "red" [film] alone formed the center of the problem, but times change and from five-six years ago, wearing a Japanese disguise, we have seen the rise of radical rightism. [According to Suga Tarō, L.L.B.:] "Generally speaking . . . they shun parliamentary methods and have recourse to extraparliamentary action, but there is a danger that this action is often tainted with an illegal, direct, terrorist, coup d'état–like coloration." (Tajima, *Ken'etsu Shitsu*, p. 271)

Thus during 1932–1933, concern with political radicalism shifted focus from the left to the right. Notice that Tajima implicitly takes the radical right to be an illegal foreign import much like the left, though this one wears a "Japanese disguise." The trend toward right-wing and military-related films began to abate in 1934, paralleling the experience of the printed media, which also saw a slackening of rightist activity in 1934 and 1935: Naimushō Keihōkyoku, *Firumu Ken'etsu Nenpō*, 1935, pp. 1–2.
64. Naimushō Keihōkyoku, *Shuppan Keisatsu Gaikan*, 1932, p. 260.

state authority.[65] Their theories were generally less systematic than those of the national socialists and often focused on vague prescriptions for spiritual renovation.

Officials did note one or two exceptions to this general portrait among the Japanist groups. Most significant was the journal *Kaizō Sensen,* published by the Great Japan Production Party. It advocated the complete elimination of capitalism for a new state-controlled economic system.[66] The police were careful to point out that the party's formal program was more moderate and that *Kaizō Sensen* was apparently run by a faction strongly influenced by Marxism. It is significant that this journal was singled out as an exception, since certain elements in the Great Japan Production Party were involved in the only plot for armed civilian insurrection in the 1930s, the Shinpeitai Incident of July 1933. Most Japanist groups, in other words, did not share such revolutionary aims. Eleven out of twelve editions of *Kaizō Sensen* were banned in 1933.[67] As the figures in table 13 indicate, the pure Japanist groups far outweighed the national socialists in terms of publishing activity.

The agrarianist journals noted for 1934 and 1935 were largely offshoots of the rural depression, which was especially cruel in northeastern prefectures. They were opposed to Western capitalism, materialism, urban culture, and the notion of a powerful central state, appealing instead for greater self-government in the farm villages.[68]

In 1934 and 1935, the publications police noted a split in the Japanist camp. One group was very conservative, reactionary, and "idealistic" (*kannenteki*), the other more "progressive" (*shinpoteki*) and outspoken on concrete political and economic questions. The progressive wing was becoming the dominant force.[69] This cleft later developed into the distinction between the idealist right and the renovationist right, the two principal labels employed for rightist groups in the late 1930s. However, although the progressive right was said to borrow more from national socialism than the idealist right, this does not imply

65. Ibid., pp. 259–61; idem, *Shuppan Keisatsu Gaikan,* 1933, p. 244, and idem, *Shuppan Keisatsu Gaikan,* 1934, p. 154, this last for the quotation on lukewarm support for a controlled economy.
66. Idem, *Shuppan Keisatsu Gaikan,* 1932, p. 209. See also Maruyama Masao, *Thought and Behavior in Modern Japanese Politics,* pp. 30–31, and, for the party mainstream's more moderate program, p. 44.
67. Naimushō Keihōkyoku, *Shuppan Keisatsu Gaikan,* 1933, pp. 192–93.
68. Idem, *Shuppan Keisatsu Gaikan,* 1934, pp. 160–61. For a full account of agrarianist politics, see Thomas R. H. Havens, *Farm and Nation in Modern Japan: Agrarian Nationalism, 1870–1940.*
69. Naimushō Keihōkyoku, *Shuppan Keisatsu Gaikan,* 1934, p. 218.

that most progressives supported violent revolution. In fact, rightist publications on the whole "markedly softened" their platforms in 1934 and 1935 in comparison to earlier years.[70] In 1935 the number of banned rightist periodicals, books, and propaganda sheets decreased for the first time in the decade, from 492 in 1934 to 282.[71]

There is an unusually detailed account of the reasons rightist publications were banned in 1935 (see table 15). The paucity of sanctions for rejecting or slandering private property, the courts, the parliamentary system, and the law and state authority indicate that few rightist groups endorsed a politico-economic program of revolutionary extremes. And although support for violence was still the main reason for sanctions in 1935, officials noted a new moderation on this point in both 1934 and 1935:

> Seeing that even in the atmosphere of popular excitement after the Manchurian Incident, the national reconstruction movement based upon direct action by *a few extremists* in the 5/15 Incident, Shinpeitai Incident, etc., ended in failure, it is evident throughout various articles that the rightist camp is aware it is now forced to make a great shift (*tenkō*) in the movement's direction . . . .[72]

This shift was a turn by some of the more extreme groups to strictly legal methods (parliamentary action, circulating petitions) in an effort to overcome a general decline in right-wing activity and effectiveness.[73] The evidence is that despite signs of sympathy with the terror of junior officers in 1932 and 1933, the great majority of rightist groups never adopted terrorist tactics as their own, and at least by 1935 most had clearly come to espouse nonviolent means to influence.

Those groups persisting in support for violence or revolution regularly ran afoul of censorship and other forms of police control. Many rightist journals treating the Minobe affair were banned for desecrating the throne or demanding military or civilian direct action against proponents of the organ theory.[74] In May 1935, police arrested numerous rightist gang members in Tokyo, and during the year 132 rightists were prosecuted under various statutes, at least 67 of whom were fined or imprisoned, compared to 113 leftists prosecuted under the Peace Preservation Law.[75] Many rightist journals saw the state's handling of the

70. Idem, *Shuppan Keisatsu Gaikan,* 1935, pp. 43, 103.
71. Idem, *Shuppan Keisatsu Gaikan,* 1934, 1935.
72. Idem, *Shuppan Keisatsu Gaikan,* 1935, p. 109 (emphasis added).
73. Ibid., p. 110.
74. Ibid., pp. 219–21.
75. *Chian Iji Hō,* p. 651, table 3.

TABLE XV   DOMESTIC RIGHTIST PERIODICAL EDITIONS AND BOOKS
BANNED FOR VIOLATING REGULAR PUBLIC-ORDER CENSORSHIP
STANDARDS IN 1935, BY SUBJECT MATTER

	Newspaper Law		Publication Law			Percent of Column Total
	News-papers	Maga-zines	Maga-zines	Books	Total	Total
Advocating						
Illegal change	12	2	1	3	18	10.9%
Direct action	29	7	0	3	39	23.6
Mass violence	1	0	0	1	2	1.2
Violent acts	3	0	0	0	3	1.8
Illegal movements	1	1	0	0	2	1.2
Crime	1	1	0	0	2	1.2
Criminals	5	0	0	0	5	3.0
Social unrest	3	1	0	0	4	2.4
War	1	1	0	0	2	1.2
Rejecting/slandering						
Imperial family	16	7	0	2	25	15.1
Private property	1	0	0	0	1	.6
Law/state authority	2	1	0	0	3	1.8
Courts	0	1	0	0	1	.6
Parliamentary system	2	0	0	0	2	1.2
Military/war	2	0	0	0	2	1.2
Foreign policy	0	1	1	0	2	1.2
Disturbing/hindering						
Constitution	5	2	0	2	9	5.4
Foundation of military	3	0	0	0	3	1.8
Military discipline	12	13	1	6	32	19.4
Foreign affairs	2	0	0	0	2	1.2
Business world	1	0	0	0	1	.6
Other	3	1	0	1	5	3.0
Total	105	39	3	18	165	99.6
Percent of row total	63.6	23.6	1.8	10.9	99.9	

Source: Naimushō Keihōkyoku, *Shuppan Keisatsu Gaikan,* 1935.

Minobe affair as a defeat, since the cabinet had survived and no adherent of the organ theory was ever convicted in court.[76]

In 1936, the attempted coup replaced the Minobe crisis as the principal story drawing sanctions to the rightist press. In March, at least twenty-eight rightist newspapers, seven magazines, and thirty propa-

76. Naimushō Keihōkyoku, *Shuppan Keisatsu Gaikan,* 1935, p. 111.

ganda sheets were banned under the press laws for their reporting of the rebellion. Principal reasons for banning the propaganda were approval for the rebellion (nineteen sanctions), reproduction of the rebels' manifesto (five), and demands for a cabinet run by the imperial family, for a military government, or for a Shōwa Restoration (five).[77] From March to July, there were eighteen indictments of rightists for violations of the Newspaper and Publication Laws connected with the 2/26 Incident. Others were tried under the special anti-radical law passed by the Diet after the revolt.[78] In one case, a college professor was prosecuted for reprinting a letter one of the rebels wrote to his mother before execution. The letter read:

> It is I, who before now have caused you countless misfortunes, and today once more I must send you sorrowful tidings. . . . However, Mother, I ask you not to grieve too much. In order for the empire to continue its advance in the way of the gods, and so that people, parents and children and brothers and sisters in harmony, may enjoy their work, rejoice in the flowers, amuse themselves with sake, and offer congratulations of "Long life!" to the imperial reign, a small number of people chosen by heaven must taste agony, suffer grief, abandon their lives, and break their bones. I, who hope for the honor of those loyal to that fate, think there is nothing I could be more thankful for than to have been born in Japan and to be able to die for the Emperor. The history of Japan is a trail of the lifeblood shed by our ancestors to protect and foster the national polity. Now our lifeblood will become the eternal prosperity of the imperial throne. . . . If an interview should be permitted one of these days, I think I would like to see your face once more. When I think that in heaven and earth the only person who could love someone like me from the heart is you, Mother, longing deeply permeates my body. . . . I beg you please to care for your health in this hot weather.[79]

Despite extra police vigilance, there was not a great rash of rightist press violations after the 2/26 Incident; the evidence points to a relatively feeble response from rightist journals. Even the Diet's special anti-radical law aimed at the right saw little service and nearly fell into disuse after March 1937. The scarcity of violations is understandable, however, in light of earlier official reports. A trend toward moderation had characterized rightist journals for the previous two years. The strategy of direct action was losing support, and the extreme national socialist

77. Idem, *Shuppan Keisatsu Hō*, no. 91, pp. 38, 46–47.
78. Some monthly police reports do not contain a complete count of administrative sanctions by rightist and leftist groups under this law. For judicial sanctions, see idem, *Shuppan Keisatsu Hō*, no. 99, p. 124.
79. Quoted in idem, *Shuppan Keisatsu Hō*, no. 95, p. 202.

groups had become almost a null factor. The young officers themselves engaged in scant propaganda efforts. As soldiers, they were forbidden by law to publish, and they showed little interest in reaching a mass audience. Even with downtown Tokyo under their control, they did not try to seize NHK's studios or to disseminate printed materials directly to the public.[80] Their goal was a political transformation engineered at the top, preferably creation of a military cabinet, not a popular uprising.

There was much sympathy for the rebels among nationalist groups, but the state had consistently censored praise for violence, and the reaffirmation of that policy after the incident gave rightists the choice of going to court or biting their tongues. Most opted for the latter. Some were no doubt chagrined by the mutiny, because political violence was very unpopular and hurt the rightist cause. The public was initially well-informed about the coup, since the pre-publication warning against press coverage was violated repeatedly by the largest national dailies in late February, and, as usual, the police failed to seize most offending editions.[81] One sign of the negative public reaction is that rightist press circulation fell by more than 50 percent in the wake of the incident, while journals associated with the left increased sales.[82]

Given the official leeway in interpreting the law, it is obvious that censorship of the right could have been much tougher. Instead of outlawing the organ theory, for example, the state might have silenced the theory's critics for disturbing public order. Yet although the data clearly reflect more sympathetic treatment for the right than the left, they do not corroborate any close-knit alliance between state officials and the civil right wing. The relatively unfettered expansion of the rightist press in the early 1930s owed less to official favor than to the legal orientation of most journals. There were no statutes prohibiting criticism of democracy, attacks on party corruption, eulogies of the Emperor, or celebration of Japan's imperialistic mission in Asia.

The evidence, then, is that most of Japan's rightist groups were not as radical as the European fascist movements to which they are often com-

---

80. Ben-Ami Shillony, *Revolt in Japan: The Young Officers and the February 26, 1936 Incident*, pp. 159–61, 183.

81. From 26 to 29 February, 206 periodical editions were banned for violating the pre-publication warning, and of 84 major newspapers among them, only 1.4 of 5.4 million copies were seized by police (26 percent): Naimushō Keihōkyoku, *Shuppan Keisatsu Hō*, no. 91, pp. 304–14.

82. From February to June, rightist "thought" newspapers watched by the Tokyo police declined in circulation from 892,340 to 267,420 copies, while leftist papers increased from 165,700 to 245,600 copies: idem, *Shuppan Keisatsu Hō*, no. 96, pp. 100–101.

pared. Except for the few national socialist elements and a small minority of the Japanists, the Japanese right differed fundamentally from fascism. Most groups embraced a more moderate politico-economic reform program, a strategy of influencing elites rather than organizing mass action, and traditional monarchical principles of legitimacy that had no parallel in fascist ideologies.[83] The critical spurt of rightist growth preceded Hitler's rise to power, and Italian fascism had little impact in Japan. In-depth evaluations of European fascism in the rightist press were few and generally critical.[84] Most Japanese groups had desisted from applauding violence well before the 2/26 Incident, which was not representative of most rightist activity and therefore not the great turning point away from violent tactics that it is often said to be.

Certainly some state officials were not above manipulating the civil right to threaten their opponents with illegal violence. Instances of such manipulation occurred both before and after the abortive coup: for example, the military's use of reservists during the Minobe crisis, or Konoe's employment of rightists to intimidate the parties in early 1938. Yet it was almost invariably the officials who fixed the terms of such engagements. Censorship records demonstrate clearly that civil rightist groups out to threaten state authority itself with violent or revolutionary challenges were punished as lawbreakers. This continued to be so to the end of the imperial era. Rightist assassinations, intimidation, and propaganda were undoubtedly crucial to the course of Japanese politics, contributing mightily to the breakdown of party government, to the pervasive sense of political crisis, and to the delegitimation of democracy, freedom, individualism, and internationalism in public discourse. But no civil rightist group ever seized power. The notion that civil rightists or junior officers were pulling the strings behind basic state policy (Maruyama Masao's *ge-koku-jō* theory) does not hold for media controls, nor has a convincing case been made for this thesis in any other *domestic* policy field.[85] It is, rather, within high officialdom that one finds the principal causes of the great transformation in state-society relations to occur in the late 1930s.

83. I have developed these points more fully in "Fascism from Below? A Comparative Perspective on the Japanese Right, 1931–1936." For a contrary point of view, see Abe Hirozumi, "Nihon Fashizumu no Kenkyū Shikaku."
84. Kasza, "Fascism from Below?" pp. 622–23.
85. Contrary views may be overly swayed by the role of middle-ranking officers in initiating the Manchurian Incident in 1931. This was an exception to the dominant pattern of state decision-making and is in any case one that cannot be attributed to any organized rightist political group.

PLANNING FOR MOBILIZATION

More important than the policy innovations of this period was a process of committee meetings and study, planning and lobbying, that laid the foundation for Japan's coming New Order. If 1940 or 1941 had seen a violent revolution, scholarly attention to the preceding years would naturally focus on civil disturbances, the growth of radical political groups, and other signs of impending upheaval. As it happened, however, the years 1940 and 1941 witnessed a policy revolution initiated from within the state. The genesis of this revolution is traceable to a cluster of new administrative committees that labored over radical policy blueprints in the 1932–1937 period.

These committees were interministerial bodies directly under cabinet authority, and they became a haven for "renovationist bureaucrats" and politically ambitious officers from the military ministries. Creation of the Cabinet Research Bureau in 1935 constituted a watershed in the development of these agencies. Initially established as the administrative arm of a political advisory council, the bureau outlived its sponsor and merged with the Natural Resource Bureau two years later to form the Cabinet Planning Board, the center of economic mobilization strategy. In retrospect, Prime Minister Okada considered his inauguration of the research bureau to have been a serious mistake,[86] but it was only the most prominent of many such committees organized in the cabinet. Several of the new cabinet agencies proved very important to the development of media policy, and the evolution of the Film Control Committee can be described as a representative example.

The original impetus for new film controls came from the Diet in February 1933, when Representative Iwase Makoto won the approval of a lower house committee for his "Motion to Create a National Film Policy." Iwase argued that film was as influential as the press or the schools and that the state should not limit itself to passive censorship while ceding production to private companies out for profit. Alluding to the Manchurian Incident, he remarked that Japan's image abroad would suffer if "truthful" films of good quality were not made and exported. Private companies were not performing this task, and so the field had been abandoned to foreign films presenting an eccentric view of the country.[87] Iwase's motion was that Japan follow the lead of other states

86. Ide, *Nihon Kanryōsei*, pp. 88–89.
87. Many foreign films were indeed biased against the Japanese: see Jacobus ten-Broek, Edward N. Barnhart, and Floyd W. Matson, *Prejudice, War, and the Constitution*, pp. 29–32.

in establishing an official organ to play an active role in the "guidance and control" (*shidō tōsei*) of the film medium.[88]

In March 1934, this initiative bore fruit when the cabinet sanctioned the Film Control Committee (*Eiga Tōsei Iinkai*). Preparatory efforts had included a thorough study of foreign film controls and numerous meetings chaired by the Home Ministry's Criminal Affairs Bureau Chief, in which Home and Education Ministry officials (most of section chief—*kachō*—rank) participated. At first glance their achievement appears deceptively modest. Despite an impressive roster of members (the Home Minister himself acted as director), the committee's only mission was "research and discussion." A long slate of topics was drawn up for investigation: proposals for an integrated film law, state film production and distribution, state subsidies to film-makers, the manufacture of negative film, compulsory showing of educational films, censorship, and so on. But there was neither the authority nor the budget to take action.[89]

Nonetheless, the Film Control Committee overcame its handicaps to play a key role in policy development. In early 1935, both Diet chambers passed a resolution calling for enlargement of the organ, more planning for controls, and creation of a body to promote public spirit in films. The committee capitalized on the last of these recommendations, and in November 1935 it created the Great Japan Film Association (*Dai Nihon Eiga Kyōkai*) to project its influence outward. The association was a bureaucratic-civil hybrid formally approved by the Home and Education Ministers. High-ranking bureaucrats on the Film Control Committee were permanent appointees to the directorate, and leading film studios participated and gave financial support. This structure was a microcosm of the dominant state control pattern to emerge later in the decade: an interministerial cabinet agency on top, formally private firms on the bottom, and an intermediate civil-bureaucratic body linking the two. The association's goals were to eliminate the ill influences of movies on the public, to further the renovation of manners and morals, and to promote the "rational" development of film.[90]

It is not clear whether the industry reacted more with passive acquiescence or active support (perhaps hoping to make the association *its* lobby

88. Iwase's remarks are cited in *Masu Media Tōsei*, vol. 1, document 51, p. 264.
89. For information on the Film Control Committee, see ibid., pp. 265–67, and document 73, pp. 402–4.
90. According to speeches at the association's inauguration; see ibid., document 84, pp. 649–51.

with the state).[91] What is certain is that over the next five years the Great Japan Film Association pumped out a steady stream of rhetoric for tougher film controls. Its magazine, *Nihon Eiga* (Japanese Film), became a clamorous mouthpiece for promoters of a special law for film, carrying numerous articles by bureaucrats who later helped to frame such legislation; one of them was Home Ministry censor Tatebayashi Mikio.[92] In 1936, Tatebayashi wrote: "As far as we are concerned, from the vantage point of film administration, our approach is blind to artistic quality. Items unwanted by the state, though they may be 'fine art,' we discard and ignore. For state officials this is the correct attitude."[93] In October 1937, the association published a 158-page translation of all laws and administrative codes pertaining to film in Nazi Germany.[94]

The Film Control Committee and the Great Japan Film Association spearheaded the campaign for a comprehensive film law in both the state and civil society, but other state agencies were also supportive of a new film control system. Military thinking is partly revealed in the Summary Working Plan for Information and Propaganda prepared by the cabinet's Natural Resource Bureau in May 1936.[95] "Natural Resource Bureau" was the euphemistic title of an interministerial agency working on contingency plans for total war. The bureau was established in May 1927 and military officers were prominent on its staff. The bureau prepared a blueprint for state propaganda activity just before and after the outbreak of a total war. It echoed the Army Ministry's pamphlet of 1934 by proposing a central state control body to lord over seven separate media associations, each embracing all active media organs in its field. One of the seven was for the film industry. All functions

91. Okada Susumu, *Nihon Eiga no Rekishi*, p. 190. Okada deduces support from the participation of Shōchiku studio's Kido Shiro. It is not illogical that some industry people welcomed the association as a new sign of recognition for them (the film business lacked social prestige at the time), saw some promise of state subsidies in the future, and otherwise found nothing objectionable in a patriotic organization that, in any case, had no legal teeth with which to bite.

92. For numerous examples of Tatebayashi's contributions to *Nihon Eiga*, see Iwasaki, *Eiga Shi*, pp. 168–71.

93. Quoted in ibid., p. 164.

94. *Doitsu Eiga Hō*. The Japanese were keen students of foreign film controls and had access to a mountain of information. In 1929, legal scholar Yanai Yoshio published his *Katsudō Shashin no Hogo to Torishimari*, a thousand-page study of state film administration around the world. Eighteen pages of the Home Ministry's *Firumu Ken'etsu Nenpō* of 1932 were devoted to an outline of censorship practices in sixty-two countries. The survey of 1933 preliminary to establishment of the Film Control Committee has already been noted. References to foreign practices were almost invariably included in arguments for stiffer state film controls.

95. This plan, *Jōhō Senden ni Kansuru Jisshi Keikaku Kōryō An*, is reprinted in *Masu Media Tōsei*, vol. 1, document 78, pp. 627–41.

of censorship and mobilization would be concentrated in the central body. The design was modeled on the Reich Chambers of Culture fashioned by Nazi Propaganda Minister Goebbels in September 1933.[96]

Another agency supportive of new film controls was the Cabinet Information Committee created in July 1936. Part of this committee's mission was to coordinate the information output of the various ministries, but it had little actual authority to do so. It was not empowered to gather information itself, to make public pronouncements, or to infringe on the jurisdiction of existing state institutions.[97] Beyond its control over the official news agency, this committee initially appeared just as innocuous as the film committee, but its corps of military and civilian bureaucrats also promoted new film legislation and later became involved in its implementation.

These antecedents, along with the Diet support already noted at several stages, created a broad constituency within the state for a new control structure. States often organize powerless commissions to bury problems rather than solve them, but in Japan legally impotent bureaucratic organs such as those just described became the cornerstones of policy innovation. This does not mean that obscure, low-ranking officials dominated policy. Eventually the cabinet agencies became important channels of recruitment to the administrative elite and acquired formal legal powers of their own, but the initial sway of bodies such as the Film Control Committee and the Cabinet Information Committee was owed precisely to the high rank of their leading members in other state institutions that were empowered to act. Regular film committee members included the Home Ministry's Criminal Affairs Bureau Chief and the Education Ministry's Social Education Bureau Chief, men near the pinnacle of administrative power. The first head of the Cabinet Information Committee was the Cabinet Chief Secretary, the most powerful bureaucrat in the government. These were the posts to which every career official aspired as the ultimate reward for distinguished service. It was the presence of such leaders on these committees, not their manipulation by subordinates, that was the key to their effectiveness.

The efforts of the Film Control Committee later resulted in the Film

96. The seven Nazi Chambers of Culture differed in only one instance from the list of proposed Japanese media control associations. Common were organs for film, radio, the press, music, fine arts, and the theater, but the seventh German chamber was for literature, while the Japanese was for a state wire service. A monopolistic state news agency was in the making in Japan at the time this plan was drawn up, and this probably accounts for the difference.

97. *Masu Media Tōsei*, vol. 1, document 80, p. 643.

Law of 1939, the only major bill enacted for a particular mass medium in the late imperial era. By 1940, the Cabinet Information Committee had evolved into a likeness of the central propaganda organ envisioned in the army's 1934 pamphlet and in the German-inspired planning of the Natural Resource Bureau.

NHK AND CREATION OF
THE UNITED NEWS AGENCY

It was only in regard to radio that officials instituted significant structural changes in this period. Party governments had left the medium under firm bureaucratic control and therefore no broader political consensus was necessary to introduce reform. In 1934, the Communications Ministry revoked most of the autonomy of NHK's branch stations. Previously, the branches had possessed their own boards of directors, dominant voting power on executive bodies, and some meaningful independence in programming and business operations. The ministry first grew unhappy with these arrangements because the ensuing redundancy of offices and functions added considerably to overhead costs.[98] The Manchurian Incident of 1931 then shifted official concern from economizing to the issue of central program control. From this point on, the military strongly supported efforts for structural change.

A plan to centralize NHK was prepared within the Communications Ministry and tactfully imposed upon directors and investors in the spring of 1934.[99] It eliminated branch boards of directors, gave the head

98. The ministry's drive for greater economy was expressed in its budget approval commands, especially in 1930 when it ordered a reduction in listeners' fees, the expansion of facilities, and a cutback in total expenses, all at the same time. This touched off a discussion of organizational reforms. In early 1932, both the Tokyo and Osaka branches proposed a reduction of employees, a mandatory retirement age, and other cost-cutting measures, but their designs did not compromise branch autonomy.

99. From 1932, the leading advocate of reform was Tamura Kenjirō, the Administrative Section Chief of the Telephone and Telegraph Bureau in the Communications Ministry. In early 1934, Tamura and two of NHK's employees secretly composed a plan to restructure the broadcasting company. As their efforts neared fruition, Tamura quietly met with various NHK executives to impress on them the imperative of change. The subject of organizational reform was then raised openly at a central NHK board of directors' meeting on 9 April 1934, and a group of NHK's top directors was charged with formulating a concrete proposal. They returned on 21 April with a copy of the plan prepared earlier under Tamura's direction. One week later, NHK's central board forwarded this plan to the Communications Ministry without major amendments, essentially asking the ministry to approve its own work, which it did on 7 May. In another week, the document was presented to a general investors' meeting with a statement stressing the new awareness of radio's influence after the Manchurian Incident and its mission of service to the nation: *Nihon Musen Shi,* 7: 201.

office control over the budget, business plans, and national relay programming, and granted central NHK executives 40 percent of the votes
at investors' meetings.[100] The architect of this reform, Communications
Ministry Section Chief Tamura Kenjirō, stated upon its approval by the
investors:

> Originally, based upon article 2 of the Wireless Telegraphic Communica-
> tions Law, NHK was specially granted a concession for a business that was
> supposed to be managed by the government. Therefore, NHK's management
> of the broadcasting business, as an extension of the Communications Minis-
> try as it were, takes the form of acting as an agent for government business.
> Consequently, I would like to ask here that it be clearly understood that
> government supervision of the management of the broadcasting business
> must naturally differ in substance from that of other public-interest juridical
> persons.[101]

Henceforward, Tamura declared, programming would not simply flatter popular desires but would promote the "Japanese spirit" and provide leadership. The new awareness of radio's influence since the Manchurian Incident was also stressed at the investors' meeting.[102] The
elimination of branch autonomy removed the last obstacle to state mobilization of radio.

The Communications Ministry reasserted direct control over personnel by appointing a completely new generation of NHK executives in
1934, again placing many ex-bureaucrats in key posts.[103] There was a
joke current within NHK that to become a company executive one had
to be a "three tei" man: teikoku daigaku—an imperial university graduate; Teishinshō—a Communications Ministry official; and teinō—an
imbecile.[104] More significant, however, was the new provision for pro-

100. *Masu Media Tōsei*, vol. 1, document 80, p. 643.
101. Quoted in NHK, ed., *Nihon Hōsō Shi*, 1: 312.
102. Another sign of war-related thinking in this period, though less direct, was a
speech by the Communications Minister at NHK's ninth anniversary celebration on 22
March 1934, when he spoke at length on the state's increasing use of radio in England, the
United States, and especially Nazi Germany; see NHK, ed., *Nihon Hōsō Shi*, 1: 314.
103. *Nihon Musen Shi*, 7: 207.
104. The crossover of state officials and the increasing involvement of active officials
were such that later wrangles over executive appointments ceased to mean much in terms
of real state control. For example, in 1940 NHK's president succeeded in resisting several
ministerial appointments. But the president, Komori Shichirō, had himself been a Communications Ministry bureaucrat in the 1920s. He had been appointed by the Communications Minister as one of NHK's first managing directors in 1926 (reportedly against his
will), promoted by the minister to senior managing director after centralization in 1934,
and voted NHK's president in 1936 by a board of directors stacked with ministry appointees. It is therefore difficult to construe Komori's rejection of several ex-bureaucrats as a
sign of decreasing state control. In any case, many ex-officials continued to make the
transition.

gram advisory committees in the centralization plan. In June 1934, a Broadcast Programming Council was created, incorporating section chiefs from the Communications, Home, and Education Ministries and later from the Cabinet Planning Board and Cabinet Information Committee. Unlike several innocuous predecessors, this council had final authority over the broadcast schedule for national relay transmissions, which constituted over 80 percent of all broadcasts.[105] So-called renovationist bureaucrats (*kakushin kanryō*), known for their statist inclinations, participated and used their influence to tilt more and more programs to state purposes.

The new articles of incorporation also authorized NHK to manage and fund other businesses related to broadcasting, and this provision anticipated plans for a state news agency. The Manchurian Incident provided the immediate inspiration for an official wire service. Japanese officials felt they were losing the battle for world opinion, and in May 1932 Army and Foreign Ministry bureaucrats organized an informal committee to bolster propaganda. One problem had been a lack of coordination in information output, with the Foreign Ministry channeling its press releases primarily through the Rengō agency, and the Army Ministry through the other major wire service, Dentsū.[106] Bureaucrats from four other ministries later joined the committee, and pursuant to its deliberations, in September 1932 the Army, Navy, and Foreign Ministries jointly called for a single national wire service.[107]

NHK had purchased its news reports from Rengō and Dentsū since 1930, and officials now strove to merge these firms into a monopolistic state enterprise. Japan's two wire services reacted very differently to this prospect. Rengō was a financially weak nonprofit company whose employees labored without pay; it offered to surrender its facilities free of charge.[108] Dentsū was a profit-making company and its president and stockholders opposed amalgamation. The Foreign and Communications Ministers finally authorized creation of the United News Agency (UNA, *Dōmei Tsūshinsha*) in November 1935 without Dentsū's participation. The UNA's bylaws required state approval for the hiring and firing of top executives and empowered the two ministers to direct the

105. On the Broadcast Programming Council see NHK, ed., *Nihon Hōsō Shi*, 1: 339–40, and NHK, ed., *Rajio Nenkan Shōwa 10-Nen*, pp. 86–88. The official documents of state authorization are reprinted in NHK, ed., *Reiki—Hōsō Hen (1)*, pp. 7–9. Membership was listed annually in the *Rajio Nenkan* volumes.
106. Naisei Shi Kenkyūkai, ed., *Yokomizo Mitsuteru-Shi Danwa Sokkiroku*, 1: 26.
107. *Masu Media Tōsei*, 2: lix.
108. Ibid., supplementary document 2, p. 542.

firm's operations when necessary for the public interest.[109] In December, the Communications Ministry took action against Dentsū. It decreed new regulations requiring a ministry permit to transmit or receive international broadcasts or telegrams. Permits were granted exclusively to personnel of the United News Agency, terminating Dentsū's services in this area. This measure took effect on 1 January 1936, and two months later Dentsū agreed to surrender its news dispatch operations to the UNA.

From the beginning, NHK supported the concept of a state wire service. The news NHK received from Rengō and Dentsū was often inferior to newspaper reporting, and a more efficient wire service would improve broadcast journalism. The state was equally anxious to see NHK participate in the project. One of the UNA's prime objectives was to bolster overseas broadcasting power, and the construction of new facilities would be costly. The large newspapers subscribing to the UNA were wary of military financing, and Foreign Ministry funding was partly vetoed by the Finance Ministry as unaffordable.[110] In this situation, the availability of capital from NHK was a godsend. In the first half of 1936, NHK invested one hundred thousand yen in the UNA and lent it another three million at low interest. One of NHK's division managers helped to prepare the news agency's articles of incorporation, and five of NHK's executives became UNA directors, at least three of them ex–Communications Ministry bureaucrats; one of these was Nakayama Ryūji, an important figure in war-related broadcast planning after the Manchurian Incident.[111]

Thereafter, all of NHK's national news came either from the UNA or straight from state offices. Without its own news-gathering facilities, radio could not independently corroborate information from these sources. During the 2/26 Incident, for example, NHK sent people only to the UNA and Metropolitan Police headquarters to gather news. Rumors abounded during the first day, but no one was sent to the site of the action. The news reports occupying every minute of air time on 26 February were all official state announcements read verbatim. Only at 2:50 A.M. on 27 February did NHK send two men around Tokyo, and their report that all was quiet was NHK's sole contribution to news of the event.[112] With press coverage limited by official constraints, radio was

109. Ibid., supplementary document 1, p. 540.
110. NHK, ed., *Nihon Hōsō Shi*, 1: 336.
111. *Nihon Musen Shi*, 7: 196–97.
112. NHK, ed., *Nihon Hōsō Shi*, 1: 392.

the country's principal source of information until the end of February, but the only real news source was the state.[113] Officials used radio first to calm public fears and then to broadcast their ultimatum to the rebels. National news broadcasts continued to originate entirely with the state until 1945. In addition, thanks to its unique international communications facilities, the UNA eventually became the almost exclusive source of foreign news carried in the press. It thus enabled officials to shape public opinion about world affairs and contributed substantially to the coming of the Pacific War.

In July 1936, the interministerial committee that originally proposed the wire service merger was formally recognized as the Cabinet Information Committee. Its only concrete task, beyond numerous advisory functions, was official supervision of the United News Agency, including provision of state funds. The state made an annual budgetary outlay for the UNA that came to 1.1 million yen in 1936; the money was furnished by the Army, Navy, and Foreign Ministries and was dispensed through the cabinet's budget by the information committee.[114] In September 1936, the committee determined its program objectives for the UNA. The wire service was described as an agent of state policy designed to disseminate information in accord with official views. Its ultimate goal was to win the "thought war" against Reuters, TASS, AP, and other wire services and to acquire a dominant position in Asia similar to that of Reuters in Western Europe.[115]

Officials succeeded, then, in isolating radio from autonomous news sources as well as in exerting greater influence over program content through the Broadcast Programming Council. These direct forms of control would be greatly expanded in later years, largely at the initiative of the Cabinet Information Committee. The state's role in forcing a merger of the two wire services turned out to be a dress rehearsal for the subsequent consolidation of thousands of media companies by military-bureaucratic elites.

MOBILIZATIONAL MILITARY REGIMES: THE FIRST GENERATION

The economic and international crises of the 1930s afflicted many countries, stimulating political radicalism in society and prompting radi-

---

113. Nakayama Ryūji, *Sensō to Denki Tsūshin*, p. 67.
114. *Masu Media Tōsei*, vol. 2, supplementary document 3, p. 546.
115. Ibid., supplementary document 4, pp. 548–50.

cal reactions from existing elites. There were only a few areas, such as Britain and most of Scandinavia, where the violent right never became a potent political force and democracy persisted with relatively little difficulty. In other countries such as Czechoslovakia and Belgium, democrats battled successfully against a more significant rightist challenge, often resorting to quasi-authoritarian tactics to control radical movements. A new conservative authoritarian right, opposed to democracy and the left but acting primarily to sustain a traditional social order, took charge in yet another group of countries. This camp usually produced military regimes initially colluding with fascist or other civil rightist elements which the military ultimately sought to defuse or destroy, as in Portugal and Brazil. Fascist movements seized power only in Germany and Italy, where single-party regimes instituted distinctively modern and mobilizational forms of autocracy approaching the totalitarian model. Interwar Japan fits none of these patterns.

Japan's political elites were divided among four principal regime preferences after 1936. A significant segment of the Diet's lower house continued to seek a restoration of *party government* led by mainstream party elites. Most proponents were members of the larger factions of the Seiyūkai and Minseitō, men anxious to regain their lost authority. A second preference was for *conservative authoritarianism*, that is, cabinets led by non-party Prime Ministers chosen by the *Genrō* and ruling within the established political structure, similar to the Saitō and Okada cabinets and the pre-democratic Meiji pattern. Backing this position were the *Genrō* Saionji and like-minded individuals in the bureaucracy and peerage (the senior statesmen block), some of the older business combines (judging from their support for Ugaki), and, in the late 1930s, select elements in the reactionary "idealist" right (for example, Hiranuma Kiichirō), who opposed any radical restructuring of the state or society.

A third preference was for a *single-party regime*, led by a new civilian elite, that would eclipse existing party groups. Most espousing this option saw Prince Konoe Fumimaro, the most popular politician of the day, as the new party's torchbearer. Advocates included some "renovationist" rightist groups (for example, Nakano Seigō's Eastern Way Society),[116] other minor Diet parties such as the Social Masses Party, some minority factions of the Minseitō and Seiyūkai, Konoe and some of his intellectual backers in the Shōwa Research Society, and some influential

---

116. Tetsuo Najita, "Nakano Seigō and the Spirit of the Meiji Restoration in Twentieth-Century Japan," p. 409.

military officers.[117] The new party concept also aroused considerable enthusiasm in the press.

The fourth regime preference was for *militarism:* a cabinet comprising active-duty officers and civilians ready to do their bidding. An organ of mass mobilization was often part of militaristic schemes, and the army was usually pictured in the leading role. Supporters included a number of senior officers, especially those with Manchurian service or involved in planning for total war, and some civil rightist groups, bureaucrats, and newer, defense-oriented industrial combines.[118] Note that the supporters of a particular regime formation were not necessarily political allies. Those seeking a restoration of party government did not agree on how to bring it about, and while Konoe desired a single-party regime to counterbalance military influence, this is not necessarily what other backers of a new party had in mind.

The interactions among these groups were very complex, and all wielded significant political influence at least through 1940, but there is no question that military rule ultimately emerged triumphant. Konoe's first premiership (June 1937–January 1939) effectively eliminated advocates of mainstream party government and conservative authoritarianism as front-runners in the struggle for power. The Minseitō and Seiyūkai held only two ministerships in the first Konoe, the Hiranuma (January–August 1939), and the Abe (August 1939–January 1940) cabinets. No ex–mainstream party men served initially in Konoe's second cabinet, organized in July 1940 (two were added belatedly), and none participated in Konoe's third cabinet (produced by a reshuffling in July 1941) or in the Tōjō government formed in October 1941.[119] Fur-

117. Some democrats and militarists also spoke of setting up a one-party regime. The single-mass-party option referred to here, however, involved a new political structure placing the state under a new and predominantly civilian elite; by contrast, a fusion of mainstream Seiyūkai and Minseitō factions was a conservative scheme to sell old goods in a new package, and militaristic plans for a mobilization organ were generally aimed at creating a loyal servant of existing military-bureaucratic elites, not a new center of power. There were, however, some military officers who genuinely desired a powerful new political organization (albeit one that would share their goals). For example, see the plan of the Kokusaku Kenkyūkai (National Policy Research Association), prepared in part by staff of the Army Ministry's Military Affairs Bureau (*Gunmukyoku*) under General Mutō Akira, in Yokusan Undō Shi Kankōkai, ed., *Yokusan Kokumin Undō Shi,* pp. 64–71.

118. For one example of a militarist proposal, see the plan of the Tōa Kensetsu Renmei (League to Establish East Asia), representing elements of the army's Control Faction, among others, in Yokusan Undō Shi Kankōkai, ed., *Undō Shi,* pp. 72–76.

119. In the cabinet initially organized by Konoe in mid-1940, all but two ministers were military officers or bureaucrats: Ide, *Nihon Kanryōsei,* pp. 96–97. Ex–Seiyūkai leader Kanemitsu Tsuneo was added to this cabinet as Welfare Minister in September 1940, and ex–Minseitō Representative Ogawa Masatsune was appointed Minister without Portfolio in April 1941 to serve for only three months. Akita Kiyoshi, appointed

thermore, in April 1938 Konoe pushed through the Diet a State Total Mobilization Law which eventually transferred most legislation to the realm of executive decrees, and his campaign for the Imperial Rule Assistance Association in 1940 finally resulted in the dissolution of all existing parties.

Konoe also opposed conservative authoritarianism. He had refused the premiership after the 2/26 Incident, out of disagreement with Saionji's goals of conservatism at home and peace abroad. He often advised Saionji that the only way to avert militarism was for civilian leadership to take the "initiative" (sente) in promoting foreign expansion.[120] Conservative authoritarianism recovered to enjoy a brief last gasp in the pro-British Yonai cabinet (January–July 1940), which was toppled by the Army Minister's resignation to return Konoe to power. Clearly the period of political transition did not end in 1937, but Konoe's first term moved the mainstream parties and supporters of conservative authoritarianism to the fringes of political influence and simultaneously broke through the policy stalemate of 1932–1937. With very few exceptions, Konoe's inauguration terminated the involvement of the Diet and major parties in the making of media policy.

The critical questions during 1937–1940 were whether or not Konoe would succeed in organizing a new ruling party, and what might be its character. Contradictory proposals for a new party were brought to Konoe throughout his first term, but the issue came to a head during his second premiership in August 1940, when he declared a New Order (Shintaisei) in Japanese politics and assembled a preparatory committee to determine its organization. Virtually every major political group sought to turn the New Order to its advantage.

Konoe himself wanted a personal power base allowing him to con-

---

Colonial Affairs Minister in September 1940, had abandoned the Seiyūkai in 1934 and thus no longer represented mainstream party interests. Biographical background data is taken from Konsaisu Jinmei Jiten: Nihon Hen.

120. Yabe Teiji, Konoe Fumimaro, 1: 224. The Elder Statesman was in a painful predicament at the time of Konoe's first appointment. Cabinets led by no-name conservatives had failed to curtail military influence. Furthermore, the army was now in a position to veto such appointees by refusing a minister. The army sought an effective ally as Prime Minister, a departure from both conservatives (Saitō, Okada) and reasonably supportive figures who lacked leverage in the Diet (Hirota, Hayashi). Saionji desired a more forceful Prime Minister who would reassert civilian leadership, yet his appointment had to have the military's approval. The impasse between these positions was broken when each side agreed upon Konoe, Saionji less willingly than the military. Perhaps due to Saionji's reticence, the Lord Privy Seal was made to take direct responsibility for advising the Emperor on Konoe's first appointment, abandoning his usual role of passive intermediary for the Genrō: Ide, Nihon Kanryōsei, p. 123 n. 43. See also Berger, Parties, pp. 120–21.

trol the military and bureaucracy, but his vision of the New Order was never fully articulated. He did anticipate a new mass mobilization structure organizing all Japanese by occupational and social activities—newspapers would comprise one of the social units—and this structure was to include a decision-making body that would dominate the Diet.[121] But exactly how it would affect the status of the cabinet, existing bureaucratic jurisdictions, the constitutional responsibility of ministers individually to the throne, and the military's political role and right of supreme command was either left undetermined or unpublicized. In August 1940, rather than champion his own design for a New Order, Konoe invited representatives of all major groups to participate in its founding. The preparatory commission included Diet members of diverse opinions, both tendencies of the civil right wing, military officers, spokesmen for the established bureaucratic ministries, and leaders from agriculture and industry. Unison among so many clashing interests was naturally unattainable.[122]

The outcome was the Imperial Rule Assistance Association (IRAA), atop a vast system of mobilization organs administered by the bureaucracy. A conscious decision to make this a "public" and not a "political" organization meant that the IRAA would have little impact on policymaking. It did not challenge the authority of the cabinet or its radical planning bodies. Nor did it interfere with bureaucratic jurisdictions, since the Home Ministry's governors doubled as prefectural IRAA heads. The IRAA did endorse 81 percent of the winning candidates in the lower-house election of 1942, but half of its nominees were incumbents, and in any case the Diet's influence remained slight. Konoe thus failed to establish an independent source of political power. He resigned in October 1941, leaving his successor, General Tōjō Hideki,

121. Berger, *Parties*, pp. 277, 303.
122. Ibid., pp. 290–91. Many explanations have been offered for why Konoe assembled this mélange and never acted to impress his own concept upon the New Order. There was his notion of a statesmanship above narrow interests, which made political infighting distasteful. This may have been reinforced by a certain weakness of character reported by his closest friends, who found him to equivocate in the face of adversity despite his political talents: Yabe, *Konoe*, 1: 228. On the other hand, a hard-nosed appraisal of the situation may have given him pause. There was no sure way of compelling the military or the bureaucracy to play second fiddle to the New Order he envisioned. Indeed, there was no organizational infrastructure upon which to build the mass mobilization system apart from the Home Ministry's local authorities and the Military Reservist Associations. Furthermore, to establish a New Order with its own structural underpinnings would undoubtedly be a time-consuming feat involving serious political conflicts. To embark on this project while engaged in an arduous war in China might undermine national unity to the point of adversely affecting the war effort, and this possibility bore heavily on Konoe's calculations: Berger, *Parties*, pp. 274–75, 297–300, 309–11.

to lead Japan into war with America, for which the planning had already begun under Konoe's own cabinet.

Tōjō's government can be portrayed straightforwardly as rule by a military-bureaucratic regime. The Prime Minister, always in uniform, at first served concurrently as Army Minister and Home Minister as well, though he was probably more a representative of the army as an institution than a personal dictator. Among other key appointments, General Suzuki Teiichi headed the Cabinet Planning Board, bureaucrat Kaya Okinori served as Finance Minister and Colonial Affairs Minister, bureaucrat Kishi Nobusuke became Commerce and Industry Minister, and bureaucrat Hoshino Naoki became Cabinet Chief Secretary. Mixed military and civilian cabinets of this sort have characterized some 40 percent of all military regimes.[123]

Although the Tōjō cabinet was Japan's first unadulterated military government, domestic policymaking was already largely controlled by military-bureaucratic elites in the earlier Konoe cabinets. Konoe was opposed to militarism in principle and was no mere pawn of the army. He successfully resisted the impositions of the General Staff on policy toward the China Incident (paradoxically, the General Staff had opposed escalation in favor of long-term plans to bolster military strength),[124] and he censured the military's right of supreme command for hampering his efforts to control policy.[125] Yet the fact remains that Konoe came to power on both occasions as the military's choice; in 1940, the Army

123. Eric A. Nordlinger, *Soldiers in Politics: Military Coups and Governments*, p. 109. Suzuki, Kaya, and Hoshino had earlier served in Konoe's governments, and Kishi and Hoshino had completed assignments in Manchukuo. The extent of Tōjō's personal power is still not conclusively documented; the argument that his personal influence was very limited is made in Ben-Ami Shillony, *Politics and Culture in Wartime Japan*.

124. Oka Yoshitake, *Konoe Fumimaro*, pp. 81–82; Crowley, *Japan's Quest for Autonomy*, pp. 360–73.

125. Yabe, *Konoe*, 1: 225. Crowley has written of the right of supreme command:

Historically, the "right of supreme command" had invested each service with complete control over all its internal administrative affairs; and it had confirmed complete control of the conduct of military operations in time of hostilities. It had not, however, been viewed as empowering the service ministers or general staffs with the right to set national policy, as witness the conduct and determination of policy during the Sino and Russo-Japanese Wars, World War I, and the Siberian intervention. The proposition that the "right of supreme command" invested the general staffs and/or the service ministers with a veto power in cabinet decisions on national defense was first articulated during the London Naval Treaty controversy. (Crowley, *Japan's Quest for Autonomy*, p. 386)

The dispute over ratification of the naval treaty occurred in 1930. The right of supreme command was subsequently used to justify the independent actions of field armies that turned the Manchurian Incident into a campaign for territorial expansion. The proper extent of this right remained a subject of controversy thereafter.

Minister resigned to bring about Konoe's second cabinet. Konoe believed that military expansion was Japan's "inevitable destiny," and he was ultimately caught in a trap between his advocacy of conquest abroad and his opposition to military rule at home.

The difficulty was how to embrace imperialistic expansion and simultaneously contain the military's policymaking role, when the one was a partial function of the other. To prepare for a full-scale war of conquest demanded policy innovations in every sector, and planning for mobilization had long been a preserve of the armed forces and their bureaucratic confederates. In fact, their enthusiasm for Konoe was rooted in the belief that he might win passsage for their legislative proposals,[126] and he did not let them down. He later recorded that his goal upon becoming Prime Minister in 1937 was to realize Japan's "destiny" for expansion, doing his best to suppress reckless military elements while adopting military demands that were "rational."[127] But as the China Incident developed into a major war, partly due to Konoe's own decisions at crucial stages, the military's statist designs were increasingly accepted as rational.

Konoe's terms in office witnessed the enlargement of hybrid military-bureaucratic policymaking organs, the passage of legislation empowering the state to execute their plans, and concrete implementation of those plans in all important policy fields. Konoe personally supported these developments. In 1938, he threatened to resign in order to win the Diet's approval for a controversial electric-power control system, the product of military-bureaucratic planning.[128] In the same year he financed a rightist gang out to intimidate the parties during consideration of the State Total Mobilization Law,[129] an executive enabling act that emasculated the role of the Diet. He also upgraded the Cabinet Planning Board and Cabinet Information Bureau, whose renovationists strongly swayed the actions of his governments.

These measures of policy and state reorganization, inextricably tied to imperialism, greatly strengthened those very mechanisms of military-bureaucratic power that had to be dismantled to restore stable civilian control. Thus Konoe's imperialism severely compromised his efforts to reassert civilian authority over the state. He himself perceived the cabi-

---

126. Oka, *Konoe*, p. 54; Crowley, *Japan's Quest for Autonomy*, pp. 323–24; Berger, *Parties*, p. 120.
127. Yabe, *Konoe*, 1: 225.
128. Itō Takashi, *Jū-go-Nen Sensō*, p. 213.
129. Berger, *Parties*, pp. 147–49.

net's new policymaking organs as devices for increasing his own control over military and bureaucratic policy input. But in fact these organs greatly amplified the military's presence in policymaking circles, formulated policy designs which Konoe then adopted as his own, and outlived Konoe's cabinets to stand as bastions of military influence within the state. Thus despite his anti-militarism and a fairly successful struggle to rule his own governments, it was perfectly logical that Konoe's last cabinet was followed by the premiership of an active-duty general. The Imperial Rule Assistance Association was but the last great tool of administrative power Konoe bequeathed to his successors.

In characterizing the regime, the key distinction to be made is that before the Tōjō cabinet the military shared power not only with bureaucrats but also with politicians. Regarding policy toward the mass media, the evidence is that Konoe generally adopted the recommendations of the cabinet's military-bureaucratic planning organs; as the work of these administrators, Japanese policy can be compared to the media policies of other military regimes. It must, however, be kept in mind that military-bureaucratic elites were governing in coalition with a civilian politician who did play an assertive, independent role in many policy areas.

Conventional analyses of military regimes indicate that they do not exhibit a distinctive policy outlook. Aggregate data studies show that military regimes are not characterized by a common set of policies or a particular level of social intervention. R. D. McKinley and A. S. Cohan found that the only consistently outstanding difference between military and civilian regimes ruling in the same country was the military's greater suppression of civil political activity. Otherwise, military regimes did not form a distinct type in terms of performance and could not be differentiated from non-military regimes on that basis.[130] Robert Jackman also concluded that "military governments have no unique effects on social change, regardless of level of economic development."[131]

It is established, however, that a sizable majority of military regimes adopt a fundamentally conservative position in regard to the existing social order. Juan Linz writes of "bureaucratic-military" regimes:

> Authoritarian regimes in which a coalition predominated by but not exclusively controlled by army officers and bureaucrats establishes control of

130. R. D. McKinlay and A. S. Cohan, "A Comparative Analysis of the Political and Economic Performance of Military and Civilian Regimes: A Cross-National Aggregate Study," pp. 8, 23.
131. Robert W. Jackman, "Politicians in Uniform," p. 1096.

government and excludes or includes other groups without commitment to specific ideology, acts pragmatically within the limits of their bureaucratic mentality, and neither creates nor allows a mass single party to play a dominant role are the most frequent subtype. They may operate without the existence of any parties, but more frequent is the creation of an official government-sponsored single party, which, rather than aiming at a controlled mobilization of the population, tends to reduce its participation in political life even in a manipulated form . . . .[132]

Eric Nordlinger has estimated that of all cases of military intervention in politics, those in which the military consolidates a regime of indefinite tenure and transcends conservative tendencies to mobilize society through new structures constitute only 10 percent.[133]

The figure might be somewhat higher but for scholarly neglect of an important cluster of mobilizational military-bureaucratic regimes appearing in Japan and Eastern Europe in the interwar period. Under military-bureaucratic auspices, Japan underwent a policy revolution between 1937 and 1945 that involved a fundamental reorganization of many social sectors. All labor unions were dissolved and replaced with joint labor-management consultation committees in each firm. Agrarian workers were mobilized into the Agricultural Patriotic Association, the first comprehensive organization in this sector. Similar bodies targeted youth, women, artists, writers, and other groups. Heavy industries were reorganized into oligopolies of large producers linked by monopolistic distribution companies, and each industrial area was supervised by a civil-bureaucratic control association. Journals and film producers were pressed into a similar format, thousands of small to medium-sized firms being systematically driven out of business. No one familiar with the structure of Japan's media industries in 1937 would have recognized them five years later.

In Eastern Europe as well, a number of military-bureaucratic regimes attempted innovative mobilization programs in this period. Some created administered mass organizations similar to the IRAA—for example, Poland's Camp of National Unity, Rumania's Front of National Rebirth—as superstructures for mobilization bodies established in particular functional or geographic areas. These countries represent a distinct response to the interwar crises as bureaucratically dominated regimes opposed to spontaneous revolution from the left or right, but also embarking upon ambitious if selective programs of social mobilization

---

132. Juan J. Linz, "Totalitarian and Authoritarian Regimes," p. 285.
133. Nordlinger, *Soldiers in Politics*, pp. 21–22, 26–27.

that clearly escape the bounds of conservatism. Due to the German conquest, none of these experiments proceeded as far as the Japanese, which stands out among them as the best test case for the mobilizational potential of military systems.

The critical questions are how and why this regime could overcome the standard image of military-bureaucratic conservatism. The conventional view is that bureaucratic organization, military or civilian, imposes rigid discipline upon its members, whose careers hinge on seniority and conformity to procedural routine.[134] Examination criteria, training, and the specialization of offices are said to encourage a piecemeal approach to problem solving according to technical and pragmatic norms, not grand ideologies demanding systemic social change.[135] Moreover, officers and civil servants are thought to place inordinate value on public order.[136] Social unrest threatens to infiltrate military ranks or bring soldiers into confrontation with their own people; it also disrupts efficient bureaucratic planning and the predictability of policy outcomes. Radical innovations likely to generate disorder are thus not to be expected from military-bureaucratic regimes.

Administrative elites are thought to view mass mobilization in particular with serious misgivings. They have little constituency to draw upon in civil society, and they more often approach the mass public as a source of antagonism to be muzzled than as a potential asset to be activated. Furthermore, the fact that the military and bureaucracy stand above society rather than penetrating it like a mass party suggests an inability to effect radical social change, which often requires the involvement of many social actors. Whereas a party can expand to absorb members from all walks of life, modern military and bureaucratic institutions tend to be closed professions lacking such flexibility.[137] A major task of the chapters that follow is, therefore, to ascertain how the Japa-

---

134. Robert Merton writes:

The bureaucrat's official life is planned for him in terms of a graded career, through the organizational devices of promotion by seniority, pensions, incremental salaries, etc., all of which are designed to provide incentives for disciplined action and conformity to the official regulations. The official is tacitly expected to and largely does adapt his thoughts, feelings, and actions to the prospect of this career. But *these very devices* which increase the probability of conformance also lead to an over-concern with strict adherence to regulations which induces timidity, conservatism, and technicism. (Merton, "Bureaucratic Structure and Personality," p. 367)

135. Aberbach, Putnam, and Rockman, *Bureaucrats and Politicians,* p. 114; Nordlinger, *Soldiers in Politics,* pp. 119–22.
136. Nordlinger, *Soldiers in Politics,* pp. 54–56.
137. Alfred Stepan, *The State and Society: Peru in Comparative Perspective,* p. 313.

nese regime overcame these apparent handicaps to engineer a profound restructuring of many social sectors, the mass media among them.

A second focus of attention is the impact of modern warfare and political ideologies on the expansion of state power. In many countries in this century, the prospect or actuality of total war has caused a greater transformation in state control over society than any other single factor. Virtually every social organization or activity comes to be reevaluated under the rubric of national defense. In Japan, war was not only a paramount element in the thinking of media policymakers, but it also emasculated potential opposition from powerful media industries inclined to accept war-related justifications as unassailable *raisons d'état*. The immediate demands of war, however, do not provide an exhaustive explanation for Japan's policy revolution.

The renovationist bureaucrats and military officers of the Cabinet Information Bureau did not understand their policies as temporary wartime expedients, but as permanent measures heralding the arrival of a new state-society system. Strongly influenced by both Marxist and fascist thought, their perception of the war as symptomatic of a vast metamorphosis in world politics, economics, and culture provides an indispensable ideological background to the changes they wrought. The way these men managed to reshape a highly advanced media system and harness it to their purposes is in many ways a microcosm of general state-society interaction in the late imperial period. It demonstrates that Prince Konoe's New Order was not only or even mainly the tale of a stillborn political party, but comprised a massive onslaught of state control policies that largely recast the organizational landscape of Japanese society.

The Press: The Consultation System

Although the most concerted effort at mobilizing the mass media was not made until 1940–1941, as part of Prince Konoe's New Order, state control advanced beyond negative censorship to positive mobilization of content and industrial restructuring shortly after the China Incident of July 1937. This apparently unplanned clash between Japanese and Chinese troops soon escalated into a major war that would ultimately see the defeat of Japanese imperialism. Prior to the New Order, new forms of press control were instituted without legal innovations, through regular consultation meetings between state officials and journalists. This chapter, focusing mainly on the 1937–1940 period, describes how these meetings were used to deliver mobilizational directives, to initiate pre-publication censorship of magazines, to blacklist writers, and to drive press organs out of business. It is a story of seemingly boundless administrative license confronted by a disorganized industry ill equipped to defend its autonomy.

EARLY WARTIME MOBILIZATION

Immediately after the China Incident, the Home Ministry used pre-publication warnings to try to shield military secrets and stop publication of articles indicating Japan was at fault.[1] The army and navy as-

1. *Masu Media Tōsei,* vol. 2, document 2, p. 2.

sisted in preparing the warnings. Police officials were to convey them in polite "consultations" (*kondan*) with media people, employing "unofficial announcements" (*naishi*) to "positively guide" (*sekkyokuteki ni shidō*) newspapers and leading magazines.[2] These became standard phrases in official documents. "Positive guidance" meant overstepping mere taboos to indicate how stories should be written.

When the incident failed of speedy resolution, the Army Ministry (31 July), Navy Ministry (16 August), and Foreign Ministry (13 December) activated their powers to ban items from publication under the Newspaper Law, just as they had during the Sino-Japanese War, the Russo-Japanese War, and World War I.[3] Their orders were added to the Home Ministry's own pre-publication warnings. The Home Ministry telegraphed them to its local offices under joint signature (for example, signed by the Home Ministry's Criminal Affairs Bureau Chief and the Army Ministry's Military Affairs Bureau Chief), and all bonded newspapers were notified. The operation worked twenty-four hours a day, and direct telephones were installed to handle urgent commands.[4] The administrative sanctions for violating Army, Navy, or Foreign Ministry warnings were the usual bans on circulation, deletions, and so forth. Special pre-publication censorship was instituted for articles treating military matters in a narrow sense, such as strategy or troop movements. These were reviewed by local Home Ministry officials before printing; if passed, they were stamped "Approved by the Army [or, Navy] Ministry."[5] When press reports were filed from a war zone, they were censored first by

2. Ibid., pp. 2–3.
3. The ministerial decrees instituting these powers are reprinted in ibid., documents 1, 3, and 7. The Army, Navy, and Foreign Ministries had not formally exercised their Newspaper Law powers during the Manchurian Incident, though the Home Ministry had incorporated their requests into the pre-publication warning system on its own authority, as was always done for other ministries as well.
4. Ibid., document 2, p. 4. The language describing pre-publication warnings from the Army, Navy, or Foreign Ministry under article 27 of the Newspaper Law was different from that of Home Ministry warnings. The "instructions" most likely to bring a ban on circulation were *shitatsu* under Home Ministry nomenclature but *genjū keikoku* if coming from the other ministries, "advice" was *keikoku* under both systems, and "consultation" was *kondan* under the former but *chūi* under the latter. These differences were significant, since a violation of article 27 could mean two years in prison, whereas violation of an injunction from the Home Ministry brought a maximum six-month sentence. When article 27 powers were first instituted, press organs receiving a *genjū keikoku* had to acknowledge it in writing so that potential liability was clear: see ibid., p. 12.
The *chūi* and *kondan* of pre-publication warnings must be distinguished from other uses of these terms. *Chūi* was also the official label for *post*-publication warnings, and the term *kondan*, originally used to describe a pre-publication warning based solely on a moral appeal, acquired new meaning in reference to the "consultation meetings" (*kondankai*) instituted after the China Incident.
5. Ibid., p. 8.

military information units in the field, then by the Home Ministry in Japan. Photographs underwent the same procedures, and film censors received instructions identical to those for publications. In its essentials, this system resembled the one used during earlier wars.

Many items banned under the Newspaper Law soon after the China Incident pertained to weaponry and the progress of hostilities. These included photos or descriptions of armored columns, troop locations, battle dates, and the identities of commanding officers.[6] Most armies try to conceal such data, but the effort can have serious political implications. For example, on 11 July 1937, Japanese and Chinese field armies agreed to a cease-fire, but the Army Ministry's Newspaper Group (*Shinbunhan*) instructed newspapers to stop special editions on the story. Meanwhile, it had NHK broadcast that the enemy's sincerity was doubtful and the accord might end as "wastepaper."[7] Such actions could check domestic pressure for peace. Prohibiting news on conscription, munitions production, and troop departures had foreign security justifications, but it also blinded the Japanese people to the conflict's rapid escalation. Reports on cruel treatment of the Chinese were banned, but stories on Chinese brutality were acceptable.[8]

The Home Ministry itself issued public-order warnings to constrict debate. On 13 July 1937, instructions were to avoid anti-war and anti-military views, portrayals of Japan as warlike or aggressive, and references to foreign press reports that might mislead the popular judgment.[9] Quotations from the foreign press and letters to the editor were methods papers sometimes used to air sensitive criticism. The catalog of injunctions from the Home Ministry grew steadily. The following list of forbidden contents was issued by the Criminal Affairs Bureau's Book Section in August 1938 (paraphrased here).

1.   Differences of opinion with the government or military on the nation's basic China policy.

2.   A lack of unified public support for China policy.

3.   Indications that we have territorial ambitions in China or that the new states in central and northern China are Japanese puppets, or doubts about the significance of this as a holy war.

4.   Contents fostering a tendency toward peace or weakening public resolve to sustain a long war.

6. See ibid., document 2 for army contents, document 4 for navy.
7. Kuroda Hidetoshi, *Chishikijin Genron Dan'atsu no Kiroku*, p. 19.
8. *Masu Media Tōsei*, vol. 2, document 15, p. 137.
9. Ibid., document 2, p. 3.

    a.   Signs of willingness to make peace with the Chiang Kai Shek government within the cabinet, the military, the senior statesmen, or political or business circles.

    b.   Reports of an intention to soften Japan's policy against negotiating with the nationalist government (*kokumin seifu o aite ni sezu*).

    c.   Impressions that the government or diplomatic authorities are planning a policy of peace toward Chiang.

    d.   Exaggerated reports that third countries may offer to mediate between Japan and China.

    e.   The view that the Hankow offensive has fulfilled Japan's military objectives, leaving an optimistic impression.

5.   Arguments hindering foreign relations, especially friendly ties with Germany and Italy.

6.   Predictions of a cabinet change or a turnover in military ministers.

7.   Rumors related to the incident.

8.   Agitation for illegal or radical means to strengthen the domestic wartime system.

9.   Encouragement for mass action to protest foreign policy or the incident's effects on the people's livelihood.

10.   Indications that Japan lacks natural resources, stories of bank failures, or any other weak points creating uncertainty about the country's ability to wage war.

11.   Singular stress on unemployment, bankruptcies, or other ill influences of the incident on the people's livelihood.

12.   Exaggerations of war profiteering or the crippled condition of the people's income that might foster anti-war sentiment.

13.   Stories of problems faced by the families of draftees, such as those related to livelihood, chastity, government compensation, or inheritance squabbles, or reports on the private lives of soldiers returning home if they tend to engender unrest or dissatisfaction among troops departing for the front.

14.   Introduction of gaudy new fashions fostering ostentation or frivolous tastes contrary to the spirit of frugality.

15.   Lascivious or suggestive accounts of bars, cafes, dance halls, or prostitution.

16.   Provocative presentations of obscenity, rape, immorality, lovers' suicides, or other sexual matters.[10]

These instructions only begin to indicate the new severity in morals censorship. From May 1938, officials strove to harden manners and morals standards by summoning for "consultation" top magazine edi-

---

10. Ibid., document 19, pp. 145–46.

tors in fields ranging from women's interests to popular entertainment. The war was sometimes cited as justification for the crackdown.[11] In late 1937, the state had begun a National Spiritual Total Mobilization Movement to modify living habits and prepare the nation psychologically for a long war, and the new moral code was part of this movement. Consultation plans for women's magazines in May 1938 called for stricter enforcement against the following (paraphrased here).

1.   Vulgar novels or those dealing with love relationships based on romantic sentiment (ren'ai), for example, stories of the love affairs of married women or those obfuscating the ideal of chastity for young women.

2.   Lovers' suicides or other incidents exerting a bad influence on women's cultural education.

3.   Stories of true confessions, especially those related to sexual desire.

4.   Provocative articles related to sex, for example, "The Worry of Not Being Able to Attain Satisfaction," "The Difference between Virgins and Non-Virgins," "Secret Advice on Hygiene for New Brides."

5.   Articles on health matters connected with sex, such as venereal disease or contraception.[12]

These standards related to public order and morals differed in form from any previously used by the Home Ministry. In the past, regular censorship standards had never been divulged to press people, much to their annoyance; only pre-publication warnings on reports of current events had been communicated. But these new strictures were regular censorship guidelines conveyed directly to editors in meetings called by police and bureaucrats. These "consultation meetings" (kondankai) soon became an institutionalized feature of press controls.

THE CONSULTATION FORMAT

Despite its innocuous title, the "consultation meeting" is a key to understanding state power in late imperial Japan. It was employed to regulate not only the mass media but the economy, religion, art, and education. Though the meaning of consultation could vary with the context, the consultation system most often referred to ongoing direct contact between officials and subjects, initiated by the former to extend state

11. For example, see ibid., document 22, pp. 154–55.
12. Ibid., document 16, pp. 137–38. For evidence that these prohibitions were actually communicated to editors, see Kuroda, Chishikijin, pp. 91–92, where the author describes a "consultation" of 5 September 1938 in which some of these very standards were discussed.

control. It involved telephone calls, individual interviews, and group meetings arranged in conference halls or private restaurant rooms; contact could be sporadic, or scheduled at fixed intervals. For the press, the largest gatherings could involve 30 to 50 editors, and most sessions were held in secret. Communication was usually oral,[13] the journalists taking notes when officials delivered a lengthy presentation.

The consultation format developed logically out of the prominent bureaucratic role in policymaking evident since the Meiji Restoration, but its institutionalized use after the China Incident signified a sharp boost in independent administrative authority. Though consultations had not been a dominant mode of control in the past, there was a stylistic similarity in the state's handling of short-term problems such as the founding of NHK in the 1920s. Consultations also resemble postwar "administrative guidance" (*gyosei shidō*), a phrase that refers to extralegal but institutionalized advice from state agencies aimed at controlling the behavior of civil associations. It has recently been documented in such areas as medicine, broadcasting, and the economy.[14] The pre-1945 consultation system was far more penetrating, but it supplies an instructive background to postwar bureaucratic methods.

Consultations allowed officials to exercise mobilizational powers they acutely desired but had no legal means to acquire. They were deeply concerned about the limited effectiveness of earlier press controls. There had been hundreds of violations of pre-publication warnings related to the Manchurian Incident in 1931, despite sweeping press support for Japan's position. The leniency of punishments, the profitability of printing hot war news, and the general enthusiasm for military success were strong inducements to ignore the warnings. When officials compared their performance in September 1931 with that in July 1937 after the China Incident, they found about the same number of violations (July 7–31: 77 banned editions, 2 deletions, and 254 post-publication warnings—data for all publications).[15] This was still some improvement, since in 1937 more violators were small local journals, which usually offended by noting the departure of hometown boys for the front or describing military equipment.[16] Nonetheless,

13. *Masu Media Tōsei*, vol. 2, document 15, p. 133, and document 30, p. 241.
14. Seven articles in the magazine *Jurisuto* 741 (1 June 1981) are devoted to administrative guidance. See also Chalmers Johnson, *MITI and the Japanese Miracle: The Growth of Industrial Policy, 1925–1975*, chapter 7.
15. *Masu Media Tōsei*, vol. 2, document 2, p. 10.
16. Ibid.

these were so many holes that could not be plugged without greater positive control.

As the China Incident escalated, the conviction also grew that favorable reports should not be left to chance but should be systematically attuned to the demands of state policy. There were no aboveboard means to accomplish this in 1937. The one prospect for new legal powers was passage of the State Total Mobilization Law in March 1938. However, to secure the Diet's approval of the law, Prime Minister Konoe had to pledge that it would not be activated in response to the China Incident, but only in case of another war. Later this promise was honored more in the breach than the observance, but in 1938 it was politically impossible to use this law against the press.

Under these circumstances, top officials from the Home, Army, Navy, and Foreign Ministries met in the spring of 1938 under the auspices of the Cabinet Information Division to explore other routes for mobilizing the press. The cabinet's decision to upgrade the information organ from a committee to a division had been made in April 1937 and effected in September. The consultation system, already instituted by the Home, Army, and Navy Ministries on a modest scale, was endorsed by the interministerial group as the readiest tool for bolstering positive press controls. The Home Ministry conveyed the group's conclusions to its local offices on 13 July 1938.[17] The ministry's preface declared that the China Incident had engaged Japan in a "total war." It asserted that the same news could be written to leave different impressions; it was therefore necessary to shape the basic editorial attitude behind the news. This could be done by supplying newspapers with material for articles and offering "positive internal guidance" (sekkyokuteki naimenteki shidō). "Internal guidance" was official jargon for the instructions imparted through consultations.

Many state offices became involved in consultations. The Home Ministry had begun periodic meetings as early as October 1937, and the military also started regular consultations shortly after the China Incident.[18] The Cabinet Information Division came to play a major role, especially from mid-1940; also involved were the Foreign Ministry, the Military Police, offices of the National Spiritual Total Mobilization

17. The Home Ministry's notifications, including a full copy of the committee's resolution titled *Shinbun Shidō Yōryō* (Outline for Newspaper Guidance), are reprinted in ibid., document 15, pp. 133–34. The Cabinet Information Division subsequently continued to produce orders for newspaper guidance under the same title in a numbered series.

18. See Kuroda, *Chishikijin*, p. 41, and Hatanaka Shigeo, *Shōwa Shuppan Dan'atsu Shō Shi*, pp. 84–85.

Movement, the Culture and Thought Divisions of the Imperial Rule Assistance Association that succeeded it, and on occasion other agencies as well.

The targets included most periodicals, and the consultation system permitted great flexibility in aiming instructions at various types of newspapers and magazines. Guidance directives might specify all bonded newspapers, major daily newspapers only, integrated magazines, economic magazines, foreign policy magazines, newspapers with foreign correspondents, major news agencies, or various combinations of these.[19] There were special consultation meetings for children's magazines, women's magazines, and other select types, not to overlook those with groups of authors (especially novelists) that were not addressed to any particular press organ.[20]

MOBILIZATION DIRECTIVES

Three mobilization directives delivered in consultations are described below, one each on the economy, foreign policy (the signing of the Axis Pact), and domestic politics (Diet proceedings in early 1941). The mix of positive mobilization and censorship in these directives typified the consultation system.

In May 1940, the Cabinet Information Division prepared consultative guidance for newspapers on the economy.[21] It stated that some recent articles had criticized the impoverishment of consumption and the transitional steps toward a wartime economy, creating uneasiness among the people. Newspapers were urged to comply with seven directives: (1) to stress the importance of price controls and avoid articles spurring inflation; (2) to portray the disequilibrium between supply and demand as normal in wartime and to convince people that discontent with commodity shortages reflected insufficient wartime consciousness; (3) to promote saving, to slow spending and beat inflation; (4) to avoid provoking unrest over the rising national debt and the declining market

---

19. See *Masu Media Tōsei*, vol. 2, document 30, pp. 239–41, for examples of such specially earmarked guidance in mid-1939.

20. Foreign-language newspapers published in Japan were often omitted from orders sent to other press organs in the late 1930s, making them better sources of information in some respects but also rendering them unrepresentative of what most Japanese were reading. For some examples in 1938, see ibid., document 15.

21. Reprinted in ibid., document 39, pp. 266–67; this was the eighth mobilizational directive put out by the Cabinet Information Division under the title *Shinbun Shidō Yōryō*.

value of bonds; (5) to present criticism of economic control policies so as to promote controls, not to foster aversion to them; (6) to condemn hoarding and black-market operations; and (7) to avoid pessimistic coverage of food supply difficulties, yet to emphasize the need to curtail rice consumption.[22]

When Japan signed the Axis Pact with Germany and Italy in September 1940, both the Home Ministry and the Cabinet Information Division prepared press guidance. The Home Ministry document issued proscriptions such as these (abbreviated and paraphrased here):

1.   No stories opposing or slandering the treaty. Examples: the pact involves the loss of an autonomous foreign policy by Japan; Germany and Italy are the only parties to benefit; the pact resulted from the machinations of pro-German and pro-Italian elements in Japan; it will distract from a resolution of the China Incident.

2.   No sign of disagreement over the treaty within Japan.

3.   No categorical condemnation of the Soviet Union or assertion that the treaty will hinder Japanese-Soviet relations, though articles denouncing the Comintern's intrigues are acceptable. (Examples omitted.)

4.   No fanning of antagonism toward the United States as an enemy country in connection with the treaty. (Examples omitted.)

5.   No insistence that the so-called South Seas Strategy be implemented militarily immediately in connection with the treaty.

6.   No exaggerated accounts of the treaty's economic effects, or any that might cause great unrest among the people, "even if the information is true" (*jijitsu no hōdō to iedomo*). Examples: hints that stock prices may plunge; views feared to make financial circles overly cautious; matters that might provoke depositors to withdraw their money; overblown treatments of the negative influence on trade.[23]

This notification was sent to local government offices for press consultations nationwide and was added to censorship standards for enforcement through administrative sanctions.

The Cabinet Information Division's draft was the twelfth in its series of "Outlines for Newspaper Guidance" and had a more mobilizational character than the Home Ministry's instructions. It aimed at dissemination of the following points (paraphrased here).

1.   The keystone of the empire's foreign policy is to establish the Great East Asian Co-Prosperity Sphere and play a leading role in creating a new world order. The treaty is predicated on German and Italian approval of our aims,

22. Ibid.
23. Ibid., document 46, pp. 274–75.

their cooperative intentions, and our common stand on forging the new world order.

2.   The empire's purport in this treaty is not immediate participation in the war in Western Europe but, rather, to halt the spread of the evils of war and promote completion of the new world order. Furthermore, cooperation with Germany and Italy is not only an appropriate and necessary policy for resolution of the China Incident but a pivotal dimension of the empire's foreign policy in conformity with the new circumstance of the great world transformation. However, to deal with the many inevitable frictions and obstacles foreseeable on the road to this transformation, it is necessary for the empire to harden its vital determination.

3.   Since we stand at a turning point in the prosperity or decline of the empire, the government is steadily advancing domestic and foreign policies with firm resolve. For the future of these policies, the nation must believe in the government, establish the state's New Order with a solemn attitude, and strive for realization of the high degree national defense state [kōdo kokubō kokka], and each subject must faithfully perform public service at his post, "One Hundred Million with One Spirit" [Ichioku Isshin].

4.   As the empire's great course has become more fixed with this treaty, refrain from posing impatient arguments, spurring narrow-minded sentiments, or exacerbating reactionary opinion, which will turn into rash antiforeign movements; properly maintain the dauntless attitude of a great people.[24]

Another pair of documents from the Home Ministry and the Cabinet Information Bureau (a bureau as of December 1940) show how a special consultation became the cornerstone of state control over press reports on the Diet in January 1941. The Diet meeting in progress was the first since Japan's political parties had dissolved themselves in August 1940.

The Home Ministry paper reviewed existing censorship, beginning with control over the Diet minutes. The minutes were an official document and therefore technically free from press restrictions, but the Diet often enforced prevailing censorship standards on its own. If a speech transgressed pre-publication warnings or general standards of public order, the presiding chairman could revise the minutes or the speaker himself could request that his remarks be stricken or changed. The Home Ministry supplied both houses with an up-to-date list of pre-publication warnings.

The press reporting of speeches delivered in the Diet was subject to all the usual censorship restrictions. What a peer or representative could

24. Ibid.

say in session was not necessarily publishable. In practice, however, the Home Ministry was slow to punish illicit reports of regular parliamentary speeches, due to the potential for controversy. There was strict enforcement if cut or revised Diet minutes were cited in their original form or if a journalist allowed into a formally closed committee meeting reported speeches violating censorship guidelines—in the lower house, reporters were often admitted to closed committee hearings. If a debate was officially declared secret or the minutes stopped, there was severe enforcement against disclosures. Diet members' statements to the press outside parliament received no special protection.

The Home Ministry's pre-publication warnings often banned coverage of the Diet's deliberations. As early as mid-1939, they were complemented by consultative guidance. In addition to total bans on reporting, some instructions ordered that only interpellations of government spokesmen and speeches by them be reported; others, that the speeches alone be covered. Most of the affected debates touched on foreign affairs or economic policy.[25]

The Cabinet Information Bureau stiffened these controls during the first non-party Diet. On 10 January 1941, the bureau was authorized to ban from publication state secrets and items hindering official policy,[26] and it used this new power during the Diet meeting. The CIB's Governor (*Sōsai*) personally conducted a consultation with top editorial staff members of Tokyo's major newspapers. With the parties' dissolution, he stated, some members might seek to advertise themselves with reelection in mind; the press must criticize such behavior. There should be nothing downbeat in treatments of the first "Imperial Rule Assistance" Diet, whether in reporting, opinions, editorials, society columns, photos, or cartoons. All should constructively promote state policy. Concrete guidance to this end was as follows (paraphrased here).

1. Do not just inform. During the Diet meeting, give plenty of space to resolving the China Incident in order to lift public consciousness and for foreign propaganda. Stories highlighting the shortage of goods, popular discontent with the living standard, or a decline in national strength have a negative impact at home and abroad.

2. Do not take an unduly critical stance toward the Diet to flatter readers' tastes, but take it up seriously.

25. Ibid., document 57, pp. 328–31. The document suggests a marked increase in prohibitions from 1940.
26. This happened by means of an imperial rescript activating article 20 of the State Total Mobilization Law: ibid., document 54, pp. 324–25.

3. Do not draw attention to questions posed merely to advertise the speaker, but criticize the inappropriateness of such practices.

4. Do not speculate on the contents of secret Diet meetings. Naturally, there must be many in the crisis situation [*jikyokuka*].

5. Confusion on the floor or purposeful obstruction of the proceedings should be treated in a simple manner calling for reflection.

6. Work to further the views that (a) Diet members should not persist in posing the same question to government spokesmen; (b) members should request secret sessions when inquiring into military, foreign, or economic affairs, because of their extensive repercussions; and (c) to expedite business, Diet members should reveal their questions informally [*naishi*] to government spokesmen before scheduled interpellations.[27]

To see that state guidance was effective, a new system of control over Diet reporting was imperative:

> The reporting of newspapers and news agencies related to discussions in the Diet has hitherto been left to the absolutely free discretion of the companies, and positive official guidance and control has not been imposed beyond the level of occasional orders prohibiting publication [i.e., pre-publication warnings]. However, it is necessary to show the people the reality of an "Assistance Diet" as this Diet comes in the first year of implementing the Imperial Rule Assistance Movement, and, further, we are facing the fourth year of the [China] incident and it is recognized at this time that various social strata have taken a rather serious shock. Therefore, it is to be expected that fairly penetrating arguments will be heard on many areas of domestic and foreign policy, starting with the natural problems of the Imperial Rule Assistance Association and the difficulties of unemployment and occupational change from small and medium-sized commercial and industrial firms. It can be seen that prior to next year's lower-house general election, there will be a mushrooming of the old style of speeches aimed at local constituencies [*omiyage enzetsu*] and irresponsible discussions. However, it is feared that today, when we must strive to overcome the hardships of our time and unify the direction the nation must follow, "One Hundred Million with One Spirit," to continue the customary noninterference with articles on the Diet would have the result of splitting public opinion and produce an unsatisfactory situation from the perspective of executing state policy.[28]

The CIB Governor recalled coverage of the Saitō Takao incident. Saitō had strongly criticized the government's China policy in the Diet in February 1940. The presiding chairman had deleted part of his speech from the minutes, and military pressure helped persuade the lower house to expel Saitō on 7 March. The governor remarked that although political col-

27. From a CIB document dated January 1941: ibid., document 58, p. 332.
28. Ibid.

umns had labeled it a traitorous speech, some society columns had hinted indirectly at sympathy for Saitō, confusing the public's judgment. "In the country's present situation one acutely senses the need to be rid of the *jiyūshugi* [freedomist] period's concept of journalism."[29]

The antidote was a *daily* CIB consultation at the Diet with both political and society page newspaper editors. Bureaucrats would attend all Diet sessions and use the consultations to ban some items from publication, discourage the printing of others, and otherwise give advice on desirable forms of coverage. This new arrangement evidences the transition from censorship to mobilization and illustrates perfectly the meaning of "positive internal guidance." The contrasting approaches of the Home Ministry and the CIB to Diet reporting reflect the relatively conservative, censorship orientation of the former compared to the activist, mobilizational character of the latter. In the eyes of the CIB, the Home Ministry's censorship had left Diet reporting "to the absolutely free discretion of the companies."

Mobilizational directives also contained editorial interference unrelated to content. Positive guidance might require that a certain size of type be used for words related to a subject such as venereal disease;[30] that editorial and opinion columns echo the state's line on issues such as foreign affairs;[31] that a particular news item, such as a Japanese-Soviet border clash near Manchuria, not be the lead story;[32] or that no special editions appear on a crucial event such as the temporary resolution of the China Incident by field armies. In consultations with book publishers, bureaucrats sometimes ordered alterations in the titles of forthcoming volumes.[33]

PRIOR CENSORSHIP OF MAGAZINES

Magazine consultations were employed to institute pre-publication censorship of galleys during 1939–1941. Officials had long been dissatisfied with magazine censorship, especially with the extensive use of blank type (X's and O's). Participants at a National Conference of Special Higher Police Section Chiefs in September 1936 argued against blank type because it aroused interest and readers could often guess the

---

29. Ibid., p. 333.
30. Ibid., document 21, p. 153, issued in the fall of 1938.
31. Ibid., document 23, p. 164, dated September 1938.
32. Ibid., document 15, p. 135, dated July 1938.
33. Ibid., document 21, p. 153.

missing words. The inspection of galleys was praised as an admirable substitute.[34] However, since the Newspaper Law did not require censor's copies until publication started, there was no immediate prospect of change.

The consultation system opened new possibilities. From late 1937, the Home Ministry ran a monthly consultation for several influential Tokyo magazines. Officials grew increasingly bold in this forum, until in 1939 they instituted the censorship of galleys, eliminating unauthorized use of blank type and the need for administrative sanctions as well. *Chūō Kōron* sustained its last ban on circulation in March 1938, its last deletion in June.[35] Thereafter, bureaucrats cut before the final printing whatever displeased them. This new policy, which had no legal foundation, marked a sharp upgrading of state control, especially considering the poor confiscation rates for journals suffering bans or deletions.

The Cabinet Information Bureau later took charge of this system. Though the Home Ministry's censors served concurrently in the bureau after 1940, the CIB's consultations were usually dominated by its own officials, who included military officers. The CIB modified prior censorship from May 1941 by demanding a description of planned contents and authors by the tenth of every month.[36] Whole articles were proscribed (and others often proffered as possible replacements) before the type was set for a galley.[37] All this occurred in the guise of "consultations" which editors had no legal obligation even to attend. The submission of contents for prior review spread to most politically significant magazines in the summer and fall of 1941, in conjunction with paper control and other adjustments to the New Order for publishers.[38]

The Home Ministry and the CIB were of course only the primary gears in a much larger consultation machine involving meetings with the military (monthly for integrated magazines like *Chūō Kōron* and *Kaizō*), the Imperial Rule Assistance Association, and many other state agencies. All were involved in "positive guidance."

34. Galleys are printed copies made for the purpose of correcting the type before the actual printing of issues to be circulated. Information on the conference is from Kuroda, *Chishikijin,* p. 111.

35. Ibid., p. 133.

36. Ibid., p. 149; Hatanaka, *Shōwa Shuppan,* p. 36.

37. Several articles blocked from *Chūō Kōron* in CIB consultations in 1941 are listed in Hatanaka, *Shōwa Shuppan,* pp. 39–40.

38. Mimasaka Tarō, Fujita Shikamasa, and Watanabe Kiyoshi, *Yokohama Jiken,* p. 59; Ōhara Shakai Mondai Kenkyūjo (Hōsei Daigaku), ed., *Taiheiyō Sensōka no Rōdō Undō,* p. 184.

THE BLACKLISTING OF WRITERS

Blacklisting was another product of consultations. In December 1937, the Home Ministry arrested about 400 intellectual and labor leaders previously classified within the legal left (the Popular Front Incident—*Jinmin Sensen Jiken*). There followed in February 1938 the arrest of about 45 intellectuals, including moderate leftist university professors and members of the Social Masses Party (the Scholars' Group Incident—*Gakusha* or *Kyōju Gurūpu Jiken*). The Peace Preservation Law was used in both cases. It was not illegal to publish articles by arrested suspects if one had a manuscript, but in consultations the Home Ministry forbade publication of anything by those arrested, regardless of content. Officials threatened administrative sanctions and possible prosecution for any violator.[39] Dubious articles or writers were to be referred to the ministry for a decision.

These arrests, enveloping the Labor-Farmer Faction (*Rōnōha*), eliminated most remaining leftist writers and cut deeply into the ranks of regular contributors to journals like *Chūō Kōron* and *Kaizō*. Among those jailed, Arisawa Hiromi had published in *Kaizō* 28 times, Mukozaka Itsuo 37 times, Ōmori Yoshitarō 37 times, Suzuki Shigesaburō 44 times, Inomata Tsunao 48 times, and Yamakawa Hitoshi close to 200 times.[40] As was related in chapter 2, Inomata had caused the November 1931 *Chūō Kōron* to be banned from circulation for his article opposing Japanese imperialism. Ōmori had criticized press controls in the September 1925 *Kaizō* and had written sympathetically of Minobe Tatsukichi in the April 1935 *Bungei Shunjū*. Officials ordered his article "Hungry Japan" (*Ueru Nihon*) totally deleted from the September 1937 *Kaizō* for reproving the war-related program of heavy industrialization; even the title was to be stricken from the table of contents.[41] Ōuchi Hyōe, editor of the journal that carried Morito Tatsuo's article on Kropotkin in 1920, was also arrested. In short, many old debts were paid with the arrests of these men. They had been journalism's leading political critics and the Peace Preservation Law was stretched beyond all

---

39. Hatanaka, *Shōwa Shuppan,* p. 37; Kuroda, *Chishikijin,* pp. 85–86.
40. Kobayashi et al., *Zasshi "Kaizō,"* p. 133.
41. Ibid., pp. 155–56. Just before his arrest, Ōmori had submitted a film review for publication in the January 1938 *Chūō Kōron.* The journal went on sale on 19 December, just days after the mass arrest and probably before the related consultation. The magazine was banned from circulation, but at the publisher's request the police consented to release it on condition that the article be completely ripped out. This incident gave teeth to the promise of sanctions.

previous interpretations to prosecute them on the trumped-up charge of aiding the Comintern.[42]

The next step was to blacklist writers not under arrest. This began in a Home Ministry consultation for major Tokyo magazines in March 1938. Editors were unofficially told to reject any articles by Oka Kunio, Tosaka Jun, Hayashi Yō, Hori Makoto, Miyamoto Yuriko, Nakano Jūji, or Suzuki Anzō.[43] Suzuki had written the boldest defense of Minobe Tatsukichi in 1935. The state said nothing to the writers themselves; all pressure was applied to the journals. The contributions of these writers, too, were marked for rejection regardless of content: press controls now transcended the censorship of substance and encompassed the writer's ideological and organizational affiliations as targets of policy.[44]

The editors of *Chūō Kōron* report a similar incident in a Cabinet Information Bureau consultation on 26 February 1941. Six *jiyūshugi* writers unassociated with the left were proscribed: Yanaihara Tadao, Yokoda Kisaburō, Baba Tsunego, Kiyosawa Kiyoshi, Tanaka Kotarō, and Mizuno Hirotoku.[45] Yanaihara had criticized the Manchurian venture in 1932, and Home Ministry officials had ordered total deletion of his pacifistic article in the September 1937 *Chūō Kōron*. He consequently lost his chair at Tokyo Imperial University and was prosecuted under the Newspaper Law.[46] These *jiyūshugi* intellectuals, who opposed militarism or imperialism or both, had supplanted the moderate leftists arrested in 1937–1938 as the main contributors to *Chūō Kōron* and *Kaizō*, but they were now muzzled as had been their predecessors. Once again officials transmitted the blacklist as an "unofficial announcement" (*naishi*) without informing the authors. Baba, one of many earning a living from political commentary, wrote of his situation:

42. Ōuchi's interrogator, Miyashita Hiroshi of the Special Higher Police, has said he was at a loss to build a solid case according to previous Peace Preservation Law standards, and he remarked on the novel use of the Comintern connection, which was untrue but nonetheless insisted on by prosecutors due to the Comintern's endorsement of the popular front strategy to oppose "fascism" in 1935: see Miyashita Hiroshi, *Tokkō no Kaisō*, pp. 145–51.

43. Hatanaka, *Shōwa Shuppan*, p. 38; Mimasaka, Fujita, and Watanabe, *Yokohama Jiken*, p. 61; Kuroda, *Chishikijin*, p. 88.

44. It is not clear whether the March 1938 blacklist was communicated to other journals as well or if police were content to strike these writers from influential journals only.

45. Mimasaka, Fujita, and Watanabe, *Yokohama Jiken*, pp. 61–62; Kuroda, *Chishikijin*, p. 146; Hatanaka, *Shōwa Shuppan*, p. 56.

46. Kuroda, *Chishikijin*, pp. 44–45; see *Masu Media Tōsei*, vol. 2, document 12, pp. 118–23, for a complete rundown of Yanaihara's prosecution under the press laws.

Until the year when the Great East Asian War started [1941], I was writing political commentary for the newspapers once a week and for so many magazines each month. Little by little I became unable to write, and during the war I was absolutely silenced. If one looks for the reason, it was that newspapers and magazines stopped accepting my manuscripts. However, no official or military man ever confronted me saying this article is bad or ordering me not to write such and such a thing, or even spoke with me.[47]

Baba had been a critic of the military.[48]

The CIB's consultations of February 1941 were organized on a company-by-company basis, and the editors of Kaizō do not recall a blacklist ordered at that time.[49] At this stage, then, the proscriptions were sometimes dictated selectively. But what is interesting is that several of these writers had already ceased to appear in Kaizō due to fear of sanctions. Yokoda had last been published in September 1939, Baba in January 1940. In 1941, their work was still carried in supplements on the crisis "situation," but editors would not risk publishing their articles in Kaizō proper. Similarly, Chūō Kōron had refused Baba's articles for almost a year before he was blacklisted.[50] "Positive guidance" had journals anticipating official commands before they were given.[51]

By January 1941, Special Higher Police offices had card files on individuals with suspicious backgrounds and editors were urged to phone in for advice if they were uncertain about a writer's suitability; officials promised to provide an answer within two minutes.[52]

---

47. Quoted in Hatanaka, Shōwa Shuppan, p. 59.
48. Notable was his 1937 article "Gunbu wa Kokumin o Shidō Shieru Ka," written during the partial respite for critics between the 2/26 Incident and the China Incident.
49. Kobayashi et al., Zasshi "Kaizō," pp. 179–80.
50. Kuroda, Chishikijin, p. 102.
51. There were other examples of this as well. In August 1940, one large magazine company sent its own list of over fifty desirable themes to contributors, e.g., novels stressing the need for counterintelligence, describing the recovery of wounded soldiers, or recounting the hearty life of Japanese immigrants in the colonies. See Takasaki Ryūji, Sensōka no Zasshi, p. 39.
52. Hatanaka, Shōwa Shuppan, pp. 57–58. In January 1942, Chūō Kōron received from the Special Higher Police Section of the Tokyo Metropolitan Police a list of some twenty authors to avoid. No specific reprisals were threatened for noncompliance, but the restructuring of the press industry then in progress and the state's control over the paper supply gave ominous overtones to any suggestions from official quarters. In addition to those already mentioned, regular contributors to disappear from the columns of Chūō Kōron due to state pressure during the Pacific War included Imanaka Jimarō, Tsuchiya Takao, Aono Kiyoshi, Ashida Hitoshi, Abe Shinnosuke, Iwabuchi Tatsuo, Ogura Kinno-suke, Ozaki Hidesane, Kimura Kihachirō, Saigusa Hiroto, Sekiguchi Yasushi, Taira Teizō, Tanigawa Tetsuzō, Tozawa Tetsuhiko, Nashimoto Yūhei, Maruyama Masao, Machida Shinsō, Masuda Toyohiko, Miyazawa Toshiyoshi, and Morito Tatsuo: Chūō Kōronsha 70-Nen Shi, p. 317.

THE ATMOSPHERE OF
THE CONSULTATION MEETING

To what extent did consultations involve coercion versus nonbinding appeals and information of the sort offered at background press briefings in many countries? Furthermore, was the personal interaction in consultations most like a friendly chat, a formal lecture, or a bitter exchange between antagonists? The consultation was a complex control mechanism and these questions do not have simple answers.

One salient feature of consultations was a blurring of the distinction between enforceable orders and non-obligatory appeals. Three main types of information were communicated: pre-publication warnings on current events, regular censorship standards (expanded to include blacklisting and other editorial restrictions), and noncompulsory guidance. Pre-publication warnings were the most distinct, because they were generally delivered in writing. However, when announced in consultations, they were often accompanied by noncompulsory advice on how to treat the subject matter; for example, the Army Ministry's warnings against sentimental coverage of families seeing off conscripts were complemented by suggestions on how to write the story.[53] The same was true of warnings on how to report Japanese soldiers' deaths in battle. The unmistakable message was "Describe it in this patriotic fashion, and you'll both help your country and evade the censor." The boundary between regular censorship standards and nonbinding pleas was even more ambiguous. Indeed, there were no "regular" censorship standards to speak of in this period; they were modified at virtually every consultation, and officials often neglected to distinguish them from optional recommendations. As before, bureaucrats could impose sanctions at their discretion, whether a standard had been identified in advance or not.

The history of press controls imbued all consultative messages with a tinge of compulsion. Administrative sanctions had always depended on bureaucratic assessments, not legal technicalities. There had never been a sharp line between parliamentary laws and the bureaucratic ordinances and conventions supplementing them. "Positive guidance" was no more legal than the pre-publication warning system, but it could be enforced just as easily. No one ever challenged the administration's legal right to blacklist authors or conduct pre-publication censorship. To repeat, there was no route of appeal against bureaucratic sanctions,

---

53. See the pre-publication warning of 15 August 1937 in *Masu Media Tōsei*, vol. 2, document 2, pp. 12–13.

regardless of whether the offender had violated a formal warning or an informal supplication. There is no record of press people boycotting a consultation because they were not legally required to attend. Critical postwar studies written by the system's victims do not generally dwell on the formal illegality of state controls as scholars are inclined to do. That bureaucrats could introduce and enforce these innovations was taken for granted. The blurring of lines between regular censorship standards, pre-publication warnings, and positive guidance mirrored the hazy boundary between statutory authority and bureaucratic discretion that had always characterized press controls. Experience taught the imprudence of ignoring any directives from the bureaucracy and lent an air of coercion even to overtly optional recommendations.

There were wide variations in the affability or tension found in consultations. The larger gatherings tended toward formality, with officials delivering prepared statements and then allowing questions or comments.[54] Though the available evidence is sketchy, there is no indication that anger or nastiness was common. The ideal of "positive guidance" was not to beat the subject into submission, but to nurture a willing collaborator by applying persuasion against the background of the wartime crisis. The possibility of sanctions was well understood but rarely flaunted. The state's goal was to influence the editorial policy that colored all of a journal's news and commentary, and bitter confrontations were thought to be counterproductive. Furthermore, almost all press people supported the war effort and willingly complied with the state's propaganda strategy. It was the few persistently independent journals that might face naked intimidation in consultations.

The integrated magazines were perhaps the biggest obstacle to press policy. They did not contravene specific instructions, but one step beyond those instructions they strove to display an autonomous orientation. They were too prestigious to be closed down before Pearl Harbor, and their status and journalistic traditions limited the penetration of "positive guidance." Regular consultations in which their line-up of stories was berated and longtime contributors blacklisted were hardly conducive to amiability. On occasion, wrathful words were exchanged.

On 26 February 1941, the Cabinet Information Bureau called in *Chūō Kōron*'s president and top editors for a consultation led by a navy captain and Army Major Suzuki Kurazō, both CIB officials. They accused the

54. See, e.g., the account of a CIB consultation of January 1941, reprinted in ibid., document 56, pp. 526–28.

journal of not cooperating and suggested a change of editorial direction to eliminate completely the evil customs of freedom. The publisher, Shimanaka Yūsaku, replied that he was willing to support official policy but that it was not possible to mold people's thinking simply by giving orders as in the military. He advised his interlocutors to leave dealings with the intellectual class to the magazine, which possessed greater expertise. At this point Suzuki flew into a rage. He stood up and shouted that it was because this sort of individual was still publishing that people had contempt for the state. He claimed Shimanaka was instilling a *jiyūshugi* attitude in his staff, that evidence was being collected from younger employees to prove it, and that he was ready to smash the magazine.[55] The other officials present were embarrassed by this tirade, but if consultations were rarely so turbulent, threats were indeed communicated more subtly in this forum on other occasions, including suggestions that particular editors should resign.[56] Thus consultations with independent-minded journalists sometimes differed sharply from the more typical soft-sell approach. The impact of Suzuki's outburst will be better appreciated when the number of periodicals that were in fact smashed by the state in this period is recounted below.

THE PHASE OF ILLEGAL CONSOLIDATIONS

The most lethal use of consultations was to compel the dissolution of undesirable journals. From August 1938, the Book Section of the Home Ministry's Criminal Affairs Bureau systematically endeavored to terminate or merge smaller newspapers and magazines nationwide. Documentation on the origins of this momentous policy is sparse, possibly because it was completely illegal. The State Total Mobilization Law of 1938 (see chapter 8) authorized the consolidation of media organs, but this law was not activated against the press until December 1941. Before that time, consolidation policy appears to have had no formal legal foundation.[57] This makes it all the more remarkable that this radical

55. Description from one of the participating editors, in Hatanaka, *Shōwa Shuppan*, pp. 24–25.
56. Ibid., pp. 81–82. This book, full of examples of various types of consultations, is the richest source on the subject. State records are usually limited to the briefing papers prepared by officials ahead of time and do not include accounts of what actually transpired in the consultations.
57. The only reason it can be asserted that this policy began in August 1938 is that the Home Ministry's *Shuppan Keisatsu Hō*, no. 141, pp. 37–40, lists the number of active periodical press organs just before consolidation started, and the date of the list is at the end of July.

scheme was pioneered by one of the oldest ministries and not by the Cabinet Information Division and its renovationists, who began to take charge of the policy only in mid-1940.[58]

If its origins are vague, the policy's effects are devastatingly clear. The Home Ministry itself tallied the periodicals vanquished by its program of "adjustment and integration" (seiri tōgō) from July 1938 (just before the project began) through November 1941. This useful terminal date narrowly precedes the Pacific War and falls just two weeks before the Newspaper Business Decree (Shinbun Jigyō Rei) first gave the state general legal authority to coerce consolidations. These were the results:[59]

	July 1938	November 1941	Number Dissolved
Newspaper Law			
Bonded Journals	7,964	3,480	4,484
Unbonded	4,979	1,105	3,874
Total	12,943	4,585	8,358
Publication Law			
Magazines	15,325	13,497	1,828
Total	28,268	18,082	10,186

As of August 1941, 528 general dailies had been merged with other papers or dissolved at state direction, leaving a national total of 202.[60] The operative goal outside metropolitan areas was to leave one general daily newspaper per prefecture (ikken/isshi); this had been achieved in sixteen of forty-seven prefectures by 1 December 1941.[61]

The main objectives of consolidation were to curtail competition (viewed as a major reason for flouting state directives), to conserve scarce materials, and to facilitate greater control over content. Publication Law magazines were much less affected in this phase than Newspaper Law press organs, because, officials explained, "Publication Law

58. Tashiro Kanenobu of the Cabinet Information Division makes it clear that when the cabinet began to use paper controls to further consolidations in May 1940, he and his colleagues worked with a plan that had been prepared earlier by the Home Ministry's Censorship Section (the old Book Section had been so renamed by the time Tashiro wrote): see Tashiro, *Shuppan Shintaisei no Hanashi*, p. 8.

59. All figures are from Naimushō Keihōkyoku, *Shuppan Keisatsu Hō*, no. 141, pp. 37–40.

60. Idem, *Shuppan Keisatsu Hō*, no. 139, pp. 39–43.

61. *Masu Media Tōsei*, vol. 2, document 97, p. 496.

magazines have less social influence than Newspaper Law magazines, and consequently their adjustment was not enforced that much."[62] The difference in the decline of Publication Law and Newspaper Law journals demonstrates that natural attrition would have claimed only a fraction of the Newspaper Law press organs disappearing in this period. State action was clearly the predominant cause for the sharp decreases.

Implementation was handled by the Home Ministry's Special Higher Police (also executors of the Peace Preservation Law), and their principal method was pressure through consultation meetings. The police would inform an owner that his journal was a drain on resources and was impeding state policy, and they would recommend dissolution or a merger. There were recalcitrants. Even after paper control was coordinated with the program, some publishers paid exorbitant prices for scarce open-market paper in order to stay in business. Rougher methods were occasionally employed against them. In some cases, journals were directed to hand over lists of their subscribers and advertisers, who would then be visited by police and ordered to discontinue patronage or be prepared to face arrest.[63] But overt coercion was the exception, pressure applied through consultations the rule.

An article in the *Chūgai Shōgyō Shinpō* of 16 August 1940 describes how Tokyo's local newspapers and trade journals were affected:

> Control over expression. From the perspective of pulp limitation, the Censorship Section of the Metropolitan Police has initiated control of the capital's newspapers and magazines. They [the police] have steadily taken resolute action to strengthen controls, starting last year in July, when they swept away the local newspapers published in the boroughs [*ku*], to February of this year, when they ordered the dissolution of pernicious [*furyō*] newspaper companies. Since June, they have started an internal study of various types of trade newspapers. . . . by September's end controls will be implemented over newspapers and magazines related to engineering, insurance, medicine, dentistry, railroads, and industry. That is, the authorities believe that the many small newspapers and magazines exact excessive subscription and advertising fees, and, furthermore, they think it a great waste in the "situation" that there be a duplication of readership due to a profusion of the same varieties [of journals]. With the aim of reducing the present number of some 8,000 newspapers and magazines by 80 percent this year, once they have obtained

62. Naimushō Keihōkyoku, *Shuppan Keisatsu Hō*, no. 141, p. 37.
63. These methods are recounted in Kuroda, *Chishikijin*, p. 118. It has been reported that in February 1941 the Cabinet Information Bureau demanded from various magazine publishers lists of their subscribers and that those on the lists were sometimes subsequently harassed by the police. Apparently subscribers to *Chūō Kōron*, *Kaizō*, and *Nippon Hyōron* in the military were singled out for attention: see Hatanaka, *Shōwa Shuppan*, p. 36.

notices to disband from the various trade newspapers at the Censorship Section, they then advise them as to respective mergers. Looking at trends among those completing dissolution notices up to the 14th [August 1940], the pattern has been to control the transportation and communications [fields] from seventy firms [i.e., journals] to fourteen, engineering from thirty to six, insurance from sixty to nine, and firms related to dentistry and medicine from thirty each to two. . . . Those not complying with mergers are made to disband.[64]

Political and economic news-agency bulletins underwent the same process.[65]

According to police, consolidations proceeded "comparatively smoothly,"[66] and one reason is that the newspaper giants did not intervene to protect the smaller firms.[67] The three leading dailies, the *Mainichi/Nichi Nichi* chain, the *Asahi*, and the *Yomiuri*, had long competed for local newspaper readership throughout Japan. Whereas the *Asahi* and *Mainichi/Nichi Nichi* published regional editions, the *Yomiuri*'s strategy was to purchase local papers. This competition accelerated after the China Incident, when all firms were squeezed by the shortage of newsprint, and the larger gained a special advantage from their ability to field war correspondents. While the three giants ignored the smaller papers' demise, the latter had no united interest group to represent them nationally. The result was that thousands of journals were eliminated without any weighty civil association rising to their defense.

Police claimed the decline of political parties also facilitated consolidation.[68] Unlike the larger metropolitan dailies, many local newspapers had retained affiliation with the Minseitō or Seiyūkai. According to police, the decay of party politics was such that party competition no longer justified more than one local newspaper for the expression of different views. An obvious corollary is that the parties were powerless to protect publications that had long advanced their fortunes. By August 1940, of course, the parties had formally disbanded. The retreat of party rivalries from newspaper columns was cited as but one facet of the

64. Quoted from *Nihon Shinbun Nenkan Shōwa 16-Nen*, pp. 8–9. The Censorship Section referred to was a branch of the Tokyo Metropolitan Police, which was organized in an exceptional manner as Japan's largest local police office. It should not be confused with the Censorship Section (also *Ken'etsu Ka*) to emerge in the Home Ministry's central Criminal Affairs Bureau when the Book Section was so renamed in December 1940.

65. Ibid., p. 9.

66. Naimushō Keihōkyoku, *Shuppan Keisatsu Hō*, no. 140, p. 4.

67. Kuroda, *Chishikijin*, p. 118.

68. Information in this paragraph is from Naimushō Keihōkyoku, *Shuppan Keisatsu Hō*, no. 140, pp. 4–5, which covered policing of the printed media during September and October 1941.

growing convergence of contents, impelled also by the centrality of official announcements in the news and the United News Agency's dominance of wireless reporting from abroad. The uniformity of content was an effective argument for restricting each area to one paper.

The newspaper industry's reaction to consolidations is illustrated by the closure of the daily *Tōkyō Yūkan Shinpō* in July 1939, one year after forced dissolutions began. Officials attributed the notable impact of this case in newspaper circles to the adjustment of "corrupt, harmful" newspapers then in progress; their harsh treatment of this paper was probably intended as an object lesson.[69] The *Tōkyō Yūkan Shinpō* dated from 1914 and circulated 12,000 to 20,000 copies. Its president and founder, Nakajima Tetsuya, had once worked at the *Asahi Shinbun* and was sixty-one years old. He was arrested along with the journal's publisher, its business manager, a writer, and an editor for violating a pre-publication warning from the Army Ministry that forbade reporting the presence in Japan of Wang Chao Ming, ex–Vice President of the Chinese Nationalist government, who was negotiating to form a new Japanese-backed state in China.[70] The *Tōkyō Yūkan Shinpō* ignored the warning and carried the story. Prosecution was initiated under both the Newspaper Law and the Law for the Protection of Military Secrets (*Gunki Hogo Hō*), which could punish violators with life imprisonment. Speaking from jail on 12 July 1939, under intense police pressure, Nakajima announced the paper's closing. This was technically a voluntary decision, like all the others terminating publications in this period. With apologies to his readers and a grateful farewell to his employees, Nakajima declared:

> Speaking frankly, for several years now, especially since the [China] incident, it has become day by day more difficult to fulfill [the terms of] our company's founding proclamation. The trend of the times no longer permits one to brandish the pen of freedom. Moreover, along with this [trend] my attachment to the newspaper business itself has gradually faded of late. The problem with the article of 14 June has done no more than to spur me on unexpectedly and accelerate my decision to discontinue publication.[71]

The *Tōkyō Yūkan Shinpō*'s dissolution was widely discussed in the newspaper industry's trade journals, but a police survey found only one

69. *Masu Media Tōsei*, vol. 2, document 31, p. 247.
70. This he later did, in Nanking in March 1941. The warning was the least severe of the three types, amounting to little more than a moral appeal, making the arrests an extraordinarily tough reaction. This case demonstrates that disobedience even to an apparently nonobligatory appeal from officials could result in harsh penalties.
71. Quoted in *Masu Media Tōsei*, vol. 2, document 31, p. 250.

article supporting Nakajima, in *Shinbunshi Nihon* on 30 June. It repeated his view that the inability to publish foreign newspaper reports had led to a secret, ambiguous politics, and it opposed the paper's closure. On 17 July, even this journal reversed itself, attacking Nakajima for not heeding the crisis "situation," and treating the paper's dissolution as a matter of course.[72] Most tabloids had taken this stance from the beginning. *Shinbun Hihan* professed "not one iota of sympathy" (*itten no dōjō wa nai*), and *Shinbun Kaihō* called Nakajima's offense an irremovable stain on journalistic history.[73] A police report noted that the *Tōkyō Yūkan Shinpō* had disregarded a pre-publication warning during the 2/26 Incident as well.[74] It is said that consultation officials kept report cards on journals that were later used for planning "adjustment and integration."[75] Past disregard for pre-publication warnings and "positive guidance" was not forgotten.

The industry's *Nihon Shinbun Nenkan* (Japan Newspaper Yearbook) of 1941 offers further newspaper reactions to consolidation policy. It reported: "Against the government's newspaper controls, while newspaper circles remain silent, only one person has daringly offered criticism, and that is Miki Bukichi, president of the *Hōchi Shinbun,* who has advocated that 'The Newspaper Policy [suitable to] the New Order is to Abolish the Regional Editions of the Large Newspapers.' "[76] The *Hōchi Shinbun,* founded in 1895, was the fourth largest Tokyo daily, but still something of a one-man operation. It was not engaged in the scramble for regional readers, and Miki defended the small firms. He argued that were the state's objective merely to save paper, it need only eliminate the regional editions of the newspaper giants. A newspaper's survival, he wrote, should not be determined simply by its circulation. If the state's purpose was to expand control over expression, this could be achieved by strengthening the United News Agency and seeking further cooperation from local papers. Finally, he argued, if the state's goal was to eliminate journals contravening the public interest, then these alone should be suppressed—there was no need for a general strategy of mergers and dissolutions.[77] Miki's questioning of official objectives was logical considering that consolidation policy had never been debated in the Diet or enunciated by any government. His *Hōchi Shinbun* was itself

72. Ibid., pp. 247–48.
73. Ibid., pp. 249–50.
74. Ibid., p. 245.
75. Hatanaka, *Shōwa Shuppan*, p. 24.
76. *Nihon Shinbun Nenkan Shōwa 16-Nen*, p. 4.
77. Ibid.

forced to merge with the *Yomiuri* (already the majority shareholder) in August 1942. Thus the *Hōchi* succumbed like so many smaller, local papers, caught in a vise between state power and the financial hegemony of the three national dailies.

The futility of contesting police powers was the main reason for compliance with consolidation directives. To repeat the refrain, there was no recourse open to subjects victimized by the police. It was vain to dispute the legality of police action when no court was competent to adjudicate complaints, and the prospects for appealing to the parties or to public opinion on such matters were obviously bleak by the late 1930s. The Cabinet Information Division's political manipulation of paper rationing from May 1940, designed "to do away with those newspapers and magazines that are harmful or whose existence is without social value," reinforced the coercive apparatus already at work.[78]

While official prerogatives were considerable, however, their ultimate limits were never really tested in this period, due to the disunity of the press. Enmities born of business competition and exacerbated by ideological differences (plainly, right-leaning journals had less to fear from mobilization and ample reason to support it) precluded formation of a common front even against consolidation policy. The same policies that eliminated so many journals greatly benefited others. Without the leverage afforded by joint action, the press industry left its members to confront state power as so many solitary enterprises. On those terms, the outcome of any engagement with the police was a foregone conclusion.

78. The division's program for paper control is reprinted in "Senzen no Jōhō Kikō Yōran." This document was prepared by ex-officials of the Cabinet Information Bureau; it was made available to the author by Professor Itō Takashi. Paper control was first instituted by the Ministry of Commerce and Industry in August 1938, pursuant to the Law for Emergency Measures on Imports and Exports, as a purely economic measure to conserve scarce resources. Although paper rationing and consolidations began at roughly the same time, the two policies were initially unrelated. In fact, the Ministry of Commerce and Industry's measures benefited the same small, local newspapers the Home Ministry was out to ruin, since those using fewer than 12,000 reams a year were not subject to its paper quotas. A completely free market would have seen them outbid by the larger companies. See Tashiro, *Shuppan Shintaisei*, p. 62; Kuroda, *Chishikijin*, p. 121. The paper supply became a political weapon only with the establishment of the cabinet's Committee for Newspaper and Magazine Paper Control in May 1940; this body was administered by the Cabinet Information Division.

The New Order for the Press, 1940–1945

"New Order" (*Shintaisei*) became the official slogan for Konoe Fumimaro's second cabinet in August 1940.[1] For the mass media and other social sectors it portended a policy revolution that drastically restructured civil associations and subjected them to penetrating positive controls. Press policy in the New Order was typical of that for most major industries: officials liquidated the vast majority of firms and herded the remainder into control bodies which exercised authority under the State Total Mobilization Law. The experience of the press thus exemplifies a much broader pattern for the expansion of state control over society. New Order policymaking provides the truest measure of the radicalism of military-bureaucratic elites in the late imperial period. It also furnishes valuable insights into the potential for civil resistance, since even the most prominent media organs were compelled to fight not just for their autonomy but for their very survival.

THE STATE TOTAL MOBILIZATION LAW

The legal underpinnings of the New Order were fixed by the State Total Mobilization Law of 1938, whose press provisions had lain dormant for nearly three years. This law was drafted by the Cabinet Planning Board's radically statist officers and bureaucrats responsible for designing wartime economic controls. For all its impact on journalism,

1. The slogans "New Order" and "national defense state" had also been used by the earlier Abe cabinet: Ide, *Nihon Kanryōsei*, p. 124.

items affecting the press were afterthoughts to a statute aimed primarily at the economy. The law was an enabling act for use only during war. It authorized sweeping state controls over labor, industry, and other civil sectors by means of executive imperial decrees, obviating the need for parliamentary laws in each case. It was not, then, just another law itself, but a new legal framework replacing regular constitutional procedures.

Passage of the bill was a major political undertaking. To secure the Diet's approval, Prime Minister Konoe declared that the law would not be evoked in response to the China Incident, and he intimated that he might organize a new party to challenge for leadership of the Diet if the bill were defeated.[2] The solid backing of this astute Prime Minister was a prerequisite for the Diet's endorsement. On 17 February 1938, during debate over the bill, several hundred rightists dressed in khakis attacked both Minseitō and Seiyūkai party headquarters. The Seiyūkai's offices were occupied overnight before police arrested the trespassers, who called for a single national party. One participant later claimed the intrusions had the prior blessing of both Konoe and Home Minister Suetsugu Nobumasa; this would explain the procrastination of the police, which was a clear warning to the parties.[3] Before this incident, rightists had visited representatives' homes to apply pressure, guided by plainclothes police.[4]

Three aspects of the mobilization law touched the press. First, it empowered the government to ban or limit the publication of information when necessary for mobilization and to seize offending copies (article 20). This clause had little meaning, however, since the same powers were already enforced under the Newspaper Law.[5] Second,

2. Kuroda, *Chishikijin*, p. 80; Berger, *Parties*, pp. 155–56.
3. Itō Takashi, *Jū-gonen Sensō*, pp. 216–17.
4. Berger, *Parties*, pp. 147–48.
5. According to rumors repeated during Diet committee hearings, the Cabinet Planning Board had not included this censorship article in the law's original draft, and neither the Home Minister nor the Army Minister opposed its removal. Rather, it was the Home Ministry's Criminal Affairs Bureau Chief who had initially urged its inclusion; see *Masu Media Tōsei*, vol. 2, document 11, pp. 94, 106, 88. The first version of the law presented to the Diet had stipulated that the government could suspend publication of any journal violating mobilizational directives twice, but to defuse potential opposition this clause had been removed by the cabinet. The real purpose of the article had been the new power of suspension, leaving the remainder rather meaningless after its exclusion.

When some Diet members asked what mobilization law censorship added to the Home Ministry's pre-publication warning system, they were told that pre-publication warnings were only administrative conveniences and mobilization powers should have a firmer legal foundation: see ibid., pp. 97, 102–3. There ensued a rather pointless discussion of the legality of pre-publication warnings—pointless because no one contested the Home Ministry's right to employ them.

businesses "related to information, enlightenment, and propaganda necessary for state total mobilization," including all publishing companies, were made subject to general mobilization powers (article 3, section 7). In wartime, the state could command the establishment, abolition, suspension, or transfer of any mobilization business, as well as changes in its functions (article 16, section 3).[6] This entailed an unqualified power of life and death over every newspaper, magazine, and book publishing company. The state could also expropriate all or part of any mobilization business (article 13), order or prohibit changes in its equipment (article 16, sections 1–2), control the hiring and firing of employees and regulate their salaries (articles 4, 6), and limit the companies' production, distribution, and consumption of goods (article 8). The gravity of these powers eluded most Diet members, who displayed their ignorance of existing press controls by lavishing attention instead upon the inconsequential censorship provision. A few members did pinpoint the implications, however, arguing that newspapers would become state organs and lose their credibility.[7]

The insertion of newspapers as mobilization businesses was characterized by official duplicity. When word leaked about their possible inclusion, some eighty-nine newspaper delegates conferred with the Cabinet Planning Board's Governor on three occasions. They were first told that the law would not apply to dailies, but when they requested a written exemption in the bill, it was eventually refused. This subterfuge deflected criticism while the law was under consideration in the Diet.[8] The only assurance given in Diet hearings was that the commandeering of newspapers was "for the most part" (hotondo) not being contemplated.[9]

Finally, the law authorized officials to set up control associations, fashioned after the Nazi *Wirtschaftsgruppen*, to regulate groups of enterprises (article 18, section 1). The state could make membership in these associations compulsory and dictate the rules they would enforce. Thus, a blueprint for intermediate state bodies governing civil organizations in different sectors was clearly outlined in law in early 1938.

The bill's principal justification was that a modern total war required total mobilization. The Justice Minister declared to the House of Representatives:

6. The State Total Mobilization Law is translated in T. A. Bisson, *Japan's War Economy*, pp. 212–21.
7. See, e.g., *Masu Media Tōsei*, vol. 2, document 11, p. 113.
8. See the exchange on this episode in upper house hearings in ibid., document 13, pp. 127–28.
9. Ibid., p. 124, in the words of the Cabinet Planning Board's Governor.

This is a matter of wartime. Because this is a situation in which the entire nation must fight for victory or defeat, subjects tender all their strength and all their goods. If one discusses this with peacetime thinking, one can speak of qualifications for a certain type of goods or a certain business. But when the nation gathers all its strength to fight, it must concentrate all of its material resources and all of its might. Consequently, regarding the composition of these regulations, one cannot stipulate what about lead or what about gold. Because everything is all right, everything that exists is put forward.[10]

No one in the lower house disputed this logic.

Opponents contended that the law was either unnecessary or unconstitutional. It seemed unnecessary because the constitution permitted emergency rule by decree as well as declaration of a wartime state of siege when regular laws and civil rights would be suspended. The government contended that the law would alert the people to future sacrifices and provide a better legal foundation for wartime measures.[11] In fact, the whole scheme was designed to eradicate the Diet's policymaking role. Konoe's pledge not to invoke the law for the China Incident had not been part of the Cabinet Planning Board's original design; if passed as initially conceived, the law would have eroded the Diet's prerogatives at once.[12] Existing constitutional mechanisms would not have nullified the Diet's authority so thoroughly. Emergency decrees required subsequent Diet approval to retain their force, whereas the terms of a state of siege were not as specific as the mobilization law; a temporary emergency could hardly justify a massive consolidation of industries. Only this law could offer blanket prior authorization for a specified but almost unlimited range of executive action.

The argument for unconstitutionality was that the law usurped the Diet's proper legislative functions, including the exclusive power to compromise subjects' rights. The Justice Minister answered as follows:

it is decided in part two of the constitution that to restrict the rights, freedoms, and property of subjects one must do so by means of law. Accordingly, it is prescribed in this bill's various clauses that we will limit or divest subjects of their rights, freedom, and property. The manner and degree are merely left to imperial decrees, but the scope of writing these decrees is

10. Ibid., document 11, p. 70.
11. Ibid., p. 72.
12. There were even inconsistencies in the Diet statements of government spokesmen on this point. For example, the Cabinet Planning Board's Governor announced the intention of employing mobilization censorship as soon as the law passed, while this was declared unnecessary by the Army and Home Ministers: see ibid., pp. 108–9.

determined in the articles [of the law] and beyond that subjects will not be troubled.[13]

It was true that civil rights had no defense from the law. It was sophistry, however, to pretend that the mobilization bill was just another law of limited scope, when it effectively transferred legislative power to the cabinet and removed virtually all limits on executive decrees.

When some Diet members compared the law to Germany's enabling legislation and claimed it would invite a "fascist" despotism as in Germany and Italy, the Home Minister replied:

> I think "fascist" politics was born in response to the necessities and special conditions of Italy. In our country there is an authorized constitution based on our grand national polity that stands proud in the world. Regardless of what sort of politics there are in other countries, in our country politics conforms to the spirit of this great authorized constitution.[14]

Yet government spokesmen wielded the German and Italian examples as a double-edged sword to promote the bill. On the one hand, German precedents added prestige and legitimacy to new mobilization powers, just as the British model had shored up policies in the 1920s. Yet government officials also pointed to the violent, revolutionary character of European fascism as a frightful inevitability should the bill fail to pass. For example, the Cabinet Planning Board's Governor stated that the law would dispel the unrest of soldiers returning home, which might otherwise culminate in an explosion as it had in Russia, Germany, and Italy.[15] This implicit threat must be evaluated in light of the 2/26 Incident and other rightist violence, the delayed police reaction to assaults on party headquarters, Konoe's feints toward forming a one-party system, and the Home Minister's reported statement that *jiyūshugi* (or freedomism) was a hotbed for communism, all of which filled in the background for intimidation.[16]

---

13. Ibid., p. 66.
14. Ibid., pp. 60–61; the prior accusation is in ibid., pp. 59–60.
15. Ibid., p. 64.
16. Ibid., p. 61. Just before passing the State Total Mobilization Law, the lower house expelled Social Masses Party Representative Nishio Suehiro for a speech including these words: "We must consider this bill from the viewpoint of the future international situation and our country's historic mission. The contradictions of the capitalistic politico-economic system have not only sprung up in this country but internationally. . . . Prime Minister Konoe must carry out renovationist policies properly in the manner of Hitler, Mussolini, and Stalin." Quoted in Itō Takashi, *Jū-gonen Sensō*, p. 214. If many mainstream party members were uncomfortable with references to Hitler and Mussolini, the mention of Stalin was anathema. But it was precisely the renown of Germany and Italy combined with the disinclination to emulate their experience *in toto* that allowed Japanese statists to exploit their example.

For all practical purposes, the State Total Mobilization Law marks the Diet's exit from press policy. The Diet did maintain a modicum of influence through a commission of fifty members, thirty drawn from the legislature, that deliberated upon mobilization decrees, but this commission never rejected or amended measures affecting the press.[17] Press policy, already largely a bureaucratic affair *de facto,* was now set to become a bureaucratic affair *de jure* as well. To repeat an earlier observation, the only constitutional guarantee of an autonomous press lay in the premise that an elected lower house would block overly repressive policies. Yet between the liberal reform of 1897 and the mobilization law of 1938, the House of Representatives had voted to harden press controls at nearly every opportunity; only the progressive newspaper bill aborted after lower-house passage in 1925 stands to its credit.

The mobilization law was critical to Japan's subsequent political course. By gradually shifting parliamentary functions to the executive branch, it allowed military-bureaucratic elites to revolutionize the state-society relationship without abandoning the Meiji constitution. Had the Diet forced a constitutional crisis by denying such legislation, state control over society could not have mushroomed as it did without a clearer break with the past, involving either the formation of a single state party under Konoe, or the organization of a military government that would dissolve the Diet altogether. The Diet's retreat and the constitution's remarkable elasticity made it possible to avoid such a showdown, facilitating the formation of a military-bureaucratic regime without a tumultuous political upheaval.

Many motives were operative in the Diet. The fear of confronting a new party led by Konoe was widespread. The major parties certainly understood how the police could sway election results, and Konoe's Home Minister, Suetsugu Nobumasa, was a known antagonist of the parties, chosen precisely to give the Prime Minister leverage against them.[18] But the threat of domestic political combat was of less moment

17. Several more severe laws on expression passed later had little impact on publications. For example, the Diet passed the *Genron, Shuppan, Shūkai, Kessha Rinji Torishimari Hō* (Law for the Emergency Control of Speech, Publications, Assembly, and Associations) in December 1941. This law required a license for all Newspaper Law periodicals, something not demanded since 1887. It also granted the power to suspend further publication of a journal if an edition were banned from circulation for a violation of content, a power that had been stricken from the original State Total Mobilization Law. The control association system was so developed by late 1941, however, that these powers had little meaning. Aspects of this law punishing rumors and requiring licenses for political associations and meetings were more significant. The law and accompanying regulations are reprinted in *Masu Media Tōsei,* vol. 2, document 74, pp. 377–78, and document 79, pp. 444–45.

18. Berger, *Parties,* pp. 141–42.

than the reality of war in China. The constellation of political forces around the mobilization law was very much a product of the war. The war helped to win support from the established ministries for a project conceived by cabinet renovationists, thus providing the government with a fair amount of internal cohesion. The war greatly reinforced the atmosphere of crisis and thereby enhanced the believability of a radical alternative (that is, a party under Konoe) should the bill fail to pass. Most important, the war supplied a nonpartisan vindication of the law that Diet members had no ideological predilections to resist. Most were staunch supporters of imperialism and free of principled liberal scruples, and the contention that total war demanded total mobilization was difficult to refute. If some representatives attacked the mobilization law, others judged it a palliative and demanded a ministry of propaganda and a new power to suspend publication.[19] Unlike many Diet members, however, the administrators who actually designed and implemented the mobilization law saw it not as a mere stopgap in response to war, but as part of an elaborate ideological program that provided the deeper inspiration for Japan's New Order.

NEW ORDER POLICYMAKERS
AND THEIR IDEOLOGY

The New Order witnessed a shift in policymaking initiative from the established ministries to the newer cabinet planning organs. In media policy, leadership transferred from the Home and Communications Ministries to the Cabinet Information Bureau. Expansion into a bureau (*kyoku*) in December 1940 brought the CIB staff up to 510 full-time employees. These included 118 ranking bureaucrats, 52 of them permanent CIB officials, 24 on temporary assignment from the Foreign Ministry, 14 from the Home Ministry, 10 each from the Army and Navy Ministries, and 8 from the Communications Ministry.[20] Within about eighteen months, they engineered a radical mobilization of the mass media.

The key administrators associated with the New Order are usually labeled "renovationist bureaucrats" (*kakushin kanryō*). They were successors to the "new bureaucrats" that appeared after 1932. The "new

19. *Masu Media Tōsei*, vol. 2, document 11, pp. 116, 83.
20. "Senzen no Jōhō Kikō Yōran," pp. 88, 187. There was one official of *shinnin* rank (personal imperial appointment), six *chokunin* (imperial appointments), thirty-eight *sōnin* (appointments approved by the Emperor), and seventy-four *hannin* (junior officials).

bureaucrats" had been so named more for their independence from the parties than for a common ideological outlook, but after the attempted coup of 1936 a number were purged as alleged sympathizers. This spawned a second generation of new bureaucrats, or the " 'new' new bureaucrats"; these came to be called "renovationist bureaucrats" as early as 1936.[21] Both terms connoted closeness to the military and support for far-reaching statist policies.

Renovationists dominated the Cabinet Planning Board, the Cabinet Information Bureau, and, by 1940, the Ministry of Commerce and Industry, whose authority increased immensely with economic mobilization. The cabinet organs were exceptional in recruiting both civilian and military officials, and they also hired some personnel from civil society, including a few ex-leftists. The most influential renovationists were career administrators originally employed by the established ministries, who served temporarily in the cabinet organs or simultaneously in their ministries and the cabinet. Many moved back and forth between the two, but it was generally in the cabinet that they had their greatest impact.

The ideology of New Order policymakers is a difficult subject. The state had no single authoritative spokesman over the entire 1937–1945 period, and many key decision-makers did not publish at the time. There is no reason to believe that all shared exactly the same assumptions. If there is no definitive statement of New Order ideology, however, some important insights into this question can be gained thanks to solid prewar documentation of the thinking of three leading administrators in the Cabinet Information Bureau: Okumura Kiwao, Miyamoto Yoshio, and Kawamo Ryūzō. All three were creative instigators of policy in their fields. Kawamo was the chief government negotiator of a New Order for the film industry. Miyamoto became the CIB's Broadcasting Section Chief in 1941, then took over the Newspaper Section in mid-1942. Okumura was appointed Vice-Governor of the CIB in October 1941, effectively taking charge of the entire operation. He was easily one of the five or six most influential bureaucrats in late imperial Japan. He had earlier helped to plan communications policy for the army administration in Manchukuo, and he had personally framed the seminal legislation to control the electric-power industry in the mid-1930s. It was then that he had enunciated his famous principle of "private

21. See "Seinen Kanshi Shain wa Nani o Kangaete Iru Ka: Zadankai," pp. 219–21; Hashikawa, "Kakushin Kanryō," pp. 251–54; Ide, *Nihon Kanryōsei*, p. 72.

ownership/state management."[22] As one author of the State Total Mobilization Law, Okumura's thought in particular transcends the media field and provides some general indication of the thinking of renovationist bureaucrats in this period. The very fact that these men were among the state's foremost propagandists speaks for the prevalence of their views in key cabinet decision-making bodies. It was Miyamoto who broadcast the call to assemble before Prime Minister Tōjō's radio address declaring war on the United States, and the Prime Minister's message was followed by Okumura's own patriotic speech.

How did these men conceive of their policy revolution? Their most basic premise was that the world was undergoing a great historical transformation that would remold every aspect of society and culture. The belief in this great historical divide has been described as the lowest common denominator of military and bureaucratic renovationist thought.[23] Okumura wrote in 1938:

> The motion of the world which mankind is experiencing at present is an historic cultural revolution that promises to correct and alter fundamentally the mode of existence we have been living in modern society. It is a revolution in law, a revolution in politics, a revolution in society and the economy.[24]

And Miyamoto:

> The world now is altogether accomplishing a great metamorphosis in terms of both states and people. Nothing shall escape it; politics and economics and culture, and thus thought and speech, and broadcasting and film that are the products of this new age, all are [undergoing this change] as one.[25]

Is their view the historical age of freedom was in its death throes. This passing epoch of *jiyūshugi* revolved around individual rights and interests, capitalism and profit, democracy and party politics. The *jiyūshugi* state was the *état-gendarme*, serving only to defend society from foreign attack, to protect life and property, and to adjudicate civil disputes. The age of freedom had begun with the French Revolution and come to Japan in modified form via the Meiji Restoration, and it had

22. On Okumura's role in drafting the electric-power legislation, see Hashikawa, "Kakushin Kanryō," pp. 257–62; Okumura Kiwao, "Denryoku Kokkan Mondai," pp. 198–209; Okumura, *Henkaku-ki Nihon no Seiji Keizai*, pp. 1–41.

23. Hashikawa, "Kakushin Kanryō," p. 264. See also Mark R. Peattie, *Ishiwara Kanji and Japan's Confrontation with the West;* William Miles Fletcher, *The Search for a New Order: Intellectuals and Fascism in Prewar Japan.*

24. Okumura Kiwao, *Nihon Seiji no Kakushin*, p. 3. This book was apparently written before police banned the word *revolution* (*kakumei*) from publication in reference to domestic politics.

25. Miyamoto Yoshio, *Hōsō to Kokubō Kokka*, p. 1.

performed a valid historical function in overthrowing the old absolutism. But this stage itself was now fraught with internal contradictions
calling for its overthrow. *Jiyūshugi* had allowed the strong to devour the
weak, making real freedom the luxury of only a few. Within countries,
this meant class struggle and the development of capitalist domination
into its final, monopolistic phase.[26] Internationally, the few great powers—the United States, Britain, and France—exploited colonies and op-
pressed their peoples. Free trade had given way to closed economic
blocs, producing conflict between nations. Both within and between
nations, then, freedom had led not to the common good but to the
selfish benefit of the few. If the old absolutist systems such as the
shogunate had elevated a private interest over the public welfare, free
societies did the same thing in a different form.

The new era in the making was identified by Miyamoto as that of the
national defense state, by Okumura as that of "totalitarianism" (*zentai-
shugi*, in this case borrowing from contemporary European usage).[27] It
was the negation of everything represented by the historical stage of
freedom. The individual was to find spiritual oneness with the whole of
society; his welfare would be realized through the nation's welfare, his
freedom through the nation's freedom and strength in world affairs.
The nation would now represent a collective will and collective ideals.
In economics, this required the introduction of a planned, controlled
economy; in law, the priority of the public over the private interest; in
politics, the end of party competition furthering narrow interests and
the concentration of power in the cabinet. The new state would play an
activist, integrating function. Unlike a socialist state, it would not represent a single class, underscore materialism, or obliterate private interests
entirely, but it would permit only those private pursuits that served the
common good. Militarily, the country would prepare to fight a total
war.

Germany and Italy were already totalitarian or national defense
states, and Japan was well fixed to enter the new age as well.[28] The
unifying concept of the family nation embodied in the Emperor, the
samurai's *bushidō* code, and the nationalistic Yamato spirit formed an
ideal moral basis for the new state-society system. General Ludendorff's

26. Ibid., pp. 12–13; Okumura, *Nihon Seiji no Kakushin*, pp. 34–43.
27. Miyamoto, *Hōsō to Kokubō Kokka*, pp. 18–24; Okumura, *Nihon Seiji no
Kakushin*, pp. 10, 99, 113–14, 133, 252.
28. Miyamoto, *Hōsō to Kokubō Kokka*, p. 21; Okumura, *Henkaku-ki Nihon*, pp.
90–93; Okumura, *Nihon Seiji no Kakushin*, pp. 51–52.

comment that of all nations Japan was the most fit to become a national defense state was a favorite citation in renovationist writings.[29] The renovationists averred, however, that *the great transformation under-way was not a return to the past but the beginning of a new stage in history.* Traditional spiritual collectivism was to be grafted onto a society embodying the bureaucratic values of order, rationality, planning, and organization. Such was the dual mentality reflected in the ideology of leading bureaucrats.

Interestingly, both spiritual traditionalism and the desire for institutional innovation contributed to a conscious rejection of the Meiji legacy. In terms of values, the Meiji Restoration was blamed for having undermined the traditional spiritual ethics the renovationists wished to revive. Thus Prince Konoe's closest advisors could declare publicly that the New Order would "cast off the poison of materialistic culture present since the Meiji Restoration and return to Japan's ancient thought and great founding spirit."[30] In terms of institutions, it was the capitalism, party politics, and civic freedoms borrowed from the West in the Meiji period that the renovationists now judged to be historically antiquated. The Meiji political enterprise was too closely associated with the imperial house to permit much forthright criticism, and renovationist writings thus conspicuously ignored Itō Hirobumi, Yamagata Aritomo, and the other Meiji state-builders. On the whole, they preferred to direct their reproaches at the more vulnerable target of party cabinets in the 1920s, but what scant mention they did make of the Meiji period was almost invariably negative.[31] This is a significant point in relation to the continuities and discontinuities in Japanese politics from the late nineteenth century to the New Order. The renovationists clearly saw their endeavor as a sharp break with the previous seventy years of their country's history, which they found spiritually too modern, but institutionally obsolete.

What did the new era portend for media policy? Freedom of thought had produced an anarchy of opinion ending in subjectivism and spiritual confusion. Public discussion degenerated into irresponsible criticism spurred by the profit motive. The *jiyūshugi* state had played a minimal, passive role, acting only to curb the worst abuses.

---

29. Miyamoto, *Hōsō to Kokubō Kokka*, p. 35. For another example, see Kikakuin Kenkyūkai, *Kokubō Kokka no Kōryō*, p. 35, a Cabinet Planning Board publication.

30. Yokusan Undō Shi Kankōkai, ed., *Undō Shi*, p. 55.

31. See, e.g., Miyamoto, *Hōsō to Kokubō Kokka*, p. 37; Kikakuin Kenkyūkai, *Kokubō Kokka*, pp. 15–16.

Cultural values had been set on a pedestal above the state and the nation and discussed in international terms. To maximize the nation's collective unity for the coming era, repression would not suffice. The will of subjects would have to be redirected from private to public interests. Public expression would have to be liberated from the profit standard so that it could progress from doubt and criticism to consent and constructiveness. The state would not manufacture all ideas and culture, but it would insist that they all serve the nation's collective purposes.

It is evident that these men did not perceive their revolution as a mere response to the demands of modern warfare. Indeed, given the nearly unanimous media support for the Japanese war effort achieved under pre-1938 regulations, it is impossible to explain much of the policy revolution that followed by reference to war alone. To these policymakers, the war was just the most visible symptom of a more profound transformation underway in politics and the social system. It was this underlying transformation that made war inevitable between the declining free societies and those exemplifying the new national defense state and that provided the deeper rationale for New Order policies. It is significant that all three men were on record as advocating mobilization policies long before Japan became embroiled in war with China in mid-1937.[32] Given Japan's aggressive role in initiating the Pacific War, it would be more correct to see the war as a product of renovationist principles and goals than to view these latter as functions of the war.

How did top renovationist policymakers come to transcend the conservative outlook usually thought to accompany a professional bureaucratic career? Okumura, Miyamoto, and Kawamo conformed in several ways to the standard portrait of the renovationist official; a closer look at their backgrounds helps to explain their iconoclastic attitudes. For one thing, all completed their educations in the law faculty of Tokyo Imperial University between 1925 and 1928. Exposure to Marxist ideas on college campuses in the 1920s is considered a vital common trait of the leading renovationist administrators and is reflected in the historicism of their world view and their censure of capitalism.[33] Some even voiced disap-

32. Okumura wrote his original electric-power-control proposal in December 1935. Kawamo criticized U.S. radio policy as too free, and praised both Nazi and Soviet control systems, in a journal circulated within the Communications Ministry in 1936: Kawamo Ryūzō, "Hōsō Jigyō no Kantoku Hōshin ni Tsuite." For Miyamoto's early statist views, see his "Tsūshin Kikan no Kōyō."

33. Hashikawa, "Kakushin Kanryō," pp. 264–65.

pointment that the subsequent suppression of communism had left their juniors in the bureaucracy without a good foundation in social criticism.[34] Second, all three were relatively young when they reached positions of authority. Okumura, the oldest, was only forty-one when he took command of the CIB. The cabinet agencies promoted younger men more quickly than the established ministries with their strict seniority system, and the unusually rapid advancement of renovationist officials was one key to Japan's administrative revolution. Finally, all three men began their careers in the lowly Communications Ministry, which had very limited policy responsibilities. Bureaucratic novices chose their ministries in the order they scored on the civil service exam, and the Communications Ministry was near the bottom in preference.

Thus the stakes of these men in instituting new state powers through cabinet superagencies like the CIB were not only ideological but occupational. All three had been founding members of the Cabinet Information Committee (the CIB's weak original nucleus) in 1936 and stood to gain considerable personal power from their efforts to promote its authority thereafter. Transfer into the cabinet body meant more attractive and consequential jobs for bureaucrats who would otherwise never have known the limelight. These career patterns demonstrate that bureaucratic structures do not invariably induce administrators to support the status quo. If some bureaucrats have a vested interest in upholding the administrative hierarchy, others may have much to gain by changing it, and reorganization within the state itself may break through the bonds of seniority that hold the prevailing policy outlook in place.

The majority of the Japanese people did not share the intensely ideological standpoint of leading New Order bureaucrats. Although the renovationists' ideas were very prominent in public discourse, the rhetoric they borrowed from Marxism and their unabashed admiration for Germany and Italy were undoubtedly less cogent to most Japanese in 1940 than the immediate demands of war. Moreover, many social leaders and state officials ready to cooperate with war-related mobilization were utterly opposed to the ideological statism of Okumura, Miyamoto, and their CIB colleagues. As renovationist officials translated their interpretation of history into concrete policy proposals, they sometimes met with considerable resistance from their patriotic but much less doctrinaire fellow countrymen.

34. "Seinen Kanshi Shain," pp. 234–35.

PLANNING FOR THE
NEW ORDER IN MID- TO LATE 1940

Prime Minister Konoe's proclamation of a "Fundamental Policy Out-line" (*Kihon Kokusaku Yōkō*) for the New Order on 1 August 1940 fueled ambitions within the cabinet bureaucracy. Originally drafted by military and bureaucratic renovationist officials, it declared the world to be at a great historical crossroads that would witness the creation of a new politics, economics, and culture, and it called for Japan to enter the new epoch by means of a "national defense state system."[35] The speech was especially pleasing to information officials, who had been avidly planning new press controls since their takeover of paper rationing in May. As one bureaucrat wrote of Konoe's proclamation, "it corre-sponded perfectly with the 'Main Points of a New Order for the Press' that we had undertaken concretely just one step ahead."[36] Despite the impatience for bold initiatives among CIB officials, however, the politi-cal climate of 1940 was not as favorable to their policy designs as it first appeared.

By mid-1940, officials were satisfied that the leading newspapers were cooperative, and patently harmful articles had been all but elimi-nated.[37] Yet they deemed the level of control to be unsatisfactory, be-cause journalism had yet to rid itself of the "critical, objective attitude of the past."[38] Due to the profit motive, papers still ran articles on the "interest standard" (*kyōmi hon'i*), that is, to appeal to the reader's interest. Therefore whenever state control was lax, criticism resurfaced, as was witnessed by the ridiculing of Prime Minister Abe Nobuyuki in the winter of 1939–1940. Most disturbing was the exacerbation of popular discontent with economic controls and the shortage of goods, where pessimistic accounts and reproofs against the state were still printed. Administrative sanctions and moral solicitation had reached the saturation point as remedies.[39] Given the newspapers' commercial

35. The source has been variously identified as the Military Section (*Gunjika*) of the Army Ministry's Military Affairs Bureau (*Gunmukyoku*) (Oka, *Konoe*, p. 121), and the Cabinet Planning Board (Berger, *Parties*, p. 273). Both were renovationist bodies. The policy outline is quoted in Yabe, *Konoe*, 2: 129–30.

36. Tashiro, *Shuppan Shintaisei*, p. 9.

37. See the cabinet opinion paper reprinted in *Masu Media Tōsei*, vol. 2, document 34, p. 261; also the decision of the CIB-managed paper control committee reprinted in "Senzen no Jōhō Kikō Yōran," p. 209.

38. "Senzen no Jōhō Kikō Yōran," p. 209.

39. *Masu Media Tōsei*, vol. 2, document 34, p. 262.

orientation, they might still run a hot news item despite maximum moral pressure from officials.[40]

CIB officials determined that the best solution was to expand their control over the business operations of the press while pushing forward with consolidations.[41] Their strategy was to emasculate the capitalistic foundation of press enterprises by checking competition for profit, the principal inducement for disregarding state policy. Moreover, the money squandered to promote competitive sales was a great waste of valuable resources. The top five newspapers of Tokyo and Osaka were said to spend six million yen annually for market expansion.[42]

Several structural changes were contemplated to root out profit incentives. One was to concentrate the marketing and distribution of all publications into two monopolistic firms supervised by the state, one for newspapers and one for magazines and books.[43] Advertising fees would also be regulated. These distribution companies and all press organs would then be corralled into industrywide control associations as provided by the State Total Mobilization Law.[44] Newspapers would belong to one such association, magazine and book publishers to another. Hereafter, newspaper policy was charged to a different group of information officials than magazine and book policy.

Planning for controls over magazines and books took concrete form very early. In August 1940, officials projected a general control body for the industry by October of that year and an integrated distribution company by February 1941.[45] Specific proposals developed more slowly for newspapers. The view that newspaper management had to be insulated from profit-hungry owners was discussed,[46] but prescriptions for change were as yet vague in late 1940. Since newspaper consolidations were already far advanced, however, officials did ponder an optimal

40. Naimushō Keihōkyoku, *Shuppan Keisatsu Hō*, no. 125, p. 12.
41. *Masu Media Tōsei*, vol. 2, document 34, pp. 262–63. Also Miyamoto Yoshio, "Senjika no Shinbun Saihensei (2)," p. 74. This was one of a five-part series of articles run under this title in the August through December editions of the journal.
42. *Masu Media Tōsei*, vol. 2, document 53, p. 322. This document, "Shinbun Tōsei Shian Danpen" [A Partial Personal Plan for Newspaper Controls], is a good source for policy planning in this period. It was prepared for Colonel Matsumura Shūitsu, the head of both the Army Ministry and Imperial Headquarters army information organs and the Newspaper Section Chief in the CIB. The author was a staff member named Ōkuma.
43. On newspapers, see ibid., pp. 322–23; on magazines and books, see Tashiro, *Shuppan Shintaisei*, p. 11.
44. Tashiro, *Shuppan Shintaisei*, p. 11; *Masu Media Tōsei*, vol. 2, document 44, pp. 272–73. The latter document, "Shinbun Tōsei Gutai An" [Concrete Plan for Newspaper Controls], was prepared in August 1940 by CIB official Onoue Hironobu.
45. Tashiro, *Shuppan Shintaisei*, p. 11.
46. *Masu Media Tōsei*, vol. 2, document 44, p. 272.

configuration for the industry. The key issue was the eventual status of the larger local and metropolitan papers as yet unaffected by "adjustment and integration." CIB opinion papers in August and December 1940 posited a target average of two general daily newspapers per prefecture.[47] There were no plans to eliminate newspaper giants such as the *Asahi, Mainichi/Nichi Nichi,* or *Yomiuri,* but other large dailies in Tokyo and Osaka were clearly earmarked for consolidation.

To attain its objectives, the CIB hoped for immediate activation of the State Total Mobilization Law's powers over the press (both mobilization censorship and business controls), and a cabinet decision to ratify a final structure for the newspaper industry.[48] Mobilization censorship was granted on 10 January 1941, but prospects for activating the law's business controls were so bleak that the issue was apparently never brought before the cabinet. When guidelines for a final newspaper structure were presented for the cabinet's approval in January 1941, they encountered steadfast opposition from Welfare Minister Kanemitsu Tsuneo and Colonial Affairs Minister Akita Kiyoshi, both ex-party men, who rejected the coercive imposition of such a scheme from above.[49] Without a consensus in the cabinet, mobilization business controls and this survival chart for newspapers were dropped as too controversial at a time when the government was struggling to launch the Imperial Rule Assistance Association and its economic mobilization programs. In sum, the CIB's renovationists were denied the legal license they needed to force media control associations, cooperative distribution, and a final newspaper structure. Their only recourse, therefore, was to use existing powers to effect these changes with the formally voluntary compliance of the press.

The CIB soon adopted the Home Ministry's tactics vis-à-vis the cabinet. True to habits of command it had acquired in the 1870s, the Home Ministry had never requested the cabinet's endorsement for consolidations; it merely implemented them on its own authority. In a period of many controversial policy innovations, it was politically more opportune to count on the cabinet's passive acquiescence than to press it for official approval. As long as the question never arose in formal debate, potential dissenters among the state elite, distracted by so many other issues, were unlikely to mount a serious challenge. The cabinet information organ was initially slow to accept this approach. Renovationist

47. Ibid., pp. 272–73, and document 53, pp. 317–24.
48. Ibid., document 53, pp. 317–18.
49. Kuroda, *Chishikijin,* p. 119.

bureaucrats tended to be political extroverts, their dynamic enthusiasm constantly seeking public outlets and approbation. Constrained by circumstances, however, they now endeavored to overstep their legal mandate and fashion "voluntary" control organs to inaugurate a New Order for the press. The operations of these voluntary control organs and their subsequent conversion into formal control associations according to the mobilization law will be described in successive sections. Since newspapers and magazines were organized into two separate systems, they are disaggregated for analysis.

A "VOLUNTARY" CONTROL ORGAN
FOR NEWSPAPERS, MAY–DECEMBER 1941

The initial promoters of a control organ for newspapers were Colonel Matsumura Shūitsu, the CIB's Newspaper Section Chief and head of the army's information organs, and Furuno Inosuke, director of the United News Agency. Furuno was a perfect middleman for dealing with the press. The news agency was financed by both the CIB and the industry, and Furuno was a fervent collaborator in renovationist designs who had worked closely with newspaper people for five years. He personally organized consultations with the large newspapers in December 1940 and with local/regional papers in January 1941, to broach the idea of a voluntary control organ. CIB and Home Ministry officials attended both meetings. Thus the first outstanding trait of the "voluntary" control organ is that it was entirely the state's idea.

Antagonism between major and local newspapers retarded creation of an integrated control body until May 1941. The local papers were represented in negotiations by just a few prominent tabloids likely to survive consolidation. Nonetheless, those participating had suffered the competition of the national dailies long enough to embitter the relationship. The possibility of dividing the rivals into two distinct control organs was entertained, but the CIB insisted on a unified endeavor.[50] With Mori Ippei of the *Nagoya Shinbun* speaking for the local/regional papers, the difficulties were ironed out in time to inaugurate the Newspaper League (*Shinbun Renmei*) on 28 May 1941. The directors (*riji*) included six representatives of local/regional newspapers, five from the largest Tokyo and Osaka papers, and Furuno Inosuke. Two supervisors (*kanji*) were drawn from medium-sized Tokyo newspapers, so in all only thirteen

50. Miyamoto, "Senjika no Shinbun (2)," p. 72.

newspaper companies had delegates on the league's decision-making council. There were also three participating directors (*san'yo riji*): the CIB's Vice-Governor and News Division Chief, and the Home Ministry's Criminal Affairs Bureau Chief.[51]

The Newspaper League's avowed purpose was "as a self-governing control group of the newspaper business, to plan the progress and development of the industry, and thereby to fulfill its state mission."[52] Specifically, it was to cooperate with state control over expression, reform newspaper editing and management, and assist in paper rationing. In short, the league was founded at the state's initiative to facilitate official control. This technically self-inflicted control had been sold to the newspapers as a preferable alternative to the state's otherwise inevitable unilateral controls. All of the league's subsequent activities were directly related to the agenda for change discussed within the CIB in 1940.

Participation in the league was formally voluntary, but since paper rationing was partly predicated on its advice, there was little choice but to join. Its founding did not halt the consolidation of member newspapers. Its decision-making rested entirely with the board of directors, and the real issue it faced was how the firms on the board and other prominent newspapers would ultimately be affected by the New Order.

On 17 September 1941, the state's participating directors placed the key questions regarding a final newspaper control system before the Newspaper League's board of directors. One set of questions concerned the structure of the industry: How should the character of newspapers and their locus of publication be fixed? Should trade or other specialized papers be allowed? Should local editions of national or regional newspapers be permitted? Should local newspapers be limited to one per prefecture? Should all newspapers be amalgamated into a single company? A second set of inquiries addressed the mode of state control: Should newspaper control be integrated into a self-governing mechanism, or be administered by state orders? Should the capital required for newspaper integration be provided by the newspapers, the state, or both? Should a national newspaper control company be established?[53]

The core of contention on the board was the prospect of consolida-

51. Miyamoto notes that the Home Ministry had retained predominant control over day-to-day censorship when the CIB was set up in December 1940, and that is why the Criminal Affairs Bureau Chief participated instead of the CIB's Censorship Division Chief. See ibid.

52. Quoted in ibid.

53. These questions are outlined in ibid., p. 74, and Kuroda, *Chishikijin*, pp. 121–22.

tion into a single national newspaper company.[54] Delegates of the *Asahi, Mainichi/Nichi Nichi,* and *Yomiuri* opposed a grand merger, since they had the most to lose in financial and material assets. Representatives of the local and regional newspapers favored the one-company plan. It would stabilize their finances and end the competitive incursions of the national papers; though their commercial autonomy would be forfeited, they would survive as branches of the new company, not a trifling matter given the background of consolidations. Tokyo's middleweight newspapers also supported amalgamation. Miki Bukichi of the *Hōchi Shinbun,* long a defender of the local papers against consolidation, now championed the single-company concept. If it were defeated, the one-paper-per-prefecture standard would probably doom middle-sized Tokyo papers such as the *Hōchi.* Even if the capital city were accorded two or three dailies, the newspaper giants would claim those slots. In short, positions taken on the one-company plan accorded perfectly with the organizational interests of each firm.

The league's directors debated for almost a month without agreement. The three big newspapers held out against amalgamation, and the discussion occasionally turned acrid. The *Mainichi/Nichi Nichi* representative, Yamada Junzō, is said to have told Miki Bukichi: "With only your own company's advantage in mind, to sell away the freedom of newspapers to bureaucrats is truly the height of shame for a newspaper man."[55] Miki, who had bravely criticized consolidations while the newspaper giants were cashing in on the disappearance of countless local papers, was understandably livid. At this stage, occasional rhetoric to the contrary, none of the newspapers seemed overly preoccupied with the ideal of a free press. The deadlock led to the chairman's designation of a subcommittee on 4 October 1941 to resolve the structural question. Its members were the United News Agency's Furuno Inosuke, the state's three participating directors, and the chairman himself, Tanaka Tokichi, who represented a middle-sized Tokyo paper and was the only newspaperman of the five.

The subcommittee reported its will to the full board on 5 November 1941. It advocated that the tangible assets and publishing rights of all newspapers be transferred to a single company. Until this company was chartered by a special law, it would be a private corporation, and

54. Though solid evidence is lacking, the Army Ministry's Military Affairs Bureau Chief, Major-General Mutō Akira, is said to have been the patron of renovationist plans to reduce all newspapers to a single national company: Kuroda, *Chishikijin,* p. 123.

55. Ibid.

the preexisting newspapers would receive stock according to their circulation, transferred assets, and business records. Furthermore, each stockholding newspaper would be internally reorganized into a juridical person comprising only its active directors and staff. The umbrella company would then entrust publication and management to these juridical persons, which would keep their previous titles (for example, *Asahi Shinbun*). In exchange, the various publishers would pay fees to the joint company. The number of newspapers allowed to continue operating would be five or fewer in Tokyo, four or fewer in Osaka, one or two in Aichi prefecture, and one per prefecture elsewhere.[56] This proposal would eliminate the newspapers' economic autonomy immediately and ultimately would compromise their managerial autonomy as well, since the state would dominate the joint company once its status was determined by special legislation. Essentially, the plan would settle the industry's final structure, thoroughly isolate management from ownership by restricting the latter to one vast holding company, and win for officials the powers promised by the State Total Mobilization Law but politically unattainable at the time. The newspapers' only consolation would be that of retaining their titles and operational staffs, at least temporarily.

The local/regional and the mid-sized Tokyo newspapers consented to this blueprint, while the *Asahi, Mainichi/Nichi Nichi,* and *Yomiuri* were dead opposed. CIB Vice-Governor Okumura Kiwao, recently appointed by Prime Minister Tōjō personally, reportedly defended the scheme before the board as follows: "Since I believe the subcommittee's plan is absolutely necessary for the state, it is not an occasion [merely] to wager my position. Even if I stake my death, I will compel its realization." To this *Yomiuri* President Shōriki Matsutarō responded: "Your earnestness to compel the realization [of this plan] shows honor. However, if I am to be told you will risk your death to force its realization, then even if I risk my life I will oppose this plan to defend the freedom of newspapers."[57] The matter thus boiled down to a struggle between a handful of Japan's most influential civil associations and CIB officials joined by a bevy of medium-sized newspapers. This was most definitely a battle over organizational autonomy, not a debate concerning the merits of Japanese imperialism. Shōriki, a former career officer of the Home Ministry's Special Higher Police (the "thought police"), had made the

56. The proposal is outlined in ibid., p. 124.
57. Quotations from ibid., pp. 126–27. For background on Shōriki Matsutarō, see Shillony, *Politics and Culture,* pp. 98–99.

Yomiuri into the foremost backer of Japan's war effort among the three national dailies. Nonetheless, he was not content to see the newspaper he had diligently nursed back to commercial health since the mid-1920s degenerate into an appendage of the bureaucracy. The impeccable nationalistic credentials of men such as Shōriki undoubtedly bolstered the efforts of the major dailies to retain their status as private entities.

On 10 November 1941, the representatives of the *Asahi* and *Mainichi/Nichi Nichi* each presented counterproposals to the Newspaper League's board. Both aimed at minimizing the capitalistic, profit-making orientation of newspapers without entirely sacrificing their financial autonomy. The *Asahi*'s plan, for example, called for newspaper stock to be wholly owned by each paper's operational staff (including directors) and prohibited editors and executives from maintaining ties with any other profit-making business. Newspaper profits were not to exceed the prevailing rate of interest. To contribute to the industry's "public character," a rescindable state license would be required to found a paper. A self-governing control body would be organized and financed by the papers, and cooperative sales and advertising would be instituted with the "objective of insuring a nonprofit orientation."[58] This proposal would presumably eliminate gain as a factor in editorial policy without transferring assets or ownership to a joint company. On this last item, the big newspapers were adamant. Furuno even promised the *Yomiuri* president executive leadership of the new national company if he would break ranks with his partners and endorse the state's proposal, but to no avail.[59]

When new subcommittees failed to resolve the dispute, the board mandated its chairman, Tanaka Tokichi, to devise an arrangement satisfactory to both parties. The delegates of the *Yomiuri, Asahi,* and *Mainichi/Nichi Nichi* met with him and pledged to abide by his settlement of all other issues if only the one-company plan were abandoned.[60] The outline Tanaka laid before the directors on 24 November closely resembled the *Asahi*'s proposal of two weeks before. Each newspaper's stock would be entirely owned by its operational staff. Permits would be required to found a paper. Staff members would sever all links with other profit-making enterprises. The profit margin would be restricted. A new control organ would be instituted for newspapers. Finally, a joint newspaper company would be formed, under the league's auspices, to oversee all

58. This plan is reprinted in Miyamoto, "Senjika no Shinbun (2)," pp. 75–76.
59. Kuroda, *Chishikijin*, p. 128.
60. Ibid.

stock transactions involved in establishing or reorganizing newspapers; the "company" form was probably window dressing to appease the state directors, whose original single-national-company concept had been rejected.[61]

The board unanimously approved Tanaka's plan, which betokened a partial defeat for CIB officials. Why had they not used the paper supply and their solid majority support on the board to realize their initial aims? Some proposed doing just that. When Furuno Inosuke got wind of Tanaka's report, he immediately advised Colonel Matsumura of the CIB that if the army stood firm they could sabotage Tanaka's design and force through the one-company plan. But Matsumura retreated, pleading that there was no consensus in the government behind that course of action. The navy was moving cautiously on the matter, and the cabinet was especially apprehensive on the subject of newspapers. The army was not prepared to press the issue alone, so if the newspapers were divided on the project, it would have to be forsaken.[62] Consequently, Tanaka's proposal encountered no resistance on the board.

The approved plan was presented to Prime Minister Tōjō, reworked into formal language, and sanctioned by the cabinet on 28 November 1941. Beyond the tenets mentioned above, it specified that membership in the new control organ would be compulsory, and that it would register and review the hiring of reporters. A transitional period was allowed for stock transfers, though the three national papers had already moved to concentrate stock within their firms.[63] This cabinet decision was the foremost product of the league's deliberations. It was followed within a month by activation of the State Total Mobilization Law's powers over newspapers. In effect, the national dailies had consented to the exercise of mobilization-law authority over the entire industry on the one condition that they retain civil ownership. Simultaneously, they sacrificed their sales and distribution networks to a single cooperative enterprise handling distribution, shipment, and the collection of revenues. It began operation in December 1941.[64]

61. Tanaka's plan is reprinted in Miyamoto, "Senjika no Shinbun (2)," p. 77.
62. This exchange is recorded in Kuroda, *Chishikijin*, p. 129.
63. Miyamoto, "Senjika no Shinbun (4)," p. 72.
64. The local/regional firms had favored cooperative distribution because it would control the regional marketing campaigns of the national newspapers: see ibid., p. 76. The national dailies had finally surrendered the point as a concession to stave off the one-company proposal. It would decrease competition, one of the CIB's principal goals, and would free workers for military conscription.

COMPLETION OF THE
NEW ORDER FOR NEWSPAPERS, 1941–1945

The Newspaper Business Decree of 13 December 1941 granted the
Prime Minister (in practice, the CIB) and the Home Minister joint
mobilization-law powers over all bonded newspapers appearing ten or
more times monthly.[65] The decision to issue this decree was implicit in
the cabinet's approval of the Newspaper League's plan for the New
Order in late November and was not related to the declaration of war
against the United States on 8 December. The Newspaper League was
replaced in February 1942 by the Newspaper Association (*Shinbunkai*),
which was chartered under the same provisions of the State Total Mobilization Law as the "control associations" (*tōseikai*) organized in most
sectors of industrial production. The word "control" was simply excluded from the title in deference to the sensibilities of newspaper people.[66] The state appointed the association's members and specified its
jurisdiction, which included controls over newspaper management and
editing, consolidations, cooperative sales, the registration of reporters,
and the distribution of newsprint and other raw materials. The control
association would exercise legal authority over its members (the newspapers), while the CIB and the Home Minister excercised legal authority
over the association. In addition to the full panoply of mobilization
business controls, the imperial decree empowered officials to ban or
suspend publication of any journal feared to impede state policy.

All imperial decrees pursuant to the mobilization law had to be
reviewed by the special commission (including Diet members) established for that purpose. When the Newspaper Business Decree was
placed before it on 10 December, one member, Nakajima Yadaji, rose
to deliver an impassioned speech for freedom of the press, urging that
the ordinance be rejected. In the middle of his discourse came the announcement that the British warships *Repulse* and *Prince of Wales* had
been sunk by the Japanese navy. All present rose to their feet, Nakajima
broke off his speech, and the decree was approved unanimously.[67] This

65. The conditions for the exercise of mobilization-law powers to be described below
refer not only to the imperial decree itself but also to its enforcement regulations (*shikkō
kisoku*) decreed by the cabinet and the Home Ministry on 20 December and the notification on enforcement sent from the CIB and Home Ministry to local officials on 5 January
1942. These documents are reprinted in *Masu Media Tōsei*, vol. 2, documents 73, 80, and
81, respectively.
66. Miyamoto, "Senjika no Shinbun (2)" p. 73.
67. Kuroda, *Chishikijin*, p. 130.

scene epitomizes some of the dominant currents of the era. It captures the patriotic support for imperialism even among convinced liberals, and it shows how the war provided such an abundant source of legitimacy for renovationist policies—at least as long as Japan was winning.

The decree gave officials for the first time full legal authority to order consolidations. However, local officials were still advised that "consultations" were the preferred method of effecting mergers and that detailed reasons should be reported if a formal order were required. It appears that the inability to handle such matters unofficially would have been counted as a failure on the part of local police. In fact, no such order was ever needed to complete the restructuring of the industry.

A decision of the cabinet on 15 June 1942 set guidelines for the last round of consolidations.[68] It ordered the merger of several medium-sized metropolitan newspapers, deprived the *Asahi* and *Nichi Nichi* of their Aichi regional editions, and called for the fusion of all trade newspapers into one daily each in Tokyo and Osaka (these survived the war as the *Nihon Keizai* and *Sankei* newspapers). A later decision permitted a small number of industrial newsletters to replace the hundreds of disappearing company publications. CIB officials communicated the cabinet's resolution to newspapers through the Newspaper Association, demonstrating how the control organ was used to convey orders from above. This action marked the first time any government had explicitly adopted a general policy of newspaper consolidations or a target structure for the industry.[69] The commitment came some four years after the Home Ministry had begun its project of "adjustment and integration" and after the great majority of daily newspapers had already been merged or destroyed.

The restructuring of newspapers for the New Order was fairly complete by late 1942. The Newspaper Association had begun with 104 members in February, but by November only 64 general daily newspa-

---

68. Miyamoto, "Senjika no Shinbun (3)," p. 85.

69. The closest any previous government had come was when the CIB's Committee for Newspaper and Magazine Paper Control reported to the Yonai cabinet in June 1940 its plan to use paper control to eliminate harmful periodicals: see "Senzen no Jōhō Kikō Yōran," p. 209. There is no evidence that this report elicited any discussion, and mere receipt of the report cannot be construed as signifying the cabinet's approval for the full range of consolidations then underway. The one-paper-per-prefecture standard had been presented to the Newspaper League for discussion but never approved. The principle had probably been accepted implicitly by the league's directors, for otherwise they would have demanded its abandonment in the final draft of terms for the New Order. The Newspaper Association's members allegedly consented to the one-paper-per-prefecture concept sometime in 1942, but solid documentation is lacking. See Miyamoto, "Senjika no Shinbun (3)," pp. 84–85.

pers remained.[70] A handful of these were in the process of consolidation. At least forty-one prefectures had been reduced to one daily newspaper apiece. In twenty-one of them, preexisting journals had absorbed
their rivals, while in the others new companies had been formed from
the merger of two or more firms.[71] The larger metropolitan centers
made out slightly better: Osaka retained four dailies; Tokyo, five plus
the English-language *Japan Times*. In addition, about forty trade newsletters were allowed. These were published by the economic control
associations or public-interest companies commissioned by the ministries. Thus a total of about one hundred newspapers survived the final
phase of consolidation.[72]

The general dailies were classified as national, regional, or local according to their range of circulation. The *Tōkyō Asahi, Tōkyō Nichi
Nichi,* and *Yomiuri* were distributed nationwide, four regional block
newspapers published in Tokyo, Nagoya, Fukuoka, and Osaka were
disseminated as far as contiguous prefectures, and by their paper rations
all others were limited to home prefectures.[73] The arrangement was also
held together by the cooperative sales and distribution company, which
was reorganized into the public-interest Japan Newspaper Distribution
Association in November 1942; membership was compulsory for all
newspapers.

There was no major tampering with the industry's structure after
1942. The final count showed that nearly seven hundred general daily
newspapers had been eradicated through state action. To the end of the
war, however, the state stood by its agreement with the national dailies
and left most remaining newspapers under civil ownership.

A "VOLUNTARY" CONTROL
ORGAN FOR MAGAZINES, DECEMBER
1940–MARCH 1943

The "voluntary" control association for magazine and book publishers was more easily created than that for newspapers because there were
no three or four companies powerful enough to impose conditions on

70. A list of 64 dailies operating as of 1 November appears in *Masu Media Tōsei*, vol.
2, document 97, pp. 495–96. Later consolidations are described in Miyamoto, "Senjika
no Shinbun (3)," pp. 80–85.
71. *Masu Media Tōsei*, vol. 2, document 97, pp. 496–97. The terms of important
mergers were often left to the companies to work out and occasionally led to extended,
acrimonious negotiations: see, e.g., ibid., documents 101 and 110.
72. Miyamoto, "Senjika no Shinbun (3)," p. 85.
73. Ibid.

the project. However, mobilization was complicated by the existence in August 1940 of over five thousand magazines regulated under the Newspaper Law and over fifteen thousand more under the Publication Law as yet undiminished by massive consolidations. Another difficulty was that while newspapers concentrated most business functions in-house, the publication, printing, distribution, and retail sale of most magazines were handled by distinct companies, demanding a more intricate network of state controls. Thus if the New Order for magazines was easier to inaugurate, it was in some ways more difficult to complete.

The editors of some major magazines greeted the New Order with genuine enthusiasm in the fall of 1940, but their expectations differed from those of renovationist bureaucrats. Early in his second cabinet, Prince Konoe appeared to many intellectuals as a godsend. He was something of an intellectual himself, and just as his new political movement could be seen as an alternative to militarism, so a self-governing control organ that might conjoin with that movement could be viewed as a shield against bureaucratic coercion. Since some form of organization to coordinate magazines appeared inevitable, one strategy was to seize the initiative and build a truly autonomous body. This thinking inspired the founding of a Japan Editors' Association (*Nihon Henshū-shakai*) in September 1940, organized by editors of the integrated magazines (*Chūō Kōron, Kaizō, Bungei Shunjū*, and *Nippon Hyōron*).[74] They quickly presented cabinet information officials with their own concept of a New Order for magazines. As one bureaucrat recalled: "From various quarters in the industry they bring in petitions without intermission. They are plans of various hues, but one may appreciate their enthusiasm. As far as possible, we decided to listen to petitions no matter how worthless."[75] There was little enthusiasm, however, for what bureaucrats were contemplating. Their New Order plans for the publishers of books and magazines had been approved by the CIB's paper control committee in August 1940, but when officials sought suitable representatives of the press to assist them, they "couldn't easily find renovationist individuals."[76] They finally had to choose their collaborators from among people nominated by the publishers.

74. Mimasaka, Fujita, and Watanabe, *Yokohama Jiken*, p. 50.
75. Tashiro, *Shuppan Shintaisei*, p. 13. The arrogance of this statement cannot be fully rendered in a literal translation. The writer's tone is one of a teacher referring to the work of pupils. On the other hand, it is hard to blame Tashiro for thinking the plan of the Japan Editors' Association to be self-serving, since it called for the little group to take the lead in editorial guidance administered through the new control organ: see ibid., pp. 170–71.
76. Ibid., p. 12.

From the first, cynicism outweighed eagerness among executives on the business side of publishing. A revealing story is told by a cabinet bureaucrat himself. He and another official set out to visit Tokyo's four largest distribution companies to discuss their integration into a single firm. En route, they happened to meet an industry man who offered to escort them. At one firm, an executive took them into an office specially furnished to his taste, and asked: "it won't be stolen from me even now, will it?"[77] Another company's director told them: "Being already an old man of the old order, I am prepared to take the seat of death at any time if the government so commands, but in exchange, if I die, please have me die for a goal I can believe in."[78] A forged industry newsletter was later circulated reporting that the bureaucrats' guide on their rounds was due for a high post in the coming control organ.[79] After relating a similar encounter with retailers in Hokkaido, the same bureaucrat admitted that such experiences were frequent: "It isn't only in Hokkaido that they refer to me as a 'devil information official' but, somehow, all over the country. I think that is just fine. Until the Publishing New Order is completed in name and reality, it will have to continue being 'devil information official.'"[80] The bureaucrat in question, Tashiro Kanenobu, had been a newspaper reporter for fifteen years before recruitment to the Cabinet Information Division in 1938.

The Japan Publishing Culture Association was launched on 19 December 1940 as an "autonomous" control organ for magazine and book publishers. It was a public-interest company with about four thousand members; the CIB decided which firms could join.[81] Among its functions were to administer paper rationing, to oversee control organs for distribution and sales, and to suppress worthless publications while promoting those that were beneficial. The CIB appointed the chairman and had to sanction all major managerial decisions. The association's charter spoke of the publishers' mission to help establish a "national defense state."[82]

The CIB also sought to establish firm control over all the businesses on which publishers had to depend, placing the magazines themselves in

77. Ibid., p. 20.
78. Ibid., p. 21.
79. Ibid.
80. Ibid., pp. 66–67.
81. Ibid., p. 88.
82. The articles of incorporation are reprinted in *Masu Media Tōsei*, vol. 2, document 50, pp. 290–93.

an economic vise. From 1941, the acquisition of paper involved the following steps.

1.   Publishers requested paper quarterly from the Japan Publishing Culture Association, which had to approve all purchases.

2.   The association processed the requests and recommended a rationing schedule to state offices.

3.   The Commerce and Industry Ministry and Cabinet Information Bureau made final decisions on paper allocation and reported them back to the culture association, which issued vouchers to publishers for their rations and forwarded rationing instructions to the paper sales cooperative.

4.   All surviving paper manufacturers belonged to the Western Paper Cooperative Sales Company, organized by the Commerce and Industry Ministry in late 1940. It dictated the distribution of its members' entire output, informing them how much paper should be sold to which wholesale outlets.

5.   The Wholesalers' Union and the Western Paper Commercial Union, two more monopolies organized by the Commerce and Industry Ministry, encompassed all wholesale and retail paper outlets, respectively. They controlled the transfer of paper from manufacturers to publishers. Publishers would present their vouchers at the local retail outlet and purchase their paper.[83]

Officials thus controlled every link in the chain from paper factory to publisher.

Paper rations were divided into one fixed portion given automatically and a second portion, conditional upon political subservience, that was often denied.[84] The fixed share was initially 90 percent of the total for magazines and 80 percent for books, but it declined steadily. After April 1942, the fixed allocation for books was eliminated; each volume required individual approval to earn a paper voucher.[85] Magazine paper was similarly manipulated. Records of paper allotments to *Chūō Kōron*

---

83. The paper allocation system is described in Tashiro, *Shuppan Shintaisei*, p. 58.
84. The second portion was granted to only 67 of 103 book publishers and 25 of 29 magazine publishers in a batch of requests handled on 14 August 1941: ibid., pp. 94–95. This meant that 4 magazine publishers would have to skip regular editions or sharply reduce the length of their journals.
85. Ōhara Shakai Mondai Kenkyūjo, ed., *Rōdō Undō*, p. 184.

and *Fujin Kōron* show that less cooperative journals saw their rations reduced. The July 1943 *Chūō Kōron* did not appear because paper was denied altogether, as a token of official displeasure.[86]

In June 1941, the monopolistic Japan Publications Distribution Company took over the distribution of all magazines and books. Its establishment followed a familiar pattern. Fifteen state officials proposed its creation at a consultation with twenty-one publishing industry figures in October 1940.[87] The participants resolved to unify distribution by means of "adjustment and integration," in order to build a new Japanese culture and a national defense state. A subcommittee then devised a plan for existing firms to transfer their assets to a single company and receive stock in return. The smaller distribution companies were not represented on the preparatory bodies, and they protested loudly when the plan was leaked. Small businessmen would be reduced to the position of salaried employees of a monopolistic company in which they held only a nominal amount of stock. As one petitioner argued, they would be stripped of their only real asset—the right to manage an independent business.[88]

Petitions related to the New Order for the press averaged eighteen per day in this period, and distributors were the most numerous dissidents.[89] Officials calculated that three thousand wholesale companies would give way before the new monopoly, some four or five hundred of them simply dissolved, the rest absorbed.[90] Publishers and retailers, however, were generally anxious to eliminate these costly and time-consuming middlemen and supported their consolidation.[91] Due to contrasting material interests, then, officials had the cooperation of two sectors of the business in victimizing a third. The monopoly was launched in May as a "state policy company" (*kokusaku kaisha*) requiring official approval for ap-

86. If *Chūō Kōron*'s paper ration in mid-1941 is counted as 1.00, by the end of 1941 it had fallen to 0.63, by the end of 1942 to 0.39, and by the end of 1943 to 0.10. See Hatanaka, *Shōwa Shuppan*, pp. 44, 94–95; Kuroda, *Chishikijin*, p. 120. Officials also threatened to cut magazines' paper rations if they refused to carry articles by certain writers suggested to them: see Hatanaka, *Shōwa Shuppan*, p. 79, where several such writers are named.

87. Tashiro, *Shuppan Shintaisei*, p. 37. The officials included six from the CIB, four from the Commerce and Industry Ministry, and one each from the Cabinet Planning Board, Home Ministry, Education Ministry, and Army and Navy Ministries.

88. Ibid., p. 196.

89. Ibid., pp. 153, 193.

90. Ibid., pp. 164, 42.

91. For example, the president of Iwanami Shoten, a book company known for publishing leftist works, was a major backer of the proposal for consolidating the wholesalers: ibid., p. 38. On the retailers, see the petition reprinted in ibid., pp. 160–62.

pointments to the senior staff and major business decisions. Stock dividends were limited to 6 percent annually.[92] The distribution monopoly was tied to the Japan Publishing Culture Association by the proviso that three of its ten directors (*torishimariyaku*) had to be culture association executives.

Having described the paper and distribution control structures, it is unnecessary to detail the similar control bodies established over book and magazine retailers, printing companies, and ink manufacturers. Suffice it to say that publishers themselves were caught in a web of official business controls regulating everything from access to raw materials to the sale of their final product. Despite the Commerce and Industry Ministry's formal authority over the purely business control organs, the system's nucleus was the Japan Publishing Culture Association, and the CIB was the principal architect of its control network.

COMPLETION OF THE NEW ORDER FOR MAGAZINES, 1943–1945

The Publishing Business Decree was proclaimed on 17 February 1943, activating the State Total Mobilization Law against book and magazine publishers. This was anticlimactic, since the basic innovations of the New Order had already been instituted under the "voluntary" Japan Publishing Culture Association. In March that body was renamed the Japan Publishing Association and became a formal control organ under the mobilization law.

The only apparent motive for the Publishing Business Decree was a desire to effect another round of extensive consolidations. This is evidenced by subsequent events and by the detailed treatment of mergers in the decree and its attendant regulations.[93] Most of the magazines affected were those administered under the Publication Law, which had not suffered much from earlier consolidations. The number active was only 38 percent lower in 1942 than at the end of 1937. By contrast, Newspaper Law publications (newspapers and magazines) had dropped 76 percent over the same years. However, the consolidation of Newspaper Law magazines could proceed no further without involving highly prestigious periodicals, and this was another reason legal authority was

92. The articles of incorporation are reprinted in *Masu Media Tōsei*, vol. 2, document 50, pp. 293–94.
93. The decree and regulations are reprinted in ibid., documents 98 and 99.

TABLE XVI   ACTIVE PERIODICALS REGISTERED UNDER THE NEWSPAPER
              AND PUBLICATION LAWS, 1937–1944

	Publication Law Magazines	Newspaper Law Periodicals
1937	16,788	13,286
1938	15,057	12,043
1939	15,953	8,676
1940	15,369	5,871
1941	13,556	4,466
1942	10,420	3,206
1943	3,081	2,621
1944	942	1,606

Source: Ōhara Shakai Mondai Kenkyūjo, ed., Rōdō Undō, p. 186.
Note: The figures comprise the number of journals active at the end of each year.

invoked. Officials clearly expected difficulties in pushing consolidations any further without formal powers. In October 1943, responding to a notification from the CIB and the Home Ministry, the Japan Publishing Association established a Headquarters for Enterprise Consolidation. In November the cabinet approved its consolidation plans, and a special council organized under the CIB's auspices began to schedule mergers and dissolutions.

Table 16 shows that Publication Law magazines were cut by 70 percent in 1943 and by 70 percent again in 1944, their number reduced by 9,478. The decrease in Newspaper Law publications (almost all of them magazines) was less (1,600), since previous consolidations had cut much deeper. Even this table exaggerates the number of major magazines remaining. The more significant journals all belonged to the Japan Publishing Association, whose members numbered 2,017 before the 1943–1944 consolidations, but only 996 in May 1944. Furthermore, 716 of the 996 were journals of occupational instruction, and only 88 were classified for popular consumption.[94] Magazines treating current events would be a fraction of the 88. From December 1943 to May 1944, "situation magazines" (that is, those covering the war) were cut from 26 to 7, cultural magazines from 200 to 62, and children's magazines from 41 to 6. The influential integrated magazines (combining reportage, social commentary, and literature) were trimmed from 6 to 3: Kaizō became a situation magazine, Bungei Shunjū a purely cultural

94. Ōhara Shakai Mondai Kenkyūjo, ed., Rōdō Undō, p. 186. See pp. 186–87 for all figures in the rest of this paragraph.

journal, and *Nippon Hyōron* an economic magazine. *Chūō Kōron* remained an integrated magazine with *Gendai* and *Kōron,* both renowned for their religious obedience to the state's direction. Companies publishing books exclusively were also diminished from over 2,000 to just 203 by May 1944. A similar decimation of bookstores began in late 1943. Beyond this wave of consolidations, the Publishing Business Decree seems to have had no novel impact upon the industry.

The consolidation of newspapers and magazines paralleled state policy in many social and economic sectors. Just as the political parties had been compressed into the Imperial Rule Assistance Association, women's groups were collapsed into the Great Japan Women's Association (*Dai Nihon Fujinkai*). Labor unions were dissolved in favor of the Industrial Patriotic League (*Sangyō Hōkoku Renmei*), and neighborhood and village organizations melted into the new *tonarigumi, burakukai,* and *chōnaikai* established by the Home Ministry. Consolidation policy reduced banks from 426 in 1938 to 69 in 1945 and cut deeply into most fields of industrial production. Clearly the fate of the press was one shared by countless civil associations in all spheres of Japanese life.[95]

STATE SANCTIONS AND
THE SCOPE OF CRITICISM

Table 17 records the administrative sanctions imposed under the Newspaper Law between 1937 and 1944. Despite official vigilance after the China Incident, the controversies surrounding economic mobilization and the New Order inflated violations during 1940 and 1941. The resolution of many domestic policy issues, the onset of the Pacific War, and the advance of consolidations led to the first sharp decline in press offenses in 1942.

A comparison of tables 17 and 18 shows that manners and morals infringements practically disappeared after 1941. Violations of prepublication warnings also decreased markedly after 1939. These warnings were given only to general daily newspapers and a few major

95. On the reorganization of women, see Fujii Tadatoshi, *Kokubō Fujinkai.* On the Industrial Patriotic League, see Andrew David Gordon, *The Evolution of Labor Relations in Japan: Heavy Industry, 1853–1955,* and Ernest J. Notar, "Japan's Wartime Labor Policy: A Search for Method." Regarding neighborhood associations, see Akimoto Ritsuo, *Sensō to Minshū: Taiheiyō Sensōka no Toshi Seikatsu,* and Thomas R. H. Havens, *Valley of Darkness: The Japanese People and World War Two.* For the figures on the consolidation of banks, see Eleanor M. Hadley, *Antitrust in Japan,* p. 118.

TABLE XVII   ADMINISTRATIVE CONTROLS ENFORCED AGAINST
DOMESTIC PERIODICALS UNDER THE NEWSPAPER LAW, 1937–1944

	Months Data Available	Press Organs	Banned Editions	Post-Publication Warnings	Deletions
1937	12	13,286	595	5,498	94
1938	10	12,043	776	2,514	104
1939	10	8,676	600	3,561	207
1940	8	5,871	655	2,917	211
1941	12	4,466	798	—[a]	337
1942	12	3,206	380		170
1943	12	2,621	174		88
1944	3	1,606	29		7

Source: Naimushō Keihōkyoku, *Shuppan Keisatsu Hō*, nos. 101–49. Nos. 116, 122, 123, 126, 127, and 129 are not extant.
Note: The numbers of press organs listed are those active at the end of each year.
[a]Post-publication warnings are not listed in official records after July 1941. In the first seven months of that year, 2,421 such warnings were given.

magazines, and the paucity of violations indicates that transgressions by important journals were infrequent. This was due to consolidations and to the concentration of "positive guidance" on influential press organs.

Which journals, then, were violating the press code, and what were their crimes? Regarding political criticism, most striking was the prominent role of right-wing publishers. They were undoubtedly the most numerous and virulent critics of the state during formation of the New Order. Tabulating banned editions and deletions related to the founding of the IRAA, rightist violations accounted for twenty-one of the thirty-five in September 1940, nine of the fifteen in October, and eleven of the twenty-two in November.[96] Rightists accused Konoe and his renovationist supporters of communist inspiration, of discrediting the national polity by adopting German and Italian models, and of violating the constitution. These attacks came primarily from the "idealist right" opposed to radical structural change, but "renovationist rightists" also joined the chorus when the IRAA did not meet their expectations.

After war began with the United States, rightist leaders were among the very few voices of forthright criticism still to be heard. Nakano Seigō, for example, severely censured Prime Minister Tōjō in January 1943 and berated the government's controlled economy as an alliance

96. Naimushō Keihōkyoku, *Shuppan Keisatsu Hō*, no. 131, pp. 32, 36, 39; no. 132, pp. 33, 39, 42; and no. 133, pp. 45, 51–52.

TABLE XVIII   ADMINISTRATIVE SANCTIONS AGAINST DOMESTIC
PERIODICALS FOR VIOLATIONS OF PUBLIC ORDER UNDER THE
NEWSPAPER LAW, 1937–1944

	Months Data Available	Total	Banned Editions		Deletions
			For Violating Regular Public-Order Standards	For Violating Pre-Publication Warnings	
1937	12	498	258	240	78
1938	10	520	398	122	62
1939	10	487	338	149	181
1940	8	619	551	68	203
1941	12	781	680	101	324
1942	12	376	282	94	160
1943	12	172	150	22	83
1944	3	29	29	0	7

Source: Naimushō Keihōkyoku, Shuppan Keisatsu Hō, nos. 101–49. Nos. 116, 122, 123, 126, 127, and 129 are not extant.

of bureaucrats and evil capitalists. Retired Colonel Hashimoto Kingorō, a veteran rightist plotter, was another critic of the cabinet.[97] These men were committed political activists who would not be silenced, and standing outside the establishment they had less to lose by such criticism than most politicians and journalists. Their opposition did not go unpunished. Nakano was driven to suicide in October 1943 when he was blacklisted from publishing and put under house arrest.

The central focus of criticism from the mainstream press was the state's economic control program and the shortage of goods. The economic situation was especially controversial in late 1939 and early 1940. Surveying available data for all publications, banned editions and deletions related to economic policy and commodity shortages numbered nineteen in December 1939, twenty-five in January 1940, twenty-eight in May 1940, forty-five in June, and twenty-one in August.[98] In June 1941 there were only eleven such violations, and officials noted a moderating trend, but economic hardship remained perhaps the most common object of public reproach throughout the war.[99] In a rare case of prosecution against a major newspaper, the Asahi Shinbun was fined

97. See idem, Shuppan Keisatsu Hō, no. 146, pp. 8–10, 13, 24–29.
98. Idem, Shuppan Keisatsu Hō, no. 124, p. 6; no. 128, pp. 2, 183; and no. 130, p. 33.
99. Idem, Shuppan Keisatsu Hō, no. 137, p. 45.

TABLE XIX   JUDICIAL VERDICTS IN TRIALS OF INDIVIDUALS
PROSECUTED FOR VIOLATING THE NEWSPAPER LAW, 1937–1940, AND
THE NUMBER OF INDIVIDUALS PROSECUTED, 1941–1943

	Sentenced to Prison	Fined	Acquitted	Prosecuted
1937	0	102	1	
1938	2	133	1	
1939	3	58	1	
1940	0	25	0	
1941				19
1942				15
1943				2

Source: Nihon Teikoku Shihōshō, Keiji Tōkei Nenpō, nos. 63–66; Hōmu Daijin Kanbō Chōsaka Tōkei Shitsu, Dai 70 Keiji Tōkei Nenpō Furoku, 1952.

in January 1942 for merely reporting the consolidation of Tokyo's sake dealers; pre-publication warnings were frequently used to block publication of such news.[100]

Table 19 records the available data on judicial sanctions under the Newspaper Law. During this period, press-law penalties were the least of a potential violator's worries. In early 1941, mass arrests and blacklisting extended even to haiku poets and stand-up comedians.[101] Some naval officers, less swayed by ideological statism than leading army bureaucrats, tried to recruit writers to promote the navy's more moderate views,[102] but after Pearl Harbor it became dangerous to play on army-navy rivalries.

A famous case was recorded in 1944. Truk Island was attacked by American troops on 21 February, and two days later the Mainichi Shinbun carried an article by journalist Niina Masuo that called for stronger naval air forces to repel such invasions. Naval officers had put him up to writing the story. It went on to warn against an unscientific approach to warfare—a slap at Prime Minister Tōjō, who was associated with an emphasis on spiritual martial qualities. Tōjō personally ordered CIB Vice-Governor Murata Gorō to take action against those behind the article. Both the newspaper's chief editor and his second-in-command accepted job suspensions to take responsibility, but the news-

100. Masu Media Tōsei, vol. 2, document 87, pp. 458–59.
101. Kuroda, Chishikijin, pp. 146, 148.
102. Ibid., pp. 143–44.

paper did not punish the reporter. Tōjō then had the journalist drafted into the army and scheduled his unit for combat duty. Niina had been exempt from military service for faulty eyesight, and he was also the first man in his age group to be drafted. When the navy pointed this out, the army proceeded to conscript another 250 men of the same age into the same regiment. Only when the Tōjō government fell in July 1944 was the navy able to retrieve Niina from the army; he was subsequently stationed with naval forces in the Philippines.[103] All journalists had to apply to the press control associations for draft exemptions, and the associations would deny releases to the uncooperative or delay processing their requests.[104]

Chūō Kōron and *Kaizō* had always spearheaded critical journalism, and their record during the Pacific War is perhaps the most fitting conclusion to this review of the New Order for the press. Though their editorial staffs saw little turnover through 1942, most of their regular social commentators had been arrested or blacklisted sometime during the previous four years. The censorship of galleys and "positive guidance" left little room for critical expression. By 1941, patently rightist authors began to appear in *Kaizō*.[105] In 1942, the principal vestiges of autonomy were occasional literary contributions unrelated to the war, articles by some of Konoe's old Shōwa Research Society brain-trusters now excluded from the military-bureaucratic establishment (by this time, Konoe himself was kept under constant surveillance by the Military Police), and work by a group of rabidly imperialist thinkers known as the Kyoto School (*Kyōto Gakuha*). The Kyoto School idealized Japan's mission of conquest, but in terms other than those of official propaganda.[106] Though the two magazines differed little in content from those self-consciously serving government purposes,[107] these faint signs of independence and the editors' antecedents sufficed to attract attention.

During the war, army information officials conducted a consultation for major magazines on the sixth of every month (the *Roku-nichikai*). In September 1942, they sharply rebuked *Kaizō*'s representatives for a two-part article carried in August and September in which Hosokawa Karoku, a writer linked to the Shōwa Research Society, had suggested that Japan adopt some of the Soviet Union's colonial policies for use in

103. Hatanaka, *Shōwa Shuppan*, pp. 98–99.
104. Ibid., p. 98.
105. Kobayashi et al., *Zasshi "Kaizō,"* p. 180.
106. Hatanaka, *Shōwa Shuppan*, pp. 61–62.
107. Mimasaka, Fujita, and Watanabe, *Yokohama Jiken*, pp. 73, 80.

the South Seas.[108] Galleys of the articles had passed the CIB's censorship, but that was immaterial to the army; the two editions were banned ex post facto. A week after the consultation, Hosokawa was arrested by Yokohama's Special Higher Police, and *Kaizō* was told it could not continue without an editorial change. Thus began the Yokohama Incident. *Kaizō*'s chief editor and the staff member handling Hosokawa's manuscript resigned immediately, and several of their co-workers followed close behind. *Chūō Kōron* had a similar experience in June 1943, having angered army officers in April and May by publishing a novel unconnected to the war. Though approved in advance by state censors, this too led to a wholesale turnover on the editorial board to avoid "adjustment and integration." The departing staff had already prepared the July edition, but the army prohibited its publication and it never appeared.

Unrelated to these events, an employee of the Manchurian Railroad was arrested in Tokyo in May 1943. Among his belongings was found a photograph of Hosokawa Karoku with three friends: one worked for *Chūō Kōron;* another had been employed by *Kaizō*. They were pictured enjoying a country outing, which the police quickly construed as a plot to revive the communist party. The three in the photograph were arrested, and their interrogation led to the roundup of others. In January 1944, five *Chūō Kōron* staff members and four from *Kaizō* were caught in the dragnet, and later several *Nippon Hyōron* editors were also picked up.[109] Before the arrests had ended, more than thirty intellectuals were being held by the Yokohama thought police.

The police had no solid case against those detained. The evidence was so flimsy that they even accused *Chūō Kōron* of abetting communism because the company song mentioned a rose (presumably a red one).[110] In lieu of hard evidence, the police set out to extract confessions. Two of *Chūō Kōron*'s employees subsequently perished under brutal treatment; a third died shortly after his release. Thirty-two of the accused claim to have suffered serious injuries; twelve report that they were beaten unconscious.[111] None was tried until several days after Japan's surrender, when they were summarily convicted of the charges against them. In July 1944, the CIB's News Division Chief Hashimoto Masami summoned the publishers of *Chūō Kōron* and *Kaizō* to demand

108. Information in this paragraph is from Hatanaka, *Shōwa Shuppan,* pp. 88–95.
109. Ibid., pp. 128–29.
110. Kuroda, *Chishikijin,* pp. 146–47.
111. Hatanaka, *Shōwa Shuppan,* pp. 128–29.

their journals' "voluntary" dissolution for hindering thought control. They complied with this order later that month—and so disappeared the "matchless twin stars" of the periodical press.

The Yokohama Incident was not typical of press policy under the New Order. It is, rather, the softer image of the consultation meeting that symbolizes the dominant pattern of state-society interaction. But in many ways the incident was a logical offshoot of the administrative despotism that reached its zenith under Japan's military-bureaucratic regime.

CHAPTER IX

Film

By the time of the China Incident in July 1937, film had become a vital factor shaping public opinion on current events. From July through December 1937, state censors inspected 14,833 pieces of film related to the war.[1] This accounted for much of the increase in the number of films inspected: from 25,008 in 1936 to 41,560 in 1937. Films attracted 440.5 million paying customers in 1940; on the average, each Japanese went to the movies six or seven times during the year.

Film policy is of particular interest because film was the only communications medium subjected to a comprehensive control law in this period, the Film Law of 1939. Sponsored by the cabinet and passed by the Diet, this bill is the best example of a statewide consensus on media controls that can be found in the 1937–1945 period, and it therefore deserves careful study.

EARLY WARTIME MOBILIZATION

Official film controls imposed between 1937 and passage of the Film Law two years later resembled those instituted against the press and thus receive only brief treatment here. The same mobilization directives issued by the Army and Navy Ministries under the Newspaper Law and communicated to periodicals were systematically relayed to film-makers; the

---

1. Naimushō Keihōkyoku, *Firumu Ken'etsu Nenpō*, 1938, pp. 40–41.

directives themselves contained specific instructions to that effect. Furthermore, they were generally conveyed through the same forum, the consultation meeting. The first consultation on China policy with news film personnel was held just one week after the incident on 14 July 1937. Consultations with the dramatic film studios to encourage "popular spiritual renovation" began the next month.[2]

If there was any difference between film and press guidance it was that the former concentrated more heavily on manners-and-morals subject matter. For example, at a five-hour consultation between film writers and Home Ministry censors on 30 July 1938, the conferees agreed to the following: the pervasive trend toward individualism due to the influence of European and American movies was to be eradicated; to elevate the Japanese spirit, the beauty of the country's typical family system would be exalted and the public spirit of sacrifice promoted; considering the trend of youth, especially modern girls, to become westernized and lose characteristically Japanese sentiments, the mass public was to be reeducated through film; frivolous language and behavior was not to be filmed; and efforts would be made to deepen the sense of respect for fathers, elder brothers, and other superiors.[3] These goals reflect the increasingly xenophobic outlook accompanying escalation of the war in China. The distinction between political concerns and questions of manners and morals, fuzzy at best in earlier years, all but disappeared after 1937, with the growing aversion to foreign social customs. Film-makers were urged to attune their art to the goals of the National Spiritual Total Mobilization Movement, launched by the state in October 1937 with an initial membership of seventy-four nationwide organizations. Producers were required to include official patriotic slogans in the film credits preceding their movies.

Wartime measures of economic stringency initially affected film more than the other mass media. In December 1937, the Home Ministry tightened restrictions on the length of movies and the duration of film entertainment programs, in order to minimize expenditures on imported negative film, to reduce the number of low-quality productions, to preserve health and morals within theaters, and to avoid lengthy entertainment programs unsuitable during war.[4] In 1938, new theater construction was banned.

Balance-of-payments pressures had more pronounced political ef-

2. Iwasaki, *Eiga Shi*, p. 165.
3. Tanaka, *Nihon Eiga Hattatsu Shi*, 2: 234.
4. Ibid., p. 233.

fects in curtailing the importation of foreign movies. Just two days after the China Incident, the Finance Ministry advised local American film company representatives to limit imports, on the authority of the Foreign Exchange Management Law. In September 1937, finance officials announced a licensing system for imports and declared that no licenses would be tendered for the rest of the year, news film excepted. In 1938 a dollar ceiling was imposed on film imports from the United States. Incoming movies from the big American studios decreased sharply due to these measures and to the Home Ministry's decision to increase foreign film inspection fees the year before:[5]

	1937	1938
Paramount	46	10
Columbia	39	20
Metro	31	16
Warner	31	7
RKO	21	18
Universal	20	6
Fox	17	9
United	17	8
Total	222	94

In January 1938, foreign-film-company representatives began to evacuate Tokyo for Shanghai.

THE FILM LAW

The Film Law offers the best overview of official thinking on media controls in this period. Though the State Total Mobilization Law had a devastating impact on the press, it was not designed primarily to regulate the mass media and therefore does not disclose a general strategy for media policy. The Film Law, however, was aimed directly at an important mass medium. Furthermore, unlike the many bureaucratic and legislative measures affecting only some single aspect of a particular medium,

5. Ibid., p. 284.

this law restructured the entire relationship between the state and the film industry. It also represents a broader state consensus than any other media policy. The bill was neither the unilateral enactment of a single ministry nor a project imposed on the regular bureaucracy by cabinet renovationists. It had solid support from the Home and Education Ministries, the military, and the Cabinet Information Division, and it easily passed the Diet, where for many years there had been calls for comprehensive film legislation. This widespread support was owed to the persistent lobbying of the Film Control Committee within the state and the Great Japan Film Association in civil society (see chapter 6). A final point is that the Film Law was one of the few bills presented in this period without a war-related justification.[6] Government spokesmen touted it as Japan's first "cultural law," and article 1 declared its purpose to be the "healthy development of the film industry and the elevation of film quality."[7] Thus, although the war was present in the background, the law was not conceived or discussed as an emergency measure.

PERSONNEL CONTROLS

The Film Law required every person working in the industry to obtain a state license, including producers, distributors, directors, cameramen and other technical personnel, actors, and theater projectionists. Unlicensed workers could not be hired. Producers and distributors violating the law or harming "the public interest" might have their work suspended or their licenses revoked altogether. This penalty was weightier than the six months in prison that courts could impose upon the law's violators.

Actors and technical personnel had to pass competency tests administered by the Great Japan Film Association, whose promotion of the Film Law was thus rewarded with an official task. This was just one among many examples of civil associations in this period undertaking official duties and thereby transforming themselves into partial state organs. The employees of private companies who served temporarily in the industrial control associations represented a related phenomenon as

6. Uchikawa Yoshimi, "Shiryō Kaisetsu," 2: xxii–xxiii.
7. The Film Law is reprinted in *Masu Media Tōsei*, vol. 2, document 28, pp. 234–36; the ministerial decree regarding its implementation is reprinted in ibid., document 32, pp. 251–59.

non-career officials exercising legal authority. Some sample questions from the competency tests for film workers are:

> 1941—What is the purpose of the Imperial Rule Assistance Movement? Why was it necessary to launch the "New Order" movement?
>
> 1942—Our country has an exalted national polity unmatched throughout the world. Why? Since the eruption of the Great East Asia War, the imperial armed forces have won consecutive victories, and now America and Britain are absolutely incapable of laying a hand on the Far East. However, it is said that "the real battle remains for the future." Why?[8]

CENSORSHIP

The Film Law instituted pre-production censorship of all dramatic movie scripts. Drama producers had to submit a request to begin work at least ten days in advance of the start of shooting. Applications, including two copies of the proposed script, went to the Home Ministry, whose censors were empowered to alter the script for reasons of public safety or manners and morals. Changes made during filming required official approval before they were put on camera. Inspection of the finished product before public showing was still mandatory for all films, but administrative sanctions plummeted once script inspection began (see table 20). Unfortunately, no records were kept of the script changes imposed by the state; after 1939, information on film cuts is obviously not very revealing. In practice, pieces of film cut by censors were classified under the same categories as before (see table 21).[9]

Another new twist to censorship was that under "special circumstances" the state could restrict or ban a film's showing even if it had already passed inspection. Hypothetically, then, the state could rewrite a dramatic movie script prior to filming, cut the film before approving it for public showing, and then ban it from circulation due to "special

---

8. Iwasaki, *Eiga Shi*, pp. 211–12.
9. Though in practice the same classification was used, a new set of standards was formally inscribed in the decree accompanying the Film Law, which prohibited the following: (1) items feared to desecrate the sanctity of the imperial family, or to harm the empire's dignity; (2) items feared to advocate thought undermining the constitution; (3) items feared to hinder the public interest in politics, military affairs, foreign relations, economics, or any other area; (4) items feared to disturb virtuous manners and morals or to corrupt public morality; (5) items feared to damage the purity of the Japanese language in a striking way; (6) items notably inferior in production techniques; and (7) any other item feared to obstruct the progress of national culture: *Masu Media Tōsei*, vol. 2, document 32, p. 255.

TABLE XX   ADMINISTRATIVE SANCTIONS IMPOSED UNDER THE
MOTION PICTURE FILM INSPECTION REGULATIONS AND THE FILM LAW,
1937–1942

	Total Films Inspected[a]	Bans[b]	Required to Reshoot[c]	Films Cut	Limited by Time/Location	With-drawn	
1937	41,560	5	21	395	63	40	
1938	46,690	8	15	221	85	65	
1939	53,323	5	40	205		60	(18)[d]
1940	51,872	18	29	35	112	107	(50)
1941	39,705	4	23	11	89	122	(40)
1942	34,247	0	0	11	338	115	(29)

Source: Naimushō Keihōkyoku, *Firumu Ken'etsu Nenpō,* 1938–1939; idem, *Eiga Ken'etsu Nenpō,* 1940–1943.

[a]The figures include Japanese and imported films, films submitted for the first time, resubmissions, and prints of previously submitted films.

[b]The figures include films withdrawn from inspection because sponsors were informed they would be banned. These films are not counted in the "withdrawn" column.

[c]These films were formally listed as having been withdrawn from inspection; they are not counted in the "withdrawn" column.

[d]Some films were withdrawn from inspection at the convenience of their sponsors, and not due to any action by officials. Those in parentheses, however, were withdrawn for the following reasons: military-related reasons (1939—10, 1940—1, 1941—0, 1942—0); unsuitable in the wartime "situation" (1939—8, 1940—44, 1941—39, 1942—25); reasons of foreign policy (1939—0, 1940—5, 1941—1, 1942—4). The numbers within parentheses are included in the total "withdrawn" figures.

circumstances." It was entirely up to officials to decide what constituted "special circumstances."

MOBILIZATION

The Film Law enabled the Education Minister to compel theater owners to show nonfiction films serving to educate the public. This power was initially used to promote "culture films." In April 1937, the Home Ministry had decreed that Japanese films that "elevate national consciousness, establish public morality, correct the understanding of Japan's domestic and international situation, serve as propaganda (*senden*) for the administration in matters pertaining to the military, industry, education, fire prevention, nutrition, etc., or contribute to the advancement of public welfare in other ways" would henceforth be inspected without charge. Nonfiction films exempted from inspection fees were referred to as *bunka eiga,* or culture films. The term, borrowed from Nazi Germany's *kulturfilm,* was generally used to describe

TABLE XXI   PIECES OF FILM CUT UNDER THE MOTION PICTURE FILM INSPECTION REGULATIONS AND THE FILM LAW, BY CENSORSHIP STANDARDS AND AREA OF PRODUCTION, 1937–1942
(J = Japanese, F = Foreign)

	1937		1938		1939		1940		1941		1942	
	J	F	J	F	J	F	J	F	J	F	J	F
Public Safety												
Imperial family	3	2	0	2	1	7	0	0	0	1	1	0
Nation	2	0	0	0	0	0	0	0	0	0	0	0
Constitution	0	0	0	0	0	0	0	0	0	1	0	0
Social organs	4	16	4	0	1	2	0	0	2	0	1	0
Class conflict	1	6	0	0	1	1	0	0	0	0	0	0
National ethos	1	0	0	0	0	8	0	0	0	0	2	0
Foreign affairs	1	8	2	1	0	0	0	0	0	0	0	0
Group conflict	0	5	0	0	0	1	0	0	0	0	0	0
Crime	14	14	8	2	3	1	1	0	0	1	0	0
Public business	9	22	3	2	8	10	0	0	0	0	0	0
Other	70	63	29	33	26	47	7	2	2	0	8	4
Area Total	105	136	46	40	41	77	8	2	4	3	12	4
Annual Total	241		86		118		10		7		16	

Manners and Morals

Religion	3	0	4	0	12	0	1	0	0	0	2	0
Cruelty/ugliness	37	31	36	16	21	7	4	17	0	1	0	0
Sex-related	190	372	168	140	99	256	26	43	0	26	0	4
Work ethic	2	0	0	0	0	0	8	0	0	0	0	0
Education	32	17	25	2	25	7	0	0	0	0	1	0
Family	7	7	2	0	6	0	0	0	1	4	0	0
Other	66	55	52	38	40	2	16	1	0	0	3	2
Area Total	337	482	287	196	203	272	55	61	1	31	6	6
Annual Total	819		483		475		116		32		12	
Grand Area Total	442	618	333	236	244	349	63	63	5	34	18	10
Grand Annual Total	1,060		569		593		126		39		28	

Source: Naimushō Keihōkyoku, *Firumu Ken'etsu Nenpō,* 1938–1943.

educational, documentary, and propaganda films that served state ends. In the last three months of 1939, 985 films received the Education Ministry's blessing as culture films; in 1940, 4,460.[10] Regulations accompanying the Film Law demanded that every film entertainment program include at least 250 meters of officially sanctioned culture film. This command was enforced nationwide by July 1940.[11]

The Education Minister was also empowered to recommend films. Each year several films would be awarded an "Education Minister's Prize," some receiving a monetary subsidy. This codified in law a recommendation system that the ministry had run more informally for several years. The first awards ceremony was held in March 1940.

The Film Law also authorized any administrative state office to order the showing of films necessary for "enlightenment or propaganda." The Home Ministry apparently anticipated that its local government offices would use this provision, though they were admonished not to burden any one theater with forced showings for more than six weeks per year. The Home Ministry continued to exempt certain films from inspection fees; with the advent of the forced showing policy, all culture and current-events films were so exempted. Twenty-six dramatic movies were also relieved of payment in 1940.[12]

FOREIGN FILMS

The law allowed the Home Minister to dictate the kind and number of imported films circulated by distributors and shown in theaters. Initial enforcement required distributors to petition each October for the next year's foreign film quota, and theaters were limited to showing fifty foreign films annually.

Beyond the above-mentioned powers, the law contained two open-ended enabling clauses. Article 18 permitted the Home and Education Ministers to regulate film production and distribution, order the improvement of facilities, and eliminate unfair competition when neces-

10. For the figures, see Naimushō Keihōkyoku, *Eiga Ken'etsu Nenpō*, 1941, p. 103. On the 1937 decree, see idem, *Firumu Ken'etsu Nenpō*, 1938, pp. 2–3. The first official use of the term *culture film* that I encountered in writing was in the *Firumu Ken'etsu Nenpō*, 1937, p. 2, which notes the number of "culture films" released in 1936. There, however, the term was given a wider meaning that included dramatic movies supportive of the state. The meaning given in the text here was the most commonly used. Tōhō studios opened the film industry's first culture film division in 1937.

11. Tanaka, *Nihon Eiga Hattatsu Shi*, 2: 236.

12. Naimushō Keihōkyoku, *Eiga Ken'etsu Nenpō*, 1941, pp. 6–8.

sary for the public good. Article 8 also empowered administrative officials to impose controls on production and on the employment of film workers, again for the public good. The Home Ministry used this authority in 1941 to limit the annual production of dramatic film studios to a specified number of feature-length and short-subject movies.[13]

The Film Law thus gave the state unconditional authority over every person and organization in the film industry. If officials wished to close a film studio, they could halt production, rescind its business permit, and revoke the licenses of its employees: The End. The law did not define bureaucratic powers so as to render film administration predictable; rather, it removed the last fetters on bureaucratic rule and placed the film industry at the mercy of whatever state policy might ensue. The concept of law as a restraint upon state action was turned on its head; this was law in the form of a blank check.

The Film Law was not only applauded in the Diet, but also well received by the film industry. Film people had once been considered less than respectable in polite society, and to many the law was long-overdue recognition of their achievements. Others expressed satisfaction at phrases such as "planning the healthy development of the film industry" and "pressing for greater film quality," which sugarcoated the less benign provisions of the bill. Apparently only *one* individual, the critic Iwasaki Akira, dared to write openly in opposition to the law; for this he was blacklisted from publishing and spent part of 1940 in prison as a violator of the Peace Preservation Law.[14] The danger of such repression makes it difficult to gauge the genuineness of public reactions, but Iwasaki himself reports that most of the support was freely given.

Foreign models were one factor legitimizing the new system. The Film Law had been partly inspired by Nazi film legislation, and in 1939 German prestige was as its peak. During the Diet's deliberation on the law, Hitler had annexed a large part of Czechoslovakia, and his ally Franco had defeated the Spanish Republican forces at Madrid. Another reason for support was the law's partial character as an enabling act,

13. This policy was presented to the movie studios at the first Film New Order Consultation Meetings, held in August and September 1940. Simultaneously, entertainment programs were further shortened to a maximum of two and one-half hours, eliminating double features, and culture films were restricted to 300 meters. See Tanaka, *Nihon Eiga Hattatsu Shi*, 2: 238.

14. On the film industry's reaction and Iwasaki's opposition, see Iwasaki, *Eiga Shi*, p. 172, and Okada, *Nihon Eiga no Rekishi*, pp. 191–93. Iwasaki had been a founder of the Japan Proletarian Film League in 1929, and after his release in 1940 he worked for the Manchurian Film Association.

that is, it granted the state broad powers without fully specifying how they would be used. Since the Home Ministry was the chief beneficiary of those powers and film people had survived under that ministry's hegemony for several decades, few feared that the state was about to dispossess them simply because it now had that legal prerogative. The State Total Mobilization Law claimed similar powers over many civil associations, but it had not yet produced much structural change. If giant combines such as Mitsui and Sumitomo were subject to such authority, how were film companies to object? The Home Ministry did not in fact impose extensive changes upon the film industry while it supervised implementation of the law. When the Cabinet Information Bureau took the lead in film policy in late 1940, however, the full ramifications of the state's new authority became painfully clear.

The Film Law reveals just how far the tide had turned toward statism by the spring of 1939. There was no institutional opposition to a law that might be used to deprive an important mass medium of all meaningful autonomy. Of course, the bill was less significant than the State Total Mobilization Law enacted one year earlier, but the defeat of liberal forces on that occasion may well have demoralized potential opponents of the film legislation. Whereas the mobilization law had been rammed through the Diet by a skillful Prime Minister over many protests, the Film Law, sponsored by the decidedly weak cabinet of Hiranuma, met with no such resistance.

CONSOLIDATION OF THE FILM INDUSTRY

Film consolidations were even more drastic than those forced upon the press. They began in April 1940 when news film companies were merged into a single firm under state direction. This company then absorbed many of the larger cultural/educational film producers in May 1941. There followed in August 1941 a more sweeping consolidation plan directed at makers of dramatic films, the remaining cultural/educational film companies, and film distributors. The final tally showed 10 drama producers reduced to 3, over 200 cultural/educational film producers amalgamated into 4 main companies and a few stragglers, and the fusion of the almost 300 film distributors into a new, monopolistic firm. In early 1942, film importers were similarly merged into a single unit.

The first step toward a New Order for film was the merger of Japan's four news film producers into the Japan News Film Company on 9 April 1940. The firms integrated were those of the *Asahi, Yomiuri,* and *Mainichi/Nichi Nichi* newspapers, and the film operations of the United News Agency. Thus the state accomplished with news film companies what it had failed to achieve with daily newspapers: a production monopoly. The Cabinet Information Division and the UNA were the prime movers behind this project. The new monopoly became a public-interest adjunct of the UNA, Furuno Inosuke serving as president of both. The Cabinet Information Division channeled all state monies to the companies—in 1940, 3.9 million yen to the UNA and 100,000 to the Japan News Film Company.[15] With production now confined to a state-organized monopoly, newsreels were made compulsory in all film entertainment programs in October 1940, just as culture films had been before them.[16]

After its upgrading in December 1940, the Cabinet Information Bureau seized the initiative in film policy. The bureau received censorship authority paralleling that of the Home Ministry, it took charge of rationing negative film, and it immediately pressed forward with plans for amalgamation.[17] Its first success was to merge the culture film departments of several newspapers and movie studios into the state's news film enterprise, renamed the Japan Film Company in May 1941.[18] For some time thereafter, this one firm produced all the newsreels and culture films legally required in each film entertainment program.

The big push for consolidation, however, began on 16 August 1940, when the CIB's Cultural Division Chief, Kawamo Ryūzō, called into his office the three dramatic-film business representatives in the Great Japan Film Association. Their companies partially financed the film association, which had promoted the Film Law and now administered state

15. *Masu Media Tōsei,* vol. 2, document 35, p. 264, and document 50, p. 306.
16. Tanaka, *Nihon Eiga Hattatsu Shi,* 2: 239. Not a single piece of current events film was cut by censors between 1939 and 1942: Naimushō Keihōkyoku, *Eiga Ken'etsu Nenpō,* 1940–1943.
17. Naimushō Keihōkyoku, *Eiga Ken'etsu Nenpō,* 1941, p. 3; *Masu Media Tōsei,* vol. 2, document 50, pp. 299, 306–8. The rationing of negative film, which consumes materials used in the manufacture of gunpowder, had begun in October 1940, when production was cut 36 percent as a measure of economic belt-tightening under the Public Livelihood Retrenchment Decree (*Kokumin Seikatsu Kinshuku Rei*); see Tanaka, *Nihon Eiga Hattatsu Shi,* 2: 302.
18. To guard against confusion: "news" film refers to reportorial coverage of the latest events, whereas "culture films," though they might take up current topics, were a step removed from the immediate. The newspaper companies had ceded their news-film operations to the Japan News Film Company but had continued to produce culture and educational films until these functions too were absorbed by the renamed Japan Film Company.

tests for film-industry workers. With this legal authority, these three men were already part-time state officials themselves. It was not in their capacity as officials, however, but as industry spokesmen that they were to be addressed. The functionary Kawamo informed them that "not one foot" more of negative film could be spared for the dramatic-film companies; all film was needed for military purposes.[19] He suggested they offer a plan for conversion of the dramatic-film sector to wartime footing. The three stunned listeners surmised correctly that the film embargo, tantamount to extinction for their studios, might prove negotiable if steps toward conversion were satisfactory, but this opening salvo illustrates the pervasive atmosphere of coercion surrounding state-society interaction during the establishment of the New Order.

The drama producers quickly formed a crisis committee to prepare a response. Seeing the futility of unyielding resistance, they prepared a minimal reform proposal to save their firms. What they offered, one week after Kawamo's would-be death sentence, was this: a state-managed "control association" would be created for the dramatic-film business according to the State Total Mobilization Law, which regulated such organs in other economic sectors. The chairman would be an individual who had the confidence of both the state and the industry, and film-makers would submit to his decisions on every facet of the association's work. The agenda of the new unit comprised control over film production and the structure of film distribution, and the rationing of resources used by the industry. The producers recommended Gotō Fumio, an ex–Home Minister and a director of the Great Japan Film Association, as the first chairman. In effect, the drama producers would swallow any medicine the state might prescribe, on one condition: that their businesses be left intact.[20] This was the same position taken by the large newspapers when confronted with the single-national-newspaper proposal. The drama producers conceded state control over the "structure" of distribution, a painful gambit since they themselves ran the largest film distribution concerns. But the control association, though it could otherwise regulate production, was not authorized to interfere with the structure of production, that is, their businesses would stay afloat.

19. For accounts of this meeting, see *Masu Media Tōsei*, vol. 2, document 68, pp. 356–57; Tanaka, *Nihon Eiga Hattatsu Shi*, 2: 241; Okada, *Nihon Eiga no Rekishi*, p. 198.
20. *Masu Media Tōsei*, vol. 2, document 68, p. 357.

This proposal was read to an audience of CIB, Army, Navy, Home, and Education Ministry personnel on 23 August 1941. They found the industry's attitude "extremely irresolute."[21] After passage of the Film Law, there was no reason for officials to rejoice at concessions they could legally exact at their pleasure. It is obvious in retrospect that the bureaucrats had their own scheme in mind from the beginning, since they offered a comprehensive counterproposal just two days later. This was the cornerstone of the August 1941 blitzkrieg, and it contained four points: (1) the ten dramatic-film companies would be merged into two new firms, each producing two movies monthly in accord with state purposes; (2) the remaining cultural/educational film companies would be combined into one firm; (3) one integrated distribution organ would control all film circulation; and (4) film administration, heretofore divided among several state agencies, would be integrated.[22] Official goals were to eliminate commercialism by segregating production from marketing, and to amplify the industry's public character. The whole package was justified in the name of the "high degree national defense state" (kōdo kokubō kokka), which demanded an end to structures inherited from the era of freedom.[23]

The state's program caused consternation among the dramatic-film studios. The two largest film-makers, Shōchiku and Tōhō, saw the two-company policy as an opportunity for their firms to survive the cut, even though the original design was for two new enterprises. They broke ranks with the other producers and refused to take an uncompromising stance against the state's proposal.[24] The next three largest companies, Nikkatsu, Shinkō, and Daitō, represented by Eida Masaichi of Shinkō, strongly opposed the plan for two firms. They argued for three studios, the last presumably involving a cooperative venture between their companies. Despite several conferences, the producers were unable to reconcile their differences.

Consultation meetings were held on 4, 6, 8, and 10 September, but if the industry was at odds, discord was also evident among officials. Though the evidence is thin, it seems the Cabinet Information Bureau wanted to hold out for two *new* drama companies, expecting that firms without an established identity or tradition would be more malleable,

21. Ibid.
22. Ibid., p. 358.
23. Ibid., pp. 358, 356.
24. Okada, *Nihon Eiga no Rekishi*, p. 203.

whereas Home Ministry officials were inclined to build the two firms around Shōchiku and Tōhō, perhaps due to their longer association with the film industry and clientelistic ties to those studios. Industry people strove to exploit this breach. Word leaked that some had secretly tried to contact Prime Minister Konoe to plead for support, and Eida went to work on the CIB group, hinting that if three companies were approved, at least the third might satisfy their desire for a perfectly obeisant organ.[25] Whether Eida's ploy was a tactic or a sell-out is unclear, but his efforts paid off. On 19 September 1941, the CIB's Kawamo made his final offer to the producers. There would be three drama studios, one consolidated around Shōchiku, one around Tōhō, and the third a merger of Nikkatsu, Shinkō, and Daitō, to be called Daiei. Each of the surviving studios would produce two movies per month. A public-interest company would monopolize distribution, absorbing technical personnel from existing distribution operations.[26] The representatives of the film industry agreed to the plan, and committees were assembled to work out the details. The biggest hurdle was calculating stock percentages in the third drama company, but this problem had been resolved by year's end. The smaller movie studios were absorbed by the large as part of the arrangement.[27]

Consolidation of the remaining cultural/educational film companies was more time-consuming. There were over two hundred such firms operating in August 1941, and the CIB initially proposed that all merge into a single company. The bureau conveyed this design to forty of the larger firms on 27 August. Negotiations were long and stock transfers complex, but finally, in January 1943, the principal companies were fused into three units: the Science Film Stock Corporation (fourteen firms), the Asahi Film Company (eight firms), and the Dentsū Film Stock Corporation (four firms). This result was but a belated and partial success for the CIB. Of the many firms excluded from the new state-sponsored triumvirate, most either sold out to larger companies or went bankrupt, since they were denied access to negative film and the official distribution system (see below). A few, however, may have pulled through with business from other state agencies. Though the CIB dispensed all negative film, various ministries received allotments to be

25. *Masu Media Tōsei*, vol. 2, document 68, p. 362; Okada, *Nihon Eiga no Rekishi*, pp. 202–4.

26. Tanaka, *Nihon Eiga Hattatsu Shi*, 2: 245.

27. For details on the smaller firms' plight, see ibid., pp. 271–84.

used at their discretion. Some may have continued to contract for films with companies other than those formed by the CIB.[28]

Film importers were combined into the Foreign Film Stock Company in early 1942.[29] The eight companies merged had little business left to perform. In 1940, the state had answered 482 petitions for import licenses with only 120 approvals; import control was now enforced under the Film Law, not as a purely economic measure. In 1941, when there were sixteen importers, only 71 licenses had been granted.[30] After Pearl Harbor, the showing of American and other enemy films was banned altogether, and those already in Japan were seized as enemy property. Even many Nazi films could not clear censorship. Scenes of scantily dressed Aryan maidens posing gracefully in the Bavarian Alps were thought too risqué for proper manners and morals, though by special permission the German Embassy was able to screen them for its staff. During the war, theaters with foreign names (for example, Palace, Odeon) were forced to change them.

As the new structures took shape, the Cabinet Information Bureau gained complete control over the public showing of films. The country's theaters were divided into two groups, and every week CIB officials composed an entertainment program for each, including a dramatic movie, a culture film promoting public policy, and a newsreel.[31] The state-organized Japan Film Company produced all news films (except for those made by other state institutions or imported) and half of the culture films, the other half coming from the three cultural/educational film companies created in January 1943, or directly from other state organs. The dramas were all produced by the three conglomerate companies authorized by the state, Shōchiku, Tōhō, and Daiei. In its essentials, this control system endured to the war's end.[32]

The CIB also rearranged the industry's finances. Small theaters paid

28. Tsumura Hideo, *Eiga Seisaku Ron*, p. 221.
29. Tanaka, *Nihon Eiga Hattatsu Shi*, 2: 297.
30. Ibid., pp. 236, 239–40.
31. Ibid., p. 307.
32. In September 1943, the Cabinet Information Bureau founded the Japan Mobile Projection League and thereby succeeded in unifying most of the rural entertainment system: see ibid., pp. 382–83. In January 1944, all production and distribution organs were enlisted in a reorganized Great Japan Film Association: *Masu Media Tōsei*, vol. 2, document 104, pp. 508–9. This association and the Film Distribution Company were then formally merged in June 1945 into the Film Public Corporation (*Eiga Kōsha*), but by this stage of the war such structural shifts had little significance.

the Film Distribution Company a flat rate for film rental, while each of the larger handed over 40 percent of its gross earnings, keeping the other 60 percent for operating expenses (35 percent), salaries (15 percent), and a 10 percent profit.[33] The portion of theater income collected by the distribution company was used to pay film producers and to cover distribution costs. Supposing the gross income of all theaters to be 100 yen in a given month, it would be allocated among the various firms as follows:[34]

Theaters	60.0 yen
Drama producers	25.6
Distribution costs	8.0
Culture-film producers	3.2
News-film producers	3.2

This method of financing did not entirely eliminate market forces, since film producers were paid according to theater earnings from the showing of their own pictures, and not from a general pool.

It was clearly the Cabinet Information Bureau and not the Home Ministry that engineered the New Order for film, planning consolidations and dealing directly with the industry. Indications are that the CIB's aims were more radical than those of the regular bureaucracy. However, although the Home Ministry hindered the dissolution of Shōchiku and Tōhō, its officials acted more as collaborators than foot-draggers in the New Order project. Their objections rarely exceeded a defense of bureaucratic turf. The Home Ministry retained its grip on the execution of regular film censorship, and so the unity of film administration became the one unfulfilled goal of the August 1941 New Order blueprint.

33. However, the state initially collected half of the operating expenses (17.5 percent) each month, along with a report of each theater's expenditures. If a theater's financial breakdown indicated exorbitant outlays, the appropriate amount would be taken out of the 17.5 percent; the remainder would be returned to the theater operator after three months. This was to insure against wasteful spending and excess profits. In May 1943, the Home Ministry launched a campaign that brought many theaters under direct state management—this was apparently done not on the basis of the Film Law but according to the traditional jurisdiction of the local police over entertainment. See Tanaka, *Nihon Eiga Hattatsu Shi,* 2: 387–88.
34. Ibid., pp. 308–9.

WARTIME MOVIES

By most accounts, Japan's wartime movies served as excellent propaganda. Production values and artistic quality were superior, eliciting praise from American directors such as Frank Capra and Alexander Korda.[35] Just as technical journalistic standards remained high during the war, indirect state control also facilitated the making of excellent films by leaving professionals in place to manufacture the final product. Movie plots and characters appealed skillfully to Japanese sensibilities. Typically, the protagonists were modest individuals of humble antecedents rather than larger-than-life heroes. The films shied away from abstract symbols of patriotism such as the Emperor or the Sun Goddess in favor of a more realistic portrayal of the hardships of war. In place of artificially happy endings, the main characters achieved personal triumph when their devotion to duty stood firm despite great suffering and led them to an honorable death for family and country.

Consider Ruth Benedict's description of the Japanese film *Chocolate and the Soldier* (1941):

> Seiki, the hero of the film, is a minor clerk in a small fishing village. Scenes of daily life in the village open the film—a beautiful sunset, the quiet evening, fishing with the children, supper at home with his wife and two children, a warm drink of sake, warm white rice. Then a messenger from the reservist corps arrives. Seiki's unit is called. The last night at home is spent going over a few mementos of school days and early life, repairing the children's toys, performing a few tasks for the family. Morning brings the hour of departure. There are flag waving and shouts of "banzai" or "long live the Emperor." Without tears and with a calm resignation in the knowledge that the end has come, the hero recognizes that the only thing required of him now is to fight and die bravely. And then China, disembarkation, mud, marching, trenches with water up to the chest, letters from home. Everywhere that Seiki goes, he picks up chocolate wrappers to send home to his little son. Trench scenes alternate with those of home where his wife ekes out a living doing embroidery work and his son has stopped attending street theater to save money. Both at the front and in the family, there are scenes of patience, courage, and fortitude. Seiki's squad is to be sent out on a suicide mission and he drinks sake with his comrades. A farewell to his family, together with the implicit symbolism of its perpetuation through his son, is shown by the last look and the drink taken from a little cup given him by his son as a parting gift. The scene shifts to the arrival of the fatal letter at his home together with a package of chocolate wrappers collected by him on the muddy roads of China. Does the wife break down? Does she

---

35. Ruth Fulton Benedict, "Japanese Films: A Phase of Psychological Warfare," p. 11.

weep? . . . Not in a Japanese film. She reads the letter quietly, braces herself as she lifts her eyes to the skies, then calls the little son to tell him that his father is dead. The only weeping which accompanies the memorial services is that of friends who weep for pity and admiration of Seiki's gallant wife and son . . . . The boy receives a prize for the chocolate wrappers. A chocolate company takes an interest in him and decides to send him to school. The street theater man comes around once more. The children play as before. But at the family altar is a white box of ashes. Seiki . . . lived and died as was proper.[36]

Upon seeing this film, which brings concreteness to much of the state's guidance regarding artistic treatment of the war, Frank Capra commented: "We can't beat this kind of thing. We make a film like that maybe once in a decade. We haven't got the actors."[37] A sample of twenty popular wartime films showed that the most common themes were the submission of the individual to his or her country (7) or to father and family (6), and the devotion of married women to their husbands (3) and widows to their in-laws (3).[38]

Wartime movies were also carefully calibrated to accommodate the propensities of foreign audiences. The film *Shina no Yoru* (China Night, 1940) was a love story involving a Japanese naval officer and the Chinese girl he rescues from destitution—a very popular combination of characters in Japanese cinema at the time. The movie was given three different endings for audiences in Japan, Southeast Asia, and China, respectively.[39] In Japanese theaters, the officer died in battle and his lover drowned herself in a river when she heard of his death. In the version screened in Malaya and the Philippines, the report of the officer's demise proved unfounded and he returned to rescue his lady from suicide in the nick of time. For Chinese audiences both death and suicide were edited out; the protagonists, personifying the two pillars of the Great East Asian Co-Prosperity Sphere, were happily bound together in matrimony. Such fanciful portrayals of friendly relations between the Japanese and conquered peoples were perhaps the most consistent distortion of reality in Japan's wartime films.[40] The Western enemy was usually depicted as morally corrupt and cowardly, and even Japanese villains exemplifying these character traits frequently sported Western

36. Ibid., pp. 3–4.
37. Ibid., p. 11.
38. Ibid., p. 5.
39. Ibid., p. 11.
40. William B. Hauser, "The Japanese War Film: National Service versus Individual Survival," pp. 6–9.

clothes, smoked American cigarettes, expressed a preference for jazz, or boasted an academic degree from a Western school.[41]

As the war progressed, the state became increasingly active as a partner in film production. Though the military had contributed to the production of culture films since 1933, it was not until after the China Incident that state-civil ventures became most visible. The first big war hit produced with military help was *Shanhai Rikusentai* (Shanghai Marines), made by Tōhō with the Navy Ministry's cooperation in 1939. In 1940, fourteen dramatic movies, eight of which involved the military, were produced with state assistance.[42] Tōhō invested the huge sum of 920,000 yen in another cooperative endeavor with the navy in 1942, *Hawai-Mare Okikaisen* (Hawaii-Malay Sea Battle), which attracted an audience of over ten million.[43] Officials also used consultation meetings and prize competitions to encourage films on favored topics.

State film control, then, encompassed the following measures: official monopolies on news-film production and film distribution; total control over film-industry personnel; pre-production censorship of dramatic-movie scripts and censorship of all finished films before public showing; management of film financing; rationing of negative film; selection of all film programs to be shown in theaters; a licensing system for imported films; a sweeping consolidation of film production companies; official collaboration in film production; and awards and various financial incentives for the production of films serving policy objectives. The only noteworthy civil autonomy to filter through this control structure was the production of a few movies with no direct connection to the war; Shōchiku, in particular, persisted in making some films purely for entertainment.[44] Occasional resort to nonpolitical artistic expression becomes the only form of protest possible in such an advanced mobilization system, where the great majority of works overtly support state interests.

41. Benedict, "Japanese Films," p. 12.
42. Naimushō Keihōkyoku, *Eiga Ken'etsu Nenpō*, 1941, pp. 7–8.
43. Iwasaki, *Eiga Shi*, p. 183.
44. Ibid., p. 180.

CHAPTER X

Radio

In the late 1930s, radio became the principal means of communication between the Japanese state and its subjects. In just three weeks after the China Incident of July 1937, there were 1,844 news items broadcast over radio, 68 percent of them related to the incident.[1] Shortly thereafter, NHK and state officials adopted the Nazi slogan of "one house/one radio" and it became national policy to provide every Japanese with access to a receiver.[2] Several ministries cooperated in poster campaigns boasting such slogans as "National Defense and Radio," and patriotic organizations, including the Great Japan Youth League, joined in the effort. In small farm villages, where receivers were a luxury item, they were installed free of charge in markets, stations, parks, shrines, and other public areas.[3] The Communications Ministry, radio's bureaucratic shepherd, had the commodity tax removed from listening sets, pushed for longer hours of electric power supply in the countryside, and scavenged for scarce raw materials to maintain production in the face of wartime rationing.[4]

Due to the profusion of small rural communities, the project to bring radio into the life of every Japanese was not entirely successful, but by

1. NHK, ed., *Nihon Hōsō Shi,* 1: 389.
2. Ibid., p. 306.
3. Ibid., p. 481. Some 25,000 radio receivers were supplied to the branches of the Great Japan Youth League (*Dai Nihon Rengō Seinendan*) nationwide: NHK, ed., *Rajio Nenkan Shōwa 13-Nen,* p. 244. By 1941, there were 346 radio towers in public parks in the larger cities: NHK, ed., *Rajio Nenkan Shōwa 17-Nen,* pp. 317–23.
4. NHK, ed., *Nihon Hōsō Shi,* 1: 482.

1941 the results were impressive. Radio receivers had multiplied from 2.9 million in 1936 to 6.6 million; following the United States, Germany, and Great Britain, this gave Japan the fourth highest number in the world.[5] Nationwide, over 45 percent of all households owned a radio.[6] Newspapers and magazines were probably more influential among political elites, and it may be argued that films make a deeper impression on most people than audio alone, but in sheer magnitude of public exposure, radio had no competitor in this period. It was indisputably the most forceful mass medium shaping public opinion on current events. Recognizing this fact, the Cabinet Information Bureau had by February 1942 adopted a policy "to make all broadcast programs conform to state purposes."[7] The mobilization of radio was not only more thorough than that of the other media, but also more easily accomplished, since the existing structure required only slight modifications to achieve complete official dominance.

THE STRUCTURE OF PROGRAM CONTROL

The Broadcast Programming Council remained the principal vehicle for program interference until 1939. After the China Incident, it was complemented by a slew of specialized program advisory committees also including state officials. There were separate committees for music, lectures, and entertainment, as well as for programs directed overseas or into the school system. Their influence, however, depended on the council's responsiveness.

This arrangement changed with the establishment of the Situation Broadcast Planning Conference within NHK in July 1939. ("Situation" was the official euphemism for the wartime crisis.) This body quickly displaced the programming council as the last court of judgment on the monthly broadcast schedule, and its grip on program policy was such that the many program advisory committees ceased to meet or matter very much within about a year. The state's programming control was codified in November 1939 when the Communications Ministry revised a decree of 1923 to read: "In times of war or incident or when otherwise necessary, the Communications Minister may command broadcast op-

---

5. Ibid., p. 306, and the table titled "*Rajio no Nendo Betsu Kanyū Haishi Zōka Genzaisū*" on an unnumbered page at the end of the volume.

6. Ibid., the table titled "*Rajio no Nendo Betsu To-Dō-Fu-Ken Fukyū Ritsu*" on an unnumbered page at the end of the volume.

7. *Masu Media Tōsei*, vol. 2, document 83, p. 451.

erators to transmit items for the public interest and order any necessary measures related to these broadcasts."[8] It was the Situation Broadcast Planning Conference that actually made use of this authority. The conference recruited members from NHK and the Communications Ministry as well as the Cabinet Information Division, but the staff of the information division exercised the greatest influence.[9]

When the information division was upgraded to bureau status in late 1940, the Communications Ministry transferred much of its substantive program authority to this new organ. The CIB was given control over broadcast contents, while the ministry continued its jurisdiction over transmission facilities. The Communications Ministry thus ceded more authority to the CIB than any of the other regular ministries.[10] This was probably due to the presence of several ex–Communications Ministry bureaucrats in the highest offices of the CIB, and to the cabinet information staff's considerable input into radio policy in earlier years. At this time, the CIB's Broadcasting Section Chief was an ex–Communications Ministry official, Miyamoto Yoshio. The mechanics of censorship were still performed mainly by NHK and ministry officials, but the CIB determined most censorship standards and the selection of programs. NHK's personnel policy, bylaws, office organization, business plans, and finances were placed under the joint authority of the ministry and the bureau.

The Situation Broadcast Planning Conference operated until war began with the United States in December 1941, when it yielded to daily meetings of CIB officials (who included military men) and personnel from the Communications Ministry and NHK. One early decision was to suspend NHK's second channel during the conflict. Program policies underwent constant revision, but a running file of orders was maintained. An Implementation Study Meeting (Sōchi Kentōkai) was held weekly to discuss changes in the file and to refine policy execution.

8. NHK, ed., Nihon Hōsō Shi, 1: 322.
9. One illustration of the Cabinet Information Division's influence in the conference was that it sponsored a major decision earmarking NHK's national channel for programs aimed at the average subject, while the second channel (operative only in Tokyo, Osaka, and Nagoya) was to focus on a more intellectual, urban audience: ibid., p. 347.
Broadcasting to the colonies and foreign countries is not treated here. However, note that an East Asian Broadcast Conference was organized in September 1939 to supervise overseas programs, its membership and functions paralleling those of the Situation Broadcast Planning Conference. Just before Pearl Harbor, NHK was broadcasting to overseas areas in sixteen languages almost twenty-four hours a day: ibid., p. 305.
10. The accord between the CIB and the Communications Ministry is reprinted in Masu Media Tōsei, vol. 2, document 49, p. 279. See also ibid., document 45, pp. 273–74.

If cooperation between the Cabinet Information Bureau and the Communications Ministry was occasionally strained,[11] friction between the CIB and the military was constant. It was the hydra-headed nature of military involvement that complicated matters. The first channel of military input was through the officers employed directly by the CIB. As of January 1942, an army major and a navy lieutenant commander both served in the CIB's office supervising radio, while simultaneously holding positions in their respective military ministries. Reportedly they pushed a hard statist line within the CIB.[12] Despite this influence, however, the information offices of the two military ministries continued to function independently. Their operations were not absorbed by the cabinet until April 1945, even though from its inception the CIB had been designed to coordinate the state's entire information output.

Beyond the ministries were the army and navy information offices serving Imperial Headquarters (*Daihon'ei*). Headquarters was responsible for combat strategy, and it was the only state organ whose propaganda authority equaled that of the cabinet. It could unilaterally make pronouncements on the war, and this power was unassailable, for it was rooted in the constitutional right of supreme command. Membership overlapped between the information offices of the military ministries and Imperial Headquarters, but they nonetheless functioned as distinct entities. As the war advanced, headquarters increasingly issued direct instructions to NHK and other media organs without filtering them through the CIB. This created agonizing predicaments when such statements duplicated or contradicted those emanating from the ministries and the cabinet, which were cleared through the CIB. The CIB and Imperial Headquarters concluded several formal agreements during the war to dispel the confusion, but disharmony in war-related pronouncements was never entirely overcome.[13]

11. NHK, ed., *Nihon Hōsō Shi*, 1: 519. On attempts to expedite ministry-bureau cooperation, see *Masu Media Tōsei*, vol. 2, documents 94 and 95.
12. This point should not be misconstrued—there were civilian bureaucrats in the CIB whose statist predilections were as radical as those of their military co-workers.
13. A program aired on Asahi Television in 1981 recounted an incident late in the war when the *Asahi Shinbun* was forced to carry conflicting state announcements on the same page of the same issue.
Note that there were a number of structural innovations late in the war in response to defeats and enemy bombing which are not treated here. The most significant was a merger of the Communications Ministry with the Railroad Ministry in November 1943, after which a Transmission Agency (*Tsūshin-in*) was detached as an external ministry office to handle radio's technical side; this office was placed under cabinet authority in May 1945. These late changes were rather desperate improvisations which did not affect the general level or method of state control.

WARTIME BROADCASTING

Since mobilizational directives on specific issues are described in chapters on the press, radio programming will be treated in a series of vignettes illustrating the transformation of content.

ENTERTAINMENT

The China Incident in mid-1937 marked a turning point in the politicization of radio entertainment; the Manchurian Incident had had less of a backlash here than in news and lecture programs. The initial reaction to the China war was less to mobilize entertainment than to moderate it, since mirthful enjoyment seemed out of step with the "situation." Even traditional dancing at the yearly Lantern Festival (*Obon*) was forbidden and did not reappear until 1942.[14] This anti-entertainment policy was reflected in radio programming. A poll published by the journal *Bungei Shunjū* in early 1941 reported that 89 percent (607) of the respondents found radio "unentertaining."[15] The journal ascribed this to the excess of serious war-related programs, though it responded patriotically by calling for a "new culture" to promote morale on the home front. Policy changed markedly after October 1940, when, in a cabinet resolution, Army Minister Tōjō called for "healthy entertainment."[16] The proportion of entertainment programs on NHK's first channel in Tokyo subsequently rose from 23 percent in 1940 to 33 percent in 1941,[17] and shortly thereafter the Imperial Rule Assistance Association even promoted a "New Rice Dance" around the country. But although the mobilization of entertainment gained steam in the early 1940s, it had been well in evidence ever since late 1937.

In the two years after the China Incident, jazz was stricken from radio for being un-Japanese, and as a rule music sung in foreign languages was banned; German and Italian songs later become exceptions. Even Japanese music composed in foreign styles was targeted for elimination. In January 1943, the CIB compiled a list of one thousand songs, both foreign and Japanese, to be banished from entertainment, and after April 1944 music played on the banjo, ukulele, and steel

14. NHK, ed., *Nihon Hōsō Shi,* 1: 635.
15. Cited in ibid., p. 490.
16. Ibid., p. 635.
17. NHK, ed., *Hōsō 50-Nen Shi,* p. 610.

guitar was outlawed altogether, while use of the saxophone was narrowly restricted.[18]

Meanwhile, radio authorities discovered patriotic virtues in the more native *shakuhachi* (a bamboo flute), which was lauded as follows:

> The *shakuhachi*, in the tune of just a single flute, reproduces the universe. It is truly a typical Oriental symbol. Those who play it must devote their entire character to it, which leads not only to the perfection of a really severe art, but also contributes to the spiritual culture of *bushidō* [the way of the samurai] and is an act of religious purification. In order to overcome our present difficulties in this dangerous time which cries out for renovation of the nation's livelihood and for self-discipline from the people, the *shakuhachi* especially is the simple art form appropriate for the country's way of life in the situation.[19]

State officials were fortunate: their desire to revive such traditional instruments as the *shakuhachi,* the *koto,* and the *shamisen* was boosted by some independent developments in the arts. The most notable was the "New Japanese Music" movement started in the early 1930s as a response by traditional artists to the invasion of Western popular music. Arrangements were written for a full orchestra, a concession to current Western tastes, but most instruments used were the traditional ones listed above. The new form was very well received. By 1940, the entire New Japanese Music movement was adopted as "one important element in 'National Music' [*Kokumin Ongaku*]," the state's term for patriotic songs it fostered on radio.[20]

The National Music campaign was in full swing by 1940. In spring and autumn, audiences were blitzed nightly with military marches, focusing on China Incident songs in the spring, and music related to the Manchurian Incident and earlier wars in the autumn; new contributions were strongly promoted at year's end to climax radio's celebration of Japan's mythical 2,600th birthday.[21] Officials sponsored contests to encourage the composition of "healthy" music. For example, between August 1942 and March 1943, a cash prize competition was held for a form of musical storytelling which typically addressed traditional moral themes (*rōkyoku*): "The [Cabinet] Information Bureau has planned to select and reward national musical storytelling of a healthy, cheerful

---

18. NHK, ed., *Nihon Hōsō Shi,* 1: 544–45.
19. NHK, ed., *Rajio Nenkan Shōwa 17-Nen,* pp. 162–63.
20. Ibid., pp. 163–64.
21. Ibid., pp. 162–65.

kind that will contribute to a wide understanding and propagation of state policy by recently establishing a National Musical Storytelling Prize."[22] The better entries to such contests were recorded and played on the radio.

To summarize regarding radio music: the state eliminated most foreign music, as well as Japanese music that duplicated foreign styles; encouraged musical trends employing native styles and traditional instruments, often infusing them with nationalistic tone or content; and actively promoted the writing of new music explicitly supportive of state policy.

Developments in dramatic radio entertainment paralleled those in music. War-related plays, precursors of a state-generated National Theater movement, were already being broadcast by late 1937.[23] In 1938, "situation dramas" began to appear regularly; these were ten-minute performances addressing the wartime crisis or related to state policy. "Culture plays" taking up themes in the service of official objectives were also broadcast. This art form took its cue from the "culture films" produced at the time, both terms having been borrowed from Nazi Germany. In February 1938, during radio's second "Emphasis Week" for the National Spiritual Total Mobilization Movement, there were nightly thirty-minute dramatic performances in which "the Japanese spirit was concretely interwoven," and these continued thereafter at least twice a week. Most comprised various kinds of storytelling, some accompanied by music. By March 1939, there had been 317 such performances carried over radio.[24] Throughout 1940, extensive radio programming celebrated the patriotic commemoration of Japan's founding, including the broadcast of a new full-length play each month of the year, from the genre of National Theater.[25]

By 1942, state programmers were working to eliminate what remnants of nonpolitical performances were left. As one official document expressed it:

> in our experience, though one cannot say that we never find absolutely impermissible entertainment beyond the reach of discretion, the most common cases are neither passable nor damnable but right in the middle. In reality, our duty and the greater part of our work lie in adding political

22. *Dai Tōa Sensō Hōsō Shirube*, no. 16, September 1942, p. 15. This document was printed by the Cabinet Information Bureau for intrastate consumption.
23. NHK, ed., *Nihon Hōsō Shi*, 1: 374.
24. Quotation and data from NHK, ed., *Rajio Nenkan Shōwa 15-Nen*, p. 169.
25. NHK, ed., *Nihon Hōsō Shi*, 1: 374.

considerations to such pieces and guiding them so that they advance along the course upon which they must advance in wartime.[26]

The state organized contests for drama as well. For example, in late 1942, prizes were offered for the best fairy-tales, stories, and dramatic scripts submitted for the "Little Subjects' Hour" (previously titled "The Children's Hour").[27] The purpose was "to contribute to the rise of little subjects' culture, to the promotion of their education, and to little subjects' sentiments during the Great East Asian War."[28] Similar contests were held for full-length plays for adults.

The attitude of many officials is epitomized in the words of the Broadcasting Division Chief of the Tokyo Communications Bureau in 1942: "Broadcasting is a political organ ... apart from its political nature, culture does not exist."[29] The more radical CIB officials wished to stop the performance and broadcast of all classical music by composers of Jewish origin or from countries at war with the Axis powers. The works of some composers (for example, those of Mendelssohn) disappeared completely, but a few music lovers apparently managed to squeeze in pieces by Debussy (France) and Chopin (Poland) without announcing the composer's name.[30] The less sophisticated CIB officials, some of whom reportedly took Dostoevsky to be the name of a new drug, failed to notice.[31]

As for sports and health programs, the regular "Radio Gymnastics" show was incorporated into the National Spiritual Total Mobilization Movement in 1938. This program had been originally modeled on an American radio show sponsored by an insurance company in the 1920s. Though young naval officers had always announced the drills, the program had not initially served any political purpose. For three weeks every August, special assemblies were organized nationwide to perform the exercises; schoolchildren on summer vacation received cards from their teachers to be stamped when they arrived at the park to participate. In the summer of 1938, these assemblies were for the first time arranged under the banner of spiritual mobilization: more than 30,000

---

26. *Masu Media Tōsei*, vol. 2, document 91, p. 483.
27. The new Japanese title was *Shōkokumin no Jikan*. There were many such language changes during the war. The English-derived *nyūsu* reverted to the Japanese *hōdō*, *anaunsā* to *hōsōin*, etc. Foreign-language lessons were stricken from radio completely.
28. *Dai Tōa Sensō Hōsō Shirube*, no. 16. p. 95.
29. *Dai Tōa Sensō Hōsō Shirube*, no. 18, November 1942, p. 79.
30. NHK, ed., *Nihon Hōsō Shi*, 1: 555–56.
31. Ibid., p. 297.

gatherings drew a total of 147 million people.[32] During the war, the drills turned from simple gymnastics to martial exercises, and from 1941 on the program was directed at the "neighborhood associations" (*tonarigumi*) at the base of the Imperial Rule Assistance Movement.

Broadcasts of the alien sport of baseball, already a growing Japanese passion in the 1930s, were restricted to holidays after the China Incident, and, by 1940, limited even on holidays. Native Japanese sumo wrestling, however, was a military favorite and received extra air time.[33]

RELIGIOUS PROGRAMS

Religious radio shows in the 1930s also reflected growing state control over programming. In the very popular series "Discourse on the Sacred Books" (*Seiten Kōgi*), running from March 1934 to January 1935, there had been fifteen programs on Buddhism, five on Christianity, three on Confucianism, and four others. In February 1935, the show was renamed "Morning Cultural Lesson" (*Asa no Shūyō*) and over the next year it carried eleven talks on Buddhism, eight on the Japanese spirit and national history, three on Confucianism, and three others— already a significant shift in content. Before the program's termination in April 1941, it had degenerated into a patriotic pep rally, expounding upon such themes as the practice of loyalty in the "situation."

A number of more limited religious programs mirrored the same trend. Starting in January 1937, a series of ten monthly religious broadcasts addressed such topics as the promotion of *bushidō* and "the Japanese view of life and death." Monthly religious lectures in 1938 carried such titles as "Commentary on Sacred Teachings to Be Heard in the Situation," and "The Great Achievement of Emperor Jinmu" (Japan's mythical first monarch).[34] This transition from purely religious to highly nationalistic spiritual content was paralleled by the growing persecution of Buddhist, Christian, and even splinter Shintō groups from about 1934, when the state had run out of communists to arrest. The same thought police and prosecutors who had worked over the leftists then turned on the clerics.

The ease with which officials could control religious groups and use spiritual exhortations to advantage reflects the absence of a powerful independent religious institution in civil society. There was no religious

32. NHK, ed., *Rajio Nenkan Shōwa 15-Nen*, p. 10.
33. NHK, ed., *Nihon Hōsō Shi*, 1: 395.
34. Ibid., p. 353.

group as weighty as the Catholic Church of interwar Italy or postwar Poland to sustain a vital sphere of autonomy from state control. Without comparable religious resistance, it was relatively easy for the Japanese state to penetrate the inner life of its subjects with its own spiritual doctrines.

NEWS

By 1937, news reports occupied 3 hours and 58 minutes of radio time daily,[35] and polls unfailingly identified the news as NHK's most popular program. In November 1937, survey research gave the 7:00 P.M. news the highest audience rating on the schedule, and listening rates for the 7:00 P.M. and 9:00 P.M. news never wavered from the 80–85 percent range during the war.[36] In 1939, people who had recently purchased radio receivers were polled for their reasons: the most common response was a desire to hear the news sooner (given by 18 percent); the second was to deepen the listener's awareness of the China Incident (12 percent).[37] This desire for information was answered with an unmitigated flow of state propaganda.

A document outlining basic state policy on radio news was prepared by the Communications Bureau in Tokyo in September 1942 and printed for intrastate consumption by the CIB. On the overall purpose of radio mobilization it stated: "Throughout all broadcasts, the basis of our approach to [program] inspection is the determination to 'complete the Great East Asian War' and for 'every broadcast to conform to the purposes of the state.' In other words, it is 'to perceive all broadcasts from an intensely political standpoint.' "[38] The document enumerated four criteria by which officials would evaluate radio news. These are especially illuminating because they establish that conscious lying was the essence of the state's information output in general, and of news broadcasts in particular:

1. Is the broadcast suitable for the nation at the present time? . . . Needless to say, in the news there are items suitable to relate to the people, and others not so. The choice must be made first and foremost judging from the state's vantage.

35. Ibid., p. 349.
36. Ibid., p. 633.
37. Ibid., p. 486.
38. *Masu Media Tōsei*, vol. 2, document 90, p. 478. Phrases in single quotation marks are apparently citations from an earlier state document or common slogans.

2.   Is the perspective that of Japan and the Axis powers? . . . [On the topic of broadcasting news from the point of view of neutral countries] It certainly cannot be said that to take the standpoint of third countries purely is fair news from the perspective of our allies, because allies and enemies would be given an equal appraisal.

Rather, the effect of reporting news to the nation from a third-country viewpoint is the opposite. Which is to say, this so-called fair standpoint is called fair because it does not discriminate between causes and does not resolve the issues, but leaves judgment to the decision of the listener's mind. This tendency concedes a freedomist viewpoint to the minds of the people. It is premised on the restoration of so-called *jiyūshugi*. This is because various factors are presented uncritically and it is left for the one who hears them to compare and examine them in his own head and arrive at his own conclusions. If one were continually to present this kind of uncritical news, and the public were to interpret events as it pleases, the result would be to open a crack in the public opinion which has finally been led at great pains to a union of belief.

Consequently, how should we treat this news from the position of a third country? We must make it beneficial for the guidance of our national opinion by adding our own subjective comments but dressing it up to the utmost just like objective news on the surface.

3.   Is it cooperative with the government? . . . [Under this item, the document warns that even facts favorable to the state can sometimes have the wrong effect if reported too objectively. For example, election coverage in 1942 had noted that electoral law violations had declined, but then went on to list the various violations, leaving a contrary impression on the listener.]

4.   Is there a danger of it being used against us by the enemy?[39]

The question "Is the story true to fact?" never arises. The disastrous naval defeat at Midway in June 1942 was judged unsuitable news for the people to hear.[40] The rendering of consciously fabricated commentary as objective reporting was official policy. It had begun at least as early as 25 December 1941, when a news item from Imperial Headquarters on the attack against Hong Kong was followed (still within the newscast) by an official explanation of its importance.[41] By 1943, news and analysis were systematically mixed without any distinction.[42]

How much, then, did the Japanese people know of the real causes of a war in which some three million of them were to die? In April 1943, Murata Gorō, a senior Home Ministry bureaucrat, was personally asked by Prime Minister Tōjō to become the new Vice-Governor of the Cabinet Information Bureau. This was the highest working post in the

39. Ibid., pp. 479–80.
40. NHK, ed., *Nihon Hōsō Shi,* 1: 565.
41. Ibid., p. 564.
42. Ibid.; *Dai Tōa Sensō Hōsō Shirube,* no. 20, January 1943, p. 6.

bureau. When he took up the assignment, Murata reports that one of the first things he did was to look into the origins of the war:

> As for me personally, I thought that Konoe's third cabinet had been wrecked mainly because the Japanese army absolutely refused to agree to America's demand for a troop withdrawal, and therefore I figured that the war had probably begun likewise as a result of the exacerbation of this troop withdrawal problem. However, there were not a few civil intellectuals who said that mere complications over the issue of troop withdrawal were not sufficient reason for Japan and America to go to war.
>
> Because so many made this claim, even I was thinking that I would like just once to ascertain clearly the real reason this war actually started.
>
> Therefore, after my transfer to the [Cabinet] Information Bureau, starting with the army and navy officers who worked there, I took aside the bureau's leading officials and asked them various questions to make sure of the real reason for the outbreak of war. However, there was not one among them who clearly understood the true cause.[43]

And indeed, state propaganda had so little to do with the truth that they could function perfectly well without comprehending the full magnitude of their distortions.

After war began with the United States, the CIB ordered news announcers to switch from the "disinterested tone" (*tan tan chō*) to the "war-cry tone" (*otakebi chō*) of speaking, and news broadcasts were punctuated with martial music to embellish their impact.[44]

THE BROADCAST DAY: 8 DECEMBER 1941

What follows is a slightly abbreviated transcription of NHK's broadcasting schedule for the day the Japanese armed forces attacked the United States. Entries marked simply "music" were recordings, most often the patriotic numbers played before and after the news during the war. All other musical pieces were performed live for radio.

6:20 A.M.	News/Music
6:40	Discourse on *Bushidō* [the way of the samurai]
7:00	Special News
7:04	Radio Gymnastics
7:18	Special News
7:20	Morning Words: "Date Masamune and the Pacific Ocean"

43. Naisei Shi Kenkyūkai, ed., *Murata Gorō-Shi Danwa Sokkiroku*, 3: 245.
44. NHK, ed., *Nihon Hōsō Shi*, 1: 495.

7:41	News/Music
7:50	Accompaniment for Work—Marching Songs: "Brilliance of the Imperial Army," "Night of the Air Force," "March of the Great Fleet," "Military March at Dawn"
8:30	Special News
8:50	Radio Gymnastics
9:00	National School Broadcast (Education Vice-Minister)
9:12	Music
9:20	Economic Market Report
9:30	Special News/Music
10:20	Women's Household Hour: "Post Office Annuities for Country and Home" (Communications Ministry Bureau Chief)
10:40	Instrumental Music: A Medley of Marching Songs
11:00	Special News/Music
11:40	Economic Market Report
12:00 noon	Announcement National Anthem Reading of an Imperial Rescript [declaring war] "To Revere the Imperial Rescript" (Prime Minister Tōjō Hideki) "Patriotic March" (music)
12:16 P.M.	Imperial Headquarters Announcement
12:17	Instrumental Music: "Spirit of the Imperial Army," "The Strength of Asia," "Patriotic March"
12:30	Reading of a Government Announcement
12:37	News/Music
1:45	Economic Market Report
2:00	Special News/Music
3:08	Broadcast to the Workplace: Music/Radio Gymnastics
3:30	News/Music
4:40	Economic Communication
5:00	Special News
5:14	Choral Music: "Annihilation of the Enemy's Character"; Music

5:50	Program Preview
6:00	Call to Assemble before the Radio (Miyamoto Yoshio, CIB)
6:04	Little Subjects' Newspaper
6:30	Choral and Orchestral Music: "March of the Warships," "If One Goes to Sea," "Annihilation of the Enemy's Character," "Let Us Carry Out the Holy War," "Protect Our Skies," "Pacific March," "I Pledge to the Country," "The Strength of Asia," "Patriotic March," "Parade March"
7:00	National Anthem Reading of an Imperial Rescript "To Revere the Imperial Rescript" (Prime Minister Tōjō Hideki)
7:13	News
7:30	"A Pledge to the Nation regarding the Declaration of War" (Okumura Kiwao, CIB Vice-Governor)
8:01	Musical Recital: "We the People of the Emperor," "From Now On" (song of the ancient military guards)
8:04	"Emergency Financial Policies" (Finance Vice-Minister)
8:15	Instrumental Music: "The Combined Fleet," "Warship"
8:24	Musical News Ballad: "The Declaration of War"
8:30	Proclamation to the Entire Nation (army general)
8:40	Instrumental Music: "If One Goes to Sea," Others
9:00	News Instrumental and Choral Music: "Military March of the Century," "The Song of Oceanic Aerial Flight," "Military March of the Sea," "Protect the Oceans," "Pacific March"
10:00	Today's War Situation and News
11:00	News[45]

Radio continued to provide unflagging support for the war effort until 15 August 1945, the day a recorded speech by the Emperor was broadcast to announce Japan's surrender.

45. *Masu Media Tōsei*, vol. 2, document 72, pp. 371–74.

Comparative Analysis

Although the political regime ruling Japan from 1937 to 1945 was not structured along the lines of a single-party totalitarian system, the New Order nonetheless witnessed a revolution in the state-society relationship. Shedding their usual image of conservatism, military and bureaucratic elites embraced radical political goals and reorganized many sectors of a highly complex society. Despite the antagonism they encountered in some quarters, they succeeded in mobilizing people and material resources on a scale rarely observed in any country, even in the twentieth century. The course of this administrative revolution contradicts many stereotypes associated with military-bureaucratic regimes and sheds light on some important questions pertaining to the problem of the modern state.

THE LESSONS OF CIVIL RESISTANCE

Civil opposition to state control was evident throughout 1868–1945, but the struggle against the New Order offers the best material for a general assessment. From about 1900 to the early 1930s, mainstream press organs and film producers generally acquiesced in the controls of the *état-gendarme;* severe sanctions fell mainly upon a radical minority little able to defend its interests. Mainstream media people certainly resented state interference—witness the movement to revise the Newspaper Law in 1924—but they normally endured state meddling as but an occasional irritant. Only in regard to radio did civil forces for autonomy play their last card before the 1930s. Despite opposition from Osaka's radio investors, however, the state won that confrontation easily, because controls were imposed before civil organizations could establish a pattern of broadcasting autonomy. The acid test of civil resistance, then, came from 1937 to 1945, when officials attempted a radical mobilization of the film and press industries, by then among the world's most advanced. The study of their efforts to retain their autonomy leads to the following conclusions: large, dominant media organs are best able to resist state power; logistical difficulties, competitive antagonisms, and the uneven impact of control policies are great barriers to civil solidarity against the state; and the public interest structure (represented by NHK) was no match for privately owned, profit-making companies in resisting mobilization. Although extensive comparative research would be needed to test the general validity of these postulates, they are unambiguously supported by the data here.

The record of newspapers, magazines, and film-makers indicates that the less pluralistic the civil sector, that is, the more it is dominated by a few powerful associations, the better it can defend its autonomy from radical mobilization.[1] Certainly no media organ could resist the state's full coercive power, but if officials do not resort to extreme coercion and civil associations have some room for maneuver, it is the large ones that can put up the best fight.

While the landscape of small local and trade newspapers was flattened illegally without much of a struggle, the three renowned national dailies preserved a modicum of operational autonomy. They had great credibility and prestige; they were functionally irreplaceable; they had official supporters in the navy and the cabinet (a by-product of their political influence); and they found it much easier to stand together than did the horde of small newspapers spread around the country. Likewise, the two dominant dramatic-film producers maintained civil ownership against the Cabinet Information Bureau's designs. In the magazine sector, however, there were no two or three firms in a superior class. No magazine had the prestige, resources, or circulation of a national newspaper. The state managed to enter the magazine business itself with its weekly *Shūhō* and unofficial sponsorship of such journals as *Gendai*

1. These comments are valid only in regard to resistance against the extreme form of state mobilization attempted in the late imperial period. A simple censorship policy out to stop radical criticism might face greater obstacles in a civil sector of thousands of small media organs.

and *Kōron,* and it finally eradicated even *Chūō Kōron* and *Kaizō,* the two foremost independent periodicals. The absence of a few clearly preeminent firms emasculated the sector's capacity to resist.

This finding points to the weakness of an ideal democratic social structure in opposing radical mobilization. The democratic ideal is for many associations to compete in the marketplace of ideas so that all groups can air their views. Dominance by just a few firms, comprising something of a civil tyranny, undercuts this ideal. However, given the frailty of all but the largest media businesses before state power, there exists a paradox that the more democratically a civil sector is organized, the more easily the state can usurp its autonomy, thereby undermining both its democratic (that is, representative) and its liberal character. While democracy is enhanced by many small to medium-sized media organs, liberal resistance to state encroachment is better served by the civil tyranny of a few large firms (assuming that all media companies have an equal desire to remain autonomous). The more oligopolistic the sector, the stronger its defenses.[2] The validity of this proposition should increase with the level of political development, for as the state's absolute power grows, so must the minimal resources of any organization capable of resisting it.

Arguably, the ideal civil sector might comprise many small to medium-sized associations united against state intervention; would this not maximize both liberal and democratic values? Unfortunately, there are practical obstacles to realizing this scenario. Given the huge size of contemporary countries, coordination among numerous small organizations in different regions requires strenuous efforts by all concerned. Their inability to act quickly in unison renders their combined resources less effective than the same resources concentrated in a few firms. The experience of the German newspaper business, which was highly decentralized into small and medium-sized firms in the 1920s, also discredits the hypothesis. Oron Hale has cited "the lack of unity among the segments of the publishing industry" as one reason the Nazis easily subjugated the sector.[3]

Japan's newspaper and film industries, each boasting several dominant firms to check the state and many smaller ones to complement the

---

2. This is not contradicted by the state's preference for an oligopolistic structure of civil associations within the control scheme it envisioned for the press and other industries. The point is that an autonomous oligopoly was best able to counter state efforts to create a completely controlled oligopoly of media organs.

3. Hale, *Captive Press,* p. 2.

large, would seem perfect if only they had closed ranks to resist mobilization. Autonomy from the state appears to be a common interest of all media organs. But their solidarity was impeded by the very competition that typifies a relatively free society. The newspapers' battle for readers had created such bad blood that most declined to protest the liquidation of their rivals—with few exceptions, none discovered the sanctity of an autonomous press until its own coals were in the fire. The national and local newspapers had vied for so long that they formed two antagonistic blocs during creation of the New Order. Thus a second paradox is: the greater competitive intensity in the marketplace, the less likely it is that the sector will unite to defend its autonomy from the state and thereby protect competitive conditions.[4] If the three largest newspapers had not overcome *their* rivalry to cooperate in 1941, there would not have remained a single newspaper owning its own printing presses or the land and buildings that housed them.

The tendency for media organs to parry the state's challenge individually instead of treating it as a sectoral problem was reinforced by the disparate effects of control measures. In the dramatic-film industry, the two largest companies, Shōchiku and Tōhō, saw a chance for survival under the state's consolidation scheme, while it meant certain dissolution for the others. If paper rationing hurt such critical magazines as *Chūō Kōron* and *Kaizō,* it favored the periodicals of forthright state supporters. The elimination of middlemen in book and magazine distribution was a boon to publishers and retailers. The one-company newspaper design would have benefited local papers, to the detriment of the national dailies. In every case, some firms stood to gain from the state's despoliation of others, and lesser incentives for cooperation such as complimentary tours of the battle front, preferential access to news sources, and official collaboration in film production were never lacking. It is not that most media people were pleased by the policy of consolidation, but when some comprehensive restructuring appeared inevitable, each firm was inclined to maximize its own advantages rather than rally to a common cause. Competitive enmity and the uneven impact of control policies were major reasons.

A final point is that NHK offered none of the resistance witnessed in the privately owned press and film sectors. The public-interest format has too many variations to permit generalizations, but regarding NHK,

---

4. To read "political party" for "media organ" in this discussion discloses many obvious parallels with the struggle to uphold political autonomy in Japan and elsewhere.

it is clear that state control over personnel and the absence of private ownership and profit left no one to resist the wartime system for ideological or material reasons. It was still possible for Shōchiku to produce a few nonpolitical films, and for the journals to publish some short stories unrelated to state policy or occasionally even to exploit conflicts within officialdom to air different viewpoints. These were humble signs of autonomy, to be sure, but even these faint vestiges of independence were denied to radio.

This underscores the fact that the principal motive for civil resistance was to protect private ownership. It was only consolidation policy that moved influential media organs to pronounced opposition. Typical was the posture of the national newspapers and the major dramatic-film studios in 1940–1941: they would concede anything so long as private ownership was respected.[5] Ownership should not be confused with profit; restrictions on profit were not a major bone of contention. There was, rather, a sense that private ownership was the minimal requirement if a company was to keep its organizational integrity and traditions intact. This desire to save the enterprise as a distinct entity was probably bolstered by the well-known Japanese tendency to project family-like loyalties and sentiment onto nonfamilial social organizations. Radio had never enjoyed the independence that comes with the full prerogatives of private ownership, so no similar threshold of resistance was there to be crossed.

Given the penetration of mobilization policies, the resistance of the mass media was feeble on the whole, and the fundamental reason was patriotic support for the country at war. War reinforces the myth that the state alone represents the public good, while "private" associations stand for selfish concerns that properly yield to this public good and its alleged spokesmen. It was this misconception above all that disarmed so many Japanese from defending even their life's work from bureaucratic ambitions. How is a businessman to confront a battery of officials telling him that his homeland's survival requires the sacrifice of his little film company or magazine, especially when he desires victory as much as they? The state rarely had to unsheathe its brute power to win compliance from its subjects. Its moral authority in wartime was the major reason that so much de-

5. Similar evidence for surviving private publishers in Nazi Germany led Oron Hale to ask: "But even in conserving and defending their property rights were they not also defending freedom?": *Captive Press*, p. 269.

struction could be wreaked upon private individuals in the quiet of the consultation meeting.

What of those few media people (not in prison) who found militarism and mobilization abhorrent and longed for the critical freedom of the past? Were all the editors of the *Asahi Shinbun* and *Chūō Kōron* nothing but naive patriots themselves? Patriots they were, naive they were not. Even among virulent opponents of militarism, it is hard to identify even one mainstream media figure who repudiated Japan's war aims.[6] Their commitment to the nation at war ultimately transcended their contempt for the regime. So by propagation of the state's one-sided views and by conscious deceit, they helped to persuade millions of people to give their lives for imperialism. Many journalists observed the rape of Nanking, but what they saw was not reported or published. What were their options? Martyrdom would do little but assuage the individual conscience, and perhaps not even that, since to denounce the regime meant abandoning fellow countrymen on the battlefield. To continue laboring at the same job entailed more compulsory support for the state's designs than opportunities for meaningful opposition. To abandon public life would be to sacrifice all influence, however small, and would probably invite replacement by a true believer in the regime. It might also mean poverty, or conscription or other mandatory, war-related work. Most chose to keep their jobs in the mass media, even at the cost of serving a government they detested. The state had placed them in a dilemma with no satisfactory route of escape.[7]

If coercion (that is, punitive sanctions—expropriation, imprisonment, execution) was not the main cause of submission, it was still a very important factor. The police worked to intimidate those struggling to protect small businesses, and they possessed virtually unlimited powers, including preventive arrest. The coercive authority of the State To-

6. This judgment is based primarily on memoirs written by editors of the integrated magazines—such men as Kuroda Hidetoshi, Hatanaka Shigeo, and Mimasaka Tarō. See Hatanaka, *Shōwa Shuppan*, p. 126.

7. Mimasaka, Fujita, and Watanabe carried out a related analysis of how intellectuals reacted to the political situation, outlining three types: (1) those who rationalized active collaboration by adopting a progressive interpretation of events (the New Order was Japan's New Deal); (2) those who opposed but felt helpless as individuals—these remained involved to earn a living and did what they could to ameliorate the system within the existing limits, but basically they kept their protests to themselves and perhaps a small circle of trusted friends; (3) those who allowed themselves to be carried away by the trend of the times, cooperating actively to secure as comfortable a place for themselves as possible, though without a sincere belief in the rightness of what they were doing. See *Yokohama Jiken*, pp. 28–34.

tal Mobilization Law and the Film Law also cast a deep shadow over the New Order's establishment. Furthermore, although executions were rare and arrests relatively few given the extent of mobilization, there were some conspicuous resisters serving time in prison. Those arrested after the China Incident were not extremists but ex-professors and colleagues of mainstream intellectuals in the media; some had contributed regularly to various journals and were thus intimate friends of editors and reporters. The seizure of these men came as a shock to those who knew them.[8]

Moreover, while punishments may appear lenient by some standards, they must be interpreted in light of cultural and geographic factors. What may seem a mild sentence could have dire consequences in Japan due to the social ostracism that frequently struck not only the defendant but his family as well. Even today a son may lose his job and a daughter have difficulty marrying if their father commits a serious crime. Furthermore, unlike Europeans, Japanese dissidents did not have the option of relatively comfortable exile in a neighboring country. The surrounding countries offered distinctly lower standards of living and most are not culturally related to Japan in the way Italy, France, and Switzerland belong to one Western culture. In the interwar period, nearby countries were controlled by the Japanese state, the Western imperial powers, or the antagonistic Chinese Nationalist government. The road to the United States was barred by racial prejudice and laws specifically proscribing Japanese immigrants. Under these circumstances, seemingly mild punishments could be strong incentives for complying with state controls.

Thus the history of late imperial Japan, like that of Fascist Italy, demonstrates that a high level of mobilization need not require extensive coercion. This is but one illustration of the tenuous relationship between coercion and state control in general. Recent military regimes in Uganda and Argentina have been inhumanly brutal, killing thousands of opponents, but their positive control over society (the imposition of desired behavioral patterns, the restructuring of social sectors) has been slight relative to that in interwar Italy or Japan, where state murders were few. Severe coercion may even be dysfunctional to state control, by provoking resistance where more subtle measures might win compliance. Certainly the mass murders in Nazi Germany and the Soviet Union were not necessary for the success of mobilization in those countries—what Hitler

---

8. Ibid., pp. 13–14. Mimasaka also discussed his own reactions with the author in an interview.

wrought by violence against the leftist press he accomplished equally well against the centrist press with tactics similar to those employed in Japan.[9] The savagery was largely gratuitous, reflecting the moral depravity of officials more than the demands of control. Although coercion is an essential aspect of all state authority and would almost certainly increase to some extent with an ambitious mobilization program, there is no necessary relationship between the absolute level of official coercion and the degree of state control over society.[10]

THE STRUCTURE OF STATE CONTROL

The essential structural innovation within the state was the creation of supra-ministerial agencies such as the Cabinet Information Bureau. These evolved gradually from ad hoc or purely advisory committees in the early 1930s to become the principal generators of state policy by 1940, seizing the initiative from the established ministries. This transfer of authority to the cabinet's superagencies surmounted most of the usual barriers to innovative bureaucratic policymaking, accounting for much of the extraordinarily radical bent of Japan's military-bureaucratic regime. The narrow jurisdiction of administrative offices and the specialization of the tasks of individual officials normally block comprehensive policy planning, but the cabinet organs possessed broad responsibilities and recruited personnel from many different agencies, allowing them to transcend the parochialism of the regular bureaucracy. Unlike the older ministries, they were free of clientelistic ties with powerful civil associations and were therefore less constrained from adopting policies that upset the established social hierarchy. They overcame the conforming pressures of seniority by promoting younger bureaucrats into top positions of authority, showing greater adaptability than the ministries with their rigid pecking order.

The political function of the new agencies was especially critical. They assembled ideological statists from all arms of the administration, thereby turning otherwise isolated renovationist elements into an organized, coherent political bloc within the state.[11] They also placed mili-

9. Hale, *Captive Press*, pp. 194–95.
10. Relevant here is the discussion of terror in totalitarian systems in Linz, "Totalitarian and Authoritarian Regimes," pp. 217–28.
11. This is not to overlook the role of renovationists remaining in the regular bureaucracy, who were especially potent in ministries with the most to gain from mobilization, e.g., the Commerce and Industry Ministry with such well-known renovationists as Minobe

tary officers in regular staff positions, greatly diminishing the isolation of the military bureaucracy and permitting a partial replication of the military-bureaucratic policy organs operating in Manchuria. The military thus acquired a direct input into domestic policy formulation beyond its usual veto power at cabinet meetings. Finally, the cabinet's new bodies sharply increased the power of the Prime Minister. He now had his own sizable staff of experts to formulate new programs, freeing him from dependence on the more conservative ministries for information and policy development. Given Konoe's statist proclivities and his influence over events, these new capabilities were extremely important.

The founding of supra-ministerial agencies to facilitate policy planning on a grand scale is now a widespread form of administrative reorganization. Other military regimes have employed such agencies as well: the SINAMOS bureaucracy that served General Juan Velasco Alvarado's government in Peru and the Ministry of National Planning organized by General Ne Win in Burma both bear comparison to Japan's wartime superagencies. Examples of such bodies can also be found in most postwar industrial states—the United States National Security Council, the Dutch Central Plan Bureau, Canada's Treasury Board Secretariate.[12] Japan's experience demonstrates that superagencies of this type can nullify the most frequently cited structural impediments to administrative radicalism, but their full significance is rarely recognized. It is still common to read that the only major bureaucratic reform in postwar Japan was to eliminate the Home Ministry, as if the disappearance or reorganization of the Cabinet Information Bureau and other comparable superagencies were unworthy of mention. Yet these organizations were the chief instigators of the New Order in their fields. The increasing concentration of power in modern bureaucracies signifies that their internal reorganization can be every bit as consequential for the polity as a major change in the party system.

Yōji and Kishi Nobusuke. But their concentration in the cabinet bureaus offered a unique opportunity to exert influence.

The cabinet agencies also hired a few reformed leftists from civil society. When ex-leftists hired into the Cabinet Planning Board became targets of attack by the big companies trying to stave off state controls (the accusation being that the administration was infiltrated with communists), some were placed under arrest to blunt the criticism (the so-called Cabinet Planning Board Incident, or *Kikakuin Jiken*, of 1941). For the account of one of those arrested, see Katsumata Seiichi, "Kikakuin Jiken o Megutte."

12. On Canada's supra-ministerial policy organs, see Colin Campbell and George J. Szablowski, *The Superbureaucrats: Structure and Behavior in Central Agencies;* others are listed in Dogan, "Political Power," p. 18.

Needless to say, the cabinet's growing authority caused friction with the established ministries. Jurisdictional battles produced an awkward duplication of functions in several areas, the consultation system foremost among them, and there were a few serious rows over the substance of policy as well. In one case, the CIB's one-company newspaper scheme was obstructed by the navy and by several civilian cabinet ministers. Although renovationists controlled the policy agenda and largely realized their aims, they did not monopolize policy input, and conservative elites blunted some of their more radical proposals. In the media field, however, such stalwart opposition was rare. Crisis conditions largely quieted substantive disputes, and although a sharp increase in state power always exacerbates interagency competition over new organizational assets, overall there was less internal conflict than often accompanies radical mobilization by single-party regimes, certainly much less than in Nazi Germany.[13]

Mobilization engineered by a political party invites greater discord because the very existence and integrity of non-party state offices are threatened by the appearance of parallel party organs and the direct penetration of party cadres. By contrast, Japan's cabinet bodies were merely additions to the bureaucracy. They did not have the resources to replace existing agencies or to usurp most tasks of policy implementation, and their relations with the regular bureaucracy were smoothed by their recruitment of personnel from the established ministries. For example, although the Home Ministry lost the initiative in media policymaking to the Cabinet Information Bureau, it largely retained its grip on policy execution; its censors doubled as CIB officials to conduct the actual inspection of most films and publications. In short, there was greater continuity in the state administration and consequently less antagonism than when a radical political party takes power to effect mass mobilization. The greatest disharmony in media policy occurred during the last two years of war, when American bombing stymied planning and coordination.

The Japanese experience demonstrates that intrastate conflicts do not necessarily mitigate state control over society; in fact, such conflicts can exacerbate control. Civil autonomy may benefit from official discord

---

13. Dietrich Orlow has chronicled the interminable struggles over power and policy between official institutions in Nazi Germany in his *The History of the Nazi Party: 1933–1945*. The recent "interest group" analyses of Soviet politics also underline the abrasive interaction between official organizations. See, e.g., H. Gordon Skilling and Franklyn Griffiths, eds., *Interest Groups in Soviet Politics*.

over statist programs, but it will suffer from jurisdictional struggles that leave in their wake a multitude of offices with overlapping control functions. A single consultation on content would have been less oppressive than the many uncoordinated encounters with the CIB, Home Ministry, army, navy, and IRAA. A pluralism of competing civil associations should not be confused with a plurality of feuding state institutions—the first is a sign of autonomy, the latter often just a squabble over who will crack the whip.[14] Common sense would advise that the greater the internal unity of a state, the greater will be its capacity to extend its power and usurp civil autonomy. Yet the most powerful states in the twentieth century have been characterized by severe internal conflicts, and these conflicts are logical offshoots of the state's size and of the predictable clash of diverse organizational interests within officialdom. Unwieldly control systems may be less efficient in working toward a coherent set of official objectives, but from the vantage of civil associations, controls are no less onerous for lack of integration.

Turning to structural innovations in civil society, officials adopted a three-pronged strategy. First, in some areas all firms over a certain size were forcibly merged into monopolistic public-interest companies. While smaller businesses were simply closed, the absorbed firms became branches of the monopoly, their former owners receiving stock according to the capital and facilities they surrendered. Necessary operating personnel were retained, and the cabinet organs and ministries were granted direct managerial controls in the new companies' charters. This monopolistic pattern was typical of distributors but rare in the production field. Distribution systems for all movies and publications as well as paper were lodged in new monopolistic concerns. Only in the all-important news sector did the CIB try to force producers into the monopolistic format, succeeding in the area of news film but failing with newspapers, due to resistance from the larger dailies.

A second approach was to reduce sectors to an oligopoly of large firms by compelling small to medium-sized companies to dissolve or merge. The survivors were left under private ownership, though the state might alter existing ownership patterns, for example, by restricting the possession of newspaper stock to each firm's active employees. This oligopolistic pattern was typical of producers. Newspapers, magazines, film-makers, and book publishers were all pressed into this mold, which was standard in many areas of industrial production.

14. This point is elaborated in Joseph LaPalombara, "Monoliths or Plural Systems: Through Conceptual Lenses Darkly."

The third component of the system was a series of sectorwide control associations (*tōseikai*), which all relevant monopolies and oligopolistic firms were forced to join. There was one such association for newspapers, another for the publishers of magazines and books, and a third for the film industry. While these associations possessed sweeping legal powers over their members, they in turn were legally subject to the authority of the cabinet bodies and regular ministries above. The control associations were thus an intermediate layer between the pure bureaucracy of career officials and the private and public-interest companies in each sector. Their personnel comprised career state administrators as well as industry people co-opted to serve as part-time or temporary officials. The most critical control decisions, such as paper rationing, were always subject to the approval and intervention of the superior bureaucratic offices.

The control associations greatly facilitated state management of the business affairs of the mass media. The associations coordinated state control over access to raw materials and the distribution of media products, forcing each member firm to work through an official filter when arranging transactions with the others. This regulation of the market lifelines leading to and from the companies constituted the state's most immediate source of material power over the media. Bureaucrats made a conscious decision to focus attention on business operations, believing that control over content necessitated control over raw materials and product distribution. The success of their approach teaches that secure autonomy for the mass media is unattainable unless the purely economic sectors on which the media depend and the market connections between firms are free of state interference.[15]

---

15. Some scholars would label Japan's control associations "corporatist." Indeed, if *corporatism* is used to signify certain institutional arrangements regardless of their ideological content, then some of the control structures did approach a corporatist model, meeting most of Philippe Schmitter's criteria, as singular, compulsory, noncompetitive, and functionally differentiated bodies licensed by the state to encapsulate their fields of endeavor. See Schmitter, "Still the Century of Corporatism?" pp. 93–94. However, such a reading may omit too much when it ignores the values of policymakers. Japan's military and bureaucratic planners did not make an explicit commitment to corporatist principles; i.e., they did not adopt the view that society was naturally divided into certain occupational or religious or other sectors, whose institutional integrity had to be respected in the political structure. Where sectoral organizations were created, this was done for purely pragmatic reasons. On those few occasions when corporatist values were discussed specifically, usually in conjunction with proposals for occupational representation in the Diet, they were rejected, because such arrangements were thought to encourage partial interests as opposed to an indivisible public good. E.g., see Yokusan Undō Shi Kankōkai, ed., *Undō Shi*, p. 69. The dominant image of society as a family nation in which the Emperor reigned over his subjects as a unified body, "One Hundred Million with One Spirit," left little

The control structures were not only consistent with the renovation-ists' ideal of the state-society relationship but were based on a pragmatic assessment of their own mobilization capabilities. Without the man-power flexibility of a political party, the success of military-bureaucratic mobilization was indeed highly contingent upon the active involvement of private individuals and firms, and Okumura Kiwao's principle of "private ownership/state management" recognized that reality. Military and civilian administrators lacked the requisite expertise to replace the staffs of most leading media organs. Unlike a mass party, they could not recruit heavily from the civil professions.[16] Moreover, they realized that to substitute bureaucrats and military officers for media personnel would mean losing the likes of the *Asahi Shinbun* as an effective propa-ganda weapon, since the credibility and professional quality of media organs would disintegrate. Yet the shallow base of military-bureaucratic institutions in civil society did not pose an insuperable obstacle to mobilization. The control associations enabled administra-tors to make full use of the personnel, expertise, plant facilities, and even the finances of privately owned companies. Furthermore, this was accomplished without vitiating the competence and discipline of regular state offices with a flood of new recruits, since those deputized to share in the exercise of legal authority were generally confined to the new intermediate control structures.

In sum, though military-bureaucratic regimes often suffer organiza-tional limitations unknown to a strong ruling party, their handicaps need not preclude the formulation and execution of radical policy pro-grams. In Japan, structural innovations in the state and civil society empowered renovationist administrators to seize control of the policy-

---

room for any ideology legitimizing distinct rights and duties for particular social sectors. For this reason, to apply to late imperial Japan a model of corporatism shorn of any ideological component could create a serious misunderstanding.

16. Alfred Stepan has written:

it is crucially important whether the state elite is a military bureaucracy or a political party. A revolutionary party may monopolize all elite functions yet be able to recruit into its top echelons members from all important career roles. In the case of Peru, regardless of the loyalty, brilliance, or technical skill of civilians, they cannot be recruited into the strategic state elite as long as that elite is a military bureaucracy, because the military carry with them their own institutional recruitment patterns. In Peru for example, recruitment to the military career occurs before 20 years of age . . . . (*The State and Society*, p. 313)

In Japan, the civilian bureaucracy was also recruited almost exclusively from among recent school graduates.

making process and to bring the prestige and technical excellence of the country's most influential media organs into the service of state policy.

WAR, IDEOLOGY, AND ADMINISTRATIVE REVOLUTION

The immense impact of war on the development of state power is one of the most striking lessons of late imperial Japanese history. War-related considerations colored almost every media policy from the Manchurian Incident in 1931 to 1945. Imperial ambition in some quarters and the fear of war in others strongly swayed policy deliberations even in years of peace. The reality of prolonged conflict after July 1937 was essential in securing widespread tolerance (if not outright support) for radical statist measures among the general public and many Diet members, businessmen, and bureaucrats. Imperialism was so popular that it is often difficult to determine whether compliance was voluntary or coerced.

Interwar Japan offers just one example of the widespread connection between war and the evolution of modern state-society systems. An influential volume on modern state-building in Western Europe asserts:

> Possibly most striking and disturbing is the finding of the authors of this volume that wars and the threats of war played such a critical part in building the strong states of Europe. The ominous phenomenon of war gave telling reality and unquestionable legitimacy to the reasons of state. What was established and learned in the mobilizing of resources for national security persisted to provide funds for peacetime allocations . . . .[17]

A study of mass media controls in the Middle East produced similar findings:

> Arab governments since World War II have increased their influence and control over the mass media in part with the justification that their newly independent nations face overwhelming external and internal problems requiring unity and purposefulness and a minimum of dissent . . . . The most common focus of such reasoning has been the Arab-Israeli conflict.[18]

When there is no ready prospect of foreign hostilities, war may be declared against real or imagined internal exploiters or revolutionaries,

17. Lucian W. Pye, "Forward," p. x.
18. William A. Rugh, *The Arab Press*, pp. 89–90.

legitimizing controls in the same way.[19] Tanzanian President Julius Nyerere has sanctioned severe controls over the mass media, by asserting that all new nations fighting underdevelopment are in the position of countries at war.[20]

It is incorrect to regard war-related policies as aberrations that are unreflective of state-society interaction in general because they are not the products of "normal" times. War or the expectation of war is a constant in many states, and war thus becomes a continual preoccupation of policymakers. Cabinet Information Bureau official Tashiro Kanenobu warned in 1942 that the Great East Asian Co-Prosperity Sphere would require twenty years to complete. Okumura Kiwao titled a section of one of his books "War Above All Is Normal."[21] The notion that politics floats into limbo during wars and returns to some underlying normality afterwards is bankrupt in the twentieth century, when war often changes the life of every human being and social institution in a combatant country. The state's wartime measures to extract greater resources and restructure society, even when packaged as emergency steps, often have a permanent character from their very inception. The thousands of Japanese businessmen who saw their journals and film companies closed or absorbed by larger firms could hardly regard their plight as a temporary inconvenience due to war. Win or lose, their businesses were gone, and they were not scheduled for resurrection once the war was over.

There is no gainsaying the long-term impact of wartime policies in Japan. Labor mobilization under the New Order is partly responsible for today's enterprise-based union system.[22] The postwar National Associa-

---

19. According to Edward Feit:

Speaking of the Middle East, Miles Copeland points out that most Arab leaders rose to power by making promises that they knew they could not keep. Once in power their skill in retaining it depended on their skill at blaming others for their failure to deliver. Thus the economies of the Arab countries remain poor because "imperialists" wish to keep them poor and are holding them back. Censorship, police control, and extraordinary disciplines on the population are justified by the threat of "Israeli aggression" and "foreign agents." Difficulties of governments with their subjects are presented as the work of the CIA. Arab unity remains a myth not because of territorial nationalisms but because "Zionist and imperialist schemes" keep the Arab states divided. (Edward Feit, *The Armed Bureaucrats: Military-Administrative Regimes and Political Development*, p. 15)

The Copeland article cited here is "The Middle East in Revolution," *New York Times Book Review*, 31 January 1971.

20. Dennis L. Wilcox, *Mass Media in Black Africa*, p. 21.

21. Tashiro, *Shuppan Shintaisei*, p. 96; Okumura, *Henkaku-ki Nihon*, p. 144.

22. Nakamura Takafusa, *The Postwar Japanese Economy: Its Development and Structure*, p. 18. For a concrete example of the transition from wartime to postwar labor organizations, see Ōhara Shakai Mondai Kenkyūjo, ed., *Rōdō Undō*, pp. 60–61.

tion of Agricultural Cooperatives (*Nōkyō*), which virtually monopolizes interest representation for farmers, was likewise built on the foundations of its wartime predecessor.[23] The postwar structure of daily newspapers, comprising five national dailies (the *Asahi, Yomiuri, Mainichi, Sankei,* and *Nihon Keizai*), three principal regional block papers (the *Hokkaidō, Chūnichi,* and *Nishi Nippon*—an additional Kantō paper operated during the war), and one major local paper in most prefectures, also reflects the official designation of national and regional dailies and the "one-paper-per-prefecture" policy during the war. While the *Asahi, Yomiuri,* and *Mainichi* had achieved prominence before the 1930s, the *Nihon Keizai* and *Sankei* newspapers were artificial offspring of consolidation policy. The ownership patterns imposed under the New Order also endure, the *Asahi, Yomiuri,* and *Mainichi* remaining completely owned by their staffs. These are just a few of the aftereffects that persist despite seven years of rule by an occupying army out to delegitimize the previous regime, purge its leaders, undo its policies, and remake the social order in a contrary image. Along with the Meiji Restoration and the American Occupation, the New Order deserves to be recognized as one of the three great intervals of change in modern Japanese history, one that profoundly altered the structure of organizations in many spheres of society despite its war-related character and premature end in defeat.

War may require domestic changes otherwise unwanted by state elites, but this was not generally true in Japan. War was less an unexpected imposition from without than a policy actively pursued by military-bureaucratic administrators. Their war aim was not simply to win material advantages within the existing domestic and international systems, as was true of earlier Japanese imperialism, but to construct a new international order predicated on a sweeping transformation of domestic political, economic, and cultural life. It was this goal that prompted most domestic structural changes accompanying the war. Seen in this light, the motives of New Order policymakers seem to reflect the primacy of ideological concerns over wartime expediency, but it is truer to say that their ideological doctrines were inseparably linked to the concrete requirements of total war; this linkage was highlighted in the concept of the "national defense state," which fused ideological principles and an interpretation of history to the immediate demands of wartime mobilization. The important point is that renovationist ideology graced mobilization with a transcendent legitimacy and

---

23. T. J. Pempel, *Policy and Politics in Japan,* p. 30.

very much determined the content of mobilization policies. Indeed, given the widespread support for imperialism, most new media control policies were unnecessary to sustain the war effort; shorn of their ideological underpinnings, they become inexplicable.

It is not surprising to find strains of ideological statism entering Japan in this period, given concurrent events in Germany, Italy, the Soviet Union, and even the United States. What is extraordinary is that this ideological trend found such enthusiastic and coherent expression among established administrative elites. This is not to say that a majority of generals or bureau chiefs embraced radical ideas; indeed, radical views rarely, if ever, win majority support in any occupation. But renovationists were numerous enough to transform the behavior of leading state institutions. These were not disgruntled civil intellectuals or a *Lumpenproletariat* disadvantaged by the status quo but, rather, men who had climbed the traditional ladders to success. Most would have held important posts even if there had been no depression, no breakdown of democracy, no war, and no New Order. That they could embrace a novel ideology demanding systemic change contradicts a prevalent stereotype of administrators as apolitical and conservative by nature. Even scholars who view military-bureaucratic regimes as potential instruments of modernizing reform have generally censured them for a lack of ideological sophistication.[24] Japan's experience shows that entrenched administrative elites apparently socialized into the establishment may be just as sensitive to revolutionary ideas in challenging times as anyone else in the political system. Their behavior invalidates almost every hypothesis of occupational determinism ever put forth regarding the military or civilian bureaucracies.

The far-reaching transformation of the state-society relationship in Japan from 1937 through 1945 is best described as an *administrative revolution*. Without the seizure of power by an external elite (without even a coup d'état), new value orientations and reorganization within the state administration itself produced policies radically altering the structure of key social sectors and subjecting them to penetrating positive control. Several important historical factors facilitated this revolution.

1.   The bureaucracy's powerful independent role in policymaking and implementation was responsible for such vital extralegal mecha-

24. For example, see Edward Shils, "The Military in the Political Development of the New States," pp. 54, 58–59.

nisms of power as consultation meetings and the first "voluntary" control associations.

2.   The military's legal prerogatives permitted a level of political intervention that the armed forces of most countries could achieve only by means of a coup. In particular, the right of supreme command heightened civil-military conflict and induced (or at least legitimized) the Manchurian Incident in 1931, and the restoration of the military's right to active-duty service ministers in 1936 enabled it to veto the formation of new cabinets and to terminate governments in office at several critical junctures.

3.   The administration of Manchuria, controlled by the Japanese military, provided a perfect incubator for the army and its bureaucratic allies to experiment with statist policies free from the interference of other elites.

4.   Prior military and bureaucratic experience with popular mobilization in Japan itself prepared administrators to direct mass mobilization in the late imperial period. Such endeavors as the Military Reservist Associations and the bureaucracy's Local Improvement Movement of 1900–1918 compare favorably with political-party organization of the general public before the late 1930s.[25]

5.   The inability of the parties, Saionji, and Konoe to reestablish a sound civilian regime went hand in hand with administrative ascendancy. The parties' scandalous corruption, their lack of interest in organizing a broader mass base, their inadequate response to a grave depression, and their failure to cooperate to restore party government after 1932 were all critical. Later, Konoe's indecisiveness, his reluctance to found an autonomous mass party, and his partly unwitting fortification of military-bureaucratic policymaking smoothed the way for a full-fledged military regime.

Nonetheless, the inefficacy of civil political forces was not merely a fortuitous circumstance for the militarists: in large measure, it was they who brought it about. Military obstructionism was the only insuperable barrier to a return to democracy. Despite the army's strident criticism of party government and democratic values, military sway over policy after 1932 did not ameliorate the agrarian crisis (if anything, heavy defense spending impeded solutions), and the mainstream parties lost little of their electoral support. Yet even after the 2/26 Incident, when it

25. See Pyle, "Technology"; Richard J. Smethurst, *A Social Basis for Prewar Japanese Militarism: The Army and the Rural Community.*

appears a restoration of party government would have been quite popular, the military blocked the way. Konoe's options, too, were narrowly constricted by the military and bureaucracy. Both of his premierships were partly owed to military support, and if the military wanted a skillful puppet to do its bidding, the ministries were determined to protect their bailiwicks from any novel political force. What, then, were the realistic prospects of subordinating these elites to a new civil party? Weak civil political institutions are often blamed for inviting military intervention in politics, but their weakness may also be the effect of such intervention.

6.   The constitution's remarkable malleability was indispensable to the course of Japan's administrative revolution. By not fixing the pool for chief executives or their method of selection, the constitution permitted military-bureaucratic elites to take charge of the cabinet. By placing no absolute limits on state control over society, it provided a pliant legal framework for mass mobilization. By granting bureaucrats independent policymaking authority, it encouraged a burgeoning of administrative discretion that eventually undermined the Diet's assigned legislative functions (which were quite specific concerning the rights of subjects) and altogether subverted rule-by-law, one of the constitution's original principles.[26]

The Diet, of course, bears its share of responsibility for the constitutionality of the New Order. The Diet's passage of bills such as the State Total Mobilization Law and the Film Law emasculated its own constitutional prerogatives, eliminating the separation of powers between legislature and administration so as to free the latter from prescribed rules of governance. In effect, these laws abrogated the constitutional legislative process without abrogating the constitution itself. While the constitution's original limits on executive action were thus jettisoned, the persistence of the constitutional system allowed military-bureaucratic elites to borrow the legitimizing formula of the imperial reign. As in Thailand, the exploitation of a relatively powerless monarch relieved a military-dominated regime from having to invent and propagate a legitimizing rationale of its own.[27] In sum, the constitution was unusually favorable to military-bureaucratic elites, and whatever obstacles it placed in their path were removed by the Diet's acts of self-destruction.

26. See Dan Fenno Henderson, "Law and Political Modernization in Japan," p. 415.
27. Ferrel Heady, *Public Administration: A Comparative Perspective*, pp. 308–9, for a description of the Thai situation.

To list these ingredients is not yet to explain how they coincided to shape late imperial politics. Many catalysts were at work, but the Manchurian Incident stands out as the central trigger mechanism in this analysis. A party government's initial reluctance to press the Manchurian hostilities hardened military opposition and aggravated the crisis of party rule. The incident ignited the violent political radicalism of junior officers and the growth of civil rightist groups espousing anti-democratic, anti-liberal, and anti-internationalist ideas, thus spurring the breakdown of democracy (which in turn freed bureaucrats from party control). The success of the Manchurian venture convinced many army officers that they knew what was best for the country, and their experience governing Manchukuo made them confident they could also govern Japan.

The process of building a new Manchurian state inspired the dreams that eventually transformed Japanese imperialism from a calculated pursuit of material advantage into an ideological crusade. The incident also isolated Japan from the international community, especially from the democratic powers whose Asian interests it threatened, dislodging them as models for domestic Japanese politics. It led to a natural sense of oneness with Germany and Italy, the other major powers that abandoned the League of Nations, and to the sympathetic study of their policies and radically statist ideologies.

The Manchurian Incident further created the atmosphere of war that permeated Japan throughout the 1930s and was so pivotal in winning broad acceptance for mobilization policies. Historian Itō Takashi has characterized the entire 1931–1945 period as a "fifteen-year war" that began with aggression in Manchuria. Certainly there was nothing inevitable about the course of events traceable to the Manchurian affair. But it seems impossible that the constellation of elements that finally produced Japan's administrative revolution could have crystallized without this central variable linking so many of them together.

THE REGIME AND CONTROL
SYSTEM IN COMPARATIVE PERSPECTIVE

A comparative framework for late imperial politics will be explored along two dimensions: one, the regime type (who governed?); the other, the structure and degree of state control over society. The two dimensions are related but not identical, since different regimes may implement similar control policies, or similar regimes adopt different forms of control. Comparisons will be drawn first with single-party regimes, then with military regimes.

A COMPARISON TO SINGLE-PARTY REGIMES

As was already indicated, late imperial Japan was never governed by a single-party regime. The Imperial Rule Assistance Association cannot be described as a ruling party; it was not a source of recruits to the top state elite or a significant policymaking body. It is probably incorrect to refer to the IRAA as a party at all, since most scholars define a political party as an organization created for the purpose of taking charge of government.[28] The mobilization structures erected by military regimes are often judged as failures because most of them do not accomplish this purpose, or even because they do not perform as democratic parties (that is, by winning popular support, or serving as meaningful conduits for mass participation). Since the application of party criteria is usually misplaced, however, these judgments are often beside the point.

The administrative elites who conceive structures such as the IRAA have almost invariably rejected government by popular mandate and they despise professional politicians and political parties; their goal is a different type of institution. Most mass organizations created and administered from above by military-bureaucratic elites are not *intended* to supply the state with leaders or to subject the military and civilian bureaucracies to the popular will. Their purposes are to propagandize for the regime, to enforce obedience to its policies, and to preempt organized opposition by replacing spontaneous participation with highly structured involvement. In Edward Feit's terms, they offer people a substitute for autonomous politics.[29]

In these respects the IRAA resembled several contemporary East European counterparts, such as Poland's Camp of National Unity, as well as postwar Peru's SINAMOS organizations, Pakistan's Basic Democracies, Burma's Socialist Program Party, and Egypt's Arab Socialist Union. Given the number and impact of these administrative structures, they should be evaluated as significant political phenomena in their own

28. William R. Schonfeld, "Political Parties: The Functional Approach and the Structural Alternative," p. 478.
29. Feit, *The Armed Bureaucrats,* p. 19.

right, not misconstrued as abortive parties.[30] The Imperial Rule Assistance Association, as it finally emerged from a complex interplay of contrary expectations in early 1941, was not a ruling party either in conception or in fact, but a tool of administrative mass mobilization, performing a function similar to that of the media control associations.

The absence of a ruling party means that Japan did not have a totalitarian system like Nazi Germany or the Soviet Union. In colloquial speech, the term *totalitarianism* is sometimes loosely applied to any extraordinarily oppressive state. In virtually all scholarly definitions, however, totalitarianism refers exclusively to a subset of single-party regimes.[31] Therefore, the totalitarian model, as it is now depicted in a large body of research, does not provide the correct comparative framework for Japan's regime configuration during the 1937–1945 period.[32]

Moving beyond the comparison of regime types to the comparison of state controls over society, however, the question arises: to what extent were the structure and penetration of Japanese controls over the mass media analogous to those of totalitarian single-party regimes? The totalitarian pattern has been for the ruling party and other official organizations to undertake direct ownership and operation of all media organs. This has been accomplished in many communist totalitarian systems, and although the Nazi structure initially tolerated private ownership, it was clearly moving in the same direction. The Nazis inherited a state monopoly over radio, nationalized all film production, and progressed steadily toward the goal of a party monopoly over the press.[33] They seized the communist and socialist press in 1933, closed or absorbed most periodicals of sizable circulation or previously linked to other parties starting in 1935, and thereafter manipulated wartime shortages to the detriment of remaining private

30. This is not to say that military regimes never try to establish genuine political parties; they have done so in such countries as Argentina (the Partido Peronista) and Turkey (the Republican People's Party). However, for administrative mobilization structures, it may be preferable to abandon the party nomenclature altogether. Another approach that makes some of the important distinctions is that of Samuel Finer, who works with a broader understanding of what constitutes a party and subdivides parties into categories based on their organizational strength and autonomy from the military: see Finer, "The Morphology of Military Regimes," pp. 287–88.

31. For example, see the influential formulation of Carl J. Friedrich and Zbigniew K. Brzezinski in *Totalitarian Dictatorship and Autocracy*, p. 9.

32. A broad review of the literature on totalitarianism is offered in Linz, "Totalitarian and Authoritarian Regimes."

33. Hale, *Captive Press*, p. 95.

companies. In 1944, there were still 625 privately owned German newspapers, but only 25 had a circulation exceeding twenty-five thousand; the 350 party-run newspapers accounted for 80 percent of all circulation.[34] As Oron Hale wrote: "What marks the newspaper development in the Third Reich as unique was the displacement of the free press by the party press of the NSDAP and the establishment of a near monopoly in the publishing field."[35]

A comparison of Nazi Germany with Japan reveals much similarity in the treatment of radio and the wire services. Neither regime ever confronted truly autonomous broadcasting companies, and both effected literally total mobilization of radio. Their radio policies were functional equivalents, bureaucrats supervising all programming in Japan, Goebbels' Propaganda Ministry doing the same in Germany. The founding of official wire-service monopolies in the two countries reads like the same play enacted by two different troupes of actors. In Germany, there were initially two dominant wire services, the semi-official Wolff Telegraph Bureau and the Hugenberg Telegraph Union. In December 1933, these were merged into the monopolistic Deutsches Nachrichten Büro, owned and managed by the Ministry of Propaganda.[36] In Japan, the public-interest Rengō and privately owned Dentsū were forcibly merged some two years later into the United News Agency, which was controlled and partially funded by the Cabinet Information Committee. A precise comparison would require further research, but the evidence suggests considerable structural as well as functional resemblance.

There were basic differences, however, between the Japanese control structures for newspapers, magazines, and producers of dramatic and educational films, and those in Germany and the Soviet Union. In the totalitarian systems, the ruling parties aimed at directly absorbing these media sectors, while in Japan intermediate bureaucratic control associations regulated an authorized oligopoly of privately owned businesses. The limited personnel and expertise available to Japan's military-bureaucratic regime largely precluded a policy of total assimilation. Thus the differences in control structure seem to reflect the differences in regime.

34. Ibid., p. 307.
35. Ibid., p. 314. The Nazi experience has been unique among highly developed societies, but of course many countries at lower levels of political development have witnessed similar ruling-party dominance.
36. Ibid., pp. 137–38.

Were these structural variations merely a matter of form, or did they significantly affect the impact of state control? Relying upon Hale's research on the Nazi press, three tentative conclusions can be offered comparing German and Japanese newspaper control: (1) the degree of positive state control over content was similar, but somewhat higher in Germany; (2) the effectiveness of state control policies in molding public opinion was greater in Japan; and (3) the persistence of civil ownership over Japan's major media organs provided a firmer basis for the reintroduction of a liberal system after the regime collapsed.

In terms of the degree of control, Germany's mobilization of content peaked with the consolidations of 1935–1937, Japan's with the New Order consolidations of 1940–1941. Beyond these points, the daily press of both countries was in all important matters an active champion of state policy, though both cases had their rare exceptions. There was the *Frankfurter Zeitung*'s survival until 1943, when this newspaper, previously under Jewish ownership and opposed to Nazism (and now owned by the party!), was finally closed for infuriating Hitler with a reference to the alcoholism and drug addiction of Nazi poet Dietrick Eckart.[37] In Japan, a similar exception was the article carried by the *Mainichi Shinbun* in 1944 echoing the navy's criticism of Prime Minister Tōjō's war strategy, in punishment for which the physically unfit reporter was drafted. For every such case there were 999 articles enthusiastically endorsing the official line; the control systems must be characterized by their dominant patterns, not by rare occurrences. Even in the Soviet Union, a more finished totalitarian system than Nazi Germany, dissidents like Alexander Solzenitsyn have been active at various times within the official writers' guild.

The prevalence of the party press imposed somewhat greater uniformity on reporting in Germany, but it also rendered controls less effective in swaying public opinion. Party newspapers lacked credibility, for they were obviously mouthpieces of the state. This, combined with the low journalistic quality of newspapers run by party hacks rather than professionals, was enough to make many Germans stop reading. Between 1933 and 1935, before the era of wartime shortages, daily newspaper circulation declined by one million annually.[38] Party leaders recog-

37. Hitler had to order the closing three times before it was finally accomplished against the express opposition and bureaucratic foot-dragging of all his subordinates, including Goebbels, who had a low opinion of the utility of the party press for propaganda activities. See ibid., pp. 289–95.

38. Ibid., p. 230.

nized this problem and sought to correct it—some traveled the country lecturing on the need for more creative renditions of the party line—but to little avail.[39] The ideological imperative of direct party control undermined the effectiveness of propaganda in convincing the reader. Japan's propaganda machine did not labor under this ideological handicap. Since those actually writing the articles and moving the presses were the same old employees of the venerable *Asahi Shinbun,* journalistic quality was as good as ever, and outside the intellectual class, until very late in the war there is little evidence of widespread skepticism about what was being written.[40] Administrative mobilization outperformed the totalitarian model in accomplishing the state's objectives precisely because it allowed the printed media a greater degree of residual autonomy.

The persistence of private ownership in Japan was even more significant after the war. When the Nazi party fell, the German press largely disappeared with it. Had the party endured to complete its ingestion of the mass media, as has the Communist Party of the Soviet Union, no foundation would have remained upon which to rebuild an autonomous civil sector. In Japan, the control structure was built around companies neither owing their origins to the state nor directly operated by officials. Their proprietors were both able and anxious to reassert full autonomy after the war. This illustrates the frequently noted distinction between totalitarian and authoritarian regimes, namely, that the totalitarian regime is out to consume civil society altogether, whereas other non-democratic systems extend control without entirely voiding the boundary between the state and civil associations.

What is unexpected is that Japan's bureaucratic mobilization could drastically restructure media industries as sophisticated as those in Germany, control content almost as rigidly as the Nazi party, and finally produce a propaganda network more effective than that of Goebbels in shaping public opinion. Regimes outside the single-party category are generally thought incapable of such feats. Regarding degrees of state control, the boundary between totalitarian and authoritarian regimes appears less well defined than in regard to control structures, though even structurally, radio and wire service controls were virtually identical in the two countries.

39. Ibid., pp. 147, 227, 230–33, 241–42, 321–23.
40. I have not been able to locate circulation figures for the late imperial period, but the paper rationing in effect from 1938 would in any case make it impossible to judge public credence with reference to such data. Public skepticism was reportedly encountered in polls conducted by the United News Agency toward the end of the war: see Katō Masuo, *The Lost War: A Japanese Reporter's Inside Story,* pp. 141–42.

A COMPARISON TO MILITARY REGIMES

It is among the minority of military-bureaucratic regimes implementing highly mobilizational policies that the closest parallels to the Japanese state-society system of 1937–1945 are to be found. A comparison between the Japanese and two other mobilizational military regimes, Egypt under Nasser (1952–1970, especially from 1960) and Peru under Velasco Alvarado (1968–1975), will illustrate the point. Like the Japanese, these regimes formulated rather sophisticated ideologies transcending narrow military matters to encompass a wide-ranging evaluation of society. Egypt adopted its own brand of socialism with proclamation of the National Charter in 1961. In Peru, the experience of leftist guerrilla warfare in the mid-1960s led the army to formulate a broad social program to eliminate the root causes of civil rebellion; it was based on an organic statist conception of the state and society and capped by the Peronist slogan "Neither capitalist nor communist."[41] These ideologies were not mere window dressing but were intimately linked to radical new policies. In Egypt, the embrace of socialism coincided with an extensive nationalization of businesses and a moderate land reform, while in Peru there was a more extensive land reform and a significant expropriation of domestic and, especially, foreign-owned companies.

Both regimes established novel administrative mobilization structures to control the population and to impede the revival of civil associations they had neutralized. In Egypt, several inclusive mass organizations were created from above: the Liberation Rally, the National Union, and finally the Arab Socialist Union. The last resembled the IRAA in form, just as the Egyptian Public Agencies (or General Organizations) managing industry in many ways mirrored Japan's control associations.[42] In Peru, several distinct mobilization networks were launched to organize urban squatters, workers, peasants, and other elements, all falling under the new SINAMOS bureaucracy. Though the Peruvian military took the goal of meaningful popular participation more seriously than did the Japanese or

41. Internal revolt has been a more common motivation than external threats for mobilizational military regimes. Some scholars have even argued that the more the military is preoccupied with external security, the less likely it is to intervene in politics, but this position is easily disproven in the century of total war. Given contemporary military technology and tactics, neither internal nor external warfare is limited in the minds of strategists to armed warriors and a field of battle. The Japanese and to a significant degree the Egyptian experience as well demonstrate that foreign enemies may propel the military into a sweeping program of social change just as easily as the domestic kind.

42. Claude E. Welch, Jr., and Arthur K. Smith, *Military Role and Rule: Perspectives on Civil Military Relations*, pp. 196–212; John Waterbury, *The Egypt of Nasser and Sadat: The Political Economy of Two Regimes*, chapters 5, 6, 13, 14.

Egyptian regimes, military-bureaucratic elites invariably commanded the upper echelons of the new structures, and policy input from below was strictly limited.[43]

Although many military regimes censor the mass media only to eliminate overt opposition, and some have occasionally permitted rather blunt criticism (for example, Ecuador 1972–1979, Brazil after 1975), the Egyptian and Peruvian regimes followed the Japanese in undertaking radical policies to restructure and mobilize mass communications. Before Nasser came to power, the Egyptian monarchy had consigned radio to "a semi-autonomous board of governors whose supervision was relatively loose."[44] The military regime transferred control of the medium to its Ministry of National Guidance (later displaced by a Ministry of Information), which greatly expanded broadcasting facilities to exploit radio's mobilizational potential, just as was done in Japan in the 1930s. The state exercised firm positive control over programming. "Regular listeners understood quite clearly from news and commentaries and from features, drama, and music programs what direction his [Nasser's] policy was taking and who his friends and enemies were."[45] The regime then created a state news agency in 1956 to convey the official line through press releases and briefings. The immediate stimulus was the perception of an anti-Egyptian bias in Western wire-service reports concerning the Suez crisis—a close parallel to the Japanese view of foreign wire service reporting of the Manchurian Incident, which also inspired the founding of an official news agency.

The Egyptian press was one of the oldest and most venerable in the Middle East before the military takeover; several daily newspapers dated back to the nineteenth century, and the civil press offered a wide variety of opinions, representing both party and nonpartisan views.[46] The Nasser government first organized its own publishing house and used censorship to tame the opposition. Journals persisting in criticism, such as *al-Misri,* the world's largest Arab-language newspaper, were ordered to close.[47] Thoroughgoing mobilization came in 1960 when the regime seized the country's four large publishing companies and made them the property of the National Union; effective control lay with the

43. This is a central theme in Stepan, *The State and Society,* especially chapters 6, 8.
44. Rugh, *The Arab Press,* p. 116.
45. Ibid., p. 121.
46. Ibid., pp. 32, 57.
47. Ibid., p. 62. *Al-Misri,* associated with the Wafd party, Egypt's leading civil political group at the time, was closed in 1954. It was the last newspaper to hazard serious criticism of the regime.

Ministry of Information.[48] Many ex-military officers took up key positions in the mass media, to the extent that one source asserts that they comprised a majority of newspaper editors.[49] As in Japan, this assault on the press was closely linked to the mobilization of other social sectors. One apparent motive was to preempt opposition to the massive nationalization of the economy planned for the following year.[50] Egypt was the first Arab country to mobilize the press to this degree. Rugh now lists six others in the same category, and five of them (Libya, Syria, Iraq, the Sudan, and Algeria) are military regimes.

The Peruvian regime also executed a radical mobilization of the mass media. In 1970, the dailies *Expreso* and *Extra* were expropriated by decree in the "social interest,"[51] and in 1971 the collapse of a business group led to the government's takeover of two more journals.[52] Official appointees were placed in charge of management, while a number of former staff members were exiled, a fate soon to be shared by other journalistic critics of the state.[53] The closing of a few opposition journals and the banishment of antagonistic reporters do not constitute extraordinary repression from a Latin American military regime, even one of the temporary, caretaker variety, but the Peruvian regime clearly broke with the norm in 1972 when a new law required majority state ownership of all television stations and 25 percent state ownership of radio stations. A new bureaucratic authority (ENTEL-PERU) was created to oversee the electronic media.

In July 1974 a similar threshold was crossed when the regime expropriated the country's six major daily newspapers. Most had been tied to business interests already prejudiced by economic control policies.[54]

48. Ibid., pp. 37–38; Iliya Harik, *The Political Mobilization of Peasants: A Study of an Egyptian Community*, p. 131.

49. Welch and Smith, *Military Role and Rule*, p. 193; also Feit, *The Armed Bureaucrats*, p. 149.

50. Rugh, *The Arab Press*, pp. 66–67.

51. Augusto Chavez-Costa, *El Perú: Un Pueblo Olvidado y sin Voz*, pp. 184–85; "Diarios y Libertad de Expresión: El Caso Peruano," p. 21—this is a publication of the Centro de Documentación MIEC-JECI in Lima. The owner of the newspapers had helped to negotiate an unpopular petroleum agreement for the previous regime.

52. Chavez-Costa, *El Perú*, pp. 192–93. These were *La Crónica* and *La Tercera*. General Juan Velasco Alvarado, the head of state, personally chose new managerial personnel for these journals.

53. One was Luis Rey de Castro of *La Prensa*, arrested while celebrating the National Prize of Journalism he had just received from the Ministry of Education. Also exiled were two leading leftist intellectuals, Aníbal Quijano and Julio Cotler, who published the magazine *Sociedad y Política*: ibid., pp. 202–3.

54. Another example of the linkage between economic and media controls, which in this case was explicitly pointed out by defenders of the action; see ibid., p. 187, and "Diarios y Libertad de Expresión," pp. 35–36.

The journals were handed over to the administrative mobilization structures organized by the state (peasant, labor, service, educational, professional, and cultural organizations),[55] and the government appointed their first directors. Most practicing journalists lost their jobs as a result of the transformation. A new bureaucratic agency, the National System of Information, was created to supervise the flow of news throughout the country. The final media control structure thus had three tiers: (1) direct state participation in all radio and television stations and two overtly official newspapers; (2) state control over the other eight national newspapers through officially sponsored and regulated corporate groups—these journals were referred to as "social property"; and (3) private publication of local newspapers circulating fewer than twenty thousand copies, and magazines.[56] Many journals in the last category suffered lengthy suspensions.[57]

It is noteworthy that both the Egyptian and the Peruvian regime went further than the Japanese in placing the mass media under direct state management. This is to be explained by the less advanced state of their communications systems, which presented more vulnerable targets than Japan's sophisticated media industries, and also by the differing objectives of policymakers. These two cases may confirm what the Japanese experience begins to suggest: that totalitarian levels of control over various social sectors may not require the type of single-party regime specified in the standard totalitarian model. The need to explore the connection between regime structures and state control over society free of preconceptions is just as evident in the authoritarian context as it was in the earlier discussion of democracies.

In sum, the essential traits of the Japanese regime and control system can all be found in these two countries: the military and bureaucracy inaugurated a revolutionary ideology, new administrative mobilization structures, and radical control policies aimed at many social sectors, including the mass media. The three cases share the important attribute that the impetus for revolution came from within the state.

It may be asked whether this brand of revolution, executed by estab-

55. See "Diarios y Libertad de Expresión," p. 36.
56. Ibid., pp. 34–35.
57. The well-known weekly *Caretas* was suspended in 1974, and many leftist magazines later suffered a similar fate. The latter are listed in *Manual de Prensa Obrera y Popular*, pp. 43–45. When the regime veered to the right in the face of impending economic collapse following Velasco's ouster in 1975, many editors of the "socialized" newspapers were replaced by the state for being out of touch with the new direction in policy.

lished state elites, is practicable only in relatively less-developed societies, where civil associations are for some reason extraordinarily weak, or whether it is feasible in more advanced social systems. In some countries, such as many of those placed under colonial rule, civil political activity has been stifled for a prolonged period while state institutions have been developed to a superior level of organizational sophistication. In that situation, the less-developed condition of civil society might indeed facilitate the execution of radical mobilization policies imposed from above. However, the experience of Japan, Peru, and Egypt demonstrates that the potential for inbred state revolution is not limited to those circumstances alone. Civil associational life was highly developed in interwar Japan, where the military had to displace a fairly institutionalized system of party governments, and the debility of civil political groups such as the Wafd in Egypt and the APRA party in Peru was also as much the artificial result of military tampering as it was an historical legacy. The appearance and impact of mobilizational military regimes in these countries are not very well explained by a prior absence of influential civil associations. Japan's administrative revolution and the similar revolutions that germinated within the state in Peru and Egypt were not archaic offshoots of underdeveloped polities. Rather, they were extreme manifestations of the very modern trend toward an enormous concentration of power in the complex of permanent state institutions.

The two essential prerequisites for a revolution from within the state are present even in the world's most highly developed political systems. The first is the absolute mastery of the state security forces over any possible armed civil opposition. This mastery is a fact of life in all but perhaps the world's least developed polities. The second is the technological and administrative capacity of the bureaucracy to plan and implement mobilization policies. At present, the perception that bureaucratic power is increasing at the expense of political parties and other civil associations is as prominent in studies of Western Europe as it is in research on the less-developed countries. The preconditions for a revolution from within officialdom, then, are not confined to certain underdeveloped areas. In many countries, permanent state institutions now possess the means to exclude outsiders from power, to restructure and control formidable civil organizations, and to redirect the course of social development. The Japanese and analogous cases demonstrate that administrators may sooner or later claim independent control of these means, and occasionally even use them for radical purposes, theories of bureaucratic conservatism notwithstanding. It is where those who possess the tools of power do not make use of them that there exists an unnatural situation, one that will constantly be strained by the internal and external crises that regularly challenge every contemporary political system.

The concept of administrative revolution belies the usual portrayal of revolutions as dramatic upheavals of mass violence, but it is revolution by the masses that has become an anachronism. The immense power wielded by contemporary states has made it extraordinary for any regime to be overthrown by civil forces unless it is divided from within or another state aids the opposition. Juan Linz concludes from his study of the breakdown of democratic regimes: "The twentieth century has seen fewer revolutions started by the populace than the nineteenth, and their fate in modern states has generally been defeat. . . . Only the direct intervention of the military seems to be able to topple regimes in modern stabilized states."[58] And Eric Nordlinger in his research on militarism: "There has not been a single instance in which civilians alone demonstrated the strength to overthrow a military regime backed by a unified officer corps intent upon retaining power. They simply do not have sufficient numbers, organization, and weapons to defeat the military."[59]

An attachment to the conventional view of revolution has led some to exaggerate the impact that political violence, the civil right wing, and rural social conditions had on the course of Japanese politics in the 1930s. Eyes overexposed to the light of turbulent insurrections and class analysis are not easily sensitized to the darker regions where new committees are formed and decrees prepared. Important elements in the social and economic environment cannot be ignored, but the record shows that the Japanese state was no mere hostage to outside influences. Officials were never compelled to take resolute action to alleviate rural poverty, and they manipulated or suppressed rightist groups that might have challenged their authority. Rightist violence and the plight of the peasantry were not the foremost concerns of the military-bureaucratic

58. Linz, *Breakdown of Democratic Regimes*, p. 15.
59. Nordlinger, *Soldiers in Politics*, p. 139. Successful popular revolutions of recent vintage have occurred mainly where the state has been organized in antiquated fashion as a personal or family domain, an arrangement Max Weber labeled *sultanism*. This was the case in Iran under the Shah, Nicaragua under the Somoza family, and the Philippines under Ferdinand Marcos. These regimes lacked the institutionalized strength of modern states, and even in these instances, divisions within the military and foreign support may have been essential to the revolutionaries' success. The fate of popular revolt confronting the modern institutionalized state is perhaps better represented by the history of the Solidarity union in Poland, where the rebels have not been favored by outside interference or military disunity, and consequently a regime has sustained itself against the evident opposition of practically the entire population of the country.

policymakers who forged the New Order. The principal causes of Japan's statist revolution were imperial ambition and a new ideology nurtured within the state itself, independently shaping the way officials interpreted events and formulated their goals. Renovationist administrators charted their course as fairly autonomous actors, not as the pawns of external forces, and although they encountered many obstacles to the realization of their designs, they overcame those obstacles well enough to institute revolutionary changes in Japanese society. To rephrase an aphorism of the Belgian socialist Henri de Man: it is no longer by revolution that one can attain power, it is the holders of power who can realize the revolution.

Appendix: Overview of State Controls

State controls over the press, radio, and film are summarized below for the 1918–1932 and 1937–1945 periods. The controls are classified according to their impact on six basic managerial decisions that might be made by a media organ:

1. *Ownership.* The decision to found, buy, sell, or continue to operate a media enterprise.

2. *Price.* The decision to set a price on media products.

3. *Content.* The decision to fix the substantive contents of media products.

4. *Output level.* The decision to expand or contract the level of output.

5. *Personnel.* The decision to hire or fire employees.

6. *Materials.* The decision to acquire materials needed to operate the enterprise.

1918–1932	1937–1945

The Press

1. *Ownership.* A security deposit and reporting formalities were required to publish a journal covering current events. The judicial power to dissolve a publication for violating censorship standards or reporting requirements was used only once.

1. *Ownership.* The state forcibly closed over six hundred newspapers and thousands of magazines to eliminate opposition, improve positive control over content, and conserve resources during wartime. The State Total Mobilization Law authorized officials to order changes in the own-

ership of press organs, and they restricted newspaper ownership to the operating personnel of each paper. No journal could be founded or could modify its ownership arrangements without prior approval. The judicial power to dissolve publications remained dormant.

2. *Price.* None.

2. *Price.* Advertising rates, profits, and the price of issues were regulated by the state's control associations.

3. *Content.* Press organs had to submit inspection copies simultaneously with publication. The state employed censorship standards related to public order, manners and morals, and current events. Administrative officials could ban a violating issue from circulation or compel the journal to make deletions as a precondition for sale. Banned issues could be confiscated by the police, but confiscation rates were generally well below 50 percent. Therefore, though pre-publication warnings on coverage of current-events had mobilizational pretensions, they succeeded only in curbing extended discussion of certain issues, not in stonewalling information. Judicial fines and imprisonment were meted out in only a small number of cases related to public order. In practice, then, the system was mainly one of moderate post-publication penalties. Leftists, however, were subject to special legislation imposing up to ten years in prison for publishing radical literature; this legislation was severely enforced. Constitutional emergency powers allowing unlimited control over press content were evoked only once, after the Tokyo earthquake in 1923, by a nonparty Prime Minister.

3. *Content.* Officials instituted regular "consultation" meetings with press personnel to issue instructions on the desired content of every type of article, from current events to fiction. They occasionally offered propagandistic articles for inclusion, and numerous pre-publication warnings on current events restricted coverage to official press releases. A thorough prior censorship system was installed for major magazines, with officials cutting all or part of articles from tables of contents or galley proofs submitted before publication. (Books had to be licensed in advance, one by one.) Press organs still had to submit inspection copies at the time of publication, but since many magazines were censored beforehand, post-publication sanctions such as bans on circulation were imposed mainly upon daily newspapers. Many writers of the center left, like the radical leftists before them, were arrested under the Peace Preservation Law, but otherwise formal judicial sanctions for violations of content were used sparingly. The ultimate penalties awaiting nonleftist offenders were forcible closure of their journals and informal administrative measures (see "Personnel" below). Magazines were re-

stricted in their range of subject matter, e.g., to cultural, scientific, or war-related topics. From about mid-1941 to at least 1944, when defeats on the battlefield began to undermine military dominance over the state, the system successfully mobilized the press into an active promoter of state policy. Frontal criticism of basic policies or top leaders was extremely rare and did not go unpunished. Toward the end of the war, a small number of mainstream magazine editors were imprisoned and tortured.

4. *Output level.* None.

4. *Output level.* The number of copies issued by each periodical was regulated through state control over the paper supply.

5. *Personnel.* Soldiers, minors, convicts, probationers, and people residing outside Japanese territory were forbidden to become publishers or editors.

5. *Personnel.* Many political and social commentators in the mainstream press were blacklisted from publishing, at official consultations with editors. While leftists were subject to the Peace Preservation Law, centrist writers were often blacklisted without suffering any further sanctions. Editors themselves were sometimes forced to resign if a journal seriously overstepped mobilization guidelines. As before, soldiers, minors, convicts, probationers, and people residing outside Japanese territory were forbidden to become publishers or editors.

6. *Materials.* None.

6. *Materials.* The state rationed paper and other necessary materials. The denial of paper was a principal means of closing undesirable journals. Magazines most supportive of official policy had their rations increased, while those testing the limits of the permissible had their supplies depleted, sometimes so drastically that scheduled editions could not appear.

Radio

1. *Ownership*. Establishment of a broadcasting company required a state license; only nonprofit firms were allowed. Officials initially compelled investors to organize joint ownership and management of single companies in each of three cities; in 1926 a merger of these three into a state-protected national monopoly was forced. Licensing of subsequent stations was restricted to branches of this firm, investors in each locale again being forced by the state to combine. Dissolution of the broadcasting company required state approval.

1. *Ownership*. The state continued to permit the radio operations only of the officially organized public-interest monopoly, NHK.

2. *Price*. The state licensed the collection of fees from the owners and producers of radio receivers and regulated the cost of the fees.

2. *Price*. No change.

3. *Content*. The state banned commercial messages. All programs had to be inspected and approved by officials before broadcast. The state could ban programs in whole or in part and could order a broadcast stopped in progress if it violated legal proscriptions. Extensive censorship guidelines were imposed on broadcasting, including both political and manners-and-morals subject matter. Political argumentation was entirely forbidden except for addresses by state officials. The state possessed a legal right to order the transmission of its announcements. Official defense of government policy over radio began in 1929 and increased sharply after the Manchurian Incident of 1931, though never exceeding a small proportion of the broadcast schedule.

3. *Content*. The state exceeded previous restrictions by taking direct control of all program selection. Official policy was to mobilize radio so that every program, from news to music, drama, and radio gymnastics, contributed to the attainment of state goals.

4. *Output level*. The length of the broadcast day and the power of radio transmissions required prior state approval.

4. *Output level*. In addition to previous restrictions, officials closed the broadcasting company's second channel during the war.

5. *Personnel*. The hiring and dismissal of broadcasting-company executives and the hiring of all employees with substantive responsibilities in the technical and programming fields were subject to prior state approval. Officials could fire executives if it was judged to be in the public interest, employees for improper behavior, and either for legal violations. The state appointed the first group of executives at each station of the consolidated broadcasting company, putting many ex-bureaucrats in key posts. Officials had a veto over all outside speakers on radio, since their names were a mandatory part of program reports to the censor.

5. *Personnel*. No change; the state continued to place ex-officials in many managerial positions.

6. *Materials*. The state did not restrict access to raw materials, but it determined the acquisition of materials by dictating certain projects of new construction, for which the broadcasting company was financially liable.

6. *Materials*. No change.

Film
Producers

1. *Ownership*. None.

1. *Ownership*. The state forced mergers of Japan's ten dramatic-film companies into three, of the four news film companies into one under state direction, and of over thirty producers of cultural and educational films into four. Official control over access to raw materials drove many other companies that produced cultural and educational films out of business.

2. *Price*. None.

2. *Price*. Officials fixed the income of film producers at a certain percentage of theater earnings from the showing of their films.

3. *Content*. All films had to pass state censorship before public release. Officials could ban films, cut objectionable parts, or return them to their producers for reshooting as a precondition for approval. This forced producers to tailor their products to censorship standards, which covered contents related to public order and to manners and morals. The state imposed limits on the length of films.

3. *Content*. Production of a dramatic movie required prior state approval of the script. Officials were authorized to rewrite a script if they judged it unsuitable. Finished films still had to pass state censorship before public showing. As before, they could be banned, cut, or returned for reshooting, and limits were imposed on the length of films. The state further exempted certain films from censorship inspection fees, gave its recommendation or monetary subsidies to others, and collaborated increasingly with film-makers to encourage the production of works serving state ends.

4. *Output level*. None.

4. *Output level*. Officials fixed the number of films to be produced by the various companies.

5. *Personnel*. None.

5. *Personnel*. State licenses were required for actors and managerial and technical personnel working in film production. Licenses were granted based on success in competency tests that included questions on political orientation, and officials might revoke them at any time.

6. *Materials*. None.

6. *Materials*. The state controlled access to negative film and used this power to drive producers of undesirable films out of business.

Distributors

1. *Ownership*. None.

1. *Ownership*. Officials forced all film-distribution companies to merge into a single firm.

2. *Price*. None.

2. *Price*. Officials fixed the income of the distribution company at a certain percentage of theater earnings.

3. *Content.* Distributors could not handle a film unless it had passed state censorship.

3. *Content.* State officials selected all films put into distribution.

4. *Output level.* None.

4. *Output level.* Officials fixed the number of films distributed each week.

5. *Personnel.* None.

5. *Personnel.* Autonomy over hiring and firing was precluded by the forced dissolution or merger of all civil distribution companies.

6. *Materials.* Not relevant.

6. *Materials.* Not relevant.

Theaters

1. *Ownership.* None.

1. *Ownership.* A state license was required to operate a movie theater. Officials forcibly took over direct management of some theaters and merged mobile film-projection companies into one firm.

2. *Price.* None.

2. *Price.* The state fixed theater admission charges and limited theater income to a specific percentage of the gate; full receipt of earnings was subject to official approval of a theater's monthly financial report.

3. *Content.* Theaters could not show a film unless it had passed state censorship and was of a permissible length. The overall length of film entertainment programs was also limited by law.

3. *Content.* Officials selected every film shown in every theater by placing theaters in one of two distribution networks, for which the state arranged all film programs.

4. *Output level.* Limits were placed on the duration of film entertainment programs.

4. *Output level.* The state fixed the number of films shown, the number of days a given film program would run, the length of each program, and which hours of the day it could be screened.

5. *Personnel.* None.

5. *Personnel.* A state license was required to operate a theater projector.

6. *Materials.* Not relevant.

6. *Materials.* Not relevant.

Works Cited

JAPANESE LANGUAGE

Abe Hirozumi. "Nihon Fashizumu no Kenkyū Shikaku" [Viewpoint on the Study of Japanese Fascism]. *Rekishigaku Kenkyū* 451 (December 1977).

Akimoto Ritsuo. *Sensō to Minshū: Taiheiyō Sensōka no Toshi Seikatsu* [War and the People: City Life during the Pacific War]. Tokyo: Gakuyō Shobō, 1974.

Baba Tsunego. "Gunbu wa Kokumin o Shidō Shieru Ka" [Can the Military Lead the Nation?]. *Kaizō* (January 1937).

Chian Iji Hō [The Peace Preservation Law], edited and introduction by Okudaira Yasuhiro. Gendai Shi Shiryō 45. Tokyo: Misuzu Shobō, 1973.

Chūō Kōronsha 70-Nen Shi [A Seventy-Year History of the Central Review Company]. Tokyo: Chūō Kōronsha, 1955.

Dai Tōa Sensō Hōsō Shirube [Broadcasting Guidelines for the Great East Asian War], nos. 16, 18, 20. September–November 1942, January 1943.

Doitsu Eiga Hō [German Film Law]. Tokyo: Dai Nihon Eiga Kyōkai, 1937.

Fujii Tadatoshi. *Kokubō Fujinkai* [The National Defense Women's Association]. Tokyo: Iwanami Shoten, 1985.

Fujimori Seikichi. "Hatsubai Kinshi Mondai ni Tsuite" [Regarding the Problem of the Ban on Circulation]. *Kaizō* (September 1926).

Futagawa Yoshifumi. *Genron no Dan'atsu* [The Suppression of Speech]. Tokyo: Hōsei Daigaku Shuppankyoku, 1959.

Hashikawa Bunzō. "Kakushin Kanryō" [Renovationist Bureaucrats]. In *Kenryoku no Shisō* [Thoughts about Authority], edited by Kamishima Jirō. Gendai Nihon Shisō Taikei 10. Tokyo: Chikuma Shobō, 1965.

Hata Ikuhiko. *Senzenki Nihon Kanryōsei no Seido-Soshiki-Jinji* [The Personnel, Organization, and System of Prewar Japanese Bureaucracy]. Tokyo: Tōkyō Daigaku Shuppankai, 1981.

Hatanaka Shigeo. *Shōwa Shuppan Dan'atsu Shō Shi* [A Short History of the Suppression of Publications in the Shōwa Period]. Tokyo: Tosho Shinbunsha, 1965.

Ide Yoshinori. *Nihon Kanryōsei to Gyōsei Bunka* [Japan's Bureaucratic System and Administrative Culture]. Tokyo: Tōkyō Daigaku Shuppankai, 1982.

Inomata Tsunao. "Dokusen Shihonshugi to Manmō no Kiki" [Monopoly Capitalism and the Crisis in Manchuria-Mongolia]. *Chūō Kōron* (November 1931).

Ishida Takeshi. " 'Fashizumu-ki' Nihon ni Okeru 'Kokumin Undō' no Soshiki to Ideorogī" [The Organization and Ideology of "Popular Movements" in Japan in the "Fascist Period"]. In *Undō to Teikō Jō* [Movements and Opposition, vol. 1], edited by the Tōkyō Daigaku Shakai Kagaku Kenkyūjo "Fashizumu to Minshushugi" Kenkyūkai. Fashizumu-ki no Kokka to Shakai 6. Tokyo: Tōkyō Daigaku Shuppankai, 1979.

Ishizeki Keizō. "Kokubō Kokka Ron to Kokutai Meichō" [The National Defense State Theory and Clarification of the National Polity]. In *Nihon no Fashizumu I: Keiseiki no Kenkyū* [Japanese Fascism I: Research on the Formative Period], edited by the Waseda Daigaku Shakai Kagaku Kenkyūjo Pure Fashizumu Kenkyū Bukai. Tokyo: Waseda Daigaku Shuppanbu, 1979.

Itō Takashi. *Jū-go-Nen Sensō* [The Fifteen-Year War]. Tokyo: Shōgakkan, 1976.

———. " 'Kyokoku Itchi' Naikaku Ki no Seikai Saihensei Mondai 1" [The Problem of Reorganizing the Political Arena in the Period of the "All-Nation" Cabinet 1]. *Shakai Kagaku Kenkyū*, vol. 24, no. 1 (August 1972).

———. *Shōwa Shoki Seiji Shi Kenkyū: Rondon Kaigun Gunshuku Mondai o Meguru Sho Seiji Shudan no Taikō to Teikei* [Research on Early Shōwa Political History: The Opposition and Cooperation of Various Political Groups related to the London Naval Arms Limitation Problem]. Tokyo: Tōkyō Daigaku Shuppankai, 1969.

Iwasaki Akira. *Nihon Gendai Shi Taikei: Eiga Shi* [Outline of Modern Japanese History: Film History]. Tokyo: Tōyō Keizai Shinpōsha, 1961.

Katsumata Seiichi. "Kikakuin Jiken o Megutte" [Regarding the Cabinet Planning Board Incident]. In *Kataritsugu Shōwa Shi: Gekidō no Hanseiki 3* [Retelling Shōwa History: A Half-Century of Tumult, vol. 3]. Tokyo: Asahi Shinbunsha, 1976.

Kawamo Ryūzō. "Hōsō Jigyō no Kantoku Hōshin ni Tsuite" [Concerning Policy for the Management of the Broadcasting Business]. *Denmu Kenkyū Shiryō*, no. 7 (April 1936).

Kikakuin Kenkyūkai. *Kokubō Kokka no Kōryō* [Principles of the National Defense State]. Tokyo: Shin Kigensha, 1941.

Kobayashi Eisaburō, Matsuura Sōzō, Daigohō Susumu, and Seki Tada, eds. *Zasshi "Kaizō" no 40-Nen* [Forty Years of the Magazine "Kaizō"]. Tokyo: Kōwadō, 1977.

Konsaisu Jinmei Jiten: Nihon Hen [Concise Biographical Dictionary: Japan Edition]. Tokyo: Sanseidō Co., 1976.

Kuroda Hidetoshi. *Chishikijin Genron Dan'atsu no Kiroku* [Record of the Suppression of Intellectuals and Speech]. Tokyo: Hakuseki, 1976.

————. *Shōwa Genron Shi e no Shōgen* [Eyewitness Account of the History of Expression in the Shōwa Period]. Tokyo: Kōbundō, 1966.

"Manmō Mondai ni Kansuru Hansei" [Reconsideration of the Manchurian-Mongolian Problem]. *Chūō Kōron* (October 1931).

Masamune Hakuchō. "Hatsubai Kinshi ni Tsuite" [Regarding the Ban on Circulation]. *Kaizō* (September 1926).

Masu Media Tōsei [Mass Media Controls], 2 vols., edited and introduction by Uchikawa Yoshimi. Gendai Shi Shiryō 40–41. Tokyo: Misuzu Shobō, 1973.

Midoro Masaichi. *Meiji Taishō Shi I: Genron Hen* [Meiji and Taishō History I: Public Expression]. Tokyo: Asahi Shinbunsha, 1930.

Mimasaka Tarō, Fujita Shikamasa, and Watanabe Kiyoshi. *Yokohama Jiken* [The Yokohama Incident]. Tokyo: Nihon Editā Sukūru Shuppanbu, 1977.

Minobe Tatsukichi. "Rikugunshō Happyō no Kokubō Ron o Yomu" [Reading the Discussion of National Defense in the Army Ministry Report]. *Chūō Kōron* (November 1934).

————. "Shuppanbutsu no Hatsubai Kinshi" [The Ban on Circulation of Publications]. *Kaizō* (September 1926).

Miyamoto Yoshio. *Hōsō to Kokubō Kokka* [Broadcasting and the National Defense State]. Tokyo: Nihon Hōsō Shuppan Kyōkai, 1942.

————. "Senjika no Shinbun Saihensei (1–5)" [The Wartime Reorganization of Newspapers (1–5)]. *Shinbun Kenkyū*, nos. 289–93 (August–December 1975).

————. "Tsūshin Kikan no Kōyō" [The Use of Organs of Communication]. *Denmu Kenkyū Shiryō*, no. 3 (August 1935).

Miyashita Hiroshi. *Tokkō no Kaisō* [Recollections of the Special Higher Police]. Tokyo: Tabata Shoten, 1978.

Naimushō Keihōkyoku. *Eiga Ken'etsu Nenpō* [Movie Inspection Annual Report], 4 vols., 1940–1943.

————. *Katsudō Shashin Firumu Ken'etsu Nenpō* [Motion Picture Film Inspection Annual Report], 13 vols., 1927–1939.

————. *Shuppan Keisatsu Gaikan* [Publications Police Survey], 6 vols., 1930–1935. Reprint ed. Tokyo: Ryūkei Shosha, 1981.

————. *Shuppan Keisatsu Hō* [Publications Police Report], 149 vols., October 1928–March 1944.

Naisei Shi Kenkyūkai, ed. *Murata Gorō-Shi Danwa Sokkiroku* [Record of a Conversation with Murata Gorō], 4 vols. Tokyo: Naisei Shi Kenkyūkai, n.d.

————. *Yokomizo Mitsuteru-Shi Danwa Sokkiroku* [Record of a Conversation with Yokomizo Mitsuteru], 2 vols. Tokyo: Naisei Shi Kenkyūkai, n.d.

Nakayama Ryūji. *Sensō to Denki Tsūshin* [War and Electronic Communications]. Tokyo: Denki Tsūshin Kyōkai, 1942.

Nihon Hōsō Kyōkai (NHK), ed. *Hōsō 50-Nen Shi Shiryō Hen* [A 50-Year History of Broadcasting, Documentary Volume]. Tokyo: Nihon Hōsō Shuppan Kyōkai, 1977.

————. *Nihon Hōsō Shi* [History of Japanese Broadcasting], 2 vols. Tokyo: Nihon Hōsō Shuppan Kyōkai, 1965.

————. *Rajio Nenkan* [Radio Yearbook], vols. 1931–1942. Tokyo: Seibundō, 1931–1942.

Nihon Hōsō Kyōkai (NHK) Sōgō Hōsō Bunka Kenkyūjo, ed. *Reiki—Hōsō Hen (1) Taishō 14-Nen–Shōwa 20-Nen* [Established Rules—Broadcasting Compilation (1) 1925–1945]. Hōsō Shiryō Shū 6. Tokyo: Nihon Hōsō Kyōkai, 1972.

Nihon Kindaishi Jiten [Dictionary of Modern Japanese History], edited by Tonodani Katsu. Tokyo: Tōyō Keizai Shinpōsha, 1958.

Nihon Musen Shi [The History of Japanese Wireless], 13 vols. Tokyo: Denpa Kanri Iinkai, 1951.

Nihon Shinbun Nenkan [The Japan Newspaper Yearbook], vols. 1940–1941. Tokyo: Shinbun Kenkyūjo, 1940–1941.

[Nihon Teikoku Shihōshō]. *Iwayuru "Tennō Kikan Setsu" o Keiki to Suru Kokutai Meichō Undō* [The Movement to Clarify the National Polity Triggered by the So-Called Emperor-as-Organ Theory]. Shisō Kenkyū Shiryō Tokushū Dai 72-Go. Reprint ed. Tokyo: Tōyō Bunkasha, 1975.

Nihon Teikoku Shihōshō. *Keiji Tōkei Nenpō* [Criminal Statistics Annual Report], nos. 1–66, 1875–1940.

Ōhara Shakai Mondai Kenkyūjo (Hōsei Daigaku), ed. *Taiheiyō Sensōka no Rōdō Undō* [The Labor Movement during the Pacific War]. Tokyo: Rōdō Junpōsha, 1965.

Okada Susumu. *Nihon Eiga no Rekishi* [The History of Japanese Films]. Kyoto: San'ichi Shobō, 1957.

Oka Yoshitake. *Konoe Fumimaro*. Tokyo: Iwanami Shinsho, 1972.

Okudaira Yasuhiro. "Ken'etsu Seido" [Censorship System]. In *Kōza Nihon Kindai Hō Hattatsu Shi 11* [Lectures on the Historical Development of Modern Japanese Law 11], edited by Ukai Kazunari, Fukushima Masao, Kawashima Takenobu, and Tsuji Kiyoaki. Tokyo: Gaisō Shobō, 1967.

———. "Nihon Shuppan Keisatsu Hōsei no Rekishiteki Kenkyū Josetsu" [Introductory Historical Research on Japan's Publications Police Laws], nos. 1–7. *Hōritsu Jihō* 39–45 (April–October 1967).

Okumura Kiwao. "Denryoku Kokkan Mondai" [The Problem of State Management of Electric Power]. In *Shōwa Seiji Keizai Shi e no Shōgen Chū* [Testimony on Political and Economic Shōwa History, vol. 2], edited by Andō Yoshio. Tokyo: Mainichi Shinbunsha, 1966.

———. *Henkaku-ki Nihon no Seiji Keizai* [Japan's Politics and Economics in a Period of Transformation]. Tokyo: Sasaki Shobō, 1940.

———. *Nihon Seiji no Kakushin* [The Renovation of Japanese Politics]. Tokyo: Ikuseisha, 1938.

Ōmori Yoshitarō. "Kekkyoku wa Keizaiteki Shihai Kankei" [In the End, the Connection with Economic Domination]. *Kaizō* (September 1926).

Ōsaka Hōsōkyoku Enkaku Shi [Historical Development of the Osaka Broadcasting Company]. Osaka: Nihon Hōsō Kyōkai Kansai Shibu, 1934.

Rikugunshō. *Kokubō no Hongi to Sono Kyōka no Teishō* [The True Meaning of National Defense and a Proposal for Its Strengthening]. In *Kokka Sōdōin Shi Shiryō Hen Dai 5* [The History of State Total Mobilization, Documentary Volume No. 5], edited by Ishikawa Junkichi. Tokyo: Kokka Sōdōin Shi Kankōkai, 1977.

"Ritton Hōkoku Sho" [The Litton Commission Report]. *Chūō Kōron* (November 1932).

"Seinen Kanshi Shain wa Nani o Kangaete Iru Ka: Zadankai" [What Are the Young Bureaucrats Thinking? A Symposium]. *Bungei Shunjū* (July 1936).

Sendai Teishinkyoku. *Hōsō Kantoku Jimu Teiyō* [Summary of the Business of Broadcast Supervision]. N.d.

"Senzen no Jōhō Kikō Yōran" [Outline of the Prewar Information Structure]. Unpublished manuscript, 1964.

Shisō Tōsei [Thought Control], edited by Kakegawa Tomiko. Gendai Shi Shiryō 42. Tokyo: Misuzu Shobō, 1976.

"Shumoku Tōkei Hyō" [Statistical Chart of Events]. Unpublished manuscripts, 1931–1932, 1932–1933.

Shunbara Akihiko, *Nihon Shinbun Tsūshi* [A History of Japanese Newspapers]. Tokyo: Gendai Jānarizumu Shuppankai, 1969.

Taikakai, ed. *Naimushō Shi* [History of the Home Ministry], 4 vols. Tokyo: Chihō Zaimu Kyōkai, 1970.

Tajima Tarō. *Ken'etsu Shitsu no Yami ni Tsubuyaku* [Murmuring in the Darkness of the Inspection Room]. Tokyo: Dai Nihon Katsudō Eisha Kyōkai, 1938.

Takasaki Ryūji. *Sensōka no Zasshi* [Wartime Magazines]. Nagoya: Fūbaisha, 1976.

Tanaka Jun'ichirō. *Nihon Eiga Hattatsu Shi* [History of Japanese Film Development], 4 vols. Tokyo: Chūō Kōronsha, 1957.

Tashiro Kanenobu. *Shuppan Shintaisei no Hanashi* [Speaking of the New Order for Publications]. Tokyo: Nihon Denpō Tsūshinsha, 1942.

"Tōyō Monroshugi no Kakuritsu" [Establishment of an Eastern Monroe Doctrine]. *Chūō Kōron* (December 1932).

Tsumura Hideo. *Eiga Seisaku Ron* [Discourse on Film Policy]. Tokyo: Chūō Kōronsha, 1943.

Uchikawa Yoshimi. "Shinbunshi Hō no Settei Katei to Sono Tokushitsu" [The Characteristics of the Legislative Process behind the Newspaper Law]. *Tōkyō Daigaku Shinbun Kenkyūjo Kiyō*, no. 5 (1956).

———. "Shiryō Kaisetsu" [Commentary on the Documents]. In *Masu Media Tōsei* [Mass Media Controls], 2 vols., edited by Uchikawa Yoshimi. Gendai Shi Shiryō 40–41. Tokyo: Misuzu Shobō, 1973.

Watanabe Osamu. "Fashizumu-ki no Shūkyō Tōsei" [Control over Religion in the Fascist Period]. In *Senji Nihon no Hōtaisei* [The Legal System of Wartime Japan], edited by Tōkyō Daigaku Shakai Kagaku Kenkyūjo, "Fashizumu to Minshushugi" Kenkyūkai. Fashizumu-ki no Kokka to Shakai 6. Tokyo: Tōkyō Daigaku Shuppankai, 1979.

Yabe Teiji. *Konoe Fumimaro*, 2 vols. Tokyo: Konoe Fumimaro Denki Hensan Kankōkai, 1951.

Yanaihara Tadao. "Manmō Shinkokka Ron" [Discourse on a New State in Manchuria-Mongolia]. *Kaizō* (April 1932).

———. "Manshū Keizai Ron" [Discourse on the Manchurian Economy]. *Chūō Kōron* (July 1932).

Yanai Yoshio. *Katsudō Shashin no Hogo to Torishimari* [The Protection and Control of Motion Pictures]. Tokyo: Yūhikaku, 1929.

Yokusan Undō Shi Kankōkai, ed. *Yokusan Kokumin Undō Shi* [History of the National Assistance Movement]. Tokyo: Kaimeidō, 1954.

Yoshino Sakuzō. "Minzoku to Kaikyū to Sensō" [Nations, Classes, and War]. *Chūō Kōron* (January 1932).

ENGLISH AND SPANISH LANGUAGE

Aberbach, Joel D., Robert D. Putnam, and Bert A. Rockman. *Bureaucrats and Politicians in Western Democracies*. Cambridge, Mass.: Harvard University Press, 1981.

Akita, George. *Foundations of Constitutional Government in Modern Japan, 1868–1900*. Cambridge, Mass.: Harvard University Press, 1967.

Allen, William Sheridan. *The Nazi Seizure of Power: The Experience of a Single German Town, 1930–1935*. New York: New Viewpoints, 1973.

Bayley, David H. "The Police and Political Development in Europe." In *The Formation of National States in Western Europe*, edited by Charles Tilly. Princeton: Princeton University Press, 1975.

Beckmann, George M., and Ōkubo Genji. *The Japanese Communist Party 1922–1945*. Stanford: Stanford University Press, 1969.

Bendix, Reinhard. *Nation-Building and Citizenship*. New York: John Wiley & Sons, 1964.

Benedict, Ruth Fulton. "Japanese Films: A Phase of Psychological Warfare." Washington, D.C.: Unpublished manuscript, 30 March 1944.

Berger, Gordon Mark. *Parties out of Power in Japan: 1931–1941*. Princeton: Princeton University Press, 1977.

Berlin, Isaiah. *Four Essays on Liberty*. New York: Oxford University Press, 1970.

Bisson, T. A. *Japan's War Economy*. New York: Institute of Pacific Relations, 1945.

Campbell, Colin, and George J. Szablowski. *The Superbureaucrats: Structure and Behavior in Central Agencies*. Toronto: Macmillan of Canada, 1979.

Chavez-Costa, Augusto. *El Perú: Un Pueblo Olvidado y sin Voz*. Lima: Programa Editorial, 1978.

Christoph, James B. "High Civil Servants and the Politics of Consensualism in Great Britain." In *The Mandarins of Western Europe*, edited by Mattei Dogan. New York: Sage, 1975.

Crowley, James B. "Japanese Army Factionalism in the Early 1930's." *Journal of Asian Studies*, vol. 21, no. 3 (May 1962).

———. *Japan's Quest for Autonomy*. Princeton: Princeton University Press, 1966.

Curran, James, and Jane Seaton. *Power without Responsibility: The Press and Broadcasting in Britain*. Glasgow: Fontana, 1981.

Dahl, Robert A. *Polyarchy*. New Haven: Yale University Press, 1971.

"Diarios y Libertad de Expresión: El Caso Peruano." *América Latina Boletín,* nos. 6–7 (January–February 1975).

Dogan, Mattei. "The Political Power of the Western Mandarins: Introduction." In *The Mandarins of Western Europe,* edited by Mattei Dogan. New York: Sage, 1975.

Dore, Ronald. *Land Reform in Japan.* London: Oxford University Press, 1959.

Dowdy, Edwin. *Japanese Bureaucracy: Its Development and Modernization.* Melbourne: Cheshire, 1972.

Duus, Peter. *Party Rivalry and Political Change in Taishō Japan.* Cambridge, Mass.: Harvard University Press, 1968.

Ehrmann, Henry W. *Politics in France.* Boston: Little, Brown, 1983.

Feit, Edward. *The Armed Bureaucrats: Military-Administrative Regimes and Political Development.* Boston: Houghton Mifflin, 1973.

Finer, Samuel. "The Morphology of Military Regimes." In *Soldiers, Peasants, and Bureaucrats: Civil-Military Relations in Communist and Modernizing Societies,* edited by Roman Kolkowicz and Andrzej Korbonski. London: George Allen & Unwin, 1982.

Fletcher, William Miles. *The Search for a New Order: Intellectuals and Fascism in Prewar Japan.* Chapel Hill: University of North Carolina Press, 1982.

Friedrich, Carl J., and Zbigniew K. Brzezinski. *Totalitarian Dictatorship and Autocracy.* New York: Frederick A. Praeger, 1956.

Gordon, Andrew David. *The Evolution of Labor Relations in Japan: Heavy Industry, 1853–1955.* Harvard East Asian Monographs 117. Cambridge, Mass.: Harvard University Press, 1985.

Grosser, Alfred. "The Evolution of European Parliaments." In *European Politics: A Reader,* edited by Mattei Dogan and Richard Rose. Boston: Little, Brown, 1971.

Hadley, Eleanor M. *Antitrust in Japan.* Princeton: Princeton University Press, 1970.

Hale, Oron J. *The Captive Press in the Third Reich.* Princeton: Princeton University Press, 1973.

Hanazono Kanesada. *The Development of Japanese Journalism.* Osaka: Ōsaka Mainichi, 1924.

Harik, Iliya. *The Political Mobilization of Peasants: A Study of an Egyptian Community.* Studies in Development 8. Bloomington: Indiana University Press, 1974.

Hauser, William B. "The Japanese War Film: National Service versus Individual Survival." Unpublished lecture, University of Rochester, February 1981.

Havens, Thomas R. H. *Farm and Nation in Modern Japan: Agrarian Nationalism, 1870–1940.* Princeton: Princeton University Press, 1974.

———. *Valley of Darkness: The Japanese People and World War Two.* New York: W. W. Norton, 1978.

Hayek, Friedrich. *Law, Legislation, and Liberty,* 3 vols. Chicago: University of Chicago Press, 1979.

Heady, Ferrel. *Public Administration: A Comparative Perspective,* 2d edition, revised and expanded. New York: Marcel Dekker, 1979.

Henderson, Dan Fenno. "Law and Political Modernization in Japan." In *Political Development in Modern Japan*, edited by Robert E. Ward. Princeton: Princeton University Press, 1968.

High, Peter B. "The Dawn of Cinema in Japan." *Journal of Contemporary History*, vol. 19, no. 1 (January 1984).

Huffman, James L. *Politics of the Meiji Press: The Life of Fukuchi Gen'ichiro.* Honolulu: University Press of Hawaii, 1980.

International Press Institute Surveys Nos. I–VI. New York: Arno, 1972.

Ishida Takeshi. "The Development of Interest Groups and the Pattern of Political Modernization in Japan." In *Political Development in Modern Japan*, edited by Robert E. Ward. Princeton: Princeton University Press, 1968.

Itō Hirobumi. *Commentaries on the Constitution of the Empire of Japan.* Tokyo: Chūō Daigaku, 1906.

Jackman, Robert W. "Politicians in Uniform." *American Political Science Review*, vol. 70, no. 4 (December 1976).

Johnson, Chalmers. *MITI and the Japanese Miracle: The Growth of Industrial Policy, 1925–1975.* Stanford: Stanford University Press, 1982.

Kakegawa Tomiko. "The Press and Public Opinion in Japan, 1931–1941." In *Pearl Harbor as History*, edited by Dorothy Borg and Okamoto Shunpei. New York: Columbia University Press, 1973.

Kasza, Gregory J. "Fascism from Below? A Comparative Perspective on the Japanese Right, 1931–1936." *Journal of Contemporary History*, vol. 19, no. 4 (October 1984).

Kato Masuo. *The Lost War: A Japanese Reporter's Inside Story.* New York: Alfred A. Knopf, 1946.

King, Anthony. "Political Parties in Western Democracies: Some Skeptical Reflections." *Polity*, vol. 2, no. 2 (Winter 1969).

LaPalombara, Joseph. "Monoliths or Plural Systems: Through Conceptual Lenses Darkly." *Studies in Comparative Communism*, vol. 8, no. 3 (Autumn 1975).

———. *Politics within Nations.* Englewood Cliffs, N.J.: Prentice-Hall, 1974.

Linz, Juan J. *The Breakdown of Democratic Regimes: Crisis, Breakdown, and Reequilibration.* Baltimore: Johns Hopkins University Press, 1978.

———. "Totalitarian and Authoritarian Regimes." In *Handbook of Political Science 3*, edited by Nelson Polsby and Fred Greenstein. Reading, Mass.: Addison-Wesley, 1975.

Loewenstein, Karl. "Legislative Control of Political Extremism in European Democracies II." *Columbia Law Review*, vol. 38, no. 5 (May 1938).

McKinlay, R. D., and A. S. Cohan. "A Comparative Analysis of the Political and Economic Performance of Military and Civilian Regimes: A Cross-National Aggregate Study." *Comparative Politics*, vol. 8, no. 1 (October 1975).

McLaren, W. W., ed. "Japanese Government Documents." *Transactions of the Asiatic Society of Japan*, vol. 42, part 1 (1914).

Manual de Prensa Obrera y Popular. Lima: Fenix Impresores, 1981.

Maruyama Masao. *Thought and Behavior in Modern Japanese Politics*, expanded ed., edited by Ivan Morris. London: Oxford University Press, 1969.

Merton, Robert. "Bureaucratic Structure and Personality." In *Reader in Bureaucracy,* edited by Robert Merton, Ailsa P. Gray, Barbara Hockey, and Hanan C. Selvin. New York: Free Press, 1952.

Miller, Frank O. *Minobe Tatsukichi: Interpreter of Constitutionalism in Japan.* Berkeley and Los Angeles: University of California Press, 1965.

Mitchell, Richard H. *Censorship in Imperial Japan.* Princeton: Princeton University Press, 1983.

——. *Thought Control in Prewar Japan.* Ithaca, N.Y.: Cornell University Press, 1976.

Najita, Tetsuo. *Hara Kei in the Politics of Compromise, 1905–1915.* Cambridge, Mass.: Harvard University Press, 1967.

——. "Nakano Seigo and the Spirit of the Meiji Restoration in Twentieth-Century Japan." In *Dilemmas of Growth in Prewar Japan,* edited by James W. Morley. Princeton: Princeton University Press, 1971.

Nakamura Takafusa. *The Postwar Japanese Economy: Its Development and Structure,* translated by Jacqueline Kaminski. Tokyo: University of Tokyo Press, 1981.

Nordlinger, Eric A. *Soldiers in Politics: Military Coups and Governments.* Englewood Cliffs, N.J.: Prentice-Hall, 1977.

Notar, Ernest J. "Japan's Wartime Labor Policy: A Search for Method." *Journal of Asian Studies,* vol. 44, no. 2 (February 1985).

Orlow, Dietrich. *The History of the Nazi Party: 1933–1945.* Pittsburgh: University of Pittsburgh Press, 1973.

Ortega y Gasset, José. *Invertebrate Spain,* translated by Mildred Adams. New York: W. W. Norton, 1937.

Peattie, Mark R. *Ishiwara Kanji and Japan's Confrontation with the West.* Princeton: Princeton University Press, 1975.

Pempel, T. J. *Policy and Politics in Japan.* Philadelphia: Temple University Press, 1982.

Peters, B. Guy. *The Politics of Bureaucracy: A Comparative Perspective.* New York: Longman, 1978.

Political Handbook of the World: 1986, edited by Arthur S. Banks. Binghamton, N.Y.: CSA Publications, 1986.

Putnam, Robert D. "The Political Attitudes of Senior Civil Servants in Britain, Germany, and Italy." In *The Mandarins of Western Europe,* edited by Mattei Dogan. New York: Sage, 1975.

Pye, Lucian W. "Forward." In *The Formation of National States in Western Europe,* edited by Charles Tilly. Princeton: Princeton University Press, 1975.

Pyle, Kenneth B. "The Technology of Japanese Nationalism: The Local Improvement Movement 1900–1918." *Journal of Asian Studies,* vol. 33, no. 1 (November 1973).

Rosenberg, Hans. *Bureaucracy, Aristocracy, and Autocracy: The Prussian Experience, 1660–1815.* Boston: Beacon, 1958.

Rousseau, Jean-Jacques. *Letter to D'Alembert,* translated by Allen Bloom. Ithaca, N.Y.: Cornell University Press, 1968.

——. *The Social Contract,* translated by Judith R. Masters. New York: St. Martin's Press, 1978.

Rubin, Jay. *Injurious to Public Morals: Writers and the Meiji State.* Seattle: University of Washington Press, 1984.

Rugh, William A. *The Arab Press.* Syracuse: Syracuse University Press, 1979.

Sandford, John. *The Mass Media of the German-Speaking Countries.* London: Oswald Wolff, 1976.

Sartori, Giovanni. *Parties and Party Systems.* Cambridge: Cambridge University Press, 1976.

Schmitter, Philippe. "Still the Century of Corporatism?" In *The New Corporatism: Social-Political Structures in the Iberian World,* edited by Frederick B. Pike and Thomas Stritch. Notre Dame, Ind.: University of Notre Dame Press, 1974.

Schonfeld, William R. "Political Parties: The Functional Approach and the Structural Alternative." *Comparative Politics,* vol. 15, no. 4 (July 1983).

Schumpeter, Joseph A. *Capitalism, Socialism, and Democracy,* 3d ed. New York: Harper Torchbooks, 1950.

Shillony, Ben-Ami. *Politics and Culture in Wartime Japan.* Oxford: Clarendon Press, 1981.

———. *Revolt in Japan: The Young Officers and the February 26, 1936 Incident.* Princeton: Princeton University Press, 1973.

Shils, Edward. "The Military in the Political Development of the New States." In *The Role of the Military in Underdeveloped Countries,* edited by John J. Johnson. Princeton: Princeton University Press, 1962.

Skilling, H. Gordon, and Franklyn Griffiths, eds. *Interest Groups in Soviet Politics.* Princeton: Princeton University Press, 1971.

Smethurst, Richard J. *A Social Basis for Prewar Japanese Militarism: The Army and the Rural Community.* Berkeley and Los Angeles: University of California Press, 1974.

Spaulding, Robert M., Jr. "The Bureaucracy as a Political Force: 1920–1945." In *Dilemmas of Growth in Prewar Japan,* edited by James W. Morley. Princeton: Princeton University Press, 1971.

———. *Imperial Japan's Higher Civil Service Examinations.* Princeton: Princeton University Press, 1967.

Stepan, Alfred. *The State and Society: Peru in Comparative Perspective.* Princeton: Princeton University Press, 1978.

tenBroek, Jacobus, Edward N. Barnhart, and Floyd W. Matson. *Prejudice, War, and the Constitution.* Berkeley and Los Angeles: University of California Press, 1968.

Terrou, Fernand, and Lucien Solal. *Legislation for Press, Film and Radio.* Paris: UNESCO, 1951.

Titus, David Anson. *Palace and Politics in Prewar Japan.* New York: Columbia University Press, 1974.

Tocqueville, Alexis de. *Democracy in America,* 2 vols., translated by Henry Reeve. New York: Vintage, 1945.

———. *The Old Regime and the French Revolution,* translated by Stuart Gilbert. New York: Doubleday Anchor, 1955.

Tsuji Kiyoaki. "Decision-Making in the Japanese Government: A Study of

Ringisei." In *Political Development in Modern Japan,* edited by Robert E. Ward. Princeton: Princeton University Press, 1968.

Waterbury, John. *The Egypt of Nasser and Sadat: The Political Economy of Two Regimes.* Princeton: Princeton University Press, 1983.

Weber, Eugen. *Varieties of Fascism.* New York: D. Van Nostrand, 1964.

Welch, Claude E., Jr., and Arthur K. Smith. *Military Role and Rule: Perspectives on Civil Military Relations.* North Scituate, Mass.: Duxbury Press, 1974.

Wilcox, Dennis L. *Mass Media in Black Africa.* New York: Praeger, 1975.

Index

Abe Hirozumi, 159
Abe Nobuyuki, 207
Abe Shinnosuke, 184n. 52
Aberbach, Joel, 107
Adachi Kenzō, 84–87
Administrative guidance, 173
Administrative revolution, 149, 266, 282–85, 294–96, 296n. 59, 297; ideology of, 200–206; origins of, 149–52
Advertising, 189; ban on, over radio, 75–76
Agitation, concept of, 41
Agrarianist right wing, 140, 143
Agricultural Patriotic Association, 165
Agriculture and Forestry Ministry, 90
Akita, George, 6
Akita Kiyoshi, 159n. 119, 209
Algeria, 293
Allende, Salvador, xiv
Al-Misri, 292
American Commission on Freedom of the Press, 56
American Occupation, 281
Anarchist publications, censorship of, 39–41
Aono Kiyoshi, 184n. 52
APRA (*Alianza Popular Revolucionaria Americana*—Peru), 295
Arab Socialist Union (Egypt), 286, 291
Argentina, 272, 287n. 30
Arisawa Hiromi, 182
Army, 26, 124, 168–69, 276, 283; navy rivalry with, and press controls,

228–29; position of, on newspaper consolidations, 215; and Yokohama Incident, 229–30. *See also* Army Ministry; Militarism, Japanese; Military, the Japanese
Army General Staff, 125, 162
Army Ministry, 105, 162, 163, 174, 185, 191, 195n. 5, 197n. 12; and appointment of active-duty ministers, 124–25; and consolidation policy, 222n. 87; and consultation meetings, 229–30; and film policy, 58, 232, 245; intervention of, in cabinet formation, 125, 160; Military Affairs Bureau of, 159n. 117, 169, 212n. 54; and Minobe crisis, 131–32, 133n. 40; Newspaper Law powers of, 19, 169, 169n. 3; 1934 pamphlet of, 124, 125, 130, 151; officials of, in CIB, 200; and radio mobilization, 95, 255, 256; support of, for law against rightist propaganda, 128; and the United News Agency, 155, 157. *See also* Army; Militarism, Japanese; Military, the Japanese
Asahi Film Company, 246
Asahi Shinbun, 44, 87, 134, 135, 136, 191, 227–28, 243, 255n. 13, 271, 281, 290; criticism of Peace Preservation Law in, 44–46; employment exams for, 28; reaction of, to consolidations, 190, 212–15, 217, 227–28; reaction of, to Newspaper Law, 16
Ashida Hitoshi, 184n. 52

319

Compositor:	Huron Valley Graphics, Inc.
Text:	10/13 Sabon
Display:	Sabon
Printer:	Edwards Brothers
Binder:	Edwards Brothers